W9-BNC-099

EUROSTAT YEARBOOK 2003

The statistical guide to Europe

Data 1991–2001

  eurostat

Published by

Office for Official Publications of the European Communities Luxembourg, 2003

Eighth edition

Edited and produced by

Eurostat, the Statistical Office of the European Communities, in Luxembourg

Unit C1: Information and dissemination

C. Botto, M. Copers, M. Kessanoglou, G. Kyi

with the assistance and support of the following Eurostat directorates:

Directorate A: Statistical information system; research and data analysis; technical cooperation with Phare and Tacis countries

A3   *Reference databases (M. Loos, S. Paganoni, A. Pasqui)*

A4   *Research and development, methods and data analysis (A. Götzfried, I. Laafia, A. Larsson)*

A5   *Technical cooperation with candidate, CARDS and Tacis countries (A. Krüger)*

Directorate B: Economic statistics and economic and monetary convergence

B2   *Economic accounts and international markets: production and analysis (J.-Ph. Arnotte, N. Thoma, J. Pasanen)*

B3   *Price comparisons, correction coefficients (M. Hussain, S. Stapel, L. Viglino)*

B4   *Accounts and financial indicators, statistics for the excessive deficits procedure (G. Amerini, O. Delobbe, G. Dierickx, G. Revelin)*

B5   *International trade in services, direct investment, balance of payments (L. Biedma, C. Kuppel, A. Lupi, S. Pantazidis, P. Passerini, M. Sautelet)*

Directorate C: Information and dissemination; transport; technical cooperation with non-member countries (except Phare and Tacis countries); external and intra-Community trade statistics

C2   *Transport (H. Strelow)*

C3   *Technical cooperation with non-member countries (except Phare and Tacis countries) (C. Bisenius)*

C4   *Methodology, nomenclature and statistics of external and intra-Community trade (A. Berthomieu, C. Corsini, H. Tyrman)*

Directorate D: Business statistics

D1   *Methodological coordination, structural indicators, classifications and registers (M. Hahn, M. Léonard, S. Jouhki)*

D2   *Structural business statistics (F. Faes-Cannito, C. Clément, P. Feuvrier, P. Sneijers)*

D3   *Production, short-term business statistics (D. Amil)*

D4   *Energy statistics (A. Gikas)*

D5   *Information society and tourism statistics (R. Deiss, G. Di Giacomo, S. Fickinger, M. Lumio, H.-W. Schmidt)*

Directorate E: Social statistics

E1   *Labour market (R. Clare, A. Franco, S. Jouhette, A. Paternoster, A. Persenaire, K. Winqvist)*

E2   *Living conditions (I. Dennis, A. C. Guio, J. Piirto)*

E3   *Health, education and culture (M. Dunne, D. Dupré, E. Kailis, K. Kühl, A. Montserrat, S. Pilos, P. Schmidt)*

E4   *Population and social protection (F.-C. Bovagnet, R. Brandenbourger, C. Cadolino, A. Laihonen, A. Melis, C. Mottet, D. Thorogood)*

Directorate F: Agricultural, environmental, food and regional statistics

F1   *Economic and structural statistics for agriculture (U. Eidmann, G. Mahon, P. Marquer)*

F2   *Land use, agricultural products and fisheries (M. Bettio, S. Bos, P. Bruyas, D. Cross, F. Weiler, F. Zampogna)*

F3   *Environment and sustainable development (D. Heal, G. Lock, L. Sanches, U. Wieland, L. Vasquez)*

F4   *Regional accounts and indicators, and geographical information system (A. Behrens, T. Carlquist)*

F5   *Food safety, rural development and forestry (A. Mariano, Y. Zanatta)*

EFTA   *(A. Ottestad)*

NACE   *(D. Delcambre)*

Geonomenclature   *(A. Ferlini, E. Jouangrand)*

Translation

Translation Service of the European Commission, Luxembourg

Cataloguing data can be found at the end of this publication.

A great deal of additional information on Eurostat is available on the Internet: http://www.europa.eu.int/comm/eurostat/

Office for Official Publications of the European Communities, 2003
ISBN 92-894-4209-3 (printed version in English and CD-ROM: English, French and German)
ISBN 92-894-4210-7 (printed version in French and CD-ROM: English, French and German)
ISBN 92-894-4208-5 (printed version in German and CD-ROM: English, French and German)

One way of better understanding our neighbours is simply by comparing them with us. Adding to this understanding is what international statistics are all about: they are a direct and down-to-earth way of comparing how we live and work.

That is why Eurostat, the Statistical Office of the European Communities, produces this yearbook on Europe and Europeans. It compares significant features of each country of the European Union and of other European countries, as well as of Canada, Japan and the United States of America. As Europe evolves, the yearbook evolves too: we have made a special effort to present data on candidate countries.

Moreover, the yearbook presents the relevant statistics on the situation of the national economies, thus giving a unique means of analysis of economic capacities of the countries that make up the European Union.

For ease of comparison, all statistics in this publication are compiled in the same way, or harmonised by Eurostat, or accepted by Eurostat as offering sensible comparisons.

We invite you to read the Eurostat yearbook, to compare for yourself, and to get to know your European neighbours better.

Eurostat

Contents

eurostat

The Eurostat yearbook as a combined product

The Eurostat yearbook 2003 is a combined product consisting of a book and a CD-ROM. The CD-ROM contains more than 1 000 statistical tables and graphs, a selection of which is presented in the book. All data can be easily extracted from the CD-ROM.

On the CD-ROM, the references for further reading are linked electronically to the Internet presentation of the respective publication, or, if the publication can be downloaded free of charge, to the publication itself. The ⌧ for the structural indicators is linked to the Internet pages presenting these indicators (see section 'Eurostat's structural indicators').

The Eurostat yearbook is easy to use

— Introductory texts for each section explain the main features and the relevance of the information presented and give an idea of what other data on the subject Eurostat has on offer.

— A glossary clarifies the statistical terms and concepts used.

— References indicate how to get more Eurostat data and analysis on the subject.

— The abbreviations used are spelled out on the bookmark to the yearbook.

Data extraction

The statistical data presented in this yearbook were extracted at the end of 2002 and represent the data availability at that time.

Symbols

-	Nil
0	Less than half the final digit shown
.	Not applicable
..	Confidential data. Data not conclusive or withheld owing to non-disclosure practice
:	Data not available
*	Provisional or estimated figures
#	Rebased, adjusted or recalculated by Eurostat
|	Break in series, because data on each side of the bar are not fully comparable

€ zone Euro zone. '€ zone', which is not an official symbol, is being used for practical reasons.

1

Statisticians for Europe

Eurostat's service

The European Union in the global context

In the spotlight: the candidate countries

Eurostat, your key to European statistics

Comparable information about Europe has a name: Eurostat

'Eurostat' is the synonym for a high-quality information service providing statistical data about, and for, the European Union. Using our data means having a finger on the pulse of current developments in Europe: we report the background figures and facts needed to understand these developments.

The Eurostat yearbook: compiled for everyone with an interest in Europe

The Eurostat yearbook opens the door to Eurostat's information service by providing an overview of the spectrum of data we offer. It shows how benchmark figures have developed during the last 10 years in the European Union, the euro zone and the EU Member States. To facilitate international comparison, some tables include the comparable data for other countries, for example Canada, Japan or the United States of America.

Introductory texts for each section give an idea of what data Eurostat has on the subject and what the relevance of this information is. We understand the yearbook not to be a mere collection of tables, but a 'portal' to European statistics. We hope it will make you curious about the data Eurostat has on offer. Our information service will provide more detailed data and advice.

How to get the data you want

Something for everyone

Eurostat's information service assists and adapts according to your requirements.

We publish our most relevant data for everybody free of charge, for example through our daily press releases which are available on our up-to-date web site.

More detailed information can be found in our compendium publications whose 'flagship' is the Eurostat yearbook. The backgrounds to specific topics are provided in our *Panorama* publications which contain thoroughly elaborated analyses, tables, graphs and maps. Briefing the public on specific topics is the objective of our *Statistics in Focus* publications.

The wide spectrum of our publications and databases on indicators is oriented to different uses.

— The 'free selection' is a selection of the tables presented in the Eurostat yearbook and aimed at providing a general overview. It is available free of charge on Eurostat's web site.

— The 'structural indicators' help to assess the longer-term progress in the policy domains of employment, innovation, economic reform, social cohesion and the environment. They are recognised to be most relevant for political discussion. Consequently, all structural indicators are presented in the Eurostat yearbook and identified here with a specific icon. For more information, please read the text 'Eurostat's structural indicators: high-quality statistics for competent governance in Europe'. All structural indicators are updated and are available free of charge on the Eurostat web site (http://www.europa.eu.int/comm/eurostat).

— The 'Euroindicators' provide a collection of the latest data which are helpful for a short-term evaluation of the economic situation in the euro zone and in the European Union as a whole. The Euroindicators are updated daily on a special web site (http://www.europa.eu.int/comm/euroindicators/).

1

The collections 'Methods and nomenclatures', 'Detailed tables' and 'Studies and research' suit the needs of specialists who are prepared to spend more time on analysing and using very detailed tables.

Eurostat's database NewCronos contains a large spectrum of data and time series that allow analysts and decision-makers to extract the information they need and in the required format.

Evidently, it is impossible to publish all data available at Eurostat in all imaginable combinations. Therefore, experts are invited to contact one of our Eurostat Data Shops if they wish to have tailor-made extractions from our databases (see below). As always, Eurostat ensures that for these extractions the confidentiality of the data is strictly guaranteed.

An address for your list of favourites: http://www.europa.eu.int/comm/eurostat

Eurostat's web site offers an up-to-date overview of its latest news and products. It contains all of Eurostat's news releases and many indicators that are available online as soon as they are released. Other reasons to visit the site are the demonstration of Eurostat's publications and services, the online catalogue and the description of the dissemination network for European statistics.

Contact your Eurostat Data Shop!

If you have any questions about the content of the yearbook, if you need more data, if you want advice about what additional data are available, or if you require more information on Eurostat's offers, please contact your Eurostat Data Shop.

The addresses of the Data Shops can be found at the end of the yearbook and on our web site. The Eurostat Data Shops are at the core of Eurostat's dissemination network and have been established in most Member States as well as in the United States.

Eurostat's service for journalists

Statistics make news. They are essential background to many news stories, features and in-depth analyses. The printed press as well as radio and TV programmes use our data intensively. Eurostat's Press Office puts out user-friendly news releases on a key selection of data covering the EU, the euro zone, the Member States and their partners, and particularly the candidate countries. About 150 press releases are published each year, of which nearly 100 are about the monthly or quarterly Euroindicators. The Press Office also coordinates interviews and press conferences on important statistical results and events. Eurostat's Media Support helps professional journalists to find data on all kinds of topics.

All Eurostat news releases are available free of charge on the web as soon as they are released.

Please contact Eurostat Media Support if you need further information on our news releases or other data (tel. (352) 43 01-33408, fax (352) 43 01-35349, e-mail: eurostat-mediasupport@cec.eu.int).

Why Eurostat data?

Equal information for a democratic society

Being informed is the first step to actively participating in a democratic Europe. Europeans demand a high-quality information service providing impartial, reliable and comparable statistical data. They want to access them easily and without exemption: no key information must be withheld; all citizens and enterprises must have equal and complete access to it. Eurostat and its partners in the European statistical system open the door and guarantee this equal and comprehensive information on social, economic and environmental developments in Europe. It is up to you to use it!

Impartiality and objectivity: two pillars of trust

Access to reliable and high-quality statistics becomes ever-more important in the information society in which we live, and trust in the source an immeasurable value. Eurostat's trustworthiness is enshrined by law. Article 285(2) of the EC Treaty says: 'The production of Community statistics shall conform to impartiality, reliability, objectivity, scientific independence, cost-effectiveness and statistical confidentiality; it shall not entail excessive burdens on economic operators.' These are not abstract words for us: they are the leading principle for our day-to-day work.

Comparability through harmonisation

It is easier to understand each other if one knows about the other's conditions of life and work. What is true for the relationship between individuals is also true for society as a whole. Comparisons, however, require comparable statistics that, in turn, demand the use of a common 'statistical language'.

The common language has to embrace concepts, methods and definitions, as well as technical standards and infrastructures. This is what statisticians call harmonisation. It is what the European statistical system is all about. And it is Eurostat's primary *raison d'être*.

The European statistical system

The European statistical system comprises Eurostat and the statistical offices, ministries, agencies and central banks that collect official statistics in the EU Member States, Iceland, Liechtenstein and Norway. The statistical authorities in the Member States collect, verify and analyse national data and send them to Eurostat. Eurostat consolidates the data and ensures their comparability. The European statistical system concentrates on EU policy areas. But, with the extension of EU policies, harmonisation has extended to nearly all statistical fields.

The European statistical system is a network in which Eurostat's role is to lead the way in the harmonisation of statistics in close cooperation with the national statistical authorities. At the heart of the European statistical system is the Statistical Programme Committee, which brings together the heads of Member States' national statistical offices and is chaired by Eurostat. The Statistical Programme Committee discusses joint actions and programmes to be carried out to meet EU information requirements. It agreed a five-year programme, which is implemented by the national authorities and monitored by Eurostat.

A matter of disposition: an attractive and relevant data assortment

Data become information when they become interesting. As a matter of disposition, Eurostat has an open ear for what people are interested in.

The statistical programme of the European statistical system does not 'fall out of the blue'. What we report on has been decided through a well-defined political process at the European level in which the EU Member States are deeply involved. Most surveys and data collections are based on European regulations that are legally binding on the national level. A central question during the political and legal discussions that lead to European statistical regulations is: 'To whom and why are the data of interest?' Every statistical regulation has to pass a critical test.

1

On the other hand, the European statistical programme is constantly revised. In view of the principle of cost-efficiency, the production of data that have been rendered less relevant by new developments will be modified or even discontinued. As a result, the statistical programme is kept lean and modern.

Our data are worth looking at.

Eurostat's structural indicators

Eurostat's structural indicators: high-quality statistics for competent governance in Europe

At the Lisbon European Council in spring 2000, the European Union set itself the following strategic goal for the next decade: to become the most competitive and dynamic knowledge-based economy in the world capable of sustainable economic growth with more and better jobs and greater social cohesion.

The Council acknowledged the need to regularly discuss and assess progress made in achieving this goal on the basis of commonly agreed structural indicators. To this end, it invited the European Commission to draw up an annual spring report on progress on the basis of structural indicators relating to employment, innovation and research, economic reform, social cohesion and the general economic background, as well as, since 2002, the environment.

Structural indicators are also set up for use in the annual communication from the Commission on structural indicators. In this communication, a new list of structural indicators is presented every autumn. Once agreed with the Council, this list is used for the report that is presented to the European Council the following spring. Thus, the structural indicators will be at the heart of political and economic discussions for many years to come.

Eurostat disseminates the full set of structural indicators on its structural indicators web site (http://www.europa.eu.int/comm/eurostat). Time series are presented for EU-15, EU Member States and, as far as possible, the EFTA countries, Japan and the United States. As accompanying information on the economic background, indicators for EU-12 are also provided. Starting from 2003, candidate countries will also be covered wherever data are available.

The 2002 set of structural indicators is listed below. All structural indicators are presented in the Eurostat yearbook. They are marked with the following icon 〰 which appears next to the title of the respective tables.

List of the 42 structural indicators

General economic background

a. GDP per capita and real GDP growth rate

b. Labour productivity (per person and per hour)

c. Employment growth (total and by gender)

d. Inflation rate

e. Unit labour cost growth

f. Public balance

g. General government debt

I — Employment

1. Employment rate (total and by gender)

2. Employment rate of older workers (total and by gender)

3. Gender pay gap

4. Tax rate on low-wage earners

5. Lifelong learning

6. Accidents at work (serious and fatal)

7. Unemployment rate (total and by gender)

1

II — Innovation and research

1. Spending on human resources (public expenditure on education)

2. R & D expenditure (BERD and GERD)

3. Level of Internet access (household and enterprise)

4. Science and technology graduates

5. Patents

6. Venture capital (early stage and expansion and replacement)

7. ICT expenditure

III — Economic reform

1. Relative price levels and price convergence

2. Prices in the network industries (telecommunications and energy)

3. Market structure in the network industries (telecommunications and electricity)

4. Public procurement

5. Sectoral and ad hoc State aid

6. Capital raised on stock markets

7. Business investment

IV — Social cohesion

1. Distribution of income (S80/S20)

2. Risk of poverty (before and after social transfers)

3. Persistent risk of poverty

4. Regional cohesion (unemployment)

5. Early school-leavers

6. Long-term unemployment

7. Population in jobless households

V — Environment

1. Greenhouse gas emissions

2. Energy intensity of the economy

3. Volume of transport (freight and passengers)

4. Modal split of transport

5. Urban air quality

6. Municipal waste (collected, landfilled, incinerated)

7. Share of renewables

The European Union in the global context

Get an idea of the EU's position in the world

Eurostat's data allow comparison between the EU and other parts of the world. They help in analysing its relation to other countries and economic zones. To demonstrate the EU's position in the world, the Eurostat yearbook presents a small statistical selection about the following.

— The EU population and its development relative to the world population.

— Some economic indicators such as gross domestic product per capita, labour productivity, unemployment rate and foreign direct investment, as well as imports, exports and the EU's current transactions broken down by partner zones.

— Information on the EU's official development assistance and official aid to other countries, to which special attention has been paid.

— Comparisons of expenditure on information technology and telecommunications as well as on the percentage of citizens who have Internet access at home provide a view of the future.

— How much energy is being used to produce the GDP in different countries? The indicator 'energy intensity of the economy' gives the answer.

The European Union wants to improve its position as a competitive and dynamic knowledge-based economy, ensuring sustainable economic growth with more and better jobs and greater social cohesion. It is up to you to consult Eurostat's data to assess the progress we Europeans make.

1

Mid-year population. 1960–2001. Millions

	1960	1965	1970	1975	1980	1985	1990	1995	1999	2000	2001
World	3 039.3	3 345.8	3 707.6	4 088.2	4 456.7	4 854.6	5 283.8	5 690.9	6 002.5	6 080.1	6 157.4
More developed countries, of which:	910.4	961.6	1 003.2	1 044.9	1 080.8	1 111.5	1 142.9	1 168.2	1 182.2	1 185.5	1 188.7
EU-15	316.2	330.2	340.2	349.2	355.3	358.8	364.6	372.0	375.9	377.3	378.8
JP	94.1	98.9	104.3	111.6	116.8	120.8	123.5	125.3	126.3	126.5	126.8
US	180.7	194.3	205.1	216.0	227.7	238.5	249.9	263.0	273.1	275.6	278.1
Russian Federation	119.6	126.5	130.2	134.3	139.0	144.0	148.1	148.1	146.5	146.0	145.5
Less developed countries, of which:	2 129.0	2 384.2	2 704.4	3 043.3	3 375.9	3 743.1	4 140.8	4 522.7	4 820.3	4 894.7	4 968.7
CN	650.7	715.5	820.4	917.9	984.7	1 054.7	1 138.9	1 204.8	1 250.5	1 261.8	1 273.1
IN	445.9	495.7	555.0	621.9	690.5	768.3	850.6	932.4	997.9	1 014.0	1 030.0
NG	39.9	45.0	51.1	58.9	69.6	79.8	92.5	107.2	120.1	123.3	126.6
BR	71.7	83.1	95.7	108.8	122.9	137.3	151.1	163.0	171.2	172.9	174.5

Source (excluding EU-15): US Bureau of the Census, International database.

Mid-year population. 1960–2001. %

	1960	1965	1970	1975	1980	1985	1990	1995	1999	2000	2001
World	100	100	100	100	100	100	100	100	100	100	100
More developed countries, of which:	30	29	27	26	24	23	22	21	20	20	19
EU-15	10	10	9	9	8	7	7	7	6	6	6
JP	3	3	3	3	3	3	2	2	2	2	2
US	6	6	6	5	5	5	5	5	5	5	5
Russian Federation	4	4	4	3	3	3	3	3	2	2	2
Less developed countries, of which:	70	71	73	74	76	77	78	80	80	81	81
CN	21	21	22	23	22	22	22	21	21	21	21
IN	15	15	15	15	16	16	16	16	17	17	17
NG	1	1	1	1	2	2	2	2	2	2	2
BR	2	3	3	3	3	3	3	3	3	3	3

Source (excluding EU-15): US Bureau of the Census, International database.

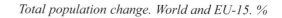

Total population change. World and EU-15. %

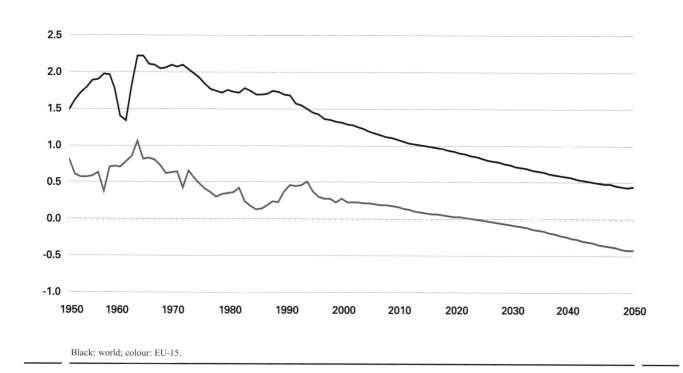

Black: world; colour: EU-15.

1

World population. 1950, 2001 and 2050. %

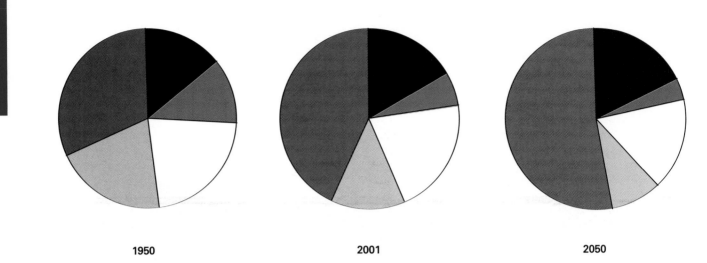

| 1950 | 2001 | 2050 |

Black: India; colour: EU-15; white: China; light grey: other developed countries; grey: other less developed countries.

Development of the share in the world population

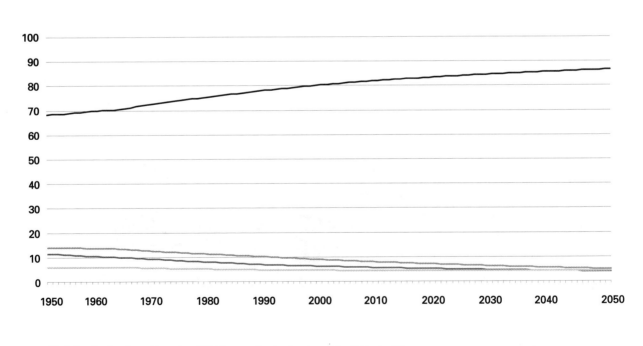

Black: less developed countries; colour: EU-15; grey: other developed countries; light grey: US.

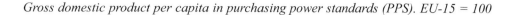

Gross domestic product per capita in purchasing power standards (PPS). EU-15 = 100

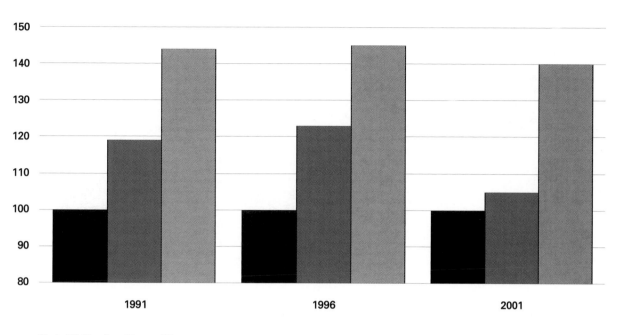

Black: EU-15; colour: JP; grey: US.

The graph compares the GDP per capita in the United States and Japan to that in the EU. Consequently, the index for the EU is, per definition, always 100.

Labour productivity. GDP in purchasing power standards (PPS) per hour worked relative to EU-15 = 100

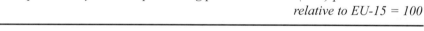

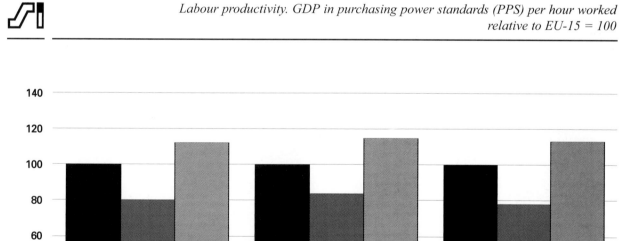

Black: EU-15; colour: JP; grey: US.

The graph compares the labour productivity in the United States and Japan to that in the EU. Consequently, the index for the EU is, per definition, always 100.

1

Total unemployment rate. Unemployed persons as a share of the total active population

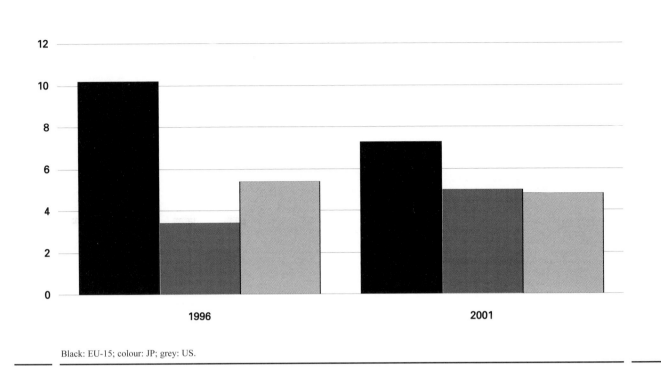

Black: EU-15; colour: JP; grey: US.

Tax rate on low-wage earners. Income tax plus employee and employer contributions less cash benefits as % of labour costs for a low-wage earner

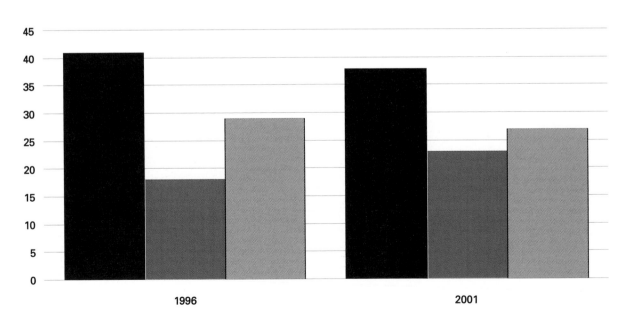

Black: EU-15; colour: JP; grey: US.

Total income tax on gross wage earnings plus employee and employer social security contributions. The tax rate applies to a single adult full-time production worker in manufacturing industry (without children) who has no income source other than wages that are equal to 67 % of the average earnings of such workers.

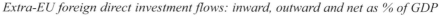

1

Extra-EU foreign direct investment flows: inward, outward and net as % of GDP

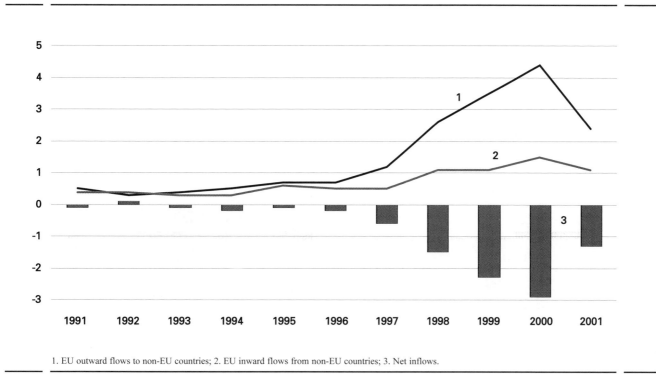

1. EU outward flows to non-EU countries; 2. EU inward flows from non-EU countries; 3. Net inflows.

EU-12 in 1991 and EU-15 from 1992; figures exclude reinvested earnings.

General government consolidated gross debt as % of GDP

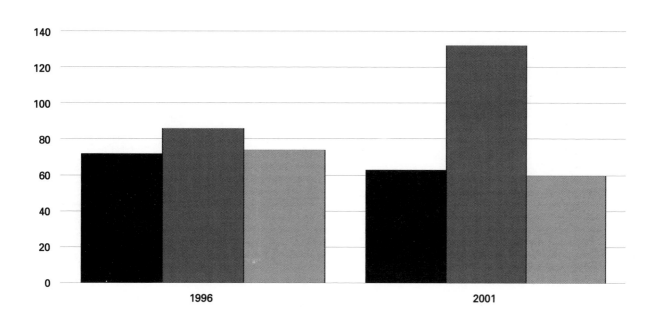

Black: EU-15; colour: JP; grey: US.

eurostat

1

Direct investment flows for the EU. Million ECU/EUR

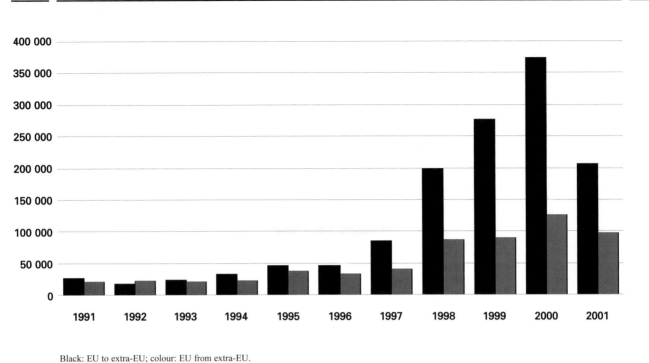

Black: EU to extra-EU; colour: EU from extra-EU.

EU-12 in 1991 and EU-15 from 1992; figures exclude reinvested earnings.

Direct investment flows for the United States. Million ECU/EUR

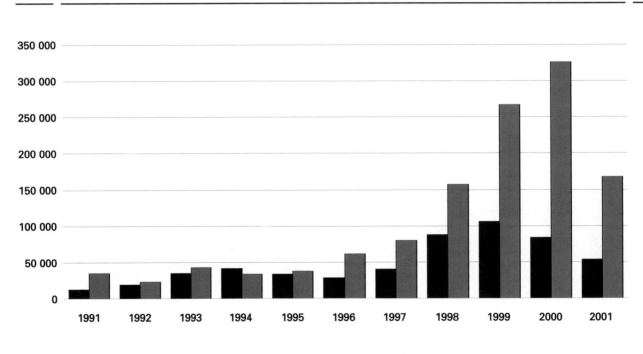

Black: United States to the rest of the world; colour: United States from the rest of the world.

Figures exclude reinvested earnings.

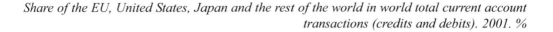

Share of the EU, United States, Japan and the rest of the world in world total current account transactions (credits and debits). 2001. %

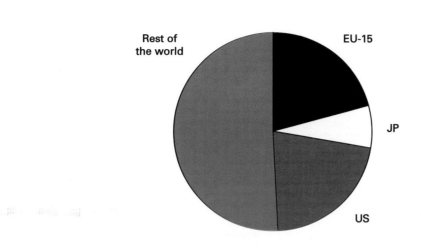

Rest of
the world

EU-15

JP

US

Evolution of EU current transactions with the extra-EU: credits and debits. 1 000 million ECU/EUR

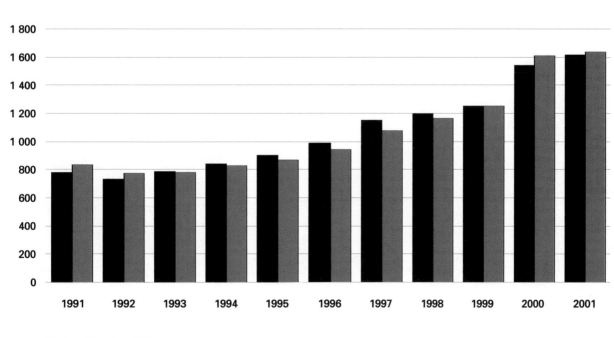

Black: credits; colour: debits.

From 1992 onwards, data for A, FIN and S are included in EU. Before 1992 the current account includes the capital account.

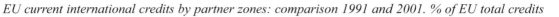
1

EU current international credits by partner zones: comparison 1991 and 2001. % of EU total credits

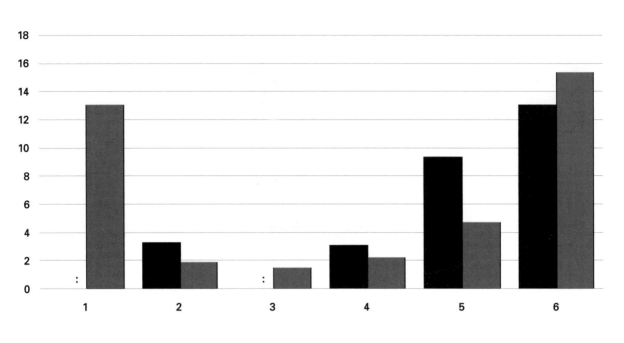

Black: 1991; colour: 2001. 1. NAFTA. 2. Japan; 3. ASEAN; 4. OPEC; 5. EFTA; 6. Rest of the world.

The partner zone 'Rest of the world' excludes EU countries.

EU current international debits by partner zones: comparison 1991 and 2001. % of EU total debits

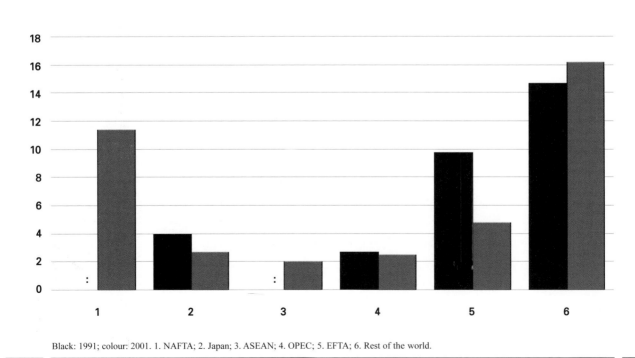

Black: 1991; colour: 2001. 1. NAFTA; 2. Japan; 3. ASEAN; 4. OPEC; 5. EFTA; 6. Rest of the world.

The partner zone 'Rest of the world' excludes EU countries.

eurostat

Official development assistance and official aid. Million EUR

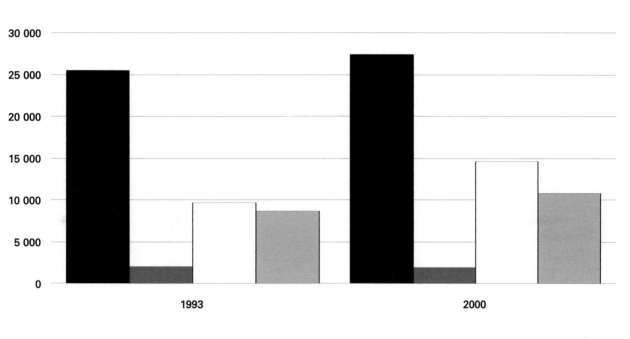

Black: EU-15; colour: CA; white: JP; grey: US.

Source: OECD-DAC tables; euro effective exchange rates calculated by the ECB (average value for 1993 and 2000); 1993: EU-15 figures without EL.

Official development assistance and official aid. Million EUR

	1993	1994	1995	1996	1997	1998	1999	2000	
EU-15	25 487	25 570	23 974	24 789	23 619	24 656	25 131	27 367	**EU-15**
B	692	611	791	719	673	787	713	887	**B**
DK	1 144	1 216	1 241	1 396	1 443	1 520	1 626	1 802	**DK**
D	5 939	5 732	5 752	5 986	5 165	4 978	5 175	5 446	**D**
EL	-	-	-	145	152	160	182	245	**EL**
E	1 114	1 097	1 031	986	1 088	1 227	1 279	1 294	**E**
F	6 759	7 117	6 455	5 868	5 561	5 121	5 291	4 444	**F**
IRL	69	92	117	141	165	177	230	254	**IRL**
I	2 599	2 274	1 241	1 902	1 116	2 032	1 694	1 490	**I**
L	43	50	50	65	83	100	111	137	**L**
NL	2 156	2 116	2 466	2 557	2 598	2 713	2 941	3 394	**NL**
A	465	551	586	439	465	407	494	458	**A**
P	201	255	197	172	221	231	259	293	**P**
FIN	303	244	297	321	334	354	391	402	**FIN**
S	1 511	1 529	1 303	1 574	1 526	1 403	1 529	1 948	**S**
UK	2 494	2 688	2 448	2 519	3 027	3 446	3 215	4 874	**UK**
NO	866	956	951	1 033	1 152	1 179	1 285	1 368	**NO**
CH	677	826	829	808	803	801	923	964	**CH**
CA	2 050	1 892	1 580	1 414	1 803	1 522	1 601	1 888	**CA**
JP	9 615	11 130	11 077	7 434	8 252	9 491	14 378	14 625	**JP**
US	8 645	8 345	5 632	7 385	6 065	7 837	8 581	10 778	**US**

Source: OECD-DAC tables; euro effective exchange rates calculated by the ECB (yearly average value); 1993–95: EU-15 figures without EL.

1

National imports and exports as % of world exports

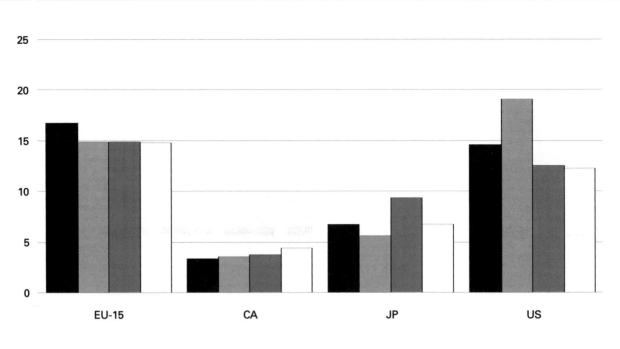

Black: imports 1991; grey: imports 2001; colour: exports 1991; white: exports 2001.

Exports/imports ratio

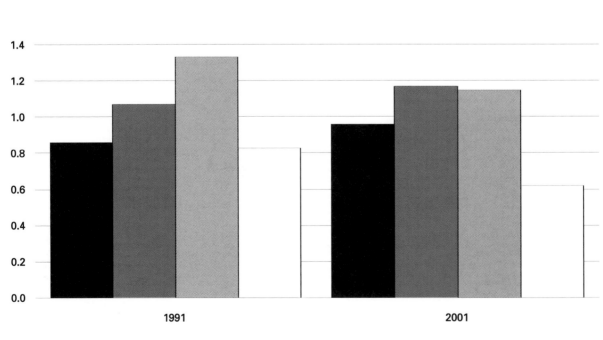

Black: EU-15; colour: CN; grey: JP; white: US.

eurostat

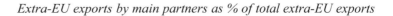

1

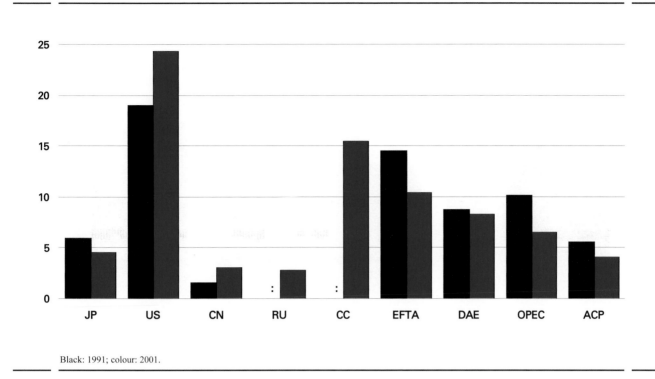

Extra-EU exports by main partners as % of total extra-EU exports

Black: 1991; colour: 2001.

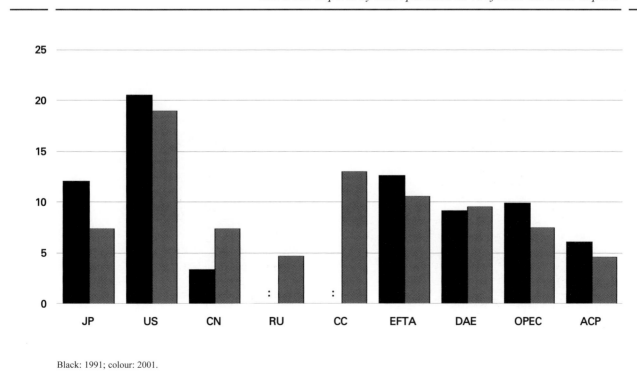

Extra-EU imports by main partners as % of total extra-EU imports

Black: 1991; colour: 2001.

1

Expenditure on information technology as % of GDP

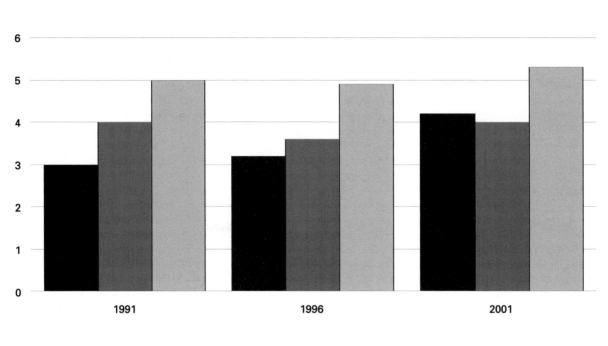

Black: EU-15; colour: JP; grey: US.

Annual expenditure on information technology hardware, equipment, software and other services as % of GDP.

Level of Internet access: households. Percentage of households which have Internet access at home

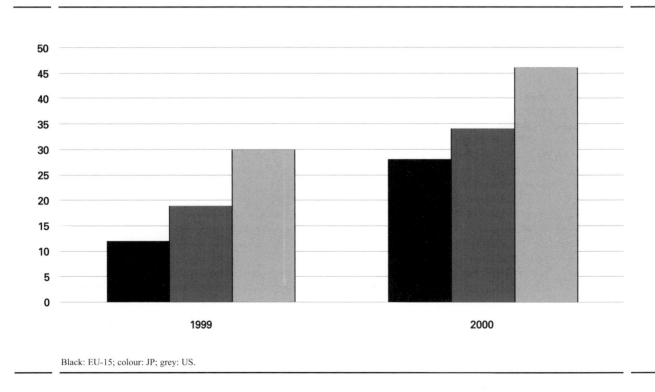

Black: EU-15; colour: JP; grey: US.

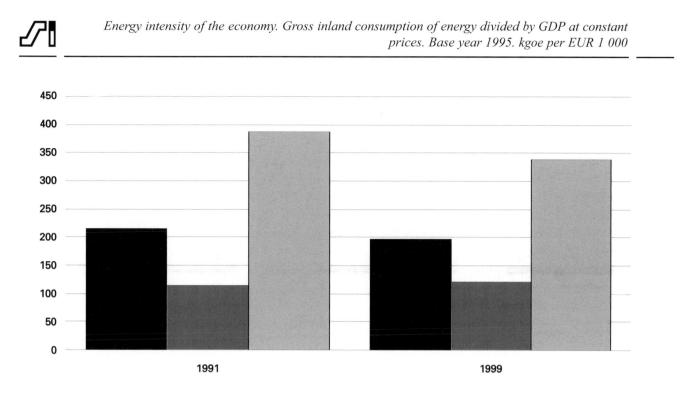

Energy intensity of the economy. Gross inland consumption of energy divided by GDP at constant prices. Base year 1995. kgoe per EUR 1 000

Black: EU-15; colour: JP; grey: US.

Ratio between the gross inland consumption of coal, electricity, oil, natural gas and renewable energy sources to GDP. GDP at constant prices in 1995 to avoid the impact of inflation.

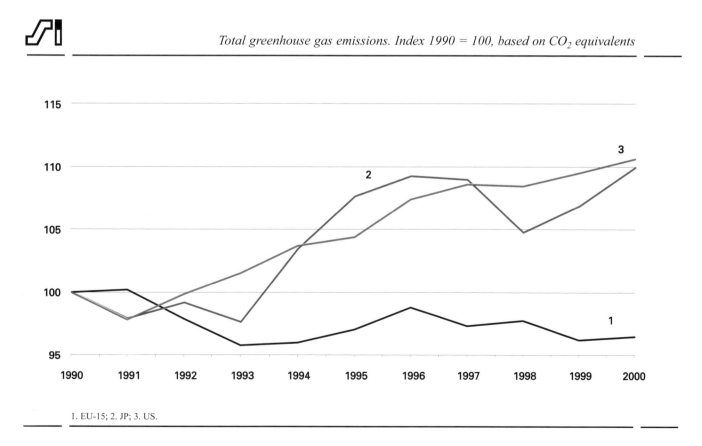

Total greenhouse gas emissions. Index 1990 = 100, based on CO_2 equivalents

1. EU-15; 2. JP; 3. US.

In the spotlight: the candidate countries

The European statistical system: in the vanguard of European integration

Thirteen countries have applied for EU membership: Bulgaria, Cyprus, the Czech Republic, Estonia, Hungary, Latvia, Lithuania, Malta, Poland, Romania, Slovakia, Slovenia and Turkey. The majority of them will join the Union in the near future as new Member States. In order to prepare for this unprecedented step in European integration, Eurostat has long been engaged in intensive technical cooperation with their statistical offices, in some countries for over 12 years. In addition, many Member States have supplied valuable technical assistance since the very beginning of this process.

Statistical offices have existed in all candidate countries for many years, although in most of them under conditions which were very different from those prevailing in EU Member States. Where the economic and legal system was that of a State trading country, many key areas of statistics did not exist at all, for example national accounts, price or labour market statistics. Statistical classifications, methods and definitions were quite different from those used in the EU. Moreover, five of the candidate countries have recently become independent nations (Estonia, Latvia, Lithuania, Slovakia and Slovenia). Their statistical offices hitherto had only been in charge of regional data collection, but after independence had to take over all the central tasks of a national statistical office.

Almost all the candidate countries have achieved impressive progress over the last 10 years. At the beginning of this process, new statistical laws were adopted, which laid the foundations for efficient statistical systems of democratic market economies, based, in particular, on the principles of independence, transparency, technical competence, accessibility of data for the public and protection of individual information. At the same time, a set of fundamental classifications had to be introduced in order to achieve a certain degree of international comparability. In parallel, the candidate countries created statistical registers, in particular for business and agricultural statistics, and began with the implementation of all the sectoral statistics that have to be operational until accession.

The candidate countries', Member States' and Eurostat's common endeavours have resulted in a continuously improving availability, comparability and timeliness of statistics on candidate countries. Most candidate countries now have an appropriate legal basis as well as administrative structure. Their data have achieved a very high degree of comparability with those of the current EU Member States.

The Eurostat yearbook presents an overview of key indicators, mostly covering 1997–2001. For those who need more detailed information, Eurostat publishes a statistical yearbook on candidate countries annually and many other publications (see 'Further reading' box below).

Population and labour market

The population of the 12 candidate countries: evolution and comparisons

On 1 January 2002, the 12 candidate countries with which negotiations have started had a combined population of 105.1 million people.

At the same time, EU-15 had 379.6 million inhabitants. This means that the enlargement of the EU to include these countries would increase its population by 28 %, to a total of about 485 million inhabitants. At the same time, its share of world population would increase from 6.1 % to about 8 %.

The 12 countries included in this study on population are Bulgaria, Cyprus, the Czech Republic, Estonia, Hungary, Latvia, Lithuania, Malta, Poland, Romania, Slovakia and Slovenia. Given the unavailability of data, the country's large population (69.2 million on 1 January 2002) and a demographic situation markedly different from the other candidate countries, Turkey is not included in this study.

Dramatic population decline of the candidate countries over the last 10 years

During the 1990s, most of the 12 candidate countries experienced dramatic demographic events. Fertility levels dropped drastically, life expectancies went down and significant net outflows were reported. Therefore, population growth has rapidly become negative in this region of Europe: since 1990, these countries have lost 1.9 million people, which is a decline of 1.8 % of their population.

Currently, the total population of these 12 countries is at the same level as in 1984; and there is still a downward trend in the population growth. Before this very eventful decade, however, population growth was quite high (about + 0.6 % per year during the 20 previous years), due to relatively high fertility levels, almost continuously increasing life expectancies and barely any (outward) migration.

No sign of recovery in most of the 12 countries in 2001

During 2001, the candidate countries as a whole continued to lose people: their combined population at the end of the year was nearly 190 000 less than at the beginning of the year. In relative terms, population decline amounted to 1.8 per 1 000.

However, not all the candidate countries were confronted with an ongoing population decline in 2001. Cyprus and Malta reported fairly strong population increases (+ 0.8 %), twice the EU-15 average, whereas Slovenia is the only central European country whose population is still growing, albeit modestly. By contrast, fairly big population decreases are still being registered in Bulgaria, Estonia, Hungary and Latvia. In all the latter countries, the number of deaths exceeds the number of live births.

Very low fertility rates in most of the 12 countries

In all the central European candidate countries, the total fertility rate remains well below the EU-15 average (1.47 children per woman). Despite the recovery in most EU countries, this indicator is falling or remaining at its low level in most central European countries.

The lowest rates are found in the Czech Republic (1.14), Bulgaria (1.20), Slovakia (1.21) and Slovenia (1.22). Cyprus (1.79) and Malta (1.51) are quite different in their reproductive behaviour. Despite a more or less continuous decline during the 1990s, total fertility rates in both countries are still well above the EU average.

Life expectancy at birth

The life expectancies of Malta and Cyprus differ considerably from those in other candidate countries. In 2000, the life expectancies of women in Cyprus (80.4 years) and Malta (79.3) were below the EU average (81.3), whereas the life expectancies of men were about the same as in the EU (75.1) in both Cyprus (75.3) and Malta (75.1).

The life expectancies in the other candidate countries are noticeably lower than the EU averages. The lowest level for females is recorded in Romania (74.2 years) and for men in Latvia (65.0).

The widest gaps between males and females are found in the Baltic States, Lithuania (10.2 years), Latvia (11.2) and Estonia (10.9) and the narrowest in Malta (4.2), where it is below the EU level of 6.1.

Further reading:

Statistics in Focus — Theme 3
— No 2   First survey of continuing vocational training in enterprises in candidate countries (-CVTS2-)
— No 12 Demographic consequences for the EU of the accession of 12 candidate countries

Do you need more information?
— Ask your Data Shop (see last page)
— http://www.europa.eu.int/comm/eurostat

Educational attainment

In the central and east European candidate countries, there is less disparity in the educational attainment levels between generations than in the EU. In the vast majority of these candidate countries, the proportion of those with tertiary education qualifications is fairly stable across at least three different age groups.

In just over half of the central and east European candidate countries, the proportion of people with tertiary education qualifications in the 30–34 year age group is lower than that in the 35–39 age group. That is a phenomenon that appears rarely in EU Member States.

Unemployment rates

Concerning the link between low education and unemployment, patterns similar to those in the EU can be observed in the candidate countries. Differences in the unemployment rates by level of education are particularly marked in Bulgaria, the Czech Republic, Estonia, Hungary, Poland and Slovakia. In Estonia and Lithuania, unemployment affects approximately one quarter of the youth labour force that has left school.

Expenditure on education as a share of GDP

In 1999, the share of expenditure for primary and secondary education in GDP was generally not much lower among the candidate countries than among the EU Member States. The difference from

the EU average is more marked for tertiary education. For this level, the total percentages are more homogeneous between the accession countries, but all but two (Bulgaria and Estonia) are below the EU average of 1.1 %. Cyprus and Romania report the lowest percentage at just over 0.4 % while the others range between 0.5 and 0.9 %.

Public expenditure per pupil or student

Generally, costs per pupil/student increase with level of education, but there is a wide variation across the countries: in 1999, the candidate countries reported, at all educational levels, less than half the EU average per student.

School expectancy

In general, school expectancy (i.e. the number of years of education that a five-year-old child can expect to receive over his or her lifetime) is lower in the candidate countries than in EU countries.

Early childhood education

In the candidate countries, on average the proportions of 4 year olds enrolled in education are lower than those in the EU.

Language learning

Between 58 and 100 % of students in general upper secondary education are taught English.

In the candidate countries, pupils are more inclined to study German at secondary level than in EU countries.

Tertiary education

For most fields of education and training, the general trends in the candidate countries are similar to those in EU Member States. However, in the fields of 'education', 'humanities and arts', 'social sciences, business and law', 'mathematics, science and computing' and 'engineering, manufacturing and construction', most candidate countries have a proportion of female graduates that is above the EU average. In Bulgaria, Latvia, Poland and Romania, more women than men obtained a qualification in 'mathematics, science and computing' (this was the case in only two EU or EEA countries). Indeed, in Bulgaria, Poland and Romania, approximately two thirds of these qualifications were gained by women compared with an EU average of 41 %. In 'engineering, manufacturing and construction', the proportion of tertiary qualifications awarded to women was between 30 and 40 % in Bulgaria, Estonia, Lithuania and Slovakia (this was the case for only one EU country). This compares to an EU average of 20 %.

Labour costs

The candidate countries have made rapid progress in setting up statistical systems that deliver data on labour costs and earnings, similar to that provided by the EU Member States. For comparison, several of the tables and graphs featured here for the Candidate Countries correspond to those presented for the EU Member States in the chapter 'Economy and ecology, Prices, wages and finance', section 'Wages and labour costs'.

The labour costs survey 2000

The term 'labour costs' refers to the expenditure necessarily incurred by employers in order to employ workers. The recent results of the four-yearly European labour costs survey (LCS) for the year 2000 are featured here. An analysis of total labour costs is presented broken down into three broad groups: 'industry', 'services' plus 'industry and services'. These aggregated labour cost figures for 2000 are presented in euro.

1

Gross annual earnings account for the largest share of total labour costs

As in the EU Member States, by far the largest component of total labour costs is accounted for by the gross annual earnings of employees (employees' remuneration before any deductions for income tax and social security contributions). As for labour costs, the aggregate gross earnings in each country are given in euro.

Tax rates on low-wage earners

In connection with low pay, one of the Commission's structural indicators is the 'tax rate on low-wage earners'. Tax rates differ markedly between the countries, but the trend across Europe in recent years is downward. A detailed description of this indicator is given in the glossary.

Further reading:

Statistics in Focus — Theme 3
— No 23 Labour Costs Survey 2000 Candidate Countries

Do you need more information?
— Ask your Data Shop (see last page)
— http://www.europa.eu.int/comm/eurostat

Business in candidate countries

Facts and figures

DATA 1995-1999

CONTENTS
- Overview of enterprises in the candidate countries
- Analysis of industrial and services activities by sector
- 15 chapters devoted to industry, 5 chapters on services
- Detailed notes on the methodology used

The first comprehensive publication on structural business statistics in the candidate countries which provides standardised data on a wide range of economic activities within these countries.

Like its counterpart dealing with the EU countries, *European business — Facts and figures*, this publication provides a wealth of information on the economies, the development patterns and the state of the different economic sectors of the countries covered. These are Bulgaria, Cyprus, the Czech Republic, Estonia, Hungary, Latvia, Lithuania, Poland, Romania, the Slovak Republic and Slovenia.

Presenting economic activity, with 20 separate chapters covering the main industries and services, and an overview of enterprises and country-specific situations, *Business in the candidate countries — Facts and figures* gives the detailed data necessary for an accurate analysis of key business areas in the candidate countries.

THIS PUBLICATION PROVIDES:
- a solid basis for analysis of business in the EU candidate countries,
- detailed coverage of the main features of business in these countries using clear graphs, tables and explanatory text.

© European Communities, 1995-2002

HOW TO ORDER THIS PUBLICATION

You can purchase *Business in candidate countries — Facts and figures* from the Eurostat Data Shop or Publications Office sales agent of your choice. A complete list of their contact details can be found at the end of this publication or is available on the Eurostat web site: www.europa.eu.int/comm/eurostat

Alternatively, you can simply visit the Eurostat web site and place your order online.

143 pages, € 30.00
Language versions: DE, EN, FR
Catalogue number:
*KS-45-02-975-**-C*
DE: ISBN 92-894-4189-5
EN: ISBN 92-894-4190-9
FR: ISBN 92-894-4191-7

ALSO AVAILABLE IN PDF FORMAT

Total population at 1 January. 1960–2001. 1 000

	1960	1965	1970	1975	1980	1985	1990	1995	1999	2000	2001	
EU-15	314 826	328 648	339 975	348 644	354 572	358 475	363 763	371 341	375 106	376 482	378 037 *	**EU-15**
BG	7 829	8 178	8 464	8 710	8 846	8 971	8 767	8 427	8 230	8 191	8 150	**BG**
CY	:	588	612	622	608	644	675	730	752 *	755	759 *	**CY**
CZ	9 638	9 756	9 907	10 024	10 316	10 334	10 362	10 333	10 290	10 278	10 295	**CZ**
EE	1 209	1 285	1 352	1 424	1 472	1 524	1 572	1 492	1 446	1 372	1 367	**EE**
HU	9 961	10 140	10 322	10 501	10 710	10 599	10 375	10 246	10 092	10 043	10 200 |	**HU**
LT	2 756	2 954	3 119	3 289	3 404	3 529	3 708	3 718	3 701	3 699	3 494 |	**LT**
LV	2 104	2 255	2 352	2 448	2 509	2 570	2 674	2 530	2 439	2 380	2 366	**LV**
MT	327	321	303	302	330	338	352	370	379	389	391	**MT**
PL	29 480	31 339	32 671	33 846	35 413	37 063	38 038	38 581	38 667	38 654	38 644	**PL**
RO	18 319	18 980	20 140	21 142	22 133	22 687	23 211	22 712	22 489	22 456	22 431	**RO**
SI	1 581	1 638	1 720	1 790	1 893	1 949	1 996	1 990	1 978	1 988	1 990	**SI**
SK	3 970	4 350	4 537	4 715	4 963	5 145	5 288	5 356	5 393	5 399	5 379 |	**SK**
TR	:	:	:	:	:	:	:	:	:	:	:	**TR**

eurostat

1

Participation rates in education for 18-year-olds, all levels. 1998–2001. %

	1998	1999	2000	2001	
EU-15	72 *	73	75	:	EU-15
BG	48	47	46	46	BG
CY	:	:	26	:	CY
CZ	64	61	70	86	CZ
EE	62	68	74	74	EE
HU	63	70	77	:	HU
LT	64	68	72	81	LT
LV	61	66	69	73	LV
MT	:	53	37	:	MT
PL	73	74	78	81	PL
RO	37	43	49	58	RO
SI	67	73	78	:	SI
SK	:	:	:	57	SK
TR	:	:	:	:	TR

CY: excludes students studying abroad. PL: estimated. Source: Unesco/OECD/Eurostat data collection.

Public expenditure on education by level of education as % of GDP. 1999

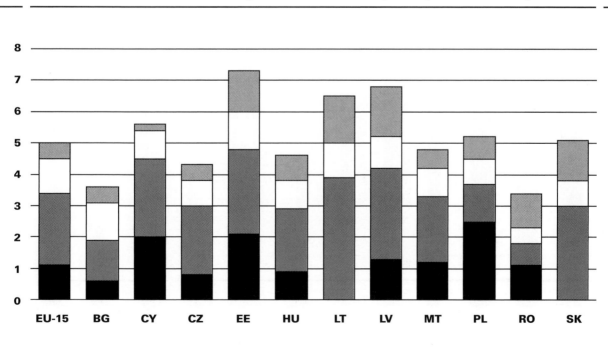

Black: primary (ISCED 1); colour: secondary (ISCED 2, 3, 4); white: tertiary (ISCED 5, 6); grey: others.

Information comes from the Unesco/OECD/Eurostat questionnaire on education finance. LT, SK: primary has been included in secondary. RO: expenditure not allocated by level has been included under 'secondary'.

1

Tax rate on low-wage earners. %. Single person without children on 67 % of the average earnings of a production worker in manufacturing. 1996–2001

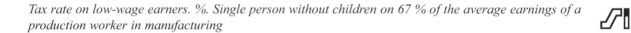

	1996	1997	1998	1999	2000	2001	
EU-15	40.6	40.8	40.3	39.1	38.6	37.8	**EU-15**
BG	40.3	37.8	39.1	37.1	39.4	36.5	**BG**
CY	16.0	16.2	16.3	16.5	16.7	17.0	**CY**
CZ	41.4	41.5	41.4	41.4	41.6	41.6	**CZ**
EE	38.5	39.5	39.8	40.0	38.2	37.4	**EE**
HU	46.8	47.8	47.4	48.2	50.1	45.8	**HU**
LT	:	39.3	39.5	39.7	42.0	42.2	**LT**
LV	39.3	41.5	41.6	41.7	41.4	41.2	**LV**
MT	15.8	15.8	15.8	16.4 *	17.3	17.4	**MT**
PL	43.6	42.9	42.1	41.9	41.9	41.7	**PL**
RO	41.6	41.9	43.8	48.9	42.3	43.5	**RO**
SI	44.2	44.2	44.2	44.2	44.2	43.6	**SI**
SK	42.0	42.1	42.2	42.3	39.1	40.4	**SK**
TR	40.2	43.5	43.0	34.5	39.1	42.0	**TR**

Tax rate on low-wage earners. %. Single person without children on 67 % of the average earnings of a production worker in manufacturing

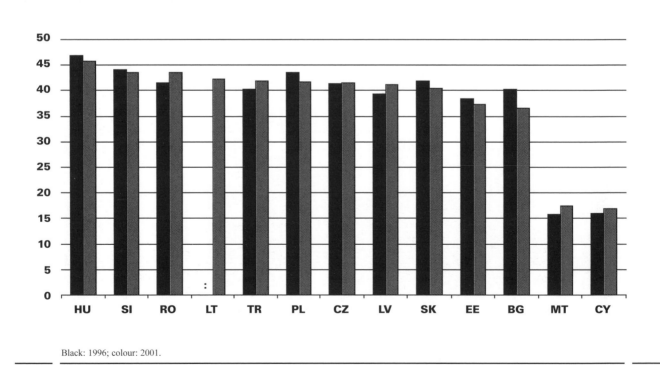

Black: 1996; colour: 2001.

1

Unemployment rate. % of labour force (labour force survey). Spring

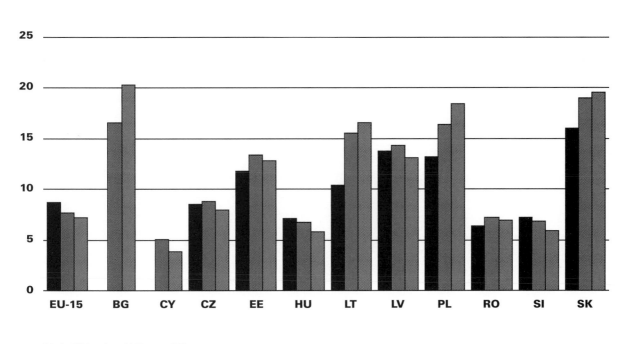

Black: 1999; colour: 2000; grey: 2001.

2001: new definition of unemployment according to Commission Regulation (EC) No 1897/2000 of 7 September 2000 except in CZ, LV, PL, RO and SK. BG: significant changes in the survey and questionnaire design (sampling and weighting procedures) make the comparability of 2001 results with previous years difficult.

Unemployment rate by sex. % of labour force (labour force survey). Spring 2001

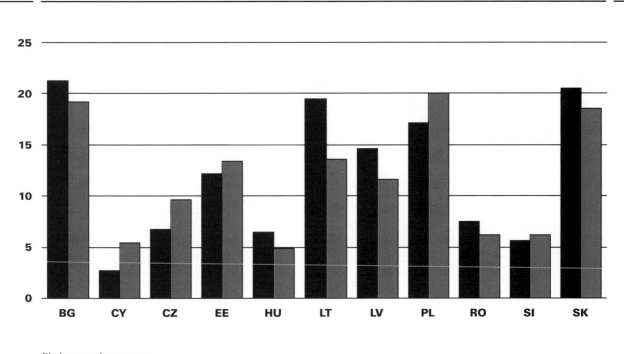

Black: men; colour: women.

Continuing vocational training in enterprises

Continuing vocational training in the candidate countries

The European Commission launched a new survey on continuing vocational training after an initial survey was carried out in 1994 in the then 12 EU Member States. The second survey was implemented in 2000–01 not only in all Member States and Norway, but also in the candidate countries Bulgaria, the Czech Republic, Estonia, Hungary, Latvia, Lithuania, Poland, Romania and Slovenia. The results for Poland apply only to the Pomorskie region.

A total of some 26 000 enterprises in these nine candidate countries took part in the survey. They provided for the first time comparable statistical data on continuing vocational training, on skills supply and demand, on training needs, on the one hand, and the forms, content and volume of continuing training, on the other. Other information is available about the enterprises' own training resources and the use of external training providers. Last but not least, the survey provides information on the costs of continuing training.

The Czech Republic: the candidate country with the highest share of training enterprises

In the nine candidate countries surveyed, the average percentage of enterprises providing continuing vocational training was 40 % in 1999. Percentages ranged from 11 % in Romania to 69 % in the Czech Republic. The average percentage of training enterprises is thus smaller than that observed in the first European continuing vocational training survey in 1993 when the average for the then 12 EU Member States was 57 %.

Great disparities between countries

In the Czech Republic and in Slovenia, the participation of employees in continuing vocational training courses was three times higher than in Lithuania or in Romania. There are only slight disparities in various countries concerning participation rate by gender. Analysis by the enterprises' size class reveals higher rates in big enterprises than in small ones. In all candidate countries, enterprises providing continuing vocational training courses organised more external than internal courses in 1999. In most of the countries, participants spent the longest time on courses in small enterprises.

High training costs in some countries despite low participation

Hungary, Bulgaria and Estonia have relatively high costs compared with their low participation rates. Only in the Czech Republic and in Slovenia are costs of courses in accordance with participation rates.

Further reading:

— First survey on continuing vocational training in enterprises in candidate countries

Statistics in Focus — Theme 3
— No 1 Working time spent on continuing vocational training in enterprises in Europe

Do you need more information?
— Ask your Data Shop (see last page)
— http://www.europa.eu.int/comm/eurostat

1

Training enterprises as % of all enterprises. 1999

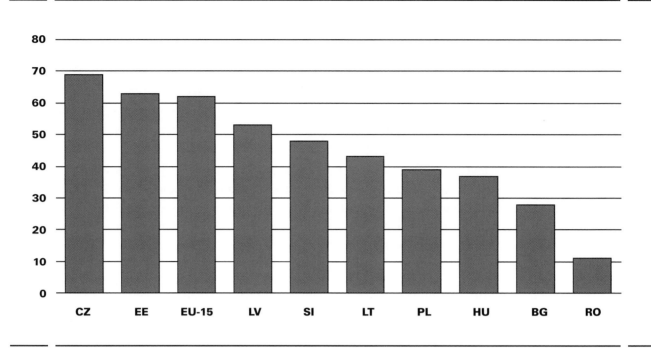

Source: CVTS2, Eurostat.

Percentage of employees (all enterprises) participating in CVT courses. 1999

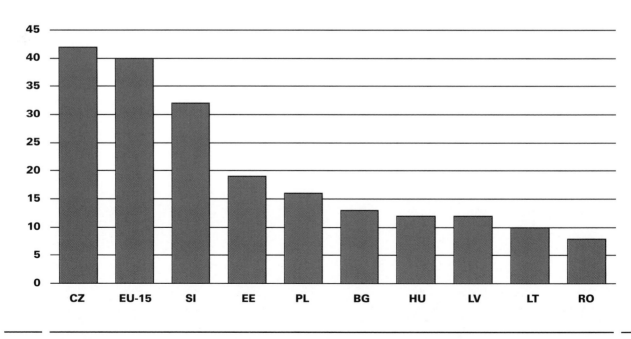

Source: CVTS2, Eurostat.

Economic position

The candidate countries' economies are very diverse in size

The combined size of the economies of the 13 candidate countries in terms of GDP in current prices was EUR 627 700 million in 2001. Even with the inclusion of relatively large countries such as Poland and Turkey, the candidate countries still have a relatively light economic weight compared with the European Union: in 2001, their GDP was 7.1 % of the EU's.

Furthermore, candidate countries' economies are very diverse in size, ranging from EUR 4 000 million in Malta to EUR 196 700 million in Poland in 2001. The Maltese economy, in euro terms, is five times smaller than that of Luxembourg, the smallest EU Member State. Adding together the GDPs of the six smallest candidate countries gives a total of EUR 57 500 million, less than 0.7 % of the EU-15 total.

2001 — a year of diverging growth rates

In 2001, the economic performance of the candidate countries was rather varied. The growth of GDP in current prices ranged from – 7.4 to + 7.7 % in comparison with the previous year. This is in stark contrast to the figures in 2000 when no country recorded negative growth. However, the growth was higher than the EU-15 average in 10 of the 13 countries, ranging from + 3.0 % in Slovenia to + 7.7 % in Latvia.

The government deficit and debt statistics of the candidate countries do not yet fully comply with EU methodological requirements. Nevertheless, the data are roughly comparable across countries.

For the time being, candidate countries notify their government deficit and debt statistics to the European Commission only once a year on 1 April as a trial exercise. Once they are members of the EU, candidate countries will have to notify their government deficit and debt statistics to the European Commission on 1 March and 1 September of each year under the 'excessive deficit procedure'.

With some exceptions, the public finance position of candidate countries does not compare unfavourably with that of EU countries, particularly in terms of debt. However, the large structural changes taking place in these economies have resulted, at least for some countries, in sharp swings in the deficit/surplus.

Exchange and day-to-day money rates are more stable

The evolution of nominal exchange rates against the ecu/euro over the years shows that for most of the candidate countries exchange rates have tended to become more stable.

The same is true for the day-to-day money rate which is a good indicator of the level of short-term market interest rates. It gives an idea of the stance of monetary policy each year.

Further reading:

Statistics in Focus — Theme 2
— No 8   Quarterly accounts Third quarter 2002   — The GDP of the Candidate Countries
— No 17 Candidate Countries' National Accounts by Industry

Do you need more information?
— Ask your Data Shop (see last page)
— http://www.europa.eu.int/comm/eurostat

1

Gross domestic product at constant prices. Change over the previous year. %

	1995	1996	1997	1998	1999	2000	2001	
EU-15	2.4	1.6	2.5	2.9	2.8	3.4	1.5	**EU-15**
BG	2.9	-9.4	-5.6	4.0	2.3	5.4	4.0	**BG**
CY	6.2	1.9	2.5	5.0	4.8	5.2 *	4.2 *	**CY**
CZ	5.9	4.3	-0.8	-1.0	0.5	3.3	3.3	**CZ**
EE	4.3	3.9	9.8	4.6	-0.6	7.1	5.0	**EE**
HU	1.5	1.3	4.6	4.9	4.2	5.2	3.7	**HU**
LT	3.3	4.7	7.3	5.1	-3.9	3.8	6.0	**LT**
LV	-1.7	3.7	8.4	4.8	2.8	6.8	7.7	**LV**
MT	6.2	4.0	4.9	3.4	4.1	4.8	-0.4	**MT**
PL	7.0	6.0	6.8	4.8	4.1	4.0	1.1	**PL**
RO	7.1	4.0	-6.1	-4.8	-1.2	1.8	5.3	**RO**
SI	4.1	3.5	4.6	3.8	5.2	4.6	3.0	**SI**
SK	6.5	5.8	5.6	4.0	1.3	2.2	3.3	**SK**
TR	7.2	7.0	7.5	3.1	-4.7	7.4	-7.4	**TR**

Gross domestic product at current prices. 1 000 million ECU/EUR

	1995	1996	1997	1998	1999	2000	2001	
EU-15	6 588.4	6 919.6	7 287.7	7 629.8	8 023.7	8 545.0	8 814.8	**EU-15**
BG	10.0	7.8	9.2	11.4	12.2	13.7	15.2	**BG**
CY	6.8	7.0	7.5	8.1	8.7	9.6 *	10.2 *	**CY**
CZ	39.8	45.5	46.8	50.6	51.6	55.8	63.3	**CZ**
EE	2.7	3.4	4.1	4.7	4.9	5.6	6.2	**EE**
HU	34.1	35.6	40.4	41.9	45.1	50.6	58.0	**HU**
LT	4.6	6.2	8.5	9.6	10.0	12.2	13.4	**LT**
LV	3.4	4.0	5.0	5.4	6.2	7.8	8.5	**LV**
MT	2.5	2.6	2.9	3.1	3.4	3.9	4.0	**MT**
PL	97.2	113.3	127.1	141.3	145.5	170.9	196.7	**PL**
RO	27.1	27.8	31.2	37.4	33.4	40.2	44.4	**RO**
SI	14.3	14.9	16.1	17.5	18.8	19.5	20.9	**SI**
SK	14.6	16.1	18.6	19.6	18.9	21.3	22.3	**SK**
TR	129.6	143.1	167.8	177.8	173.1	216.7	164.6	**TR**

Gross domestic product per capita at current prices in PPS. EU-15 = 100

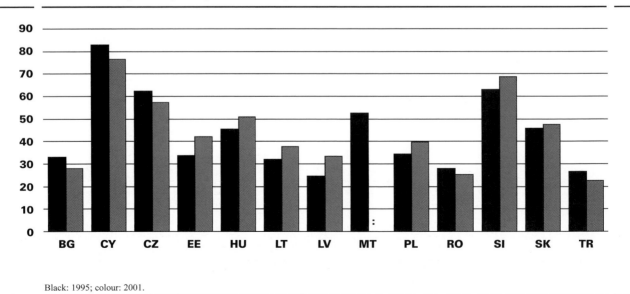

Black: 1995; colour: 2001.

For the calculation of per capita GDP, population data are taken from the national accounts and may be different from those obtained via demographic statistics. CY: 2001 estimated data.

Short-term interest rates: day-to-day money rates. %

	1993	1994	1995	1996	1997	1998	1999	2000	2001	
EU-15	8.7	6.3	6.5	5.1	4.7	4.5	3.3	4.5	4.5	**EU-15**
BG	:	:	69.9	286.4	136.8	2.4	2.6	2.9	3.7	**BG**
CY	:	:	:	6.9	4.7	4.8	5.2	6.0	4.9	**CY**
CZ	9.6	7.9	10.6	11.6	19.2	13.6	6.8	5.3	5.0	**CZ**
EE	:	5.7	4.9	3.5	6.5	11.7	4.9	4.8	4.5	**EE**
HU	15.4	25.6	31.3	23.8	20.8	18.0	14.8	11.1	10.9	**HU**
LT	:	:	:	:	:	6.1	6.3	3.6	3.4	**LT**
LV	:	37.2	22.4	13.1	3.7	4.4	4.7	3.0	5.2	**LV**
MT	:	:	:	:	5.2	5.5	5.0	4.7	4.7	**MT**
PL	:	18.7	26.4	21.2	22.7	21.1	14.1	18.1	17.1	**PL**
RO	:	92.9	48.6	53.4	86.0	80.9	80.8	44.8	41.0	**RO**
SI	38.6	28.7	12.0	13.8	9.6	7.4	6.8	6.8	6.7	**SI**
SK	:	13.1	5.7	11.6	24.6	14.5	11.5	8.0	7.4	**SK**
TR	62.2	131.0	72.4	76.2	70.3	74.6	73.5	56.7	92.0	**TR**

Ecu/euro exchange rates: annual averages. ECU/EUR 1 = ...

	1991	1992	1993	1994	1995	1996	1997	1998	1999	2000	2001	
BG	0.034	0.051	0.032	0.064	0.088	0.225	1.902	1.969	1.956	1.948	1.948	**BG**
CY	0.5734	0.5837	0.5829	0.5839	0.5916	0.5919	0.5826	0.5774	0.5789	0.5739	0.5759	**CY**
CZ	:	:	34.169	34.151	34.696	34.457	35.930	36.320	36.884	35.600	34.069	**CZ**
EE	:	:	15.491	15.396	14.990	15.276	15.715	15.753	15.647	15.647	15.647	**EE**
HU	142.202	172.777	107.611	125.030	164.545	193.741	211.654	240.573	252.767	260.045	256.591	**HU**
LT	:	2.143	5.087	4.732	5.232	5.079	4.536	4.484	4.264	3.695	3.582	**LT**
LV	:	0.8961	0.7936	0.6641	0.6895	0.6996	0.6594	0.6602	0.6256	0.5592	0.5601	**LV**
MT	0.3998	0.4130	0.4470	0.4489	0.4614	0.4582	0.4375	0.4350	0.4258	0.4041	0.4030	**MT**
PL	2.017	2.975	2.122	2.702	3.170	3.422	3.715	3.918	4.227	4.008	3.672	**PL**
RO	145.4	673.7	885.8	1971.6	2661.8	3922.2	8111.5	9984.9	16345.2	19921.8	26004.0	**RO**
SI	36.969	98.434	132.486	152.766	154.880	171.778	180.996	185.958	194.473	206.613	217.980	**SI**
SK	:	:	36.032	38.118	38.865	38.923	38.106	39.541	44.123	42.602	43.300	**SK**
TR	5153	8931	12879	35535	59912	103214	171848	293736	447237	574816	1102430	**TR**

Consumer price index. Annual average rate of change. %

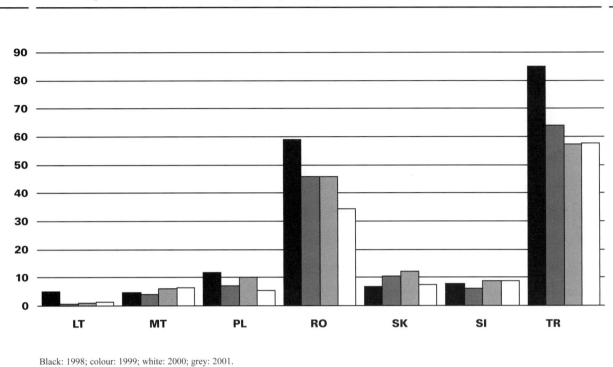

Black: 1998; colour: 1999; white: 2000; grey: 2001.

Interim HICP for BG, CY, CZ, EE, HU, LT, LV, PL, RO and SL. MT and TR calculate national indices. National index for SK in 2001.

Consumer price index. Annual average rate of change. %

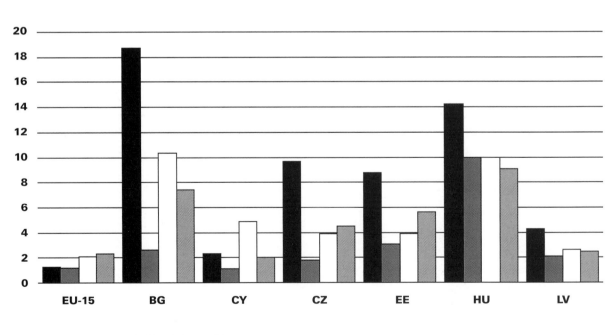

Black: 1998; colour: 1999; white: 2000; grey: 2001.

Interim HICP for BG, CY, CZ, EE, HU, LT, LV, PL, RO and SL. MT and TR calculate national indices. National index for SK in 2001.

Gross value added at current basic prices and current exchange rates. Manufacturing.
% of all branches

1

	1991	1992	1993	1994	1995	1996	1997	1998	1999	2000	2001	
BG	:	:	:	:	:	20.8	18.3	18.3	15.6	16.6	:	BG
CY	:	:	:	:	12.5	12.2	11.9	11.4	11.0	10.7 *	10.4 *	CY
CZ	28.5	29.1	24.5	25.4	26.0	28.0	28.2	26.8	26.3	27.0	27.5	CZ
EE	:	:	20.5	20.3	19.0	18.1	18.0	17.7	16.5	18.1	18.4	EE
HU	21.5	22.2	21.9	21.6	22.5	22.5	23.9	24.1	23.5	24.9	23.5	HU
LT	44.4	33.3	30.1	24.1	22.2	21.8	20.5	18.8	17.6	20.9	22.5	LT
LV	35.7	28.2	23.1	19.9	22.7	21.1	22.3	17.9	15.3	14.6	14.8	LV
MT	:	:	:	:	:	:	:	:	:	:	:	MT
PL	:	28.1	27.4	22.4	23.6	22.5	22.4	21.5	21.1	20.6	:	PL
RO	33.1	29.2	27.5	29.8	28.7	30.8	28.0	23.5	21.2	0.0	0.0	RO
SI	34.3	31.8	29.5	30.0	28.3	27.7	27.6	27.4	27.0	27.2	26.8	SI
SK	:	:	19.8	22.0	27.2	25.6	22.6	22.7	23.9	24.0	24.0	SK
TR	21.4	20.9	20.0	21.2	21.8	20.2	20.6	18.3	18.2	18.6	19.0	TR

Further reading:

Statistics in Focus — Theme 2
— No 8 Quarterly accounts Third quarter 2002 — The GDP of the Candidate Countries
— No 17 Candidate Countries' National Accounts by Industry

Do you need more information?
— Ask your Data Shop (see last page)
— http://www.europa.eu.int/comm/eurostat

Gross value added at current basic prices and current exchange rates. Wholesale and retail trade;
repair of motor vehicles, motorcycles and personal and household goods. % of all branches

	1991	1992	1993	1994	1995	1996	1997	1998	1999	2000	2001	
BG	:	:	:	:	:	10.8	8.4	7.3	7.0	9.1	:	BG
CY	:	:	:	:	13.9	13.6	13.4	13.6	12.9	13.0 *	12.9 *	CY
CZ	12.0	12.5	11.7	11.3	11.5	10.3	13.2	14.0	14.3	14.3	14.8	CZ
EE	:	:	15.2	13.9	14.8	15.8	15.1	14.9	14.4	13.9	14.2	EE
HU	13.4	10.8	11.3	10.7	11.3	11.3	11.5	11.6	11.0	10.9	11.0	HU
LT	6.1	9.2	14.0	17.6	17.8	16.8	16.5	16.3	15.4	15.7	15.6	LT
LV	9.1	11.6	8.5	9.8	11.4	15.5	16.1	16.8	17.7	18.0	18.8	LV
MT	:	:	:	:	:	:	:	:	:	:	:	MT
PL	:	13.7	16.2	20.2	20.0	20.9	21.0	20.7	20.6	20.9	:	PL
RO	12.0	11.8	8.7	7.1	9.4	9.8	9.8	12.1	12.5	16.1	51.3	RO
SI	9.8	10.5	11.1	11.8	12.1	11.6	11.5	11.4	11.5	11.3	11.4	SI
SK	:	:	17.8	15.4	12.8	11.9	14.0	14.4	14.4	15.8	15.7	SK
TR	15.4	15.2	15.3	15.9	16.8	16.4	16.4	15.5	15.0	16.0	15.6	TR

Imports of goods. Cif valuation in million ECU/EUR

	1991	1992	1993	1994	1995	1996	1997	1998	1999	2000	2001	
BG	:	:	:	:	4 169,3	3 996,0	4 349,0	4 455,6	5 098,3	7 084,9	8 127,8	**BG**
CY	2 114,6	2 542,5	2 165,6	2 533,8	2 824,0	3 135,9	3 260,9	3 288,1	2 802,8	3 386,2	3 744,1	**CY**
CZ	:	:	10 848,8	12 568,9	19 345,0	21 829,0	23 970,5	27 227,3	26 706,0	34 619,2	40 528,6	**CZ**
EE	:	:	:	:	1 946,7	2 539,0	3 912,8	4 269,7	3 224,2	4 617,3	4 798,0	**EE**
HU	:	8 376,5	9 714,8	12 234,9	11 609,7	12 634,5	18 724,2	8 217,7	26 285,6	34 832,8	37 535,3	**HU**
LT	:	:	:	2 176,5	2 789,5	3 590,3	4 976,5	5 168,0	4 349,2	5 681,3	6 692,2	**LT**
LV	:	:	:	1 043,7	1 389,9	1 826,7	2 399,4	2 846,7	2 771,5	3 466,4	3 915,0	**LV**
MT	:	:	:	2 051,8	2 249,0	2 207,0	2 251,7	2 378,4	2 667,4	3 695,9	2 826,2	**MT**
PL	:	12 258,6	16 084,1	18 132,6	22 209,1	29 247,3	37 306,9	41 971,3	43 050,8	53 084,6	56 034,5	**PL**
RO	4 675,2	4 822,1	5 569,3	5 976,4	7 857,7	9 005,9	9 946,5	10 557,1	9 773,7	14 235,4	17 383,3	**RO**
SI	:	4 730,8	5 551,6	6 140,2	7 256,6	7 419,3	8 258,7	9 018,4	9 478,4	10 986,6	11 344,5	**SI**
SK	:	:	:	5 557,7	6 239,9	7 410,9	10 340,9	11 559,6	10 619,7	13 815,3	16 480,8	**SK**
TR	16 984,9	17 618,8	25 131,8	19 560,8	27 299,1	33 810,1	42 842,5	40 949,6	38 175,6	58 734,8	46 223,4	**TR**

Trade balance for 2001. Million EUR

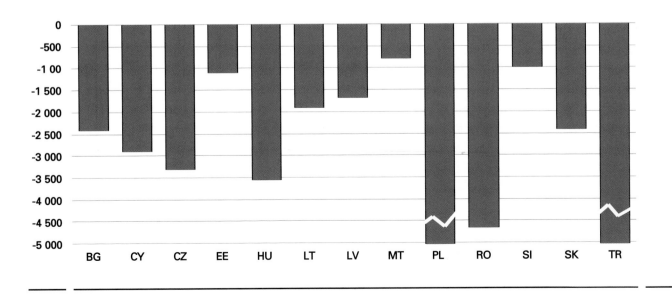

Balance of the current account at current prices. % of GDP

	1994	1995	1996	1997	1998	1999	2000	2001	
BG	-0.3	-1.5	1.6	10.1	-0.5	-5.3	-5.5	-6.0	BG
CY	:	-1.8	-5.2	-4.0	-6.7	-2.4	-5.2	-4.3	CY
CZ	-1.9	-2.6	-7.4	-6.1	-2.3	-2.9	-5.3	-4.6	CZ
EE	-7.2	-4.4	-9.2	-12.2	-9.2	-5.7	-6.0	-6.2	EE
HU	-9.8	-5.3	-3.7	-2.1	-4.9	-4.4	-3.2	-2.1	HU
LT	-2.1	-10.2	-9.2	-10.2	-12.1	-11.2	-6.0	-1.3	LT
LV	5.5	-0.4	-5.5	-6.1	-10.6	-9.6	-6.9	-9.7	LV
MT	:	-11.2	-12.2	-5.9	-6.2	-3.4	-14.9	-4.7	MT
PL	1.0	0.7	-2.3	-4.0	-4.4	-8.1	-6.3	-3.0	PL
RO	-1.4	-5.0	-7.3	-6.0	-7.1	-3.6	-3.7	-6.5	RO
SI	4.0	-0.4	0.2	0.3	-0.6	-3.5	-3.0	0.2	SI
SK	4.4	2.0	-10.2	-9.3	-9.7	-5.7	-3.6	-8.5	SK
TR	2.0	-1.4	-1.3	-1.4	1.0	-0.7	-4.9	2.3	TR

Balance of international trade in goods and services at current prices. % of GDP

	1994	1995	1996	1997	1998	1999	2000	2001	
BG	-0.1	0.8	4.6	11.2	-0.1	-5.9	-5.3	-7.5	BG
CY	:	-2.3	-5.3	-4.2	-6.7	-2.9	-6.3	-4.2	CY
CZ	-2.2	-3.5	-6.9	-5.2	-1.3	-1.5	-3.3	-2.7	CZ
EE	-10.9	-8.0	-11.5	-11.6	-10.4	-5.9	-4.2	-3.8	EE
HU	-8.6	-1.7	-0.4	0.7	-1.2	-1.6	-0.7	0.3	HU
LT	-6.0	-11.8	-9.8	-10.6	-11.9	-10.3	-6.4	-1.5	LT
LV	1.6	-2.4	-8.1	-8.5	-13.5	-10.3	-8.7	-11.3	LV
MT	:	-13.2	-13.4	-7.9	-6.0	-5.4	-10.9	-4.8	MT
PL	2.3	1.5	-2.7	-4.6	-5.4	-8.8	-6.9	-3.9	PL
RO	-1.9	-5.4	-8.1	-6.8	-7.8	-4.2	-5.2	-8.9	RO
SI	2.1	-1.9	-1.0	-0.7	-1.5	-4.4	-3.7	-0.6	SI
SK	4.7	1.6	-11.0	-9.5	-10.6	-5.2	-2.4	-8.0	SK
TR	2.2	-2.1	-2.2	-2.4	-0.4	-1.6	-5.5	3.1	TR

International trade in goods and services, cover rates. %

	1994	1995	1996	1997	1998	1999	2000	2001	
BG	99.9	101.5	107.4	120.0	99.9	88.3	91.3	88.1	BG
CY	:	95.5	90.0	92.0	86.9	94.0	88.1	91.9	CY
CZ	95.9	93.9	88.3	91.5	97.8	97.6	95.4	96.3	CZ
EE	87.4	90.0	85.3	87.1	88.4	92.8	95.8	96.0	EE
HU	75.2	96.1	99.1	101.4	97.9	97.2	99.0	100.4	HU
LT	90.2	81.8	84.4	83.8	79.9	79.4	87.6	90.3	LT
LV	103.7	95.1	86.3	85.7	79.1	81.0	84.1	79.9	LV
MT	:	87.5	86.4	91.4	93.5	94.2	90.2	94.7	MT
PL	109.9	105.6	90.6	85.6	83.4	73.7	81.0	88.3	PL
RO	92.5	83.2	77.2	80.6	74.4	86.7	86.2	80.8	RO
SI	103.7	96.6	98.2	98.7	97.4	92.2	94.1	99.0	SI
SK	108.7	102.9	82.8	85.5	84.9	92.0	96.7	90.4	SK
TR	110.6	91.0	92.0	92.1	98.6	93.8	82.2	110.0	TR

1

Business structure

Working on comparability

The EU's future enlargement raised the need for the extension of the SBS data coverage to the candidate countries. The collection process for SBS data from the candidate countries has started recently.

Inevitably, there are still a few methodological divergences between the various candidate countries' data that need to be smoothed out over the coming years.

All the candidate countries' data are expressed in current ecu/euro, which does not reflect the actual purchasing power of the candidate countries' currencies. Nevertheless, the available data present useful gauges for an analysis of the candidate countries' economic sectors.

Further reading:

Eurostat publications
— R & D and innovation statistics in candidate countries and the Russian Federation

Statistics in Focus — Theme 1
— No 6 Regional population change in candidate and EU countries
— No 8 Regional unemployment rates in the central European candidate countries 2000
— No 2 Regional gross domestic product in candidate countries 1999

Statistics in Focus — Theme 4
— No 6 Information society statistics — Data for central European candidate countries (CEC)
**— No 37 Information society statistics — Rapid growth of Internet and mobile phone usage in
         candidate countries in 2000**

Statistics in Focus — Theme 6
— No 8 The 13 candidate countries' trade with the EU in 2000
— No 6 Specialisation of candidate countries in relation to the EU

Statistics in Focus — Theme 7
— No 4 Transport in central European countries 1993–1998

Do you need more information?
— Ask your Data Shop (see last page)
— http://www.europa.eu.int/comm/eurostat

1

Industrial production volume index. Previous year = 100

		1997	1998	1999	2000	2001	
BG		81.7	91.5	90.3	110.3	97.6 *	**BG**
CY		99.8	102.6	102.1	104.5	99.7	**CY**
CZ		104.5	101.9	96.9	105.4	106.5	**CZ**
EE		114.6	104.1	96.6	114.6	107.8 *	**EE**
HU		111.1	112.5	110.4	118.1	104.1	**HU**
LT		103.3	108.2	88.8	105.3	116.9	**LT**
LV		113.8	103.1	94.6	104.7	108.4 *	**LV**
MT		98.5	110.5	107.0	116.2	93.2	**MT**
PL		111.5	103.5	103.6	106.7	99.9 *	**PL**
RO		92.8	86.2	97.8	107.6	108.2 *	**RO**
SI		101.0	103.7	99.5	106.2	102.9	**SI**
SK		101.3	103.6	97.3	108.6	106.9	**SK**
TR		111.5	101.3	97.5	103.4	94.5	**TR**

MT: 1999–2001 estimated, since the index compiled according to ISIC was discontinued. RO: 1997–2000 based on the structure of 1995; 2001 based on the structure of 1998. SK: 1997–98 calculated from industrial goods production; 1999–2001 based on EU methodology.

1

Value added at factor cost of mining and quarrying. Million EUR

	1997	1998	1999	
BG	:	:	211	**BG**
CY	19	24	:	**CY**
CZ	:	:	:	**CZ**
EE	54	48	54	**EE**
HU	:	110	106	**HU**
LT	23	25	32	**LT**
LV	8	8	:	**LV**
MT	:	:	:	**MT**
PL	4 193	3 573	:	**PL**
RO	1 334	1 674	1 121	**RO**
SI	119	126	:	**SI**
SK	165	143	122	**SK**
TR	:	:	:	**TR**

Value added at factor cost of manufacturing. Million EUR

	1997	1998	1999	
BG	:	:	1 647	**BG**
CY	779	813	:	**CY**
CZ	:	:	:	**CZ**
EE	621	655	618	**EE**
HU	:	7 514	8 236	**HU**
LT	1 003	1 057	939	**LT**
LV	825	872	:	**LV**
MT	:	:	:	**MT**
PL	25 700	28 713	:	**PL**
RO	6 744	6 303	5 479	**RO**
SI	3 169	3 372	:	**SI**
SK	2 551	2 595	2 147	**SK**
TR	:	:	:	**TR**

Value added at factor cost of electricity, gas and water supply. Million EUR

	1997	1998	1999	
BG	:	:	471	**BG**
CY	152	165	:	**CY**
CZ	:	:	:	**CZ**
EE	128	166	149	**EE**
HU	:	1 383	1 511	**HU**
LT	246	355	299	**LT**
LV	253	253	:	**LV**
MT	:	:	:	**MT**
PL	3 853	4 196	:	**PL**
RO	1 874	1 470	1 221	**RO**
SI	199	211	:	**SI**
SK	1 133	1 257	1 136	**SK**
TR	:	:	:	**TR**

Value added at factor cost of construction. Million EUR

	1997	1998	1999	
BG	:	:	375	**BG**
CY	598	621	:	**CY**
CZ	:	:	:	**CZ**
EE	164	192	155	**EE**
HU	:	655	784	**HU**
LT	315	390	339	**LT**
LV	199	264	:	**LV**
MT	:	:	:	**MT**
PL	5 109	5 927	:	**PL**
RO	1 110	1 276	1 026	**RO**
SI	601	644	716	**SI**
SK	463	425	294	**SK**
TR	:	:	:	**TR**

1

Value added at factor cost of wholesale and retail trade; repair of motor vehicles, motorcycles and personal and household goods. Million EUR

Value added at factor cost of hotels and restaurants. Million EUR

	1997	1998	1999		1997	1998	1999	
BG	:	:	648		:	:	141	BG
CY	991	1 072	:		618	681	:	CY
CZ	:	:	:		:	:	:	CZ
EE	400	427	433		39	43	47	EE
HU	:	2 102	:		:	268	273	HU
LT	614	757	645		36	48	48	LT
LV	:	668	:		39	42	:	LV
MT	:	:	:		:	:	:	MT
PL	13 035	13 358	:		713	742	:	PL
RO	2 197	:	:		168	193	180	RO
SI	1 388	1 419	1 479		202	217	221	SI
SK	659	826	674		52	60	58	SK
TR	:	:	:		:	:	:	TR

Value added at factor cost of transport, storage and communication. Million EUR

Value added at factor cost of real estate, renting and business activities. Million EUR

	1997	1998	1999		1997	1998	1999	
BG	:	:	894		:	:	177	BG
CY	:	:	:		:	:	:	CY
CZ	:	:	:		:	:	:	CZ
EE	371	511	566		151	213	223	EE
HU	:	2 424	2 907		:	967	1 226	HU
LT	514	638	588		167	210	254	LT
LV	664	742	:		177	320	:	LV
MT	:	:	:		:	:	:	MT
PL	6 735	7 650	:		4 808	6 741	:	PL
RO	:	1 806	:		425	564	548	RO
SI	740	792	814		604	704	805	SI
SK	843	938	772		417	422	357	SK
TR	:	:	:		:	:	:	TR

Total production of primary energy. 1 000 toe

	1993	1994	1995	1996	1997	1998	1999	2000	
EU-15	709 157	722 802	736 563	762 177	755 772	750 633	764 535	758 694	EU-15
BG	9 165	9 318	10 187	10 578	10 104	10 139	8 923	9 831	BG
CY	6	6	5	6	4	4	4	37	CY
CZ	34 992	32 388	31 820	32 500	32 810	30 790	27 500	29 635	CZ
EE	3 824	3 881	3 538	3 932	3 830	3 421	3 977	3 162	EE
HU	13 476	13 210	13 507	13 091	12 913	12 105	11 551	11 459	HU
LT	3 947	2 795	3 553	4 103	3 908	4 439	3 481	3 178	LT
LV	1 331	1 400	910	1 025	1 660	1 781	1 516	1 251	LV
MT	0	0	0	0	0	0	0	0	MT
PL	96 618	96 546	98 504	101 861	99 428	87 025	83 442	78 911	PL
RO	31 895	30 407	30 647	33 856	30 367	27 890	26 811	29 630	RO
SI	2 869	2 967	3 019	2 938	3 036	3 037	2 864	3 047	SI
SK	4 452	4 861	5 439	5 357	5 235	5 378	5 873	5 877	SK
TR	17 507	17 705	18 087	18 727	19 662	20 898	28 244	27 365	TR

CY: 2000 data include solar heat. TR: 1993–98 data do not include renewables.

Total gross electricity generation. GWh

	1993	1994	1995	1996	1997	1998	1999	2000	
EU-15	2 231 695	2 269 160	2 327 233	2 411 194	2 426 436	2 493 349	2 531 725	2 601 237	EU-15
BG	37 997	38 133	41 789	42 716	42 803	41 711	38 248	40 924	BG
CY	2 581	2 681	2 473	2 592	2 711	2 954	3 139	3 370	CY
CZ	58 881	58 705	60 847	64 257	64 589	65 112	64 693	73 466	CZ
EE	9 119	9 154	8 694	9 103	9 218	8 520	8 267	8 512	EE
HU	32 915	33 515	34 017	35 089	35 396	37 188	37 154	35 191	HU
LT	14 232	10 057	13 942	16 789	14 861	17 631	13 535	11 424	LT
LV	3 924	4 440	3 979	3 124	4 502	5 797	4 110	4 136	LV
MT	1 500	1 541	1 632	1 658	1 686	1 721	1 792	1 917	MT
PL	133 867	135 347	138 993	143 173	142 790	142 789	142 128	145 183	PL
RO	55 476	55 136	59 266	61 350	57 148	53 496	50 710	51 934	RO
SI	11 692	12 631	12 654	12 778	13 176	13 728	13 262	13 624	SI
SK	23 417	24 740	26 306	25 290	24 547	25 465	27 743	30 685	SK
TR	73 808	78 321	86 247	94 862	103 296	111 022	116 440	124 922	TR

Final energy consumption. 1 000 toe

	1993	1994	1995	1996	1997	1998	1999	2000	
EU-15	885 307	880 281	898 608	936 009	927 834	943 644	952 421	952 261	EU-15
BG	10 602	10 668	11 219	11 347	9 980	9 470	8 432	8 160	BG
CY	1 213	1 243	1 012	1 072	1 090	1 120	1 142	1 613	CY
CZ	25 090	24 096	25 400	26 330	24 420	23 950	21 454	24 058	CZ
EE	3 092	3 070	2 680	2 839	2 764	2 555	2 544	2 405	EE
HU	15 290	15 147	16 349	16 837	16 005	15 795	15 962	15 695	HU
LT	4 772	4 426	4 510	4 426	4 514	4 445	4 079	3 744	LT
LV	3 799	3 345	3 542	3 877	3 868	3 695	3 373	3 011	LV
MT	422	415	435	420	455	411	554	664	MT
PL	63 785	61 324	62 079	65 910	63 924	59 175	58 396	55 291	PL
RO	26 269	25 328	25 104	30 608	27 661	24 670	21 136	22 352	RO
SI	3 556	3 796	3 889	4 313	4 448	4 202	4 289	4 407	SI
SK	11 519	10 899	12 241	12 399	11 927	11 918	12 326	11 242	SK
TR	33 314	31 576	35 981	39 556	41 333	40 772	48 852	53 954	TR

TR: 1993–98 data do not include renewables.

eurostat

1

Total length of motorways in km

	1996	1997	1998	1999	2000
EU-15	46 423	47 663	49 173	50 714	51 559
BG	314	314	319	324	324
CY	194	199	204	216	240
CZ	423	485	499	499	499
EE	66	68	74	87	93
HU	365	381	448	448	448
LT	404	410	417	417	417
LV	-	-	-	-	-
MT	:	:	:	:	:
PL	258	264	268	317	358
RO	113	113	113	113	113
SI	310	330	369	399	427
SK	215	219	292	295	296
TR	1 405	1 528	1 726	1 749	1 773

Total length of railway lines in km

	1996	1997	1998	1999	2000	
159 044	157 291	159 784	156 542	156 353	**EU-15**
4 293	4 291	4 290	4 290	4 320	**BG**
-	-	-	-	-	**CY**
9 430	9 430	9 430	9 444	9 444	**CZ**
1 020	1 018	968	968	968	**EE**
7 619	7 593	7 642	7 651	7 679	**HU**
:	:	:	:	:	**LT**
2 413	2 413	2 413	2 413	2 331	**LV**
:	:	:	:	:	**MT**
23 420	23 328	23 210	22 891	22 560	**PL**
11 385	11 380	11 010	10 981	11 015	**RO**
1 201	1 201	1 201	1 201	1 201	**SI**
3 673	3 673	3 665	3 665	3 665	**SK**
8 607	8 607	8 607	8 682	8 671	**TR**

Passenger cars. 1 000s

	1996	1997	1998	1999	2000
EU-15	161 925	165 303	169 194	173 772	177 377
BG	1 707	1 731	1 809	1 908	1 993
CY	227	235	249	257	268
CZ	3 192	3 392	3 493	3 440	3 439
EE	407	428	451	459	464
HU	2 264	2 297	2 218	2 256	2 365
LT	785	882	981	1 089	1 172
LV	380	432	483	526	557
MT	166	184	175	182	189
PL	8 054	8 533	8 891	9 283	9 991
RO	2 392	2 606	2 822	2 980	3 129
SI	741	778	813	848	868
SK	1 058	1 136	1 196	1 236	1 274
TR	3 274	3 570	3 838	4 072	4 422

Passenger cars per 1 000 inhabitants

	1996	1997	1998	1999	2000	
434	441	450	461	469	**EU-15**
205	209	220	233	245	**BG**
306	315	332	340	353	**CY**
310	329	339	335	335	**CZ**
278	294	312	335	340	**EE**
223	227	220	225	236	**HU**
212	238	265	294	317	**LT**
153	176	198	221	235	**LV**
444	488	453	468	483	**MT**
208	221	230	240	259	**PL**
106	116	125	129	139	**RO**
373	392	411	427	436	**SI**
197	211	222	229	236	**SK**
53	57	60	63	67	**TR**

Goods transport by road. Million tonne-km

	1996	1997	1998	1999	2000
EU-15	1 129 100	1 173 000	1 240 600	1 297 500	1 327 200
BG	27 305	26 505	22 514	19 164	6 404
CY	:	:	:	:	:
CZ	30 052	40 640	33 911	36 964	39 036
EE	1 897	2 773	3 791	3 975	2 690
HU	14 325	14 856	18 674	18 599	19 124
LT	4 191	5 146	5 611	7 740	7 769
LV	2 208	3 352	4 108	4 161	4 789
MT	:	:	:	:	:
PL	55 461	62 590	68 450	69 792	72 174
RO	19 807	21 750	15 785	13 456	14 288
SI	1 548	1 599	1 714	1 649	1 845
SK	15 850	15 350	17 879	18 516	21 369
TR	135 781	139 789	152 210	150 974	161 552

Persons killed in road accidents

	1996	1997	1998	1999	2000	
43 626	43 312	42 643	41 967	41 116	**EU-15**
1 014	915	1 003	1 047	1 012	**BG**
128	115	111	113	111	**CY**
1 562	1 597	1 360	1 455	1 486	**CZ**
213	280	284	232	204	**EE**
1 370	1 391	1 371	1 306	1 200	**HU**
667	725	829	748	641	**LT**
550	525	627	604	588	**LV**
19	18	17	4	15	**MT**
6 359	7 310	7 080	6 730	6 294	**PL**
2 845	2 863	2 778	2 505	2 499	**RO**
389	357	309	334	313	**SI**
640	828	860	671	647	**SK**
5 428	5 125	6 083	5 713	5 510	**TR**

Persons who die within 30 days of the accident. For the countries that do not follow this definition, a correction factor has been applied.

eurostat

1

Tourist accommodation: hotels and similar establishments

	1995	1996	1997	1998	1999	2000	2001	
EU-15	190 061	189 318	186 851	186 484	198 492	198 063	:	EU-15
BG	526	523	477	513	518	648	679	BG
CY	538	573	568	580	580	583	594	CY
CZ	1 387	2 737	3 509	3 669	3 614	3 690	3 576	CZ
EE	160	174	200	237	329	350	353	EE
HU	1 501	1 687	1 739	1 817	1 851	1 928	1 993	HU
LT	143	173	182	201	221	227	231	LT
LV	135	151	152	148	150	166	:	LV
MT	256	255	261	133	130	123	130	MT
PL	1 068	1 247	1 397	1 576	1 535	1 449	1 391	PL
RO	2 294	2 362	2 446	2 535	2 660	2 533	2 681	RO
SI	307	398	404	402	398	448	381	SI
SK	447	476	397	543	570	582	764	SK
TR	1 769	1 843	1 914	1 935	1 862	1 814	:	TR

Nights spent by residents in hotels and similar establishments

	1995	1996	1997	1998	1999	2000	2001	
EU-15	587 163 908	587 073 684	601 624 459	608 822 769	660 730 665	734 550 681	:	EU-15
BG	3 735 094	3 237 997	2 537 918	2 921 278	2 662 146	3 036 033	2 855 602	BG
CY	345 770	480 221	523 998	569 828	585 437	597 429	726 828	CY
CZ	6 952 469	9 907 743	10 736 614	9 919 000	10 608 000	12 358 000	8 514 752	CZ
EE	325 000	292 000	333 000	413 000	439 000	459 109	489 443	EE
HU	3 972 000	4 135 000	4 334 000	4 714 000	5 196 000	5 479 073	5 320 713	HU
LT	331 146	292 708	321 828	363 931	319 137	302 647	292 788	LT
LV	599 960	543 545	580 073	551 258	583 307	669 338	637 956	LV
MT	:	:	:	:	:	:	:	MT
PL	:	:	9 358 870	10 169 085	7 674 069	9 352 546	8 297 145	PL
RO	18 128 000	16 254 000	14 313 000	14 832 000	13 942 000	13 861 798	14 070 872	RO
SI	2 066 377	2 004 096	1 786 942	1 727 996	1 852 396	1 859 990	1 715 336	SI
SK	2 179 741	3 102 821	2 205 446	2 830 480	2 996 549	2 843 286	2 952 743	SK
TR	9 649 492	10 333 000	14 830 640	15 413 062	16 715 245	16 350 976	14 147 282	TR

Nights spent by non-residents in hotels and similar establishments

	1995	1996	1997	1998	1999	2000	2001	
EU-15	477 215 345	481 892 270	500 541 903	516 664 931	567 992 384	587 505 500	:	EU-15
BG	5 299 262	5 783 875	5 301 493	5 042 987	4 326 486	5 103 931	6 122 143	BG
CY	14 181 358	12 688 653	13 148 263	14 430 172	16 110 328	16 790 458	18 066 132	CY
CZ	8 385 611	10 857 852	11 726 060	11 547 000	11 921 000	12 811 000	13 647 495	CZ
EE	608 000	693 000	835 000	926 000	1 045 000	1 253 000	1 423 373	EE
HU	6 894 000	7 449 000	7 619 000	7 714 000	7 539 000	8 061 859	8 405 017	HU
LT	417 510	491 609	536 205	638 512	600 390	579 075	671 847	LT
LV	661 505	675 489	744 179	725 005	717 676	690 810	836 507	LV
MT	7 632 039	7 327 807	7 694 052	8 078 542	8 235 371	7 016 080	7 474 880	MT
PL	:	:	5 594 813	5 324 847	3 973 433	4 944 670	4 918 271	PL
RO	2 326 000	2 210 000	2 384 000	2 125 000	1 960 000	2 084 897	2 300 661	RO
SI	2 058 933	2 166 981	2 499 965	2 477 855	2 267 183	2 757 751	2 878 885	SI
SK	2 339 704	2 446 492	2 144 221	2 400 747	2 557 039	2 761 064	3 101 381	SK
TR	18 438 373	25 518 014	36 011 894	30 286 907	20 358 220	28 377 334	36 307 368	TR

1

Total research and development expenditure as % of GDP. All sectors (GERD)

	1990	1991	1992	1993	1994	1995	1996	1997	1998	1999	2000	
BG	2.38	1.53	1.65	1.18	0.88	0.62	0.52		0.51	0.57	0.57		0.52	BG
CY	:	:	:	:	:	:	:	:	0.23	0.25	0.26	CY
CZ	:	2.02	1.72	1.21	1.10	1.01		1.04	1.16	1.24	1.24	1.33	CZ
EE	:	:	:	:	:	:	:	:	0.61	0.75	0.66	EE
HU	:	1.07	1.05	0.98	0.89	0.73	0.65	0.72	0.68	0.69	0.80	HU
LT	:	:	:	:	0.52	0.48	0.52		0.57	0.57	0.52	0.60	LT
LV	:	:	0.59	0.49	0.42	0.53	0.47	0.43	0.45	0.40	0.48	LV
MT	:	:	:	:	:	:	:	:	:	:	:	MT
PL	0.96	0.81	0.83	0.83	0.77	0.69	0.71	0.71	0.72	0.75	0.70	PL
RO	:	0.79	0.85		0.91	0.77	0.80		0.71	0.58	0.49	0.40	0.37	RO
SI	1.87	2.31	1.91	1.60		1.76	1.70	1.44	1.42	1.48	1.51	1.52	SI
SK	:	:	:	:	0.92	0.95	0.94	1.09	0.79	0.66	0.67	SK
TR	:	:	:	:	:	:	:	:	:	:	:	TR

The GDP denominator is taken from Theme 2 in NewCronos. BG: before 1996 only two sources of funds were available: business and government. CZ: 1990 GERD data estimated only total expenditure available. Data 1991–94 not in line with the Frascati Manual. HU: before 1994, data not in line with the Frascati Manual. For all years, total GERD data not equal to the sum of R & D expenditure by sectors and by source of funds (GERD is calculated on the basis of three data sources). Classification by sources of funds is not totally compatible with OECD standards. LT: from 1996, data collected according to the Frascati Manual. LV: 1998 and 1999 revised values. RO: 1991–94 data include only current expenditure. SI: 1990–92 data not in line with the Frascati Manual. 1993–95 data overestimated in the higher education sector.

Business research and development expenditure as % of GDP. Business enterprise sector (BERD)

	1991	1992	1993	1994	1995	1996	1997	1998	1999	2000	2001	
EU-15	1.25 *	1.26 *	1.25 *	1.28 *	1.28 *	1.28 *	1.30 *	1.34 *	1.36 *	1.38 *	1.41 *	EU-15
BG	:	:	:	:	0.72	:	:	:	:	0.48 *	:	BG
CY	:	:	:	:	:	:	:	0.42	0.48	0.51 *	:	CY
CZ	:	:	:	0.73	0.86	0.91	0.91	0.88	0.90	0.93	:	CZ
EE	:	:	:	:	:	:	:	0.97	0.99	0.98	:	EE
HU	:	0.97	0.94	0.95	0.94	0.93	1.00	1.04	1.03	1.11	:	HU
LT	:	:	:	:	:	0.40	0.39	0.39	0.38	0.36	0.37	LT
LV	0.94	0.54	0.66	0.53	0.54	0.48	0.50	0.50	0.52	0.69	0.70	LV
MT	:	:	:	:	:	:	:	:	:	:	:	MT
PL	:	:	:	0.69	0.70	0.75	0.75	0.75	0.74	0.73	:	PL
RO	:	:	0.67	0.58	0.61	0.62	0.58	0.58	0.50	0.39	:	RO
SI	:	1.28	1.11		1.29	1.30	1.34	1.20	1.22	1.28	1.36 *	:	SI
SK	:	:	:	1.02	0.97	0.96	0.98	0.97	0.87	0.86 *	:	SK
TR	:	:	:	:	:	:	:	:	:	:	:	TR

Personal computers per 100 inhabitants

	1991	1992	1993	1994	1995	1996	1997	1998	1999	2000	2001	
EU-15	8.1	9.7	10.9	12.4	14.3	16.7	19.4	22.4	25.0	28.2	31.0	**EU-15**
BG	0.9 *	1.0	1.2	1.4	166.1	1.9	2.2	2.4	2.7	4.4	4.9 *	**BG**
CY	1.5	2.1	2.8	3.5	4.8	6.8	10.1	12.1	17.3	19.9	22.4	**CY**
CZ	1.4	2.4	2.9	4.4	5.3	6.8	8.2	9.7	10.7	12.2	13.6 *	**CZ**
EE	2.2 *	2.6 *	3.3 *	4.0 *	4.7 *	6.8	9.6	11.3	13.5	16.0	18.3	**EE**
HU	1.2	1.9	2.7	3.4	3.9	4.4	5.8	6.5	7.4	8.7	10.0	**HU**
LT	0.2 *	0.3 *	0.4 *	0.5	0.6	2.7	3.4	5.4	5.9	6.5	7.0	**LT**
LV	0.1 *	0.2 *	0.2 *	0.3	0.8	2.0	4.0	6.1	8.2	14.3	15.2	**LV**
MT	2.8	4.2	5.5	6.8	8.1	10.8	13.4	15.9	18.5	21.0	23.0	**MT**
PL	1.0	1.3	1.8	2.2	2.9	3.1	3.9	4.9	6.2	6.9	8.5	**PL**
RO	0.4	0.7	0.9	1.1	1.3	1.5	1.8	2.1	2.7	3.2	3.6	**RO**
SI	0.3 *	0.4 *	5.0	7.5	10.1	12.6	18.9	21.2	25.3	27.6	27.6	**SI**
SK	0.9 *	1.5 *	1.9	2.8	4.1	4.7	7.0	8.7	10.9	13.7	14.8	**SK**
TR	0.7	0.9	1.1	1.3	1.5	1.7	2.1	2.7	3.4	3.8	4.1	**TR**

Internet hosts per 100 inhabitants

	1998	1999	2000	2001	
EU-15	1.7	2.1	2.8	3.3	**EU-15**
BG	0.1	0.2	0.2	0.3	**BG**
CY	0.7	0.8	0.8	1.1	**CY**
CZ	0.7	1.0	1.4	1.7	**CZ**
EE	1.4	1.9	2.3	3.0	**EE**
HU	0.9	1.1	1.2	1.3	**HU**
LT	0.2	0.3	0.4	0.8	**LT**
LV	0.4	0.7	0.8	0.9	**LV**
MT	0.5	1.5	1.7	1.8	**MT**
PL	0.3	0.4	0.6	1.3	**PL**
RO	0.1	0.1	0.2	0.2	**RO**
SI	1.0	1.2	1.1	1.4	**SI**
SK	0.3	0.5	0.5	1.0	**SK**
TR	0.1	0.1	0.1	0.1	**TR**

Internet users per 100 inhabitants

	1992	1993	1994	1995	1996	1997	1998	1999	2000	2001	
EU-15	0.3	0.4	0.8	1.7	3.1	5.6	9.0	15.5	23.8	31.6	**EU-15**
BG	:	:	0.0	11.9	0.7	1.2	1.8	2.9	5.2	7.4	**BG**
CY	0.1	0.1	0.1	0.4	0.7	4.5	9.1	11.7	15.9	19.8	**CY**
CZ	:	0.6	1.3	1.5	1.9	2.9	3.9	6.8	9.7	13.6	**CZ**
EE	0.1	0.3	1.1	2.7	3.4	5.5	10.3	13.8	28.6	31.5	**EE**
HU	0.0	0.2	0.5	0.7	1.0	2.0	3.9	5.9	7.1 *	14.7	**HU**
LT	:	:	:	0.1 *	0.3	0.9	1.9	2.8	6.1	6.8	**LT**
LV	:	:	:	0.4 *	0.8	2.0	3.3	4.3	6.3	7.2	**LV**
MT	:	:	:	0.2	1.1	4.0	6.6	7.9	16.0 *	25.3	**MT**
PL	0.1	0.1	0.4	0.6	1.3	2.1	4.1	5.4	7.2	9.8	**PL**
RO	:	0.0	0.0	0.1	0.2	0.4	2.2	2.7	3.6	4.5	**RO**
SI	:	0.4	1.1	2.9	5.0	7.5	10.1	12.6	15.1	30.1	**SI**
SK	:	0.1	0.3	0.5	1.9	3.5	9.3	11.1	12.0	16.7 *	**SK**
TR	:	0.0	0.0	0.1	0.2	0.5	0.7	2.3	3.0	3.8	**TR**

Main telephone lines per 100 inhabitants

	1995	1996	1997	1998	1999	2000	2001	
EU-15	49.0	51.0	52.0	53.0	54.0	:	:	**EU-15**
BG	30.0	32.0	32.0	33.0	34.0	35.0	:	**BG**
CY	47.0	50.0	59.0	54.0	54.0	57.0	:	**CY**
CZ	23.0	27.0	32.0	36.0	38.0	38.0	:	**CZ**
EE	28.0	30.0	32.0	34.0	36.0	26.0	:	**EE**
HU	21.0	26.0	30.0	33.0	36.0	38.0	:	**HU**
LT	25.0	27.0	28.0	30.0	31.0	32.0	:	**LT**
LV	29.0	30.0	31.0	33.0	34.0	34.0	:	**LV**
MT	46.0	48.0	50.0	51.0	51.0	54.0	:	**MT**
PL	15.0	17.0	20.0	23.0	26.0	28.0	:	**PL**
RO	13.0	14.0	15.0	16.0	17.0	17.0	:	**RO**
SI	31.0	33.0	36.0	37.0	38.0	39.0	:	**SI**
SK	21.0	23.0	26.0	29.0	31.0	32.0	:	**SK**
TR	21.0	22.0	25.0	25.0	26.0	27.0	:	**TR**

Mobile phone subscribers per 100 inhabitants

	1995	1996	1997	1998	1999	2000	2001	
EU-15	5.0	9.0	14.0	23.0	41.0	:	:	**EU-15**
BG	0.0	0.0	0.0	2.0	4.0	9.0	:	**BG**
CY	6.0	10.0	14.0	16.0	19.0	27.0	:	**CY**
CZ	0.0	2.0	5.0	9.0	19.0	41.0	:	**CZ**
EE	2.0	5.0	10.0	17.0	27.0	39.0	:	**EE**
HU	3.0	5.0	7.0	10.0	16.0	31.0	:	**HU**
LT	0.0	1.0	4.0	7.0	9.0	14.0	:	**LT**
LV	1.0	1.0	3.0	7.0	11.0	16.0	:	**LV**
MT	3.0	3.0	5.0	5.0	6.0	30.0	:	**MT**
PL	0.0	1.0	2.0	5.0	10.0	17.0	:	**PL**
RO	:	:	1.0	2.0	5.0	9.0	:	**RO**
SI	1.0	2.0	5.0	10.0	31.0	55.0	:	**SI**
SK	0.0	1.0	4.0	9.0	12.0	21.0	:	**SK**
TR	0.0	1.0	1.0	5.0	11.0	22.0	:	**TR**

Number of Internet hosts. 1 000s

	1998	1999	2000	2001	
EU-15	6 417.0	7 954.0	10 477.0	12 354.0	**EU-15**
BG	9.1	15.2	18.4	24.0	**BG**
CY	5.5	6.2	6.3	7.4	**CY**
CZ	70.1	102.2	143.7	176.8	**CZ**
EE	20.6	27.2	33.3	44.6	**EE**
HU	89.3	105.5	119.1	129.5	**HU**
LT	7.4	11.9	16.3	29.1	**LT**
LV	9.6	16.0	19.7	23.2	**LV**
MT	1.8	6.0	6.5	6.9	**MT**
PL	109.6	142.1	228.7	516.1	**PL**
RO	18.5	28.5	36.3	44.9	**RO**
SI	20.3	22.8	21.5	28.1	**SI**
SK	18.3	26.1	29.1	53.3	**SK**
TR	48.9	78.9	90.9	89.7	**TR**

Source: International Telecommunication Union.

Agriculture, forestry and fisheries

Agriculture is socially important

Compared with the European Union, the agricultural population in the candidate countries accounts for a larger proportion of the total population and the agricultural workforce for a larger proportion of the total workforce. Furthermore, agricultural production accounts for a greater proportion of the output of the whole economy.

Utilised agricultural area (UAA)

Arable land made up more than 60 % of the UAA in almost all candidate countries. Indeed, it exceeded 80 % in Lithuania and Estonia and reached 90 % in Malta. Slovenia was an exception, as arable land was only 35 % of UAA. Permanent grassland was 60 % of UAA in Slovenia, and between 30 and 40 % in Bulgaria, Romania, Slovakia and Turkey. There was little permanent grassland in Cyprus and Malta. However, these two countries had notable areas under permanent crops (30 and 10 % respectively).

Production

Cereals are the most important group of crop products. The harvested production of cereals including rice in 2001 (or 2000) was 12 000 and 127 000 tonnes in Malta and Cyprus respectively. Production was about 0.5 million tonnes (mt) in Slovenia and Estonia. It reached nearly 1 mt in Latvia, 2.3 mt in Lithuania, 3.1 mt in Slovakia, 7.3 mt in the Czech Republic, 10.0 mt in Hungary, 18.9 mt in Romania and 27.1 mt in Poland. For comparison, in the European Union, production ranged from 144 000 tonnes in Luxembourg, through 4.8 mt in Greece (the median production volume), to 60.3 mt in France.

As regards animal production, Poland has the largest cattle herd with 5.5 million head which would make it the seventh largest Community beef producer after France (20.3 million), Germany (14.1 million), the United Kingdom (10.2 million), Italy (7.4 million), Ireland (6.5 million) and Spain (6.3 million). Romania has 2.9 million head of cattle, which is roughly equivalent to the Belgian figure. Poland is also the most important candidate country with regard to pig stocks (17.5 million head) and would become the EU's third largest pigmeat producer after Germany (25.8 million) and Spain (24.7 million). Romania has the largest sheep flock (7.7 million head) and Bulgaria the greatest number of goats (675 000).

Data on the production of crop and animal products in the candidate countries may be found in the theme 5 Zpal_cc domain of the NewCronos database.

Prices

From the provisional data available to Eurostat, most candidate countries had a series of years with negative price trends, which were halted or reversed in 2000. The trend became more positive in 2001 for both output and input price indices in real terms (i.e. corrected for inflation, often quite high). The real output price index rose slightly (< 1 %) in Slovenia, Slovakia and Bulgaria. It increased moderately (3–6 %) in Latvia, Romania, Malta and Lithuania, and strongly (+ 10 %) in the Czech Republic and Estonia. In contrast, the real output price index declined in Poland (– 1.1 %) and Hungary (– 3.8 %). By comparison, the real output price index in the EU rose 1.9 % in 2001, with changes ranging from – 1.9 % in Finland to + 6.6 % in the United Kingdom.

Prices and price indices for many products are stored in the theme 5 Prag domain of the NewCronos database.

1

Agricultural income

The so-called 'Indicator A' measures the change in real agricultural factor income (corresponding to the net value added at factor cost) related to the change in total agricultural labour input (in annual work units). Indicator A was available from eight candidate countries. For 2001 relative to 2000, there was a steep fall in agricultural income in Slovenia (– 14.4 %) and Poland (– 10.3 %), and a moderate decline in Malta (– 1.6 %). In contrast, agricultural income rose strongly in Lithuania (+ 13.6 %), Slovakia (+ 14.1 %), Estonia (+ 17.2 %), the Czech Republic (+ 20.5 %) and Hungary (+ 26.8 %). By comparison, agricultural income rose 3.3 % in the European Union with changes ranging up to + 12.3 % for Denmark.

Detailed data on agricultural accounts in candidate countries may be found in the theme 5 Cosa_cc domain of the NewCronos database.

Forests

Forests and wooded land cover around 30 % of the candidate countries' territory and represent the equivalent of approximately 40 % of the EU's forest and wooded land area. The main areas are in Turkey, Poland, Romania and Bulgaria.

In 2000, the roundwood production of the candidate countries represented approximately the equivalent of 41 % of the EU's production. The main production is in Poland, Turkey, the Czech Republic, Latvia and Romania.

Data on forestry come from different sources

— The data on forests (e.g. structure, areas) are provided by the forest resources assessment (FRA) managed by the Food and Agriculture Organisation (FAO). To meet the requirements at the European level, the United Nations Economic Commission for Europe (UNECE) in Geneva manages a temperate and boreal forest resources assessment (TBFRA) which covers all the members of the UNECE, including all candidate countries. The Commission is involved in the preparation of this TBFRA.

— The data on wood and wood-based products come from the joint questionnaire managed by the Intersecretariat Working Group on the Forestry Sector including the FAO, UNECE, ITTO (International Tropical Timber Organisation) and Eurostat. Each organisation is fully responsible for the management of data of a group of countries (Eurostat for the data for EU and EFTA countries).

Further reading:

Eurostat publications
— **Income from agricultural activity in 2001 (2002 edition), European Union and Candidate Countries**

Statistics in Focus — Theme 5
— **No 19/2002** **Agricultural price trends of eleven Candidate Countries**
— **No 9/2002** **EU-15 agricultural income up by 3.3% in 2001 (contains also results for a number of Candidate Countries)**

Do you need more information?
— **Ask your Data Shop (see last page)**
— **http://www.europa.eu.int/comm/eurostat**

Gross agricultural production volume index. Previous year = 100

	1997	1998	1999	2000	2001	
EU-15	:	:	:	:	:	EU-15
BG	112.4	98.5	102.7	90.9	99.7 *	BG
CY	88.3	109.4	107.4	91.5	106.4 *	CY
CZ	94.9	100.7	100.6	95.5	102.5	CZ
EE	98.1	96.4	89.6	108.2	90.3 *	EE
HU	96.2	97.9	103.9	93.7	113.2 *	HU
LT	108.6	94.8	85.5	105.4	91.5	LT
LV	103.8	92.1	89.4	104.7	105.0 *	LV
MT	110.2	102.5	98.3	98.6	96.4	MT
PL	99.8	105.9	94.8	94.4	105.7	PL
RO	103.4	92.5	105.2	85.8	:	RO
SI	99.0	102.2	98.7	102.4 *	:	SI
SK	99.0	94.1	97.5	87.7	107.8 *	SK
TR	97.7	110.6	94.7	104.2	93.5	TR

EE: in 2000 prices. LV: in 1993 prices. MT: *Source:* Economic accounts for agriculture.

eurostat

Utilised agricultural area. 1 000 ha

	1991	1992	1993	1994	1995	1996	1997	1998	1999	2000	2001	
EU-15	140 799	:	139 762	139 126	138 590	137 422	:	:	132 071	:	:	**EU-15**
BG	6 159	6 159	6 159	6 159	6 164	6 164	6 203	6 203	5 696	5 582	5 498	**BG**
CY	141	144	143	133	134	136	133	134	:	144	143	**CY**
CZ	4 285	4 283	4 282	4 281	4 280	4 279	4 280	4 272	4 283	4 282	4 280	**CZ**
EE	1 375	1 374	1 321	1 101	991	1 005	1 024	457	1 001	986	891	**EE**
HU	6 460	6 136	6 129	6 122	6 179	6 184	6 195	6 193	6 186	5 854	5 853	**HU**
LT	3 512	3 524	3 519	3 513	3 507	3 504	3 502	3 497	3 496	3 489	3 487	**LT**
LV	2 523	2 466	2 292	2 052	2 540	2 541	2 521	2 508	2 488	2 486	2 485	**LV**
MT	11	:	:	:	:	:	:	:	:	:	11	**MT**
PL	18 601	18 535	18 477	18 450	18 412	18 275	18 266	18 229	18 222	18 220	18 246	**PL**
RO	14 802	14 790	14 793	14 798	14 797	14 787	14 787	14 784	14 807	14 767	14 897	**RO**
SI	842	567	565	522	538	524	494	491	:	486	:	**SI**
SK	2 417	2 419	2 421	2 446	2 446	2 446	2 444	2 445	2 444	2 446	2 444	**SK**
TR	:	:	:	:	:	39 051	38 834	38 977	38 817	38 883	38 883	**TR**

Arable land. 1 000 ha

	1991	1992	1993	1994	1995	1996	1997	1998	1999	2000	2001	
EU-15	76 741	:	77 438	75 991	75 844	75 097	:	:	74 576	73 692	:	**EU-15**
BG	3 864	4 047	4 063	4 001	3 998	4 203	4 298	4 287	3 431	3 400	3 350	**BG**
CY	92	96	96	91	92	93	90	92	:	:	:	**CY**
CZ	3 184	3 175	3 173	3 158	3 143	3 098	3 091	3 090	3 107	3 100	3 085	**CZ**
EE	1 118	1 115	1 066	949	874	884	889	445	861	843	745	**EE**
HU	4 714	4 707	4 713	4 714	4 716	4 713	4 711	4 710	4 708	4 500	4 504	**HU**
LT	3 004	3 008	2 980	2 958	2 947	2 940	2 946	2 945	2 936	2 932	2 930	**LT**
LV	1 644	1 588	1 443	1 225	1 710	1 713	:	1 800	1 841	1 851	1 845	**LV**
MT	10	:	:	:	:	:	:	:	10	10	10	**MT**
PL	14 360	14 337	14 305	14 300	14 286	14 087	14 059	14 114	14 134	14 063	14 046	**PL**
RO	9 426	9 355	9 340	9 336	9 335	9 336	9 352	9 333	9 332	9 366	9 470	**RO**
SI	246	201	202	196	196	191	173	172	171	171	:	**SI**
SK	1 510	1 509	1 486	1 483	1 483	1 479	1 476	1 472	1 469	1 461	:	**SK**
TR	:	:	:	:	:	26 674	26 457	26 600	26 440	26 506	:	**TR**

Wheat production. 1 000 t

	1991	1992	1993	1994	1995	1996	1997	1998	1999	2000	2001	
EU-15	93 996	87 803	83 939	85 696	87 686	99 669	94 881	103 705	97 656	105 191	91 848	**EU-15**
BG	4 497	3 443	3 618	3 754	3 435	1 802	3 575	3 171	3 155	3 406	4 077	**BG**
CY	6	11	12	8	11	13	12	12	14	10	11	**CY**
CZ	4 081	3 413	3 304	3 714	3 823	3 727	3 640	3 845	4 028	4 084	4 476	**CZ**
EE	62	89	106	57	77	101	111	118	88	147	131	**EE**
HU	6 008	3 453	3 021	4 874	4 614	3 910	5 258	4 895	2 638	3 693	5 226	**HU**
LT	855	834	891	549	637	936	1 127	1 031	871	1 238	1 076	**LT**
LV	190	332	338	199	244	358	395	385	352	427	452	**LV**
MT	:	:	:	:	:	:	:	:	9	10	:	**MT**
PL	9 270	7 368	8 243	7 659	8 668	8 576	8 193	9 537	9 051	8 503	9 283	**PL**
RO	5 473	3 206	5 314	6 135	7 667	3 144	7 157	5 182	4 661	4 434	7 735	**RO**
SI	181	153	143	155	156	137	139	117	:	162	:	**SI**
SK	2 124	1 697	1 529	2 145	1 938	1 713	1 886	1 789	1 187	1 254	1 894	**SK**
TR	:	:	:	:	:	18 500	18 650	21 000	18 000	21 000	:	**TR**

Gross value added at basic prices of the agricultural industry. Million ECU/EUR

	1991	1992	1993	1994	1995	1996	1997	1998	1999	2000	2001	
EU-15	:	:	129 504	136 926	140 575	147 051	147 243	144 942	142 933	146 051	152 299	**EU-15**
BG	:	:	:	:	1 423	989	2 022	1 794	1 669	1 629	1 749	**BG**
CY	:	:	:	:	:	:	:	316	327	:	:	**CY**
CZ	:	:	:	:	:	:	:	930	775	868	1 064	**CZ**
EE	:	:	:	:	:	:	:	175	150	:	:	**EE**
HU	:	:	:	:	:	:	:	2 212	1 949	1 965	2 198	**HU**
LT	:	:	:	:	322	510	643	476	410	374	416	**LT**
LV	:	:	:	:	:	:	:	175	164	212	256	**LV**
MT	:	:	:	:	:	:	:	83	80	89	:	**MT**
PL	:	:	:	:	:	:	:	5 178	4 258	4 757	6 035	**PL**
RO	:	:	:	:	:	:	:	5 152	4 220	4 217	5 709	**RO**
SI	:	:	:	:	463	452	508	489	464	473	:	**SI**
SK	:	:	:	:	534	569	590	483	415	:	:	**SK**
TR	:	:	:	:	:	:	:	:	:	:	:	**TR**

1

Total roundwood production. 1 000 m³

	1992	1993	1994	1995	1996	1997	1998	1999	2000	2001	
EU-15	226 734	226 283	248 647	263 928	247 749	259 930	261 314	261 813	286 271	259 735	**EU-15**
BG	3 545	3 547	2 685	2 838	3 205	3 041	3 231	3 205	4 784	3 992	**BG**
CY	45	53	47	48	45	41	35	36	21	18	**CY**
CZ	9 800	10 406	11 950	12 365	12 600	13 491	13 991	14 203	14 441	14 374	**CZ**
EE	2 146	2 439	3 550	3 709	3 901	5 505	6 061	6 704	8 910	12 000	**EE**
HU	5 006	4 496	4 527	4 331	3 652	4 251	4 167	5 775	5 902	5 811	**HU**
LT		2 329	3 992	5 960	5 540	5 149	4 879	4 924	5 500	5 700	**LT**
LV	2 471	4 931	5 700	6 890	8 080	8 922	10 030	14 008	14 304	14 037	**LV**
MT	0	0	0	0	0	0	0	0	0	0	**MT**
PL	18 778	18 590	18 776	20 651	20 287	21 635	23 107	24 268	26 025	25 268	**PL**
RO	12 440	8 840	11 925	12 178	12 250	13 529	11 649	12 704	13 148	12 424	**RO**
SI	1 671	1 065	1 944	1 866	1 991	2 208	2 133	2 068	2 253	2 257	**SI**
SK	4 755	5 249	5 316	5 323	5 461	5 943	5 530	5 268	5 213	5 240	**SK**
TR	16 818	18 877	16 845	19 279	19 411	18 050	17 668	17 615	16 787	16 162	**TR**

Total sawnwood production. 1 000 m³

	1992	1993	1994	1995	1996	1997	1998	1999	2000	2001	
EU-15	61 521	59 901	66 573	68 953	68 035	71 710	72 668	75 145	79 136	77 964	**EU-15**
BG	329	257	257	257	257	257	257	325	312	312	**BG**
CY	14	17	15	15	16	14	11	12	9	9	**CY**
CZ	2 652	3 029	3 158	3 498	3 412	3 398	3 432	3 584	4 106	3 889	**CZ**
EE	300	300	305	353	403	732	853	1 200	1 436	1 670	**EE**
HU	674	481	418	231	288	320	301	308	291	219	**HU**
LT	1	699	760	940	1 450	1 250	1 150	1 150	1 300	1 250	**LT**
LV	740	446	950	1 300	1 614	2 700	3 200	3 640	3 900	3 840	**LV**
MT	0	0	0	0	0	0	0	0	0	0	**MT**
PL	4 165	4 308	5 321	3 870	3 747	4 214	4 320	4 137	4 262	3 550	**PL**
RO	2 518	2 518	1 727	1 777	1 693	1 865	2 204	2 818	3 396	3 059	**RO**
SI	407	515	515	513	498	512	666	455	439	460	**SI**
SK	:	550	700	661	633	774	1 272	1 265	1 265	1 265	**SK**
TR	4 909	5 289	4 037	4 331	4 074	3 833	3 990	4 300	5 743	5 036	**TR**

1

Total catches of fishery products. 1 000 t live weight

	1991	1992	1993	1994	1995	1996	1997	1998	1999	2000	2001	
EU-15	6 386	6 713	6 420	6 824	7 233	6 672	6 827	6 711	6 292	6 062	:	**EU-15**
BG	50	24	14	6	8	9	11	19	11	7	:	**BG**
CY	3	3	3	3	3	5	16	19	5	2	:	**CY**
CZ	:	:	3	4	4	4	3	4	4	5	5	**CZ**
EE	349	131	147	124	133	109	126	122	113	113	106	**EE**
HU	8	9	8	8	7	8	7	7	8	7	:	**HU**
LT	470	188	117	49	57	89	44	67	34	79	:	**LT**
LV	414	157	142	138	149	143	106	102	125	136	117	**LV**
MT	1	1	1	2	4	9	1	1	1	1	:	**MT**
PL	428	476	404	438	426	341	353	238	235	205	212	**PL**
RO	95	71	14	22	49	18	8	9	8	7	:	**RO**
SI	:	4	2	2	2	2	2	2	2	2	:	**SI**
SK	:	:	1	2	2	1	1	1	1	2	:	**SK**
TR	357	448	549	590	634	528	459	487	574	503	:	**TR**

Total aquaculture production. 1 000 t live weight

	1991	1992	1993	1994	1995	1996	1997	1998	1999	2000	2001	
EU-15	946	917	909	1 012	1 095	1 277	1 318	1 298	1 336	1 295	:	**EU-15**
BG	8	8	8	6	5	5	5	4	8	4	:	**BG**
CY	0	0	0	0	0	1	1	1	1	2	2	**CY**
CZ	:	:	20	19	19	18	18	17	19	19	20	**CZ**
EE	1	1	0	0	0	0	0	0	0	0	0	**EE**
HU	14	14	9	10	9	8	9	10	12	13	:	**HU**
LT	5	4	3	2	2	2	2	2	2	2	2	**LT**
LV	3	1	0	1	1	0	0	0	0	0	0	**LV**
MT	0	1	1	1	1	2	2	2	2	2	:	**MT**
PL	30	30	19	25	25	28	29	30	34	36	:	**PL**
RO	30	25	21	20	20	14	11	10	9	10	:	**RO**
SI	:	1	1	1	1	1	1	1	1	1	:	**SI**
SK	:	:	2	2	2	1	1	1	1	1	:	**SK**
TR	8	9	12	16	22	33	45	57	63	79	:	**TR**

Environment

The environment in the candidate countries

The European Commission has systematically monitored transposition and implementation of the environmental *acquis communautaire* since 1998. It has supported the candidate countries' progress towards compliance and assisted them in their efforts.

Progress remained slow in 1999 and 2000. In 2001, however, it developed considerably as a result of major efforts by the candidate countries and the 'road map' for enlargement. Nevertheless, transposition still needs to be completed regarding the management of wastewater, waste and industrial pollution (air emissions).

The data on water, waste, environmental protection expenditure and air emissions for candidate countries are compiled by the same methods and bodies as for the EU Member States. Water, waste and environmental protection statistics are compiled through the joint Eurostat/OECD questionnaire. For air emissions, the responsible body is the European Environment Agency (EEA) and data are reported through the obligatory reporting mechanisms related to air emissions.

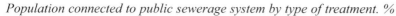

Population connected to public sewerage system by type of treatment. %

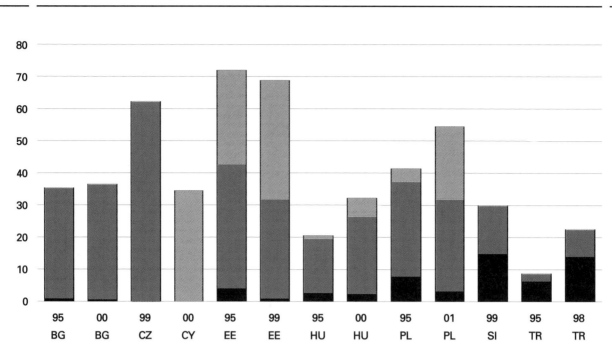

Black: primary treatment; colour: secondary treatment; grey: tertiary treatment.

Treatment of municipal waste. 1999. 1 000 t

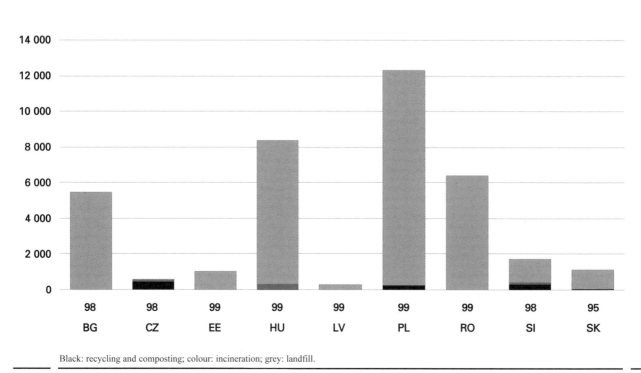

Black: recycling and composting; colour: incineration; grey: landfill.

CZ: estimates. BG, CZ, SI: 1998. SK: 1995.

eurostat

Please find the complete information of the Eurostat Yearbook on the annexed CD-ROM.

Population and labour market

- Total area in km². 2000
- Density of the population. Persons per 1 km². 1999
- Crude rate of natural increase
- Crude rate of net migration
- Crude rate of increase
- Crude rate of population increase and its components. 2000
- Total fertility rate
- Total fertility rate. 2000
- Life expectancy at birth: males
- Life expectancy at birth: females
- Life expectancy at birth for males and females. 2000
- Infant mortality rate
- Infant mortality rates. 2000
- School expectancy. 1999/2000
- Participation rate of four-year-olds in education. 1998–2001
- Duration of compulsory schooling (age). 2000
- Percentage of pupils in upper secondary education enrolled in vocational stream. By gender. 1999/2000
- Average number of foreign languages learnt per pupil in secondary general education. 2000
- Percentage of pupils in upper secondary general education learning English
- Percentage of pupils in upper secondary general education learning German
- Percentage of pupils in upper secondary general education learning Russian
- Women among tertiary students in mathematics, science and computing. 2000
- Women among tertiary students in engineering, manufacturing and construction. 2000
- Percentage of the total population aged 25 to 64 having completed at least upper secondary education
- Unemployment rates for total population aged 25 to 59 having completed no more than lower secondary education
- Unemployment rates for total population aged 25 to 59 having completed upper secondary education

- Unemployment rates for total population aged 25 to 59 having completed tertiary education
- Average hourly labour cost in industry and services. Enterprises with 10 or more employees. 2000. EUR
- Average annual labour cost in industry and services. Enterprises with 10 or more employees. 2000. EUR
- Unemployment rate. % of labour force (labour force survey). Spring
- Unemployment rate by age group. % of labour force (labour force survey). Spring 2001
- New: Structure of labour costs as % of total costs. Industry and services. Enterprises with 10 or more employees. 2000. %

Continuing vocational training in enterprises

- Percentage of employees (all enterprises) participating in CVT courses by sex. 1999
- Hours in CVT courses per participant in small and large enterprises. 1999
- Percentage of enterprises providing CVT courses by type of course. 1999
- Total costs of CVT courses per employee in enterprises with CVT courses. PPS. 1999
- Percentage of employees in small and large enterprises participating in CVT courses. 1999
- Total costs of CVT courses as % of total labour cost (all enterprises). 1999
- Hours in CVT courses per employee (all enterprises). 1999
- Hours in CVT courses per employee (all enterprises) by sex. 1999

Economic position

- Gross domestic product at constant prices. Change over the previous year. %
- Gross domestic product at current prices. 1 000 million PPS
- Gross domestic product per capita at current prices in PPS. EU-15 = 100
- Deficit (−) or surplus (+) of general government. Million ECU/EUR

- Deficit (–) or surplus (+) of general government as % of GDP
- Gross debt of general government. Million ECU/EUR
- Gross debt of general government as % of GDP
- Food and non-alcoholic beverages at current prices. % of total household consumption expenditure
- Housing, water, electricity, gas and other fuels at current prices. % of total household consumption expenditure
- Transport at current prices. % of total household consumption expenditure
- Recreation and culture at current prices. % of total household consumption expenditure
- Health, at current prices. % of total household consumption expenditure
- Gross value added at current basic prices and current exchange rates. Agriculture, hunting and forestry. % of all branches
- Gross value added at current basic prices and current exchange rates. Construction. % of all branches
- Gross value added at current basic prices and current exchange rates. Real estate, renting and business activities. % of all branches
- Exports of transport services as % of services total exports
- Imports of transport services as % of services total imports
- Exports of travel services as % of services total exports
- Imports of travel services as % of services total imports
- International trade in services other than transport and travel, cover rates. %

Bussiness structure

- Turnover of mining and quarrying. Million EUR
- Turnover of manufacturing. Million EUR
- Turnover of electricity, gas and water supply. Million EUR
- Turnover of construction. Million EUR
- Turnover of wholesale and retail trade; repair of motor vehicles, motorcycles and personal and household goods. Million EUR

- Turnover of hotels and restaurants. Million EUR
- Turnover of transport, storage and communication. Million EUR
- Turnover of real estate, renting and business activities. Million EUR
- Personnel costs of mining and quarrying. Million EUR
- Personnel costs of manufacturing. Million EUR
- Personnel costs of electricity, gas and water supply. Million EUR
- Personnel costs of construction. Million EUR
- Personnel costs of wholesale and retail trade; repair of motor vehicles, motorcycles and personal and household goods. Million EUR
- Personnel costs of hotels and restaurants. Million EUR
- Personnel costs of transport, storage and communication. Million EUR
- Personnel costs of real estate, renting and business activities. Million EUR
- Number of persons employed in mining and quarrying
- Number of persons employed in manufacturing
- Number of persons employed in electricity, gas and water supply
- Number of persons employed in construction
- Number of persons employed in wholesale and retail trade; repair of motor vehicles, motorcycles and personal and household goods
- Number of persons employed in hotels and restaurants
- Number of persons employed in transport, storage and communication
- Number of persons employed in real estate, renting and business activities
- Nights spent by residents in other collective accommodation establishments
- Nights spent by non-residents in other collective accommodation establishments
- Number of personal computers. 1 000s
- Personal computers per 100 inhabitants. 2001
- Internet hosts and Internet users per 100 inhabitants

- Number of Internet users. 1 000s
- Number of mobile phone subscribers. 1 000s
- Number of main telephone lines. 1 000s
- Mobile phone subscribers and main telephone lines per 100 inhabitants. 2001

Agriculture, forestry and fisheries

- Production of barley. 1 000 t
- Production of potatoes. 1 000 t
- Production of tomatoes. 1 000 t
- Production of apples, including cider apples. 1 000 t
- Collection of cow's milk. 1 000 t
- Production of cow's milk in farms. 1 000 t
- Production of butter. 1 000 t
- Production of cheese. 1 000 t
- Producer price indices, deflated; total agricultural production. 1995 = 100
- Purchase price indices of goods and services currently consumed in agriculture. 1995 = 100
- Forest categories (TBFRA 2000)
- Total paper and paperboard production. 1 000 t

Environment

- Total freshwater abstractions (surface- and groundwater). Million m^3
- Total freshwater abstractions (surface- and groundwater). m^3/capita
- WWater abstracted by public water supply. Million m^3/year
- Water abstracted by sector. m^3/capita
- Population connected to public sewerage system in % of total population
- Population connected to public sewerage system with treatment in % of total population
- Waste generated by economic sector. 2001. 1 000 t
- Total expenditure by public sector. Million ECU
- Total environmental expenditure by public sector by domain. %. 2000
- Total expenditure by industry by domain. %. 2000
- Emissions of greenhouse gases. Index 1990=100
- Emissions of acidifying pollutants. 1 000 t
- Emissions of tropospheric ozone precursors. 1 000 t

2

The population of the European Union: changes, comparisons, projections

On 1 January 2002, the EU had 379.6 million inhabitants

One year earlier, the total population of the European Union had been just over 378 million. The EU thus has the world's third largest population, way behind China (1 279 million) and India (1 038 million), but ahead of the United States (279.3 million), Brazil (175 million) and Japan (126.9 million).

In 2001, the EU's population increased by over 1.5 million

The increase was much the same in 2000 (1 554 900 as against 1 564 000 in 2001). The crude rate of increase in the EU's population thus remained stable at 4.1 ‰. In 2000 to 2001, however, there was a fairly sharp rise in the growth rate compared with the years immediately before then (4.1 ‰ in 2000 and 2001 as against 2.7 ‰ on average for the period 1995 to 1999).

This change was due partly to a more rapid natural increase (387 000 in 2000 and 404 000 in 2001 compared with 298 000 on average for the period 1995 to 1999), but more particularly to a substantial increase in net migration compared with the previous period (1 168 000 in 2000 and 1 160 000 in 2001 as against an average of 710 000 for 1995 to 1999).

More than ever, **net migration** is a vital component of population increase. It has been responsible for some three quarters of the increase in the EU since 1999, equalling or even overtaking the record post-war levels of 1993 and 1995. The sharp rise over the past three years is due mainly to the upward revision of population data (new estimates and census results) which Eurostat received recently from some countries (from Spain, in particular, but also from Germany, Portugal and the United Kingdom) which chiefly affected the balance of migration.

Owing to the general fall in the number of deaths over the past two years, the rate of **natural increase** has risen in virtually all EU countries, with the number of births remaining fairly stable at a little over 4 million. The natural increase was still negative, however, in three EU countries (Germany, Sweden and Greece). The figure of 404 000 recorded in 2001 should be compared with the 2.5 million which was the average for the early 1960s. At that time, natural increase was almost 8 ‰, as against only 1.1 ‰ in 2001.

The EU accounts for only around 2 % of the increase in the world's population

In 2001, the total population of the world rose by almost 78 million. China accounted for almost 14 % of that increase and India for over 20 %. At the same time, the United States (+ 9.0 ‰) had a rate of increase over twice as high as the EU's. However, in most of the other developed regions, the population increase was lower than in the EU (for example, Japan: + 1.7 ‰; Russia: − 5.1 ‰ in 2000).

In the near future, the total population of the EU is expected to stagnate or even decline

If present trends in fertility, mortality and international migration continue (Eurostat's basic scenario; see population graphs), the population is likely to peak in 2023 and then return in 2050 to a level close to the present figure.

More Eurostat data on population

If you are interested in data that are more detailed than those presented in the Eurostat yearbook, please contact your Data Shop. The addresses can be found at the end of the yearbook.

The publication *European social statistics — Demography* is also available from your Data Shop. This is a more complete yearbook exclusively about population statistics. The data presented in the 2002 edition cover the period 1960 to 2001 (2002 for population) and refer to the EU Member States

and the EFTA countries, as well as to many central European countries, Cyprus and Malta. The information includes a large range of demographic indicators, especially on:

— the European Union in the world;

— the population change;

— the structure of the population;

— the EU and its regions;

— fertility;

— marriages;

— mortality;

— international migration flows;

— population projections.

2

Further reading:

Eurostat publications
— **Key indicators — Population and social conditions**
— **European social statistics — Demography**

Other publications
— **World population prospects: the 1998 revision. United Nations**

Statistics in Focus — Theme 3
— **No 19 First results of the demographic data collection for 2001 in Europe**
— **No 17 First demographic estimates for 2001**
— **No 7(1997) Beyond the predictable: demographic changes in the EU up to 2050**

Do you need more information?
— **Ask your Data Shop (see last page)**
— **http://www.europa.eu.int/comm/eurostat**
— **Eurostat's data serves the political discussion in Europe. Have a look at the website of the "DG Justice and Home Affairs": http://europa.eu.int/comm/justice_home/index_en.htm**

Total population at 1 January. 1 000s

	1960	1965	1970	1975	1980	1985	1990	1995	2000	2001	2002	
EU-15	314 826	328 648	339 975	348 644	354 572	358 475	363 763	371 341	376 482	378 037 *	379 601 *	**EU-15**
B	9 129	9 428	9 660	9 788	9 855	9 858	9 948	10 131	10 239	10 263	10 307 *	**B**
DK	4 566	4 741	4 907	5 054	5 122	5 111	5 135	5 216	5 330	5 349	5 368	**DK**
D	72 543	75 591	78 269	78 882	78 180	77 709	79 113	81 539	82 164	82 260	82 431 *	**D**
EL	8 300	8 529	8 780	8 986	9 588	9 920	10 121	10 443	10 554	10 565 *	10 598 *	**EL**
E	30 327	31 776	33 588	35 338	37 242	38 353	38 826	39 197	39 733	40 122	40 409	**E**
F	45 465	48 562	50 528	52 600	53 731	55 157	56 577	57 753	58 749	59 037 *	59 344 *	**F**
IRL	2 836	2 873	2 943	3 164	3 393	3 544	3 507	3 598	3 777	3 826 *	3 884 *	**IRL**
I	50 026	51 907	53 685	55 293	56 389	56 588	56 694	57 269	57 680	57 844	58 018 *	**I**
L	313	330	339	357	364	366	379	407	436	441	446 *	**L**
NL	11 417	12 212	12 958	13 599	14 091	14 454	14 893	15 424	15 864	15 987	16 100 *	**NL**
A	7 030	7 248	7 455	7 592	7 546	7 574	7 690	8 040	8 103	8 121	8 140 *	**A**
P	8 826	9 029	8 698	8 879	9 714	10 009	9 920	10 013	10 198	10 263	10 336 *	**P**
FIN	4 413	4 558	4 614	4 702	4 771	4 894	4 974	5 099	5 171	5 181	5 195	**FIN**
S	7 471	7 695	8 004	8 177	8 303	8 343	8 527	8 816	8 861	8 883	8 909	**S**
UK	52 164	54 170	55 546	56 231	56 285	56 596	57 459	58 500	59 623	59 894 *	60 114 *	**UK**
IS	174	191	204	217	227	241	254	267	279	283	287	**IS**
NO	3 568	3 709	3 863	3 998	4 079	4 146	4 233	4 348	4 479	4 503	4 524	**NO**
EEA	318 584	332 567	344 063	352 882	358 903	362 889	368 279	375 987	381 272	382 856 *	384 445 *	**EEA**
CH	5 296	5 829	6 169	6 356	6 304	6 456	6 674	7 019	7 164	7 204	7 259 *	**CH**
CA	:	:	:	:	:	25 818	27 567	29 437	:	:	:	**CA**
JP	94 302	99 209	104 665	110 940	117 060	121 049	123 611	125 570	126 550	126 772	:	**JP**
US	:	:	:	:	:	236 938	248 143	261 687	275 563	278 059	:	**US**

JP: 1 October.

Total population. EU-15. Millions

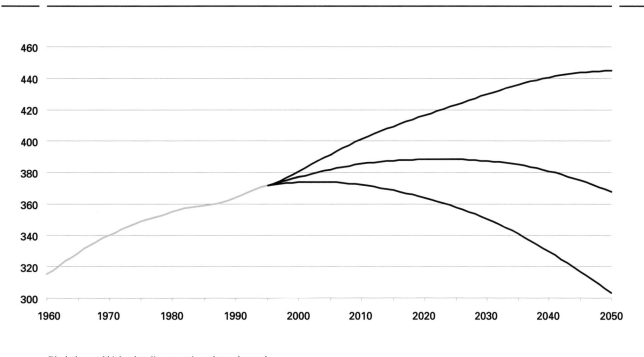

Black: low and high + baseline scenario; colour: observed.

Population projections

	2000	2005	2010	2015	2020	2025	2030	2035	2040	2045	2050	
EU-15	376 171 534	380 193 589	383 397 480	385 185 543	385 983 991	385 866 103	384 572 643	381 909 923	377 615 032	371 718 258	364 484 871	**EU-15**
B	10 223 128	10 278 591	10 352 142	10 418 949	10 482 861	10 529 973	10 538 383	10 494 042	10 394 240	10 258 116	10 104 425	**B**
DK	5 332 247	5 416 959	5 476 288	5 514 258	5 553 964	5 603 020	5 642 279	5 651 592	5 630 124	5 594 475	5 554 555	**DK**
D	82 138 397	82 994 177	83 435 049	83 476 674	83 294 567	82 817 741	81 982 719	80 915 941	79 641 170	77 980 813	76 005 825	**D**
EL	10 542 404	10 661 067	10 768 282	10 817 476	10 805 773	10 761 301	10 710 233	10 651 451	10 561 833	10 421 591	10 230 899	**EL**
E	39 432 336	39 654 236	39 856 918	39 823 814	39 528 475	39 093 032	38 606 673	38 050 291	37 328 915	36 369 941	35 145 081	**E**
F	59 198 595	60 319 965	61 369 078	62 192 287	62 839 563	63 336 194	63 669 017	63 754 932	63 466 744	62 891 960	62 153 296	**F**
IRL	3 775 974	3 970 484	4 141 222	4 294 922	4 427 309	4 533 312	4 616 512	4 681 193	4 727 692	4 754 399	4 756 653	**IRL**
I	57 588 170	57 471 793	57 276 735	56 761 388	55 984 651	55 069 404	54 042 596	52 883 739	51 520 269	49 913 580	48 071 993	**I**
L	434 254	455 056	471 136	485 301	499 744	514 840	529 150	540 758	549 051	554 804	559 310	**L**
NL	15 859 184	16 319 381	16 689 906	16 993 474	17 270 375	17 519 422	17 718 034	17 836 356	17 850 873	17 786 530	17 679 241	**NL**
A	8 089 187	8 121 830	8 148 784	8 163 293	8 169 513	8 159 020	8 113 132	8 027 690	7 916 048	7 776 941	7 612 371	**A**
P	10 002 463	10 144 858	10 308 690	10 437 341	10 526 174	10 602 554	10 679 982	10 745 193	10 771 626	10 746 542	10 669 368	**P**
FIN	5 172 569	5 226 842	5 267 213	5 295 244	5 313 503	5 317 472	5 291 658	5 229 772	5 139 439	5 043 056	4 951 245	**FIN**
S	8 861 628	8 902 734	8 951 475	9 016 565	9 114 683	9 213 430	9 257 324	9 243 895	9 209 521	9 192 823	9 197 455	**S**
UK	59 520 998	60 255 616	60 884 562	61 494 557	62 172 836	62 795 388	63 174 951	63 203 078	62 907 487	62 432 687	61 793 154	**UK**
IS	:	:	:	:	:	:	:	:	:	:	:	**IS**
NO	:	:	:	:	:	:	:	:	:	:	:	**NO**
EEA	:	:	:	:	:	:	:	:	:	:	:	**EEA**

World population. 1950, 2001 and 2050. %

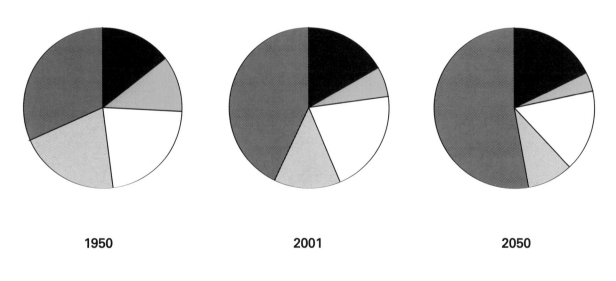

1950　　　　　　　　2001　　　　　　　　2050

Black: India; colour: EU-15; white: China; light grey: other developed countries; grey: less developed countries.

Population density. Inhabitants per km²

	1970	1975	1980	1985	1990	1995	1997	1998	1999	
EU-15	:	:	:	107	114	117	117	117	118	**EU-15**
B	316	321	323	323	327	332	334	334	335	**B**
DK	114	117	119	119	119	121	123	123	123	**DK**
D	170	173	172	171	222	229	230	230	230	**D**
EL	67	69	73	76	77	79	80	80	80	**EL**
E	67	70	74	76	77	78	78	78	79	**E**
F	93	97	99	101	104	106	107	107	108	**F**
IRL	42	45	48	50	50	51	52	53	53	**IRL**
I	178	184	187	190	188	190	191	191	191	**I**
L	131	139	141	142	147	158	163	165	167	**L**
NL	385	403	418	428	441	456	461	464	467	**NL**
A	:	:	:	90	92	96	96	96	97	**A**
P	98	103	106	109	108	109	110	110	111	**P**
FIN	:	:	:	16	16	17	17	17	17	**FIN**
S	:	:	20	20	21	22	22	22	22	**S**
UK	228	231	231	232	236	240	242	243	244	**UK**

D: includes in all years data on the former GDR. F: excluding ODs.

National population as % of EU-15 population

	1970	1975	1980	1985	1990	1995	1997	1998	1999	
EU-15	100.0	100.0	100.0	100.0	100.0	100.0	100.0	100.0	100.0	**EU-15**
B	2.8	2.8	2.8	2.7	2.7	2.7	2.7	2.7	2.7	**B**
DK	1.4	1.4	1.4	1.4	1.4	1.4	1.4	1.4	1.4	**DK**
D	23.0	22.6	22.0	21.7	21.7	22.0	22.0	21.9	21.9	**D**
EL	2.6	2.6	2.7	2.8	2.8	2.8	2.8	2.8	2.8	**EL**
E	9.9	10.1	10.5	10.7	10.7	10.6	10.5	10.5	10.5	**E**
F	14.9	15.1	15.2	15.4	15.6	15.5	15.6	15.6	15.6	**F**
IRL	0.9	0.9	1.0	1.0	1.0	1.0	1.0	1.0	1.0	**IRL**
I	15.8	15.9	15.9	15.8	15.6	15.4	15.4	15.4	15.4	**I**
L	0.1	0.1	0.1	0.1	0.1	0.1	0.1	0.1	0.1	**L**
NL	3.8	3.9	4.0	4.0	4.1	4.2	4.2	4.2	4.2	**NL**
A	2.2	2.2	2.1	2.1	2.1	2.2	2.2	2.2	2.2	**A**
P	2.6	2.5	2.7	2.8	2.7	2.7	2.7	2.7	2.7	**P**
FIN	1.4	1.3	1.3	1.4	1.4	1.4	1.4	1.4	1.4	**FIN**
S	2.4	2.3	2.3	2.3	2.3	2.4	2.4	2.4	2.4	**S**
UK	16.3	16.1	15.9	15.8	15.8	15.7	15.8	15.8	15.8	**UK**
IS	0.1	0.1	0.1	0.1	0.1	0.1	0.1	0.1	0.1	**IS**
LI	0.0	0.0	0.0	0.0	0.0	0.0	0.0	0.0	0.0	**LI**
NO	1.1	1.1	1.2	1.2	1.2	1.2	1.2	1.2	1.2	**NO**
EEA	101.2	101.2	101.2	101.2	101.2	101.3	101.3	101.3	101.3	**EEA**
CH	1.8	1.8	1.8	1.8	1.8	1.9	1.9	1.9	1.9	**CH**
CA	6.4	6.6	6.9	7.2	7.6	7.9	8.1	8.1	8.1	**CA**
JP	30.8	31.8	33.0	33.8	34.0	33.8	33.4	33.7	33.6	**JP**
US	61.8	63.1	65.0	66.1	68.2	70.5	71.4	71.9	72.4	**US**

D: includes in all years data on the former GDR.

Population increase. 1991 = 100

	1991	1992	1993	1994	1995	1996	1997	1998	1999	2000	2001	
EU-15	100.0	100.4	100.9	101.3	101.6	101.9	102.2	102.4	102.7	103.0	103.5	**EU-15**
€-zone	100.0	100.4	101.0	101.4	101.6	101.9	102.2	102.4	102.6	103.0	103.4	**€-zone**
B	100.0	100.4	100.8	101.1	101.4	101.6	101.8	102.1	102.3	102.5	102.8	**B**
DK	100.0	100.3	100.7	101.0	101.3	102.0	102.5	102.9	103.2	103.6	103.9	**DK**
D	100.0	100.7	101.5	102.0	102.2	102.6	102.8	102.9	102.9	103.0	103.1	**D**
EL	100.0	100.9	101.5	102.1	102.4	102.6	102.8	103.0	103.2	103.5	103.6	**EL**
E	100.0	100.2	100.5	100.7	100.8	101.0	101.1	101.3	101.7	102.2	103.2	**E**
F	100.0	100.5	100.9	101.3	101.6	101.9	102.2	102.6	102.9	103.4	103.9	**F**
IRL	100.0	100.8	101.4	101.8	102.2	102.8	103.7	104.9	106.1	107.3	108.7	**IRL**
I	100.0	100.0	100.4	100.7	100.9	101.0	101.3	101.4	101.5	101.6	101.9	**I**
L	100.0	101.4	102.8	104.3	105.8	107.4	108.8	110.2	111.7	113.3	114.8	**L**
NL	100.0	100.8	101.5	102.2	102.8	103.2	103.7	104.3	105.0	105.7	106.5	**NL**
A	100.0	101.3	102.5	103.2	103.5	103.7	103.8	103.9	104.0	104.3	104.5	**A**
P	100.0	100.8	100.9	101.1	101.4	101.7	101.9	102.3	102.8	103.2	103.9	**P**
FIN	100.0	100.6	101.1	101.6	102.0	102.4	102.7	103.0	103.2	103.5	103.7	**FIN**
S	100.0	100.6	101.2	101.8	102.6	102.9	103.0	103.0	103.1	103.2	103.4	**S**
UK	100.0	100.4	100.7	101.1	101.4	101.8	102.1	102.4	103.0	103.4	103.8	**UK**
IS	100.0	101.5	102.5	103.6	104.3	104.7	105.5	106.4	107.7	109.0	110.7	**IS**
NO	100.0	100.6	101.2	101.8	102.3	102.8	103.4	103.9	104.6	105.4	106.0	**NO**
EEA	100.0	100.4	101.0	101.3	101.6	101.9	102.2	102.4	102.7	103.1	103.5	**EEA**
CH	100.0	101.4	102.3	103.2	104.0	104.6	104.9	105.1	105.5	106.1	106.7	**CH**
CA	100.0	101.3	102.8	104.0	105.3	106.6	107.7	108.8	109.9	110.9	112.1	**CA**
JP	100.0	100.3	100.6	100.8	101.2	101.2	100.5	101.7	101.6	102.0	102.2	**JP**
US	100.0	101.2	102.3	103.4	104.4	105.4	106.3	107.4	108.4	109.9	110.9	**US**

Natural increase and net migration, including corrections, per 1 000 inhabitants. EU-15

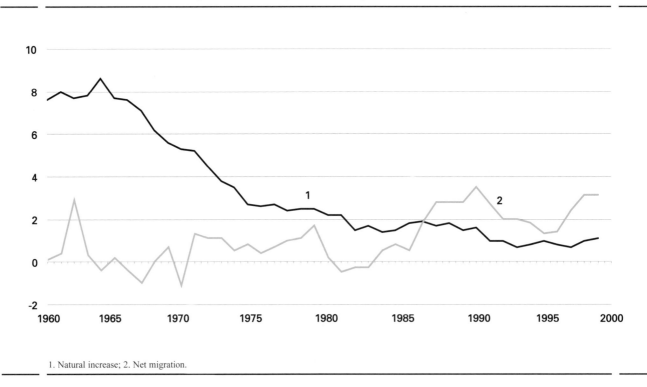

1. Natural increase; 2. Net migration.

Just over 4 million babies were born in the EU in 2001

In 2001, the number of live births in the European Union was provisionally estimated at around 4.01 million, i.e. approximately 45 000 fewer than in 2000.

The year 1999 was the only year in which the number of births fell to (just) below 4 million. In the mid-1960s, there were over 2 million more births, i.e. an average of 6 million a year. There was a sharp fall in fertility over the next decade, and in, the immediate future, the number of births is expected to continue to fall, with women born during the baby boom of the mid-1960s reaching the end of the reproductive period, to be replaced by the smaller number of women born between 1965 and 1975.

After a sharp fall, fertility in the EU has been stable since 1995

The average fertility indicator in the EU hit a post-war high in the mid-1960s (around 2.75 children per woman between 1963 and 1966) before falling sharply up to the end of the 1970s and then more gradually until the middle of the 1990s. This indicator reached a record low of 1.42 children per woman in 1995 before climbing back slightly and stabilising at between 1.45 and 1.50 children per woman over the past six years or so. In 2001, the figure was virtually the same as in the previous year, at 1.47 children per woman (as against 1.48 in 2000).

Those Member States which had the highest fertility rates at the beginning of the 1980s (Ireland and the countries of southern Europe) are those which have since recorded the steepest falls (by over 30 %), and thus the lowest levels in the fertility indicator are currently in Italy (1.24), Spain (1.25) and Greece (1.29), with the last now on a par with Germany and Austria. The highest figures are in Ireland (1.98) and France (1.90), with Denmark, Finland, Luxembourg and the Netherlands some way behind (between 1.69 and 1.74).

Completed fertility below the replacement level

The lifetime fertility of the post-war generations in the EU has been falling steadily, stabilising at around 1.70 children per woman, which is much lower than the generation replacement level (2.10 children per woman). However, the most recent data seem to indicate that fertility has reached its lowest level after decades of almost continuous decline and that the two indicators (annual birth rate and completed fertility of the generations) should move closer together in the future.

The Member States have recorded varying completed fertility figures. Women in Austria, Germany and Italy born in 1960 are expected to have under 1.70 children on average, whereas their contemporaries in France and Sweden are likely to have more than two children. Fertility will probably be highest in Ireland, with around 2.40 children per woman.

These differences are mainly due to the percentages of women with no children and families with one child. In countries where completed fertility is lowest, over 40 % of women will have only one child or no children at all, whilst in countries with the highest completed fertility rates, this figure is under 30 %.

More births outside marriage throughout the EU

Whereas 40 years ago most children born outside marriage lived with single mothers, nowadays most of them live with couples who are not married, this being a reflection of modern patterns of living together.

Although all EU Member States have recorded an increase in births outside marriage since the middle of the 1970s, there are some striking differences. At 4.1 %, Greece has the lowest rate, followed by Italy (9.6 %) and Spain (17 %). At the other end of the scale, the highest percentages are in France (42.6 %), Denmark (44.6 %) and, even more strikingly, Sweden, where over half (55.5 %) of all children are born outside marriage.

More Eurostat data on population

If you are interested in data that are more detailed than those presented in the Eurostat yearbook, please contact your Data Shop. The addresses can be found at the end of the yearbook.

The publication *European social statistics — Demography* is also available from your Data Shop. This is a more complete yearbook exclusively about population statistics.

Further reading:

Eurostat publications
— European social statistics — Demography

Statistics in Focus — Theme 3
— No 17 First results of the demographic data collection for 2001 in Europe

Do you need more information?
— Ask your Data Shop (see last page)
— http://www.europa.eu.int/comm/eurostat

Marriages per 1 000 people

	1960	1965	1970	1975	1980	1985	1990	1995	1999	2000	2001	
EU-15	7.9	7.8	7.7	7.2	6.3	5.8	6.0	5.2	5.1 *	5.1 *	:	EU-15
B	7.2	7.0	7.6	7.3	6.7	5.8	6.5	5.1	4.3	4.4	4.1 *	B
DK	7.8	8.8	7.4	6.3	5.2	5.7	6.1	6.6	6.7	7.2	6.6	DK
D	9.5	8.2	7.4	6.7	6.3	6.4	6.5	5.3	5.3	5.1	4.7 *	D
EL	7.0	9.4	7.7	8.5	6.5	6.4	5.8	6.1	5.8	4.3 *	5.4 *	EL
E	7.7	7.1	7.4	7.6	5.9	5.2	5.7	5.1	5.3 *	5.3	5.2 *	E
F	7.0	7.1	7.8	7.4	6.2	4.9	5.1	4.4	4.9 *	5.2 *	5.1 *	F
IRL	5.5	5.9	7.0	6.7	6.4	5.3	5.1	4.3	4.9	5.0 *	5.0 *	IRL
I	7.7	7.7	7.4	6.7	5.7	5.3	5.6	5.1	4.8	4.9	:	I
L	7.1	6.6	6.4	6.8	5.9	5.4	6.1	5.1	4.8	4.9	4.5 *	L
NL	7.8	8.8	9.5	7.3	6.4	5.7	6.4	5.3	5.7	5.5	5.1 *	NL
A	8.3	7.8	7.1	6.1	6.2	5.9	5.9	5.3	4.9	4.8	4.2 *	A
P	7.8	8.4	9.4	11.3	7.4	6.8	7.2	6.6	6.8 *	6.2	5.7 *	P
FIN	7.4	7.9	8.8	6.7	6.2	5.3	5.0	4.7	4.7	5.1	4.8	FIN
S	6.7	7.8	5.4	5.4	4.5	4.6	4.7	3.8	4.0	4.5	4.0	S
UK	7.5	7.8	8.5	7.7	7.4	6.9	6.5	5.5	5.1	5.1 *	:	UK
IS	7.4	8.1	7.8	7.8	5.7	5.2	4.5	4.6	5.6	6.3	5.2 *	IS
NO	6.6	6.5	7.6	6.5	5.4	4.9	5.2	5.0	5.3	5.6	:	NO
EEA	7.9	7.8	7.7	7.2	6.3	5.8	6.0	5.2	:	:	:	EEA
CH	7.8	7.7	7.6	5.6	5.7	6.0	6.9	5.8	5.7	5.5	5.0 *	CH
CA	:	:	:	:	:	:	:	:	:	:	:	CA
JP	:	:	:	:	:	:	:	:	:	:	:	JP
US	:	:	:	:	:	:	:	:	8.4	:	:	US

Divorces per 1 000 people

	1960	1965	1970	1975	1980	1985	1990	1995	1999	2000	2001	
EU-15	:	:	:	:	:	:	1.7	1.8	:	1.9 *	:	EU-15
B	0.5	0.6	0.7	1.1	1.5	1.9	2.0	3.5	2.6	2.6	2.9 *	B
DK	1.5	1.4	1.9	2.6	2.7	2.8	2.7	2.5	2.5	2.7	2.7	DK
D	1.0	1.1	1.3	1.9	1.8	2.3	2.0	2.1	2.3	2.4	:	D
EL	0.3	0.4	0.4	0.4	0.7	0.8	0.6	1.1	0.9	0.9 *	0.9 *	EL
E	0.0	0.0	0.0	0.0	0.0	0.5	0.6	0.8	:	1.0 *	:	E
F	0.7	0.7	0.8	1.1	1.5	1.9	1.9	2.1	2.0	:	:	F
IRL	:	:	:	:	:	:	:	:	:	:	:	IRL
I	0.0	0.0	0.0	0.2	0.2	0.3	0.5	0.5	0.6	0.7	:	I
L	0.5	0.4	0.6	0.6	1.6	1.8	2.0	1.8	2.4	2.3	2.3 *	L
NL	0.5	0.5	0.8	1.5	1.8	2.3	1.9	2.2	2.1	2.2	2.3 *	NL
A	1.1	1.2	1.4	1.4	1.8	2.0	2.1	2.3	2.3	2.4	:	A
P	0.1	0.1	0.1	0.2	0.6	0.9	0.9	1.2	1.8 *	1.9	1.8 *	P
FIN	0.8	1.0	1.3	2.0	2.0	1.8	2.6	2.7	2.7	2.7	2.6	FIN
S	1.2	1.2	1.6	3.1	2.4	2.4	2.3	2.6	2.4	2.4	2.4	S
UK	0.5	0.7	1.1	2.3	2.8	3.1	2.9	2.9	2.7	2.6 *	:	UK
IS	0.7	0.9	1.2	1.8	1.9	2.2	1.9	1.8	1.7	1.9	1.9 *	IS
NO	0.7	0.7	0.9	1.4	1.6	2.0	2.4	2.4	2.0	2.2	:	NO
EEA	:	:	:	:	:	:	1.7	1.8	:	:	:	EEA
CH	0.9	0.8	1.0	1.4	1.7	1.8	2.0	2.2	2.9	1.5	2.2 *	CH
CA	:	:	:	:	:	:	:	:	:	:	:	CA
JP	:	:	:	:	:	:	:	1.6	:	:	:	JP
US	:	:	:	:	:	:	:	:	4.2	:	:	US

IRL: divorce was not allowed before 1996.

Mean age at first marriage: women

	1960	1965	1970	1975	1980	1985	1990	1995	1999	2000	
EU-15	24	24	23	23	23	25	25	27	:	:	**EU-15**
B	23	23	22	22	22	23	24	25	26	26	**B**
DK	23	23	23	24	25	26	28	29	30	29	**DK**
D	23	24	23	22	23	24	25	26	27	:	**D**
EL	25	25	24	24	:	:	25	26	27	:	**EL**
E	26	25	25	24	23	24	25	27	28	:	**E**
F	23	23	23	23	23	24	26	27	28	:	**F**
IRL	28	26	25	25	25	25	26	27	:	:	**IRL**
I	25	24	24	24	24	25	26	27	:	:	**I**
L	:	:	:	:	:	:	25	27	27	27	**L**
NL	24	24	23	23	23	24	26	27	28	28	**NL**
A	24	23	23	23	23	24	25	26	27	27	**A**
P	25	25	24	24	23	23	24	25	25	25	**P**
FIN	24	23	23	24	24	25	25	27	28	28	**FIN**
S	24	24	24	25	26	27	27	29	30	30	**S**
UK	:	:	:	:	:	25	25	26	27	:	**UK**
IS	:	:	:	23	24	26	27	28	30	30	**IS**
NO	24	23	23	23	24	24	26	27	29	:	**NO**
EEA	24	24	23	23	23	25	25	27	:	:	**EEA**
CH	25	25	24	24	25	26	27	27	28	28	**CH**
CA	:	:	:	:	:	25	26	27	:	:	**CA**
JP	24	25	24	25	25	26	26	:	:	:	**JP**
US	:	:	:	:	:	24	25	:	:	:	**US**

Mean age at first marriage: men

	1960	1965	1970	1975	1980	1985	1990	1995	1999	2000	
EU-15	27	27	26	26	26	27	28	29	:	:	**EU-15**
B	25	25	24	24	24	25	26	27	28	28	**B**
DK	26	25	25	26	27	29	30	31	32	32	**DK**
D	25	26	25	25	26	27	28	29	30	:	**D**
EL	29	30	29	29	28	28	29	30	30	:	**EL**
E	29	29	27	27	26	27	28	29	30	:	**E**
F	26	25	25	25	25	26	28	29	:	:	**F**
IRL	31	29	27	27	27	27	28	30	:	:	**IRL**
I	29	28	27	27	27	28	29	30	:	:	**I**
L	:	:	:	:	:	:	27	29	30	30	**L**
NL	27	26	25	25	25	27	28	29	30	30	**NL**
A	27	26	26	26	26	27	27	29	29	30	**A**
P	27	27	27	26	25	26	26	27	27	27	**P**
FIN	26	25	25	25	26	27	27	29	30	30	**FIN**
S	27	26	26	27	29	30	30	31	32	32	**S**
UK	:	:	:	:	25	28	27	28	29	:	**UK**
IS	:	:	:	25	26	28	29	30	32	32	**IS**
NO	27	26	26	25	26	27	29	30	31	:	**NO**
EEA	27	27	26	26	26	27	28	29	:	:	**EEA**
CH	28	27	27	27	27	28	29	30	30	30	**CH**
CA	:	:	:	:	:	27	28	29	:	:	**CA**
JP	27	27	27	27	28	28	28	:	:	:	**JP**
US	:	:	:	:	:	26	27	:	:	:	**US**

Total fertility

	1960	1965	1970	1975	1980	1985	1990	1995	1999	2000	2001	
EU-15	2.59	2.72	2.38	1.96	1.82	1.60	1.57	1.42	: *	1.48 *	1.47 *	**EU-15**
B	2.56	2.62	2.25	1.74	1.68	1.51	1.62	1.55 *	1.61 *	1.66	1.65 *	**B**
DK	2.57	2.61	1.95	1.92	1.55	1.45	1.67	1.80	1.73	1.77	1.74	**DK**
D	2.37	2.50	2.03	1.48	1.56	1.37	1.45	1.25	1.36	1.36 *	1.29 *	**D**
EL	2.28	2.30	2.39	2.32	2.21	1.67	1.39	1.32	1.28 *	1.29 *	1.29 *	**EL**
E	2.86	2.94	2.90	2.79	2.20	1.64	1.36	1.18	1.20 *	1.23 *	1.25 *	**E**
F	2.73	2.84	2.47	1.93	1.95	1.81	1.78	1.70	1.79 *	1.88 *	1.90 *	**F**
IRL	3.76	4.03	3.93	3.40	3.25	2.47	2.11	1.84	1.88 *	1.89 *	1.98 *	**IRL**
I	2.41	2.66	2.42	2.20	1.64	1.42	1.33	1.18	1.23 *	1.24 *	1.24 *	**I**
L	2.28	2.42	1.98	1.55	1.49	1.38	1.61	1.69	1.73	1.80	1.70 *	**L**
NL	3.12	3.04	2.57	1.66	1.60	1.51	1.62	1.53	1.65 *	1.72	1.69 *	**NL**
A	2.69	2.70	2.29	1.83	1.62	1.47	1.45	1.40	1.32 *	1.34	1.29 *	**A**
P	3.10	3.14	2.83	2.58	2.18	1.72	1.57	1.40	1.49 *	1.52	1.42 *	**P**
FIN	2.72	2.47	1.82	1.68	1.63	1.65	1.78	1.81	1.74	1.73	1.73	**FIN**
S	2.20	2.42	1.92	1.77	1.68	1.74	2.13	1.73	1.50	1.54	1.57	**S**
UK	2.72	2.89	2.43	1.81	1.90	1.79	1.83	1.71	1.68 *	1.64	1.63 *	**UK**
IS	4.17	3.71	2.81	2.65	2.48	1.93	2.30	2.08	1.99 *	2.10 *	1.95 *	**IS**
NO	2.91	2.94	2.50	1.98	1.72	1.68	1.93	1.87	1.84 *	1.85	:	**NO**
EEA	2.59	2.72	2.38	1.96	1.82	1.60	1.58	1.43	:	:	:	**EEA**
CH	2.44	2.60	2.10	1.61	1.55	1.52	1.59	1.48	1.48 *	1.50	1.41 *	**CH**
CA	:	:	:	:	:	1.61	1.71	1.62	:	:	:	**CA**
JP	2.00	2.10	2.10	1.90	1.75	1.76	1.54	1.42	1.40	1.41	:	**JP**
US	:	:	:	:	1.84	1.84	2.08	2.02	2.05	2.06	:	**US**

Completed fertility by generation

	1930	1935	1940	1945	1950	1955	1959	1960	1961	1964	
EU-15	2.40	2.40	2.20	2.10	2.00	1.90	1.80	1.80	1.80	:	**EU-15**
B	2.30	2.30	2.20	1.90	1.80	1.80	1.80	1.90	1.80	1.80	**B**
DK	2.40	2.40	2.20	2.10	1.90	1.80	1.90	1.90	1.90	1.90	**DK**
D	2.20	2.20	2.00	1.80	1.70	1.70	1.70	1.70	1.60	1.50	**D**
EL	2.20	2.00	2.00	2.00	2.10	2.00	1.90	2.00	1.90	1.80	**EL**
E	2.60	2.70	2.60	2.40	2.20	1.90	1.80	1.80	1.70	1.60	**E**
F	2.60	2.60	2.40	2.20	2.10	2.10	2.10	2.10	2.10	2.00	**F**
IRL	3.50	3.40	3.30	3.30	3.00	2.70	2.40	2.40	2.30	2.20	**IRL**
I	2.30	2.30	2.10	2.10	1.90	1.80	1.70	1.70	1.60	1.50	**I**
L	2.00	2.00	1.90	1.80	1.70	1.70	1.70	1.70	1.70	1.70	**L**
NL	2.70	2.50	2.20	2.00	1.90	1.90	1.90	1.90	1.80	1.80	**NL**
A	2.30	2.50	2.10	1.90	1.90	1.80	1.70	1.70	1.70	1.60	**A**
P	3.00	2.90	2.60	2.30	2.10	2.00	1.90	1.90	1.90	1.80	**P**
FIN	2.50	2.30	2.00	1.90	1.90	1.90	2.00	2.00	2.00	1.90	**FIN**
S	2.10	2.10	2.10	2.00	2.00	2.00	2.00	2.10	2.00	2.00	**S**
UK	2.40	2.40	2.40	2.20	2.00	2.00	2.00	2.00	1.90	1.90	**UK**
IS	3.50	:	3.20	2.90	2.70	2.50	2.50	2.50	2.50	2.40	**IS**
NO	2.50	2.60	2.50	2.20	2.10	2.10	2.10	2.10	2.10	2.10	**NO**
EEA	2.40	2.40	2.30	2.10	2.00	1.90	1.80	1.80	1.80	:	**EEA**
CH	2.20	2.20	2.10	1.90	1.80	1.80	1.80	1.80	1.70	1.60	**CH**
JP	:	:	:	:	2.00	2.00	2.00	2.10	:	:	**JP**
US	3.20	3.20	2.80	2.30	2.00	:	:	:	:	:	**US**

D: includes in all years data on the former GDR.

Mean age of women at childbearing

	1960	1965	1970	1975	1980	1985	1990	1995	1999	2000	2001	
EU-15	28.2	27.9	27.5	27.2	27.1	27.6	28.2	28.9	:	:	:	EU-15
B	28.0	27.6	27.2	26.6	26.6	27.2	27.9	28.5 *	:	:	:	B
DK	26.9	26.8	26.7	26.4	26.8	27.8	28.5	29.2	29.6	29.7	:	DK
D	27.5	27.1	26.6	26.3	26.4	27.1	27.6	28.3	28.7	:	:	D
EL	:	:	:	26.8	26.1	26.3	27.2	28.2	28.9	:	:	EL
E	:	30.1	29.6	28.7	28.2	28.5	28.9	30.0	30.7	:	:	E
F	27.6	27.3	27.2	26.7	26.8	27.5	28.3	29.0	29.4	29.4	:	F
IRL	:	:	:	29.6	29.7	29.8	29.9	30.2	30.5	30.6	:	IRL
I	29.2	28.7	28.3	27.6	27.4	28.0	28.9	29.7	:	:	:	I
L	:	:	27.2	27.1	27.5	27.9	28.4	28.9	29.4	29.3	:	L
NL	29.8	29.0	28.2	27.4	27.7	28.4	29.3	30.0	30.3	30.3	:	NL
A	27.6	27.3	26.7	26.3	26.3	26.7	27.2	27.7	28.1	28.2	:	A
P	29.6	29.5	29.0	28.3	27.2	27.2	27.3	28.1	28.6	28.7	:	P
FIN	28.3	28.0	27.1	27.1	27.7	28.4	28.9	29.3	29.6	29.6	:	FIN
S	27.5	27.2	27.0	26.7	27.6	28.4	28.6	29.2	29.8	29.9	:	S
UK	27.8	27.1	26.3	26.5	26.9	27.3	27.7	28.2	28.4	28.5	:	UK
IS	27.7	26.9	26.0	25.7	26.2	26.8	27.6	28.7	28.7	28.9	:	IS
NO	27.9	27.7	27.0	26.4	26.9	27.5	28.1	28.9	29.3	29.3	:	NO
EEA	28.2	27.9	27.5	27.2	27.1	27.6	28.2	28.9	:	:	:	EEA
CH	28.7	28.2	27.8	27.6	27.9	28.4	29.0	29.4	29.7	29.8	:	CH
CA	:	:	:	:	:	27.3	28.1	28.8	:	:	:	CA
JP	27.6	27.4	27.5	27.4	28.1	28.6	28.9	:	:	:	:	JP
US	:	:	:	:	:	26.3	26.9	:	:	:	:	US

Live births outside marriage as % of all live births

	1960	1965	1970	1975	1980	1985	1990	1995	1999	2000	2001	
EU-15	5	5	6	7	10	15	20	24	: *	28 *	:	EU-15
B	2	2	3	3	4	7	12	17 *	: *	22 *	:	B
DK	8	9	11	22	33	43	46	46	45	45	45	DK
D	8	6	7	8	12	16	15	16	22 *	23	24 *	D
EL	1	1	1	1	2	2	2	3	4 *	4 *	:	EL
E	2	2	1	2	4	8	10	11	16 *	17 *	:	E
F	6	6	7	9	11	20	30	38	42 *	43	:	F
IRL	2	2	3	4	5	8	15	22	31	32 *	31 *	IRL
I	2	2	2	3	4	5	6	8	:	10 *	:	I
L	3	4	4	4	6	9	13	13	19	22	22	L
NL	1	2	2	2	4	8	11	16	23 *	22	28 *	NL
A	13	11	13	14	18	22	24	27	30	31	33	A
P	9	8	7	7	9	12	15	19	21	22	24	P
FIN	4	5	6	10	13	16	25	33	39	39	40	FIN
S	11	14	19	33	40	46	47	53	55	55	56	S
UK	5	7	8	9	12	19	28	34	39 *	40	40 *	UK
IS	25	27	30	33	40	48	55	61	62 *	65	63 *	IS
NO	4	5	7	10	15	26	39	48	49	50	:	NO
EEA	5	5	6	7	10	15	20	24	:	:	:	EEA
CH	4	4	4	4	5	6	6	7	10 *	11	12	CH
CA	:	:	:	:	:	:	:	:	:	:	:	CA
JP	:	:	:	:	:	:	:	:	:	:	:	JP
US	:	:	:	:	:	:	:	:	:	:	:	US

Comprehensive information on migration, asylum and citizenship

Eurostat compiles statistics on:

— international migration flows;

— asylum-seekers;

— resident foreign population;

— acquisition of citizenship;

— migrant workers.

If you would like more information on these topics than is provided in the Eurostat yearbook, please contact one of the Data Shops the addresses of which can be found at the end of the yearbook. The migration statistics yearbook *European social statistics — Migration* is also available from your Data Shop.

The EU remains attractive to migrants

Migration is influenced by a combination of economic, political and social factors. These factors may act in a migrant's country of origin ('push' factors) or in the country of destination ('pull' factors).

The relative economic prosperity and political stability of the EU exert a considerable pull effect. Various push factors in many parts of the world have also continued to have a strong effect on migrant flows.

Net migration has been the largest component of population change in the EU since 1989. It is estimated that net migration added approximately 1.16 million to the EU population in 2001, contributing three quarters of the total population increase. Net migration is calculated as the difference in the population at the beginning and end of the year, minus the difference between births and deaths in that year.

For many Member States, non-EU nationals form the largest group in the immigration flows. The second largest immigration group is generally national citizens. Except for Belgium, Ireland and Luxembourg, the smallest immigration group consists of citizens of other EU Member States.

The number of applications for asylum remains well below the 1992 peak

There were around 360 000 applications for asylum in the EU in 2000. The figures for the last few years have been higher than those seen in the mid-1990s, but remain well below the levels recorded in the early 1990s when the annual total was above half a million for several years.

Measuring migration

Statistics on migration, asylum, the resident foreign population, and the acquisition of citizenship are supplied to Eurostat by national statistical institutes and by the Ministries of Justice and the Interior. Most of these statistics are sent to Eurostat as part of a joint migration data collection organised by Eurostat in cooperation with the United Nations Statistical Division, the United Nations Economic Commission for Europe, the Council of Europe and the International Labour Office.

Countries differ in the way they produce migration statistics and who they consider to be a migrant. In some countries, migration statistics are based on administrative data taken, for example, from systems for issuing residence permits or from a population register. Some other countries use survey-based data. These variations in data sources and definitions result in problems when comparing the migrant counts for different countries.

Not all EU Member States produce statistics on immigration and emigration. Although an estimation can be made of net migration for the EU, it is not possible to provide a complete picture of immigration and emigration flows for all Member States or for the EU as a whole. For more information, refer to the glossary entries 'Immigrants' and 'Emigrants'.

Citizenship

Around 1 in 20 people in the EU are not citizens of their country of residence: 1.6 % are citizens of another EU Member State and 3.4 % are non-EU citizens. There are, however, large differences between the Member States. Luxembourg has by far the largest proportion of non-nationals: in 2001, 36.9 % of the population were not Luxembourg citizens.

Acquisition of citizenship is sometimes viewed as an indicator of the formal integration of migrants into their destination country, often requiring a period of legal residence together with other factors such as language proficiency. In the past decade, the annual number of people acquiring citizenship of an EU Member State has more than doubled.

2

Further reading:

Eurostat publications
— **Patterns and trends in international migration in western Europe**
— **European social statistics — Migration**

Statistics in Focus — Theme 3
— **No 1   Why do people migrate?**
— **No 15 First results of the demographic data collection for 2000 in Europe**
— **No 7   Migration keeps the EU population growing**

DG Employment and Social Affairs and Eurostat
— **The social situation in the European Union 2002**

Do you need more information?
— **Ask your Data Shop (see last page)**
— **http://www.europa.eu.int/comm/eurostat**
— **Eurostat's data serves the political discussion in Europe. Have a look at the website of the "DG Justice and Home Affairs": http://europa.eu.int/comm/justice_home/index_en.htm**

eurostat

Total immigration

	1990	1991	1992	1993	1994	1995	1996	1997	1998	1999	
B	62 662	67 460	66 763	63 749	66 147	62 950	61 522	58 849	:	68 466	**B**
DK	40 715	43 567	43 377	43 400	44 961	63 187	54 445	50 105	51 372	50 236	**DK**
D	1 651 593	1 198 978	1 502 198	1 277 408	1 082 553	1 096 048	959 691	840 633	802 456	874 023	**D**
EL	42 021	24 346	32 133	27 472	:	:	:	:	12 630	:	**EL**
E	33 966	24 320	38 882	33 026	34 123	36 092	29 895	57 877	81 227	127 365	**E**
F	:	:	:	:	64 102	:	:	:	100 014	57 846	**F**
IRL	33 300	33 300	40 800	35 000	30 100	:	39 200	44 000	:	47 522 *	**IRL**
I	166 754	126 935	113 916	100 401	99 105	96 710	171 967	162 849	:	:	**I**
L	10 281	10 913	10 696	9 857	10 030	10 325	10 027	10 423	11 630	12 794	**L**
NL	117 350	120 249	116 926	119 154	92 143	96 099	108 749	109 860	122 407	119 151	**NL**
A	:	:	:	:	:	:	69 930	70 122	72 723	86 710	**A**
P	:	:	:	:	:	:	:	:	6 485	14 476	**P**
FIN	13 558	19 001	14 554	14 795	11 611	12 222	13 294	13 564	14 192	14 744	**FIN**
S	60 048	49 731	45 348	61 872	83 598	45 887	39 895	44 818	49 391	49 839	**S**
UK	267 000	267 000	216 000	210 000	253 000	245 000	258 000	285 000	332 390 *	354 077	**UK**

Data exclude unrecorded migration. EL: only non-nationals from 1994 onwards. F, P: only non-nationals. IRL: labour force survey. UK: international passenger survey.

2

Total emigration

	1990	1991	1992	1993	1994	1995	1996	1997	1998	1999	
B	32 502	33 752	33 707	44 811	36 530	36 044	36 674	39 320	:	41 307	**B**
DK	32 383	32 629	31 915	32 344	34 710	34 630	37 312	38 393	40 340	41 340	**DK**
D	610 595	596 455	720 127	815 312	767 555	698 113	677 494	746 969	755 358	672 048	**D**
EL	:	:	:	:	:	:	:	:	:	:	**EL**
E	:	:	:	:	:	:	:	:	:	:	**E**
F	:	:	:	:	:	:	:	:	:	:	**F**
IRL	56 300	35 300	38 900	41 000	:	33 900	:	:	:	:	**IRL**
I	55 989	57 730	56 967	:	65 548	43 303	47 510	46 273	:	:	**I**
L	:	:	:	:	6 113	5 715	6 355	6 591	7 574	8 075	**L**
NL	57 344	57 328	58 834	59 222	53 579	63 321	65 325	62 220	60 441	59 023	**NL**
A	:	:	:	:	:	:	66 050	68 585	64 272	:	**A**
P	:	:	22 300	22 324	:	6 901	10 148	:	:	:	**P**
FIN	6 477	5 984	6 055	6 405	8 672	8 957	10 587	9 854	10 817	11 966	**FIN**
S	25 196	24 745	25 726	29 874	32 661	33 984	33 884	38 543	38 518	35 705	**S**
UK	231 000	239 000	227 000	213 000	191 000	192 000	212 000	225 000	198 934	245 340	**UK**

Data exclude unrecorded migration. EL, F: no data on emigration are available. UK: international passenger survey.

Asylum applications

	1990	1991	1992	1993	1994	1995	1996	1997	1998	1999	
B	12 945	15 444	17 675	26 717	14 340	11 409	12 433	11 788	21 965	35 778	B
DK	5 292	4 609	13 884	14 347	6 652	5 104	5 896	5 100	5 699	6 530	DK
D	193 063	256 112	438 191	322 599	127 210	127 937	117 333	104 353	98 644	94 776	D
EL	4 100	2 700	2 108	862	1 107	1 282	1 640	4 376	2 950	1 528	EL
E	8 647	8 138	11 712	12 645	11 992	5 678	4 730	4 975	4 934	8 405	E
F	54 813	47 380	28 872	27 564	25 959	20 415	17 405	21 416	22 375	30 907	F
IRL	60	30	40	90	360	420	1 180	3 880	4 626	7 724	IRL
I	3 570	24 490	2 590	1 320	1 830	1 760	680	1 890	13 100	18 450 *	I
L	114	238	120	225	260 *	280	263	433	1 709	2 930	L
NL	21 208	21 615	20 346	35 399	52 576	29 258	22 857	34 443	45 217	39 274	NL
A	22 789	27 306	16 238	4 744	5 082	5 920	6 991	6 727	13 805	20 137	A
P	61	233	655	2 090	614	332	269	251	355	307	P
FIN	2 743	2 137	3 634	2 023	836	849	711	972	1 272	3 106	FIN
S	29 420	27 351	84 018	37 581	18 640	9 047	5 774	9 678	12 841	11 220	S
UK	38 200	73 400	32 300	28 500	32 830	43 965	29 640	32 500	46 014	71 158	UK
IS	7	19	15	0	:	:	:	:	:	:	IS
NO	3 962	4 569	5 238	12 876	3 379	1 460	1 778	2 271	8 374	10 160 *	NO
CH	35 836	41 629	17 960	24 739	16 134	17 021	17 936	23 982	41 302	46 068 *	CH

B: excluding dependent children. Figure for 1999 is calculated as the sum of monthly data supplied to Eurostat. DK: excluding applications made outside Denmark and rejected applications at the border. D: excluding repeat applications. Includes dependent children if the parents requested asylum for them. EL: figures for 1989–92 are the sum of the applications registered with the Greek authorities and those registered with the UNHCR. E: up to 1998 — excluding dependants; 1999 — including dependants. F: excluding children and some accompanying adults. I: excluding dependent children. NL, A: excluding displaced persons from the former Yugoslavia granted exceptional leave to remain. S: excluding repeat applications. UK: excluding dependants. CH: partly excluding persons rejected at the border (especially those lacking proper identity papers).

Population by citizenship. Non-EU nationals

	1994	1995	1996	1997	1998	1999	2000	
EU-15	:	:	:	:	13 100 000 *	:	:	EU-15
B	372 032	370 012	355 252	352 309	341 074	288 096	289 813	B
DK	146 690	152 095	176 222	188 749	198 404	203 081	205 539	DK
D	5 127 906	5 210 656	5 362 118	5 474 195	5 515 801	5 465 272	5 484 919	D
EL	106 280	109 166	111 111	116 128	121 543	:	:	EL
E	229 880	240 976	263 365	286 300	349 214	424 388	489 126	E
F	:	:	:	:	:	2 067 688	:	F
IRL	:	:	:	:	:	27 877	34 324	IRL
I	508 836	560 552	609 310	751 043	:	:	1 122 047	I
L	:	:	:	15 030	16 290	:	:	L
NL	585 929	564 084	534 347	491 553	487 960	470 135	455 646	NL
A	:	:	:	:	:	739 837	753 528	A
P	:	:	:	129 175	129 551	129 966	138 469	P
FIN	43 086	49 111	54 841	59 625	65 673	69 329	71 352	FIN
S	324 919	357 160	352 837	348 365	345 234	322 890	309 745	S
UK	:	:	:	1 321 000	:	1 438 809	1 603 778	UK

Mortality rates are down ...

In 1976, the number of deaths in the EU reached a post-war high of nearly 3.8 million. Since then, the annual figures have fluctuated. They were slightly down at 3.6 million in 2001, the lowest for almost 35 years. Thus, the impact on the mortality figures of the increasing number of elderly persons and of the rise in the population (up 14 % since 1967) has been fully offset by the fall in mortality rates.

The decline in infant mortality (deaths of live-born children before the age of one year) is one of the most striking demographic changes. In just under 40 years, this rate has dropped by a factor of almost seven in the European Union, from 34.5 ‰ in 1960 to 4.8 ‰ in 2001.

Although the risk of death is already very low for young children, it is likely that infant mortality will continue to fall, since the biological minimum for this indicator is between 2 and 3 ‰. Given that Sweden, Finland and Iceland are already close to or have reached these values, and that the rest of the EU is likely to follow the same trend, the infant mortality rate is expected to lose its value as a demographic and social indicator in the near future.

The countries which have made the greatest progress in this respect are the southern Member States of the European Union, where rates were over 40 ‰ in 1960 and as high as 77.5 ‰ in Portugal. In 2001, they fell to below 6.0 ‰ in these countries. Spain, at 3.9 ‰, now has one of the lowest levels in the Union. The differences between Member States are now very much less pronounced, with rates varying from 3.2 ‰ for Sweden and Finland to 5.9 ‰ for Greece.

... and life expectancy up

Since 1945, life expectancy at birth has, with very few exceptions, increased steadily in every EU country. Despite a slowing-down in the rate of increase at the start of the 1960s, the overall pattern has continued, albeit with a less rapid rise since that time. For the Union as a whole, the figures are now at an all-time high, with life expectancy at birth being around 81.4 years for women and 75.3 years for men as against 72.9 and 67.4 years respectively in 1960.

Over the past four decades, the life expectancy of men aged 65 years has risen by over 20 % in the EU, from 12.7 years in 1960 to 15.8 years in 1999. Thanks to improvements in health services and social conditions, it is now well over 15 years in several countries. The life expectancy of women aged 65 years has risen by almost 30 % over the past 40 years, from 15.1 to 19.7 years.

Further reading:

Eurostat publications
— European social statistics — Demography

Do you need more information?
— Ask your Data Shop (see last page)
— http://www.europa.eu.int/comm/eurostat
— Eurostat's data serves the political discussion in Europe. Have a look at the website of the "Health and Consumer Protection DG": http://europa.eu.int/comm/dgs/health_consumer/index_en.htm

Life expectancy at birth: females

	1960	1965	1970	1975	1980	1985	1990	1995	1999	2000	2001	
EU-15	72.9	:	74.7	:	77.2	78.4	79.4	80.4	81.1 *	81.4 *	:	EU-15
B	73.5	:	74.2	:	76.8	78.0	79.4	80.2 *	80.8	80.8	:	B
DK	74.4	:	75.9	:	77.3	77.5	77.7	77.8	79.0	79.3	79.0	DK
D	:	:	:	:	76.1 *	:	78.4	79.7	80.7	:	:	D
EL	72.4	:	73.8	:	76.8	78.4	79.5	80.3	80.6	:	80.7	EL
E	72.2	:	74.8	:	78.6	79.6	80.3	81.5	82.1	82.7	82.9	E
F	73.6	:	75.9	:	78.4	79.4	80.9	81.8	82.5	82.7	83.0	F
IRL	71.9	:	73.5	:	75.6	76.7	77.6	78.4	79.1	79.2	78.5	IRL
I	72.3	:	74.9	:	77.4	78.7	80.1	81.3	82.3	82.4	82.9	I
L	72.2	:	73.4	:	75.9	77.9	78.5	80.2	81.1	81.3	:	L
NL	75.3	:	76.5	:	79.3	79.6	80.9	80.4	80.5	80.5	80.6	NL
A	72.7	:	73.4	74.7	76.1	77.4	78.9	80.1	81.0	81.2	:	A
P	66.8	:	70.8	:	75.2	76.4	77.4	78.6	79.2	79.7	80.3	P
FIN	72.5	:	75.0	:	77.6	78.7	78.9	80.2	81.0	81.0	81.5	FIN
S	74.9	76.1	77.1	77.9	78.8	79.7	80.4	81.4	81.9	82.0	82.1	S
UK	73.7	:	75.0	:	76.2	77.6	78.5	79.2	79.8	80.2	80.4	UK
IS	76.4	:	77.3	:	80.1	80.3	80.5	80.0	81.5	81.4	:	IS
NO	76.0	:	77.5	:	79.2	:	79.8	80.8	81.1	81.4	:	NO
EEA	72.9	:	74.7	:	77.2	78.6	79.4	80.4	81.1 *	81.4 *	:	EEA
CH	74.5	:	76.9	:	79.6	:	80.7	81.7	82.5	82.6	82.8	CH
CA	:	:	:	:	:	79.9	81.0	81.3	82.9	83.0	83.1	CA
JP	70.2	72.9	74.7	76.9	78.8	80.5	81.9	83.0	83.9	84.0	84.2	JP
US	:	:	:	:	77.4	78.2	78.8	78.9	79.7	79.9	80.0	US

D: includes in all years data on the former GDR.

Life expectancy at birth: males

	1960	1965	1970	1975	1980	1985	1990	1995	1999	2000	2001	
EU-15	67.4	:	68.4	:	70.5	71.8	72.8	73.9	74.9 *	75.3 *	:	EU-15
B	67.7	:	67.8	:	70.0	71.1	72.7	73.4 *	74.4	74.6	:	B
DK	70.4	:	70.7	:	71.2	71.5	72.0	72.7	74.2	74.5	74.3	DK
D	:	:	:	:	69.6 *	:	72.0	73.3	74.7	:	:	D
EL	67.3	:	70.1	:	72.2	73.5	74.6	75.0	75.5	:	75.4	EL
E	67.4	:	69.2	:	72.5	73.1	73.3	74.3	75.1	75.5	75.6	E
F	66.9	:	68.4	:	70.2	71.3	72.8	73.9	75.0	75.2	75.5	F
IRL	68.1	:	68.8	:	70.1	71.0	72.1	72.9	73.9	74.2	73.0	IRL
I	67.2	:	69.0	:	70.6	72.3	73.6	74.9	75.6	76.3	76.7	I
L	66.5	:	67.1	:	69.1	70.6	72.3	73.0	74.6	74.9	:	L
NL	71.5	:	70.7	:	72.7	73.1	73.8	74.6	75.3	75.5	75.7	NL
A	66.2	:	66.5	67.7	69.0	70.4	72.4	73.6	75.1	75.4	:	A
P	61.2	:	64.2	:	67.7	69.4	70.4	71.2	72.2	72.7	73.5	P
FIN	65.5	:	66.5	:	69.2	70.1	70.9	72.8	73.8	74.2	74.6	FIN
S	71.2	71.7	72.2	72.1	72.8	73.8	74.8	76.2	77.1	77.4	77.5	S
UK	67.9	:	68.7	:	70.2	71.7	72.9	74.0	75.0	75.4	75.7	UK
IS	71.3	:	71.2	:	73.4	74.9	75.4	75.9	77.7	78.0	:	IS
NO	71.6	:	71.2	:	72.3	:	73.4	74.8	75.6	76.0	:	NO
EEA	67.4	:	68.5	:	70.5	72.0	72.8	73.9	74.9 *	75.3 *	:	EEA
CH	68.7	:	70.7	:	72.8	:	74.0	75.3	76.8	76.9	77.2	CH
CA	:	:	:	:	:	73.1	74.6	75.3	75.9	76.0	76.2	CA
JP	65.3	67.7	69.3	71.7	73.3	74.8	75.9	76.6	77.4	77.5	77.6	JP
US	:	:	:	:	70.0	71.1	71.8	72.5	74.1	74.2	74.4	US

D: includes in all years data on the former GDR.

Life expectancy at 60: females

	1960	1965	1970	1975	1980	1985	1990	1995	1999	2000	
EU-15	19.0	:	19.8	:	21.2	:	22.5	23.3	:	:	**EU-15**
B	18.7	:	19.2	:	20.9	21.6	22.7	23.3	23.7	23.8	**B**
DK	19.3	:	20.6	:	21.4	21.6	21.6	21.3	22.0	22.3	**DK**
D	:	:	:	:	:	:	21.7	22.7	23.4	:	**D**
EL	18.5	:	19.1	:	20.8	21.6	22.3	22.8	23.1	:	**EL**
E	19.2	:	20.0	:	22.1	22.6	23.3	24.2	24.5	:	**E**
F	19.5	:	20.8	:	22.4	23.0	24.1	24.9	25.3	:	**F**
IRL	18.1	:	18.7	:	19.5	:	20.9	21.4	21.8	21.9	**IRL**
I	19.3	:	20.2	:	21.2	21.9	23.0	24.0	:	:	**I**
L	18.3	:	18.8	:	19.9	:	22.4	23.2	23.8	24.1	**L**
NL	19.7	:	20.5	:	22.6	22.8	23.1	23.2	23.3	23.4	**NL**
A	:	:	18.8	19.6	20.3	21.0	22.2	22.9	23.6	23.9	**A**
P	19.1	:	18.9	:	20.6	20.9	21.3	21.9	22.2	22.6	**P**
FIN	:	:	:	:	20.5	21.4	21.9	22.9	23.5	23.6	**FIN**
S	19.3	20.1	20.9	21.4	22.1	22.7	23.2	23.9	24.1	24.3	**S**
UK	18.9	:	19.8	:	20.4	:	21.8	22.2	22.6	23.0	**UK**
IS	:	:	:	:	22.9	22.8	23.6	23.3	23.5	23.7	**IS**
NO	20.2	:	21.0	:	22.2	:	22.7	23.3	23.7	23.9	**NO**
EEA	19.0	:	19.8	:	21.2	:	22.6	23.3	:	:	**EEA**
CH	:	:	:	:	:	:	23.7	24.5	25.0	25.0	**CH**
CA	:	:	:	:	:	:	:	:	:	:	**CA**
JP	:	:	:	:	:	:	:	:	:	:	**JP**
US	:	:	:	:	:	:	:	:	:	:	**US**

Life expectancy at 60: males

	1960	1965	1970	1975	1980	1985	1990	1995	1999	2000	
EU-15	15.9	:	15.9	:	16.8	:	18.2	18.9	:	:	**EU-15**
B	15.5	:	15.2	:	16.3	16.7	17.9	18.5	19.1	19.3	**B**
DK	17.1	:	17.1	:	17.0	17.2	17.4	17.6	18.6	18.9	**DK**
D	:	:	:	:	:	:	17.4	18.2	19.2	:	**D**
EL	16.9	:	17.5	:	18.2	18.9	19.4	19.8	20.1	:	**EL**
E	16.5	:	16.8	:	18.4	18.5	19.1	19.7	19.8	:	**E**
F	15.6	:	16.2	:	17.3	17.9	19.0	19.7	20.2	:	**F**
IRL	15.8	:	15.6	:	15.9	:	16.7	17.3	18.0	18.3	**IRL**
I	16.7	:	16.7	:	16.8	17.6	18.6	19.5	:	:	**I**
L	15.5	:	15.2	:	15.5	:	17.8	18.2	19.1	19.3	**L**
NL	17.7	:	16.8	:	17.5	17.6	18.1	18.5	19.0	19.1	**NL**
A	:	:	14.9	15.6	16.3	17.0	17.9	18.7	19.5	20.0	**A**
P	16.2	:	15.5	:	16.3	17.0	17.5	17.9	18.2	18.5	**P**
FIN	:	:	:	:	15.6	16.2	17.1	18.1	18.8	19.2	**FIN**
S	17.3	17.5	17.8	17.6	17.9	18.4	19.1	19.8	20.4	20.7	**S**
UK	15.0	:	15.2	:	15.9	:	17.5	18.3	19.1	19.4	**UK**
IS	:	:	:	:	19.3	19.4	20.1	20.2	20.9	22.2	**IS**
NO	18.0	:	17.3	:	17.7	:	18.2	18.9	19.5	20.0	**NO**
EEA	15.9	:	15.9	:	16.8	:	18.2	18.9	:	:	**EEA**
CH	:	:	:	:	:	:	19.0	19.9	20.7	20.9	**CH**
CA	:	:	:	:	:	:	:	:	:	:	**CA**
JP	:	:	:	:	:	:	:	:	:	:	**JP**
US	:	:	:	:	:	:	:	:	:	:	**US**

2

Infant mortality per 1 000 live births

	1960	1965	1970	1975	1980	1985	1990	1995	1999	2000	2001	
EU-15	34.5	27.5	23.4	18.1	12.4	9.5	7.6	5.6 *	: *	4.7 *	4.6 *	EU-15
B	31.2	23.7	21.1	16.1	12.1	9.8	8.0	6.1 *	4.9	4.8 *	5.0 *	B
DK	21.5	18.7	14.2	10.4	8.4	7.9	7.5	5.1	:	5.3	4.9	DK
D	35.0	24.1	22.5	18.9	12.4	9.1	7.0	5.3	4.5	4.4	4.5 *	D
EL	40.1	34.3	29.6	24.0	17.9	14.1	9.7	8.1	6.2	6.1 *	5.9 *	EL
E	43.7	37.8	28.1	18.9	12.3	8.9	7.6	5.5	4.5 *	3.9 *	3.9 *	E
F	27.5	22.0	18.2	13.8	10.0	8.3	7.3	4.9	4.3 *	4.6 *	4.6 *	F
IRL	29.3	25.2	19.5	17.5	11.1	8.8	8.2	6.3	5.5	5.9 *	5.8 *	IRL
I	43.9	36.0	29.6	21.2	14.6	10.5	8.2	6.2	:	4.5	4.3 *	I
L	31.5	24.0	24.9	14.8	11.5	9.0	7.3	5.5	4.6	5.1	5.9	L
NL	17.9	14.4	12.7	10.6	8.6	8.0	7.1	5.5	5.2	5.1	5.3 *	NL
A	37.5	28.3	25.9	20.5	14.3	11.2	7.8	5.4	4.4	4.8	4.8	A
P	77.5	64.9	55.5	38.9	24.3	17.8	11.0	7.5	5.6	5.5	5.0	P
FIN	21.0	17.6	13.2	10.0	7.6	6.3	5.6	3.9	3.6	3.8	3.2	FIN
S	16.6	13.3	11.0	8.6	6.9	6.8	6.0	4.1	3.4	3.4	3.2	S
UK	22.5	19.7	18.5	16.1	12.1	9.3	7.9	6.2	5.8	5.6 *	5.5 *	UK
IS	13.0	15.0	13.2	12.5	7.7	5.7	5.9	6.1	2.4	3.0	2.7 *	IS
NO	18.9	16.8	12.7	11.1	8.1	8.5	7.0	4.0	3.9	3.8	3.8 *	NO
EEA	34.4	27.4	23.3	18.0	12.4	9.5	7.6	5.6 *	:	:	:	EEA
CH	21.1	17.8	15.1	10.7	9.1	6.9	6.8	5.0	4.6	4.9 *	:	CH
CA	:	:	:	:	:	7.9	6.8	6.1	:	:	:	CA
JP	30.7	18.5	13.1	10.0	7.5	5.5	4.6	4.3	4.0	3.9	:	JP
US	:	:	:	:	12.6	10.6	9.2	7.6	6.9	6.8	:	US

Proportion of population aged 65 and over. 1960–2001. %

	1960	1965	1970	1975	1980	1985	1990	1995	1999	2000	2001	
EU-15	11	11	12	13	14	14	15	15	16	16	:	EU-15
B	12	13	13	14	14	14	15	16	17	17	17	B
DK	11	11	12	13	14	15	16	15	15	15	15	DK
D	12	12	14	15	16	15	15	15	16	16	17	D
EL	9	8	11	12	13	13	14	15	17	17	:	EL
E	8	9	10	10	11	12	13	15	17	17	17	E
F	12	12	13	13	14	13	14	15	16	16	16	F
IRL	11	11	11	11	11	11	11	11	11	11	11	IRL
I	9	10	11	12	13	13	15	16	18	18	18	I
L	11	12	13	13	14	13	13	14	14	14	14	L
NL	9	10	10	11	12	12	13	13	14	14	14	NL
A	12	13	14	15	16	14	15	15	16	16	16	A
P	8	8	9	10	11	12	13	15	16	16	16	P
FIN	7	8	9	11	12	12	13	14	15	15	15	FIN
S	12	13	14	15	16	17	18	18	17	17	17	S
UK	12	12	13	14	15	15	16	16	16	16	:	UK
IS	8	8	9	9	10	10	11	11	12	12	12	IS
NO	11	12	13	14	15	16	16	16	16	15	15	NO
EEA	11	11	12	13	14	14	15	15	16	16	:	EEA
CH	10	10	11	12	14	14	15	15	15	15	15	CH
CA	:	:	:	:	:	:	:	:	:	:	:	CA
JP	:	:	:	:	:	:	:	:	:	:	:	JP
US	:	:	:	:	:	:	:	:	:	:	:	US

eurostat

Reporting on health: a complex and sensitive task

Reporting on health and safety requires Eurostat to have a clear concept of where the collection, harmonisation and presentation of data add value to the overall statistical picture. Eurostat evaluates the wide range of statistical sources on health-related issues and chooses the appropriate ones from which to extract a rich assortment of data. To optimise the flow and analysis of the information, Eurostat cooperates closely with expert institutions and organisations in that field.

Do you feel well?

One of the ways used by governments to assess health aspects is through population surveys of self-rated health status. Subjective or self-reported health status is not a substitute for more objective indicators but rather complements these. The European Community household panel (ECHP) is a longitudinal, multi-subject survey covering many aspects of daily life, particularly employment and income, but also demographic characteristics, environment, education and health. According to 1998 results, 60.2 % of Europeans perceive their own health as very good or good, 12.3 % report a bad or very bad health status, and the rest perceive their own health as fair. Almost 9.7 % of the European population report 'being severely hampered in their daily activities by any chronic physical or mental health problem'.

Smokers

According to *Eurobarometer* estimates, 33.8 % of the EU's population aged 15 years and over smoked in 1999. Percentages were highest in the youngest age groups (15 to 24 years and 25 to 34 years).

Do Europeans eat well?

The recommended dietary allowances (RDAs) for most EU countries are about 2 900 kcal for males (25 to 50 years, about 176 cm and 79 kg) and 2 200 kcal for women (25 to 50 years, about 163 cm and 63 kg). The average consumption per person is above 3 000 kcal/day in all EU countries (except Finland); trends are not decreasing. A similar trend of unhealthy overconsumption can be observed in fat intake.

Severe diseases

AIDS is surveyed by the European Centre for the Epidemiological Monitoring of AIDS (EuroHIV — supported by the European Commission). Cases are recorded according to the AIDS case definition of 1993 and later revisions. Due to reporting delays (time between diagnosis on an AIDS case and report to national level), the incidence trends are best assessed by examining data by year of diagnosis (with adjustment for reporting delays) rather than by year of report. The annual number of cases reported continues to decrease. The last increase was in 1995. Annual AIDS incidence per million (adjusted for reporting delays) is estimated at 21.4 in 2001 with a cumulative total of cases in the EU of 232 407.

Cases of cancer are collected by the European Network of Cancer Registries and the International Agency for Research on Cancer (IARC)/WHO, with the support of the 'Europe against cancer' programme of the European Union. Both incidence and mortality rates were higher in males than in females in all countries. Even if fewer men have been dying of lung cancer since the 1980s, in 1997 it was this type of cancer which was the most common amongst men. Amongst women, it was breast cancer, which occurred most frequently in 1997.

Some of the communicable diseases preventable by immunisation can be considered practically eradicated in the EU (tetanus, poliomyelitis and diphtheria). Mumps, rubella, pertussis and measles remain a health problem in some Member States. Food diseases (salmonellosis), airborne diseases (tuberculosis, legionellosis, meningococcal disease), viral hepatitis (notably hepatitis C) and others emerge (or re-emerge) as important problematic infectious diseases.

Causes of death

Analysis of causes of death is based on the underlying cause as indicated in Section B of the death certificate. For more details, please refer to the glossary.

Total health expenditure

Data on total health expenditure can be retrieved from the OECD Ecosanté database. For more information, please refer to the glossary.

How many health professionals work in the EU?

The figures on manpower in healthcare cannot be fully compared because the EU Member States base their statistics on different concepts (e.g. only 'active' practitioners or practitioners 'entitled to practise' including practitioners who are unemployed or work without directly practising medicine).

Fewer hospital beds

A reduction in the number of hospital beds per capita could be observed virtually everywhere. This reduction is more marked for beds in psychiatric hospitals. The reduction in beds can be explained by developments in medical technologies, which have made it possible to reduce the average length of hospitalisation. Another reason is the financial constraints of the 1980s, which led to rationalisation of the health services. The average length of stay is defined as the number of bed-days in hospitals divided by the number of admissions or discharges.

Solid organ transplantation

The Council of Europe has developed the ethical principles governing organ transplantation. Eurostat collects information on this issue on the basis of results disseminated from different specialised national and international organisations. Kidney transplants remain the most frequent type of transplant.

Further reading:

Eurostat publications
— **Key data on health 2000 — Data 1985–1995**

Statistics in Focus — Theme 3
— **No 11 Causes of death among young people aged 15 to 24 1994/1997**
— **No 16 Accidents at work in the EU 1998–1999**
— **No 17 Work-related health problems in the EU 1998–1999**

Do you need more information?
— **Ask your Data Shop (see last page)**
— **http://www.europa.eu.int/comm/eurostat**
— **Eurostat's data serves the political discussion in Europe. Have a look at the website of the "Health and Consumer Protection DG" : http://europa.eu.int/comm/dgs/health_consumer/index_en.htm**

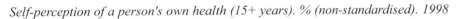

Self-perception of a person's own health (15+ years). % (non-standardised). 1998

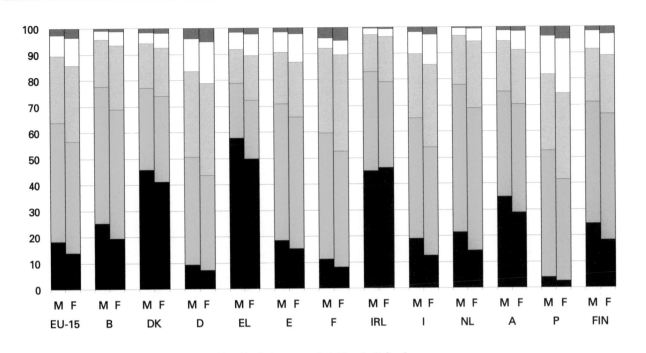

Black: very good; colour: good; light grey: fair; white: bad; grey: very bad. M: male; F: female.

2

Hospital beds per 100 000 inhabitants

	1990	1991	1992	1993	1994	1995	1996	1997	1998	1999	2000	
EU-15	779	757	733	713	702	:	:	:	:	630	:	EU-15
B	810	795	777	772	764	744	734	729	722	716	712	B
DK	567	546	519	511	504	494	475	465	455	440	:	DK
D	1 034	1 015	993	969	972	970	958	938	929	920	:	D
EL	507	503	500	497	498	500	503	500	499	489	:	EL
E	427	423	415	407	402	395	391	423	417	413	409	E
F	977	960	944	927	906	890	872	853	850	834	820	F
IRL	619	609	590	563	546	539	525	507	495	485	:	IRL
I	723	680	686	668	654	622	650	582	549	487	:	I
L	1 182	1 155	1 136	1 154	1 108	:	:	:	:	562	:	L
NL	583	573	565	555	535	523	517	514	504	497	475	NL
A	786	776	770	756	761	755	746	737	724	878	699	A
P	558	542	532	515	507	504	510	481	495	480	:	P
FIN	919	886	854	827	811	804	803	791	778	761	754	FIN
S	1 249	1 189	764	705	654	609	560	522	380	374	359	S
UK	592	563	537	506	486	468	451	436	425	413	408	UK
IS	1 053	1 011	981	973	937	911	:	:	:	:	:	IS
NO	465	442	430	420	407	406	401	398	398	390	381	NO
CH	807	796	774	751	702	701	666	664	637	630	:	CH

D, NL, P, IS: nursing homes and daycare beds are not included. EL, I: beds in military hospitals are not included. E: nursing homes and daycare beds are partially included. IRL, S, UK: only beds in public hospitals are included. UK: Eurostat estimates.

Total number of physicians (practising or licensed) per 100 000 inhabitants

	1991	1992	1993	1994	1995	1996	1997	1998	1999	2000	2001	
EU-15	316	:	:	:	:	:	:	368	375	:	:	EU-15
B	352	361	366	374	379	381	386	395	405	411	419	B
DK	297	304	307	306	309	310	309	314	317	:	:	DK
D	306	314	321	329	336	341	345	350	355	359	362	D
EL	365	376	388	389	393	397	410	426	438	:	:	EL
E	394	401	408	414	415	422	428	436	444	454	:	E
F	309	313	317	320	322	324	325	326	328	329	:	F
IRL	170	200	202	199	210	211	214	219	227	250	:	IRL
I	488	502	550	559	566	571	578	583	589	599	:	I
L	203	209	215	217	280	288	300	307	313	315	:	L
NL	260	:	:	:	:	:	:	295	311	321	:	NL
A	310	321	328	339	347	354	362	373	373	:	:	A
P	287	290	292	294	296	301	306	312	318	325	:	P
FIN	247	257	264	270	277	285	296	300	306	308	:	FIN
S	270	274	275	281	279	280	278	278	283	:	:	S
UK	141	147	151	152	158	162	168	172	176	180	:	UK
IS	287	297	297	301	303	313	328	334	340	:	:	IS
LI	100	106	107	106	105	107	132	141	:	:	:	LI
NO	258	257	263	272	279	285	253	274	280	:	:	NO
CH	160	163	167	170	176	180	184	188	191	195	:	CH
CA	213	214	215	213	211	208	207	210	210	:	:	CA
JP	:	197	:	203	:	210	:	207	:	194	:	JP
US	:	228	230	234	239	244	249	248	246	:	:	US

B, DK, EL, F, A, S, UK, IS, NO, CH, US, CA: in activity. E, I, NL, P, FIN: entitled to practise. D, LI, JP: practising doctors. IRL, UK: NHS only.

Discharges from hospitals by main group of diagnosis per 100 000 inhabitants. EU-15. 2000

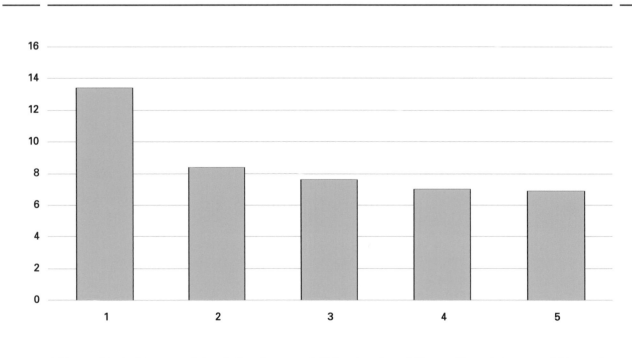

1. Diseases of the circulatory system; 2. Complications of pregnancy; 3. Malignant neoplasms; 4. Diseases of the respiratory system; 5. Diseases of the musculoskeletal system.

Standard death rates. All causes of death per 100 000 women. EU-15

	1995	1996	1997	1998	1999	
EU-15	553.8	545.3	529.9	525.1	521.9	EU-15
B	564.4	:	:	:	:	B
DK	710.8	681.5	:	:	:	DK
D	595.0	587.3	566.2	556.3	544.6	D
EL	571.2	559.6	542.7	:	:	EL
E	497.8	492.2	478.7	480.7	483.7	E
F	473.5	469.3	443.0	461.0	:	F
IRL	698.7	676.3	668.2	645.7	642.6	IRL
I	502.5	488.5	483.0	484.6	:	I
L	538.5	543.7	557.6	528.5	505.7	L
NL	564.6	565.4	556.4	552.6	564.2	NL
A	582.4	576.0	552.3	539.3	538.0	A
P	676.4	682.6	666.6	667.2	674.3	P
FIN	578.2	560.6	559.8	540.1	532.3	FIN
S	510.7	508.4	496.6	493.0	499.7	S
UK	617.8	610.2	603.0	596.3	595.1	UK
IS	576.7	539.0	:	:	:	IS
NO	550.1	534.6	538.8	523.9	531.9	NO
CH	472.3	462.2	461.8	444.2	459.7	CH

Standard death rates. All causes of death per 100 000 men. EU-15

	1995	1996	1997	1998	1999	
EU-15	949.9	930.1	896.2	923.3 *	876.1 *	EU-15
B	995.3	:	:	:	:	B
DK	1 080.7	1 046.5	:	:	:	DK
D	1 012.0	989.2	951.9	926.9	902.1	D
EL	846.0	836.3	811.2	:	:	EL
E	896.7	892.0	865.8	872.3	880.4	E
F	911.6	900.7	838.4	862.9	:	F
IRL	1 120.7	1 081.2	1 045.7	1 027.9	1 007.6 *	IRL
I	881.9	852.0	837.4	835.0	:	I
L	990.1	1 010.4	923.8	956.3	885.1	L
NL	954.2	950.4	911.1	910.2	903.3	NL
A	977.6	952.4	932.2	901.9	872.9	A
P	1 138.4	1 168.7	1 134.8	1 146.6	1 156.3	P
FIN	1 045.9	1 024.4	993.0	992.8	975.8	FIN
S	825.5	805.8	793.7	787.2	777.4	S
UK	981.0	948.7	918.5	907.7	893.6	UK
IS	809.8	810.3	:	:	:	IS
NO	929.5	880.9	878.4	863.3	864.4	NO
CH	810.9	775.7	762.2	759.6	763.2	CH

Standardised incidence rate of accidents at work with more than three days' absence per 100 000 persons employed

	1994	1995	1996	1997	1998	1999	
EU-15	4 539	4 266	4 229	4 106	4 089	4 088	EU-15
€-zone	:	5 061	4 966	4 826	4 801	4 764	€-zone
B	4 415	5 616	5 059	4 933	5 112	4 924	B
DK	2 653	2 621	2 704	3 217	3 203	3 031	DK
D	5 583	5 249	5 098	5 021	4 958	4 908	D
EL	3 702	3 468	3 783	3 309	2 936	2 740	EL
E	5 736	6 021	6 217	6 225	6 546	7 027	E
F	5 515	5 123	4 964	4 992	4 920	4 991	F
IRL	852	889	1 494	1 654	1 433	1 291	IRL
I	4 641	4 193	4 179	4 089	4 105	4 067	I
L	4 508	4 640	4 741	4 627	4 719	4 973	L
NL	4 287	4 236	4 251	4 168	3 909	4 223	NL
A	5 259	5 451	3 554	3 501	3 321	3 301	A
P	7 361	7 363	6 949	5 523	5 505	5 048	P
FIN	3 914	3 628	3 372	3 374	3 435	3 137	FIN
S	1 123	1 012	1 217	1 074	1 329	1 425	S
UK	1 915	1 806	1 550	1 535	1 512	1 606	UK
NO	:	4 605	4 352	3 933	4 866	4 421	NO

Employment figures are based on the Eurostat LFS. DK, IRL: 1998 = 1997. F: 1997 = 1998. NL: estimation from 1994 data. P: 1996 = 1997 and 1998 estimated from 1999.

Standardised incidence rate of fatal accidents at work per 100 000 persons employed

	1994	1995	1996	1997	1998	1999	
EU-15	3.9	3.7	3.6	3.4	3.4	2.9	EU-15
€-zone	4.6	4.2	4.1	3.8	4.0	3.3	€-zone
B	6.0	5.9	5.5	3.1	3.1	3.3	B
DK	2.8	3.3	3.0	2.3	3.1	2.2	DK
D	3.7	3.0	3.5	2.7	3.0	2.4	D
EL	4.3	4.3	3.7	2.8	3.7	6.3	EL
E	7.0	7.0	5.9	6.3	5.5	5.0	E
F	4.3	3.5	3.6	4.1	4.0	3.4	F
IRL	3.9	4.2	3.3	7.1	5.9	7.0	IRL
I	5.3	4.8	4.1	4.2	5.0	3.4	I
L	:	:	:	:	:	:	L
NL	:	:	:	3.0	:	2.3	NL
A	5.3	6.7	6.0	5.3	5.1	5.1	A
P	8.4	7.9	9.8	8.3	7.7	6.1	P
FIN	3.6	2.8	1.7	2.8	2.4	1.8	FIN
S	2.1	2.3	2.1	2.2	1.3	1.1	S
UK	1.7	1.6	1.9	1.6	1.6	1.4	UK
NO	:	:	:	1.4	4.3	2.4	NO

Excluding road traffic accidents and transport accidents in the course of work. Employment figures are based on the Eurostat LFS. DK, IRL: 1998 = 1997. F: 1997 = 1998. P: 1996 = 1997 and 1998 estimated from 1999.

Education opens opportunities

Eurostat provides a wide range of data on general and vocational education in Europe, for example on:

— the educational attainment of the population. These data come from the European Community labour force survey;

— entrants, enrolment and graduates. The data cover full- and part-time students at all levels of education, general and vocational, in public and private institutions. The data are broken down by age and gender;

— level and type of education;

— fields of study;

— non-national students;

— study of foreign languages;

— education staff;

— expenditure on education.

Eurostat's data on education: a basis for evaluating progress

Eurostat's statistical information on education is the basis for expert analysis, for example of:

— the participation of girls and women in education programmes;

— the age of entry to education programmes and their duration;

— the relationship between education and employment;

— the differences between States and regions.

Indicators facilitate comparisons

Eurostat calculates indicators that give a general and valid picture, for example:

— the participation rate in education (defined as the number of pupils/students enrolled as a percentage of the total population of a given age group);

— the pupil/teacher ratio which shows the number of pupils per teacher (both expressed in full-time equivalents) at a given level of education;

— the average number of foreign languages learnt by pupils at a given level of education. This figure is obtained by dividing the number of pupils studying modern languages, in a given year, by the total number of pupils enrolled in that year. All foreign languages studied in a country are taken into account.

If you would like more information, ask your Data Shop for the publication *Education across Europe — Statistics and indicators*. The addresses of the Data Shops can be found at the end of the yearbook.

International comparability through cooperation

The main source of data presented in this section is the joint Unesco/OECD/Eurostat (UOE) annual questionnaire that constitutes the core database on education. Additional Eurostat tables provide regional data and information on the study of foreign languages. As a result, the data from all EU Member States as well as the EEA and candidate countries are internationally comparable.

Some interesting findings

— During the past 10 years, there has been a very large increase in the number of students in tertiary education in EU-15 (above 50 %). For some countries, the increase has been even bigger: in Ireland, Finland and the United Kingdom, it was above 70 %. Numbers have doubled in Greece and almost trebled in Portugal.

— Germany and the United Kingdom attract most of the foreign students studying in the EU-15 area. In Belgium, Luxembourg, Austria and the United Kingdom, foreign students from other EU countries, EEA countries and candidate countries make up more than 6 % of all tertiary students.

— Luxembourg, Liechtenstein, Iceland, Greece and Ireland have a very large proportion of students studying abroad (10 % or more).

2

Further reading:

Eurostat publications
— **Education across Europe — Statistics and indicators 1999**
— **Key data on education in Europe – 1999/2000, 2002, European Commission, DG Education and Culture and Eurostat**
— **The social situation in the European Union, 2002**
— **The transition from education to working life: Key data on vocational training in the European Union**
— **Living conditions in Europe, statistical pocketbook, 2000 edition**

Statistics in Focus — Theme 3 (Population and social conditions)
— **No 4   Foreign language teaching in schools in Europe, 2001**
— **No 6   Education in the regions of the European Union, 2001**
— **No 7   Educational attainment levels in Europe in the 1990s — some key figures, 2001**
— **No 8   Public expenditure on education in the EU in 1997**
— **No 13 Employment in the EU regions 2000: Job creation is driven by the service sector — education is essential**
— **No 14 Educating young Europeans — Similarities and differences between the EU Member States and the PHARE countries, 2000**
— **No 18 Women and men in tertiary education, 2001**

Do you need more information?
— **Ask your Data Shop (see last page)**
— **http://www.europa.eu.int/comm/eurostat**
— **Eurostat's data serves the political discussion in Europe. Have a look at the website of the "Directorate General for Education and Culture": http://europa.eu.int/comm/dgs/education_culture/index_en.htm**

Pupils and students (excluding pre-primary). 1 000s

	1993	1994	1995	1996	1997	1998	1999	2000	2001	
EU-15	72 345	73 014	73 027	73 380	73 296	72 809 *	72 582	74 323	:	EU-15
B	2 087	2 113	2 153	2 160	2 168	2 137 *	2 207	2 235	:	B
DK	938	942	943	942	955	973	988	1 003	:	DK
D	13 629	13 858	14 035	14 210	14 441	14 497	14 509	14 549	14 515	D
EL	1 892	1 889	1 850	1 840	1 833	1 904	1 859	1 884	:	EL
E	8 813	8 778	8 637	8 509	8 239	8 087	7 898	7 769	7 597	E
F	11 998	12 145	12 148	12 137	12 131	12 008	11 936	11 934	:	F
IRL	892	897	893	885	886	1 000	994	990	:	IRL
I	9 467	9 572	9 099	9 300	9 306	9 203	9 151	9 049	:	I
L	:	:	54	57	60	62	68	69	70	L
NL	3 539	3 241	3 201	3 179	3 116	3 136	3 123	3 171	:	NL
A	1 372	1 387	1 402	1 412	1 416	1 426	1 443	1 459	:	A
P	2 099	2 145	2 166	2 134	2 085	2 076	2 020	2 016	:	P
FIN	1 025	1 044	1 047	1 059	1 077	1 101	1 126	1 152	1 172	FIN
S	1 623	1 656	1 698	1 753	1 814	1 962	2 075	2 090	2 107	S
UK	12 931	13 298	13 700	13 802	13 232	13 238	14 835	14 955	:	UK
IS	:	:	67	67	68	71	72	74	:	IS
LI	:	:	:	:	:	:	:	5	:	LI
NO	:	895	858	856	884	957	981	989	993	NO

D: ISCED 6 missing. I: data for ISCED 1, 2 and 3 for 1999/2000 are provisional. L: since 1998/99, private institutions have been included in ISCED 0, 1, 2 and 3; most tertiary students study abroad. UK: break in series in 1999/2000 due to change in national methodology.
Source: Unesco/OECD/Eurostat data collection.

Average number of foreign languages learnt per pupil in secondary general education. 1999/2000

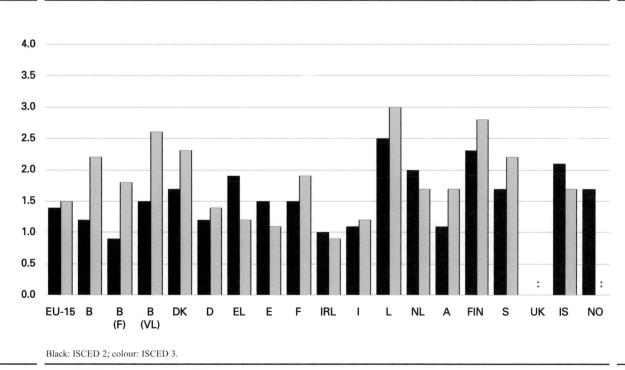

Black: ISCED 2; colour: ISCED 3.

EL, A: 1998/99. IRL, NL: data refer to full-time students only. NL: data do not include students in special schools. FIN: the national language taught in schools where it is not the teaching language is counted as a foreign language. S: in ISCED 3, only graduates are included. *Source:* Eurostat.
B (F): French community (includes small German-speaking community). B (VL): Flemish community.

Participation rates in education for 18-year-olds, all levels. 1993–2001. %

	1993	1994	1995	1996	1997	1998	1999	2000	2001	
EU-15	:	59.6	60.2	62.3	71.6	72.4	73.2	74.5	:	EU-15
B	86.2	86.8	87.7	86.3	85.7	85.4	85.3	84.9	:	B
DK	69.3	70.0	71.7	74.5	74.0	74.6	76.2	76.8	:	DK
D	80.0	84.9	84.3	85.3	85.5	85.7	85.1	85.8	82.6	D
EL	56.5	58.3	46.5	63.4	62.2	71.4	68.8	93.5	:	EL
E	56.4	61.5	62.8	64.6	66.8	65.8	66.0	68.7	70.5	E
F	:	85.2	84.4	84.6	83.6	82.6	81.6	81.5	:	F
IRL	61.7	77.7	73.8	79.4	80.6	72.2	74.0	72.7	:	IRL
I	:	:	:	:	61.9	67.7	69.6	67.1	:	I
L	:	20.7	70.3	72.2	73.9	69.5	65.6	70.1	74.1	L
NL	:	79.8	82.5	82.3	79.8	78.6	79.9	78.4	:	NL
A	:	60.9	62.5	67.6	67.6	67.7	66.7	67.2	:	A
P	52.7	54.1	55.0	54.6	61.9	64.3	64.1	67.3	:	P
FIN	82.3	82.5	81.5	83.2	84.0	84.5	85.3	87.3	88.5	FIN
S	72.4	82.6	87.9	93.7	94.6	96.0	95.5	95.5	94.7	S
UK	51.0	53.5	54.5	55.0	49.7	49.2	53.4	55.5	:	UK
IS	:	66.8	65.5	68.5	:	66.8	67.0	68.2	:	IS
LI	:	:	:	83.7	:	:	:	84.5	:	LI
NO	:	83.0	83.0	83.3	88.5	88.3	87.7	86.8	86.1	NO

B: includes social advancement courses. L: does not have a complete university system. LI: data are from national source.
Source: Unesco/OECD/Eurostat data collection.

Students in tertiary education. 1991–2001. 1 000s

	1991	1992	1993	1994	1995	1996	1997	1998	1999	2000	2001	
EU-15	9 614	10 114	10 854	11 528	11 790	11 934	12 266	12 329 *	12 438	12 563	:	EU-15
B	276	286	307	322	353	358	361	357 *	352	356	:	B
DK	143	150	164	170	170	167	180	183	190	189	:	DK
D	2 049		2 034		2 113		2 148		2 156		2 144		2 132		2 098		2 087		2 055		2 084		D
EL	195	200	299	314	296	329	363	374	388	422	:	EL
E	1 222	1 302	1 371	1 469	1 527	1 592	1 684	1 746	1 787	1 829	1 834	E
F	1 699	1 840	1 952	2 083	2 073	2 092	2 063	2 027	2 012	2 015	:	F
IRL	90	101	108	118	122	128	135	143	151	161	:	IRL
I	1 452	1 533	1 615	1 770	1 792	1 775	1 893	1 869	1 797	1 770	:	I
L	1		1		:	:	:	2		2		2		3		2		3		L
NL	479	494	507	532	503	492	469	461	470	488	:	NL
A	206	217	221	227	234	239	241	248	253	261	:	A
P	186	191	248	276	301	320	351	352	357	374	:	P
FIN	166	174	188	197	205	214	226	250	263	270	280	FIN
S	193	207	223	234	246	261	275	281	335		347	358	S
UK	1 258	1 385	1 528	1 664	1 813	1 821	1 891	1 938	1 994	2 024	:	UK
IS	5	6	:	:	7	7	8	8	9	10		:	IS
LI	:	:	:	:	:	:	:	:	:	1	:	LI
NO	142	154	:	177	173	180	185	183	188	191	190	NO

D: ISCED 6 missing. L, LI: most students study abroad. S: since 1998/99 data refer to academic year. In previous years data refer to the autumn term. *Source:* Unesco/OECD/Eurostat data collection.

Science and technology graduates. Tertiary graduates in science and technology per 1 000 population aged 20 to 29

	1993	1994	1995	1996	1997	1998	1999	2000	2001	
EU-15	:	:	:	:	:	:	:	:	:	EU-15
B	9.2	:	:	:	:	:	:	9.7	10.1	B
DK	9.8	:	9.6	9.4	:	8.1	8.2	11.1	:	DK
D	8.2	8.9	9.3	9.3	9.1	8.8	8.6	8.2	8.0	D
EL	3.8	:	:	:	:	:	:	:	:	EL
E	4.4	5.1	5.8	6.6	7.6	8.0	9.5	9.9	11.3	E
F	14.2	:	:	:	17.5	18.5	19.0	19.6	:	F
IRL	19.1	21.0	21.4	21.9	21.8	22.4	:	23.2	:	IRL
I	2.9	2.8	2.9	4.1	5.0	5.1	5.4	5.7	:	I
L	:	:	:	:	:	1.4	:	1.8	:	L
NL	5.5	5.4	5.6	6.6	:	6.0	5.8	5.8	6.1	NL
A	:	3.2	3.3	3.6	4.3	7.7	6.8	7.1	7.2	A
P	2.4	3.8	3.9	4.1	4.8	:	:	6.3	6.4	P
FIN	13.2	13.0	13.0	13.1	15.8	15.9	17.8	16.0	:	FIN
S	6.2	6.3	7.3	7.4	7.8	7.9	9.7	11.6	12.4	S
UK	12.9	13.7	13.5	14.3	14.5	15.2	15.6	16.2	19.5	UK
IS	:	:	:	7.9	7.7	7.0	6.3	8.4	9.1	IS
NO	:	:	8.5	9.1	8.4	7.5	7.2	7.9	8.6	NO
JP	:	:	12.7	12.5	:	:	:	:	:	JP
US	10.3	10.9	11.2	11.5	:	9.6	9.7	10.2	:	US

L: does not have a complete university system; refers only to ISCED 5B first degree. A: ISCED 5B refers to previous years except for 2001;
Sources: Eurostat, Unesco/OECD/Eurostat data collection and population statistics.

2

Early school-leavers not in further education or training. Share of the population aged 18 to 24 with only lower secondary education and not in education or training. %

	1991	1992	1993	1994	1995	1996	1997	1998	1999	2000	2001	
EU-15	:	:	:	:	:	21.7 *	20.8 *	:	20.7 *	19.7 *	19.4 *	EU-15
B	:	18.1	17.4	16.1	15.1	12.9	12.7	14.5	15.2	12.5	13.6	B
DK	:	15.2	8.5	8.6	6.1	12.1	10.7	9.8	11.5	11.6	16.8	DK
D	:	:	:	:	:	13.3	12.9	:	14.9	14.9	12.5	D
EL	:	25.2	25.0	23.2	22.4	20.7	19.9	19.8	17.8	17.1	16.5	EL
E	:	40.4	37.7	36.4	33.8	31.5	30.3	29.8	29.5	28.8	28.6	E
F	:	:	17.2	16.4	15.4	15.2	14.1	14.9	14.7	13.3	13.5	F
IRL	:	27.1	24.0	22.9	21.4	18.9	18.9	:	:	:	:	IRL
I	:	37.7	36.9	35.1	32.4	31.3	29.9	28.4	27.2	25.3	26.4	I
L	:	42.2	36.8	34.4	33.4	35.3	30.7	:	19.1	16.8	18.1	L
NL	:	:	:	:	:	17.6	16.0	15.5	16.2	15.5	15.3	NL
A	:	:	:	:	13.6	12.1	10.8	:	10.7	10.2	10.2	A
P	:	50.0	46.7	44.3	41.4	40.1	40.6	46.8	45.5	43.1	45.2	P
FIN	:	:	:	:	:	11.1	8.1	7.9	9.9	8.9	10.3	FIN
S	:	:	:	:	:	7.5	6.8	:	6.9	7.7	10.5	S
UK	:	:	:	:	:	:	:	:	:	:	:	UK
IS	:	:	:	:	:	:	:	:	29.8	28.6	30.0	IS
NO	:	:	:	:	:	10.9	:	:	:	13.3	9.2	NO

EU-15 from 1996 only. Estimated values — EU: 1996, 1997, 1999, 2000, 2001. UK not included because of unreliable or uncertain data.
Source: LFS.

Percentage of the total population aged 25 to 64 having completed at least upper secondary education

	1992	1993	1994	1995	1996	1997	1998	1999	2000	2001	
EU-15	:	:	:	55.4	55.8	57.3	:	62.3 *	63.5 *	63.9	EU-15
B	49.8	50.8	52.8	54.5	56.6	57.8	56.7	57.4	58.3	59.2	B
DK	74.1	81.5	76.4	79.5	77.6	78.6	78.5	79.6	79.8	80.2	DK
D	79.9	79.4	81.9	81.2	78.5	80.4	:	79.9	81.3	82.5	D
EL	36.6	39.1	41.4	42.6	44.3	45.7	47.5	49.9	51.2	51.6	EL
E	24.0	25.5	27.5	29.5	32.1	33.5	34.4	36.1	38.3	40.0	E
F	:	56.0	57.6	58.8	58.8	60.0	59.9	60.9	62.2	63.2	F
IRL	42.3	44.5	45.2	47.3	50.0	49.3	:	:	:	59.2	IRL
I	33.0	31.9 |	33.9	35.4	36.9	38.6	41.5	43.2	45.2	43.2	I
L	34.7	39.8	47.4	42.9	45.4	46.0	:	62.3	60.9	59.2	L
NL	:	:	:	:	63.1	64.5	64.4	64.7	66.1	66.9	NL
A	:	:	:	68.9	70.5	73.1	74.1	74.8	76.2	77.3	A
P	19.9	20.0	20.9	21.9	21.8	22.0	19.9 |	21.2	21.6	19.8	P
FIN	:	:	:	66.8	67.9	69.6	70.1	71.5	73.2	73.5	FIN
S	:	:	:	74.1	73.9	74.7	75.5	77.0	77.2	80.5 |	S
UK	49.3	49.9	51.7	52.8	52.5	54.7	:	79.8	80.7	81.1	UK
IS	:	:	:	:	:	:	:	63.0	62.4	63.0	IS
NO	:	:	:	:	80.7	82.2	83.5	84.7	85.5	85.7	NO

All programmes at ISCED 3C shorter than three years are included. (e.g. GCSE in th UK). *Source:* LFS.

Expenditure per pupil/student in public institutions by level of education in PPS. 1999

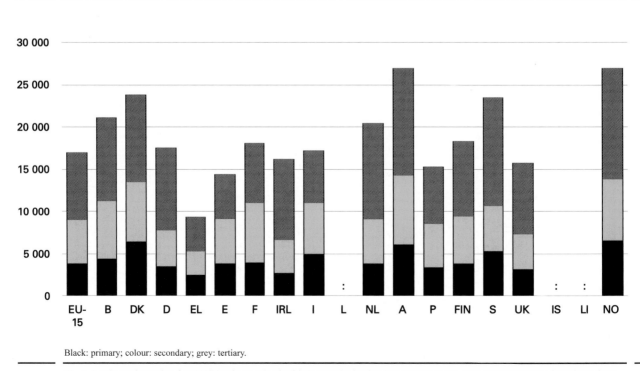

Black: primary; colour: secondary; grey: tertiary.

EL, A, P, NO: enrolment data for 1998/99 only. B: only Flemish Community is taken into account. B, NL, UK: only government-dependent private institutions are included. NO: 'secondary' covers lower secondary only.

Labour market statistics are at the heart of EU policies

Employment is having an ever-important political profile for the European Union. Labour market statistics are now at the heart of many EU policies.

An employment chapter was introduced into the Amsterdam Treaty in 1997. The extraordinary European Council of Luxembourg in November 1997 endorsed an ambitious European employment strategy aiming at the reduction of unemployment and the sustainable increase of employment rates, as well as the reduction of gender gaps.

The Lisbon Summit (spring 2000) put full employment with more and better jobs on the European agenda. For the year 2010, it set targets for the total and female employment rate:

— 70 % for the total employment rate;

— 60 % for the female employment rate.

The Stockholm Council (spring 2001) subsequently added the employment target for persons aged between 55 and 64 years to reach 50 % by 2010. It also fixed the intermediate objectives (for 2005) of 67 % for the total employment rate and 57 % for the female employment rate.

The labour force survey: an indispensable tool for observing the labour market

In this context, the role of the Community labour force survey (LFS) has gained steadily in importance. It is now universally recognised as an indispensable tool for observing labour market developments and for taking the appropriate policy measures. The LFS is the only source of information in these areas to provide data that are truly comparable. The definitions and methods are harmonised for all Member States. The LFS is the main source of data for this section.

Comparable data on Europe's labour market

An objective of the LFS is to report on the EU's population of working age (15 to 64 years) which is composed of persons in employment, unemployed persons and economically inactive persons.

The LFS provides comprehensive information on these three categories. It describes the employment situation of employees by reporting, for example, on their education, the branches in which they work, and their occupation, as well as on part-time work, the duration of the work contract and the search for a new job. The data presented in the Eurostat yearbook refer to the situation in spring.

The yearly publication *European social statistics — Labour force results* and numerous *Statistics in Focus* show the wide range of information that the LFS provides. The complete list of LFS variables (more than 100) can be consulted in the 1998 edition of *Labour force survey — Methods and definitions*. Users with specific requirements that are not met by the existing publications and databases may ask for customised tables. For more information, please contact your Data Shop. The addresses of the Data Shops can be found at the end of the yearbook.

Approaching the Lisbon Council targets slowly but steadily

The EU continued to make progress towards reaching the Lisbon Council targets. In 2001, the total employment rate in the EU reached 64.1 %, 3.4 percentage points more than in 1997 when the employment strategy was launched. The increase was more pronounced for women (4.2 percentage points); the female employment rate is now 55.0 %.

Unemployment still decreasing

The overall increase in the employment rate has led to a decrease in the unemployment rate, though not all new jobs have been filled by those previously unemployed. The EU unemployment rate for 2001 was 7.3 %, still above the rate in the United States and Japan (4.8 and 5 %, respectively).

In most of the countries, the unemployment rates for men are lower than those for women. In Greece, the gap reaches more than 8 percentage points.

Youth unemployment (15 to 24 years old) is twice the overall unemployment rate, ranging from 28.1 % in Italy and Greece to 5.5 % in the Netherlands.

Long-term unemployment affects 3.2 % of the EU labour force and represents 44 % of the unemployed. However, since 1996, the proportion of the long-term unemployed has been decreasing.

Part-time work remains a predominant feature for working women

The percentage of persons working part-time increased persistently in the last decade. In 2001, women had slightly more than 1 in 3 jobs, but close to 8 in every 10 part-time jobs. The Netherlands is the country showing the highest percentage of part-time employment with 42 % of employment (71 % of female employment). The distinction between full-time and part-time work is made on the basis of a spontaneous answer given by the respondents to the LFS.

Fixed-term contracts are more frequent for women and young people

Fixed-term contracts are prevalent in many EU labour markets with just over 13 % of all employees working in temporary jobs. These contracts are more frequent for women and young people.

Further reading:

Eurostat publications
— **European social statistics — Labour force survey results 2000**
— **Regions: Statistical yearbook 2001**

Statistics in Focus — Theme 3
— **No 8   Employment rates in Europe — 2000**
— **No 10 Labour force survey — Principal results 2000**
— **No 13 Employment in the EU regions 2000**

Do you need more information?
— **Ask your Data Shop (see last page)**
— **http://www.europa.eu.int/comm/eurostat**
— **Eurostat's data serves the political discussion in**
   Europe. Have a look at the website of the "DG Employment and Social Affairs":
   http://europa.eu.int/comm/dgs/employment_social/index_en.htm

Total employment growth. Annual percentage change in total employed population

	1991	1992	1993	1994	1995	1996	1997	1998	1999	2000	2001	
EU-15	:	:	:	:	1.0	0.6	0.9	1.7	1.6	1.8	1.2	EU-15
€-zone	:	- 0.8	- 1.6	- 0.3	0.6	0.4	0.8	1.7	1.7	2.0	1.7 *	€-zone
B	0.1	- 0.5	- 0.7	- 0.4	0.7	0.4	0.8	1.2	1.4	1.6	1.2	B
DK	- 0.6	- 0.8	- 1.5	1.4	0.5	0.6	1.2	1.7	1.5	0.7	0.2	DK
D	:	- 1.5	- 1.4	- 0.2	0.2	- 0.3	- 0.2	1.1	1.3	1.6	0.2	D
EL	- 1.4	1.0	1.2	1.7	0.5	- 0.4	- 0.5	4.1	- 0.7	- 0.3	- 0.1	EL
E	1.2	- 1.4	- 2.8	- 0.5	1.9	1.3	2.9	3.6	3.5	3.1	2.5	E
F	0.4	- 0.5	- 1.2	0.2	0.6	0.5	0.4	1.6	1.8	2.4	2.0	F
IRL	0.4	1.1	1.3	4.3	4.3	3.6	5.5	8.7	5.9	4.7	2.9	IRL
I	1.9	- 0.5	- 2.5	- 1.5	- 0.1	0.6	0.4	1.0	1.1	1.9	1.6	I
L	4.1	2.5	1.7	2.5	2.6	2.7	3.2	4.3	5.0	5.6	5.6	L
NL	1.8	1.6	0.0	0.7	1.5	2.3	3.2	2.7	2.5	2.3	2.1	NL
A	1.4	0.2	- 0.6	- 0.1	0.0	- 0.6	0.6	0.7	1.2	0.5	0.2	A
P	2.8	- 0.9	- 1.9	- 0.2	- 0.7	0.5	1.7	2.7	1.7	2.0	1.6	P
FIN	- 5.7	- 7.2	- 6.2	- 1.1	1.6	1.4	3.3	2.1	2.7	1.9	1.2	FIN
S	- 2.0	- 4.3	- 5.3	- 0.8	1.4	- 0.6	- 1.1	1.2	2.2	2.1	1.9	S
UK	:	:	:	:	3.1	1.2	1.8	1.3	1.2	1.1	0.9	UK
IS	- 0.7 *	- 0.3 *	0.2 *	1.3 *	2.1 *	2.1 *	2.9 *	2.5 *	0.6 *	0.5 *	:	IS
NO	0.0 *	- 1.6 *	- 0.8 *	0.8 *	0.8 *	2.4 *	1.6 *	3.1 *	3.0 *	:	:	NO
JP	1.9 *	1.1 *	0.2 *	0.1 *	0.1 *	0.4 *	1.1 *	- 0.6 *	- 0.8 *	- 0.2 *	:	JP
US	- 0.9 *	0.6 *	1.5 *	3.2 *	1.5 *	1.4 *	2.2 *	1.5 *	1.5 *	1.3 *	:	US

Persons in employment: men and women. Annual average. 1 000s

	1991	1992	1993	1994	1995	1996	1997	1998	1999	2000	2001	
EU-15	:	:	:	153 662	155 169	156 051	157 509	160 188	162 813	165 792	167 851	EU-15
€-zone	124 149	123 150	121 181	120 824	121 532	122 047	123 059	125 211	127 351	129 885	:	€-zone
B	3 748	3 731	3 703	3 688	3 714	3 729	3 757	3 802	3 856	3 918	3 965	B
DK	2 621	2 600	2 562	2 599	2 611	2 628	2 659	2 704	2 745	2 765	2 771	DK
D	38 454	37 878	37 365	37 304	37 382	37 270	37 208	37 611	38 081	38 706	38 773	D
EL	3 658	3 695	3 738	3 800	3 820	3 805	3 784	3 940	3 910	3 898	3 894	EL
E	13 966	13 772	13 381	13 318	13 572	13 745	14 147	14 653	15 161	15 633	16 026	E
F	22 927	22 808	22 544	22 592	22 719	22 839	22 922	23 290	23 719	24 292	24 788	F
IRL	1 154	1 166	1 182	1 232	1 285	1 331	1 405	1 526	1 617	1 693	1 743	IRL
I	23 032	22 920	22 348	22 017	21 993	22 130	22 215	22 448	22 701	23 129	23 505	I
L	195	200	203	208	214	220	227	236	248	262	277	L
NL	6 873	6 986	6 986	7 036	7 144	7 309	7 541	7 741	7 938	8 122	8 291	NL
A	3 949	3 957	3 932	3 926	3 926	3 902	3 924	3 950	3 999	4 019	4 028	A
P	4 691	4 647	4 557	4 546	4 515	4 538	4 615	4 739	4 818	4 914	4 994	P
FIN	2 337	2 168	2 033	2 010	2 042	2 072	2 139	2 184	2 243	2 285	2 313	FIN
S	4 485	4 294	4 065	4 034	4 088	4 065	4 022	4 071	4 161	4 247	4 326	S
UK	:	:	:	25 354	26 145	26 470	26 945	27 295	27 616	27 910	28 160	UK
IS	:	:	:	:	:	:	:	:	:	:	:	IS
NO	:	:	:	:	:	:	:	:	:	:	:	NO
JP	:	:	:	:	:	:	:	:	:	:	:	JP
US	:	:	:	:	:	:	:	:	:	:	:	US

Total employment rate. Employed persons aged 15 to 64 as a share of the total population aged 15 to 64. %

	1991	1992	1993	1994	1995	1996	1997	1998	1999	2000	2001	
EU-15	62.2	61.1	60.0	59.7	59.9	60.1	60.5	61.2	62.3	63.2	64.0	EU-15
€-zone	60.0	59.1	58.0	57.6	57.7	57.9	58.2	59.0	60.1	61.2	61.9 *	€-zone
B	55.9	56.3	55.8	55.7	56.1	56.3	56.9	57.5	59.3	60.5	:	B
DK	74.2	73.7	72.1	72.3	73.4	73.8	74.9	75.1	76.0	76.3	76.2	DK
D	:	66.4	65.1	64.7	64.6	64.1	63.7	63.9	64.8	65.4	:	D
EL	53.4	53.7	53.7	54.2	54.7	55.0	55.1	55.5	55.3	55.7	55.4	EL
E	49.2	47.9	45.6	45.0	45.9	46.8	48.2	49.9	52.5	54.8	56.3	E
F	60.4	59.9	59.3	59.1	59.5	59.5	59.5	60.0	60.8	62.0	:	F
IRL	51.4	51.2	51.7	53.0	54.4	55.4	57.5	60.6	63.3	65.2	65.7	IRL
I	:	:	52.1	51.2	50.8	51.1	51.2	51.9	52.6	53.7	54.8	I
L	60.8	61.4	60.8	59.9	58.7	59.2	59.9	60.5	61.7	62.7	:	L
NL	62.5	63.6	63.6	63.9	64.5	65.9	68.0	69.8	71.1	72.9	74.1	NL
A	:	:	:	68.3	68.7	67.8	67.8	67.9	68.5	68.4	68.4	A
P	68.0	66.3	64.6	63.4	62.6	62.8	64.0	66.6	67.4	68.3	68.8	P
FIN	70.5	65.3	61.1	60.4	61.7	62.5	63.3	64.6	66.4	67.3	68.1	FIN
S	78.1	74.7	70.3	69.2	69.9	69.3	68.1	68.7	70.1	70.8	71.7	S
UK	70.0	68.7	68.0	68.1	68.5	69.1	70.0	70.6	71.0	71.5	71.7	UK
IS	:	:	:	:	81.8 *	82.2 *	81.1 *	83.1 *	85.4 *	87.1 *	:	IS
NO	:	:	:	:	71.9 *	74.4 *	76.3 *	78.1 *	77.9 *	77.9 *	77.5 *	NO
JP	:	:	:	:	:	:	:	:	:	:	:	JP
US	:	:	:	:	:	:	:	:	:	:	:	US

Employment rate: females. Employed persons aged 15 to 64 as a share of the females aged 15 to 64. %

	1991	1992	1993	1994	1995	1996	1997	1998	1999	2000	2001	
EU-15	50.2	49.8	49.3	49.3	49.7	50.1	50.6	51.5	52.8	54.0	54.9	EU-15
€-zone	47.0	46.6	46.1	46.1	46.5	47.0	47.5	48.4	49.9	51.2	52.1 *	€-zone
B	42.9	44.3	44.5	44.6	45.1	45.4	46.5	47.6	50.4	51.5	:	B
DK	69.9	69.8	68.2	66.9	66.7	67.4	69.1	70.2	71.1	71.6	72.0	DK
D	:	55.9	55.1	55.1	55.3	55.3	55.3	55.8	57.1	57.9	:	D
EL	35.4	36.2	36.6	37.3	38.1	38.7	39.3	40.2	40.6	41.2	40.9	EL
E	31.2	31.2	30.3	30.3	31.2	32.3	33.6	35.0	37.6	40.3	41.9	E
F	51.4	51.4	51.5	51.6	52.1	52.2	52.4	53.0	53.9	55.1	:	F
IRL	35.9	37.1	38.5	40.1	41.6	43.2	45.9	49.0	52.0	54.1	55.0	IRL
I	:	:	35.8	35.4	35.4	36.0	36.4	37.3	38.3	39.6	41.1	I
L	44.0	45.7	44.8	44.4	42.6	43.8	45.3	46.2	48.6	50.1	:	L
NL	48.9	51.1	51.9	52.9	53.6	55.3	57.4	59.5	61.5	63.5	65.2	NL
A	:	:	:	58.9	59.1	58.4	58.6	58.8	59.6	59.6	60.1	A
P	56.9	56.0	55.1	54.4	54.3	54.7	56.1	58.0	59.4	60.3	61.1	P
FIN	68.3	63.7	59.5	58.7	59.0	59.4	60.3	61.2	63.4	64.3	65.4	FIN
S	77.2	74.4	70.5	69.1	69.2	68.3	66.6	66.6	68.4	69.3	70.4	S
UK	61.6	61.4	61.4	61.5	61.8	62.5	63.2	63.6	64.2	64.8	65.1	UK
IS	:	:	:	:	78.2 *	78.0 *	76.3 *	78.3 *	81.3 *	83.8 *	:	IS
NO	:	:	:	:	67.7 *	69.9 *	71.6 *	73.7 *	74.0 *	73.9 *	73.8 *	NO
JP	:	:	:	:	:	:	:	:	:	:	:	JP
US	:	:	:	:	:	:	:	:	:	:	:	US

Employment rate: males. Employed persons aged 15 to 64 as a share of the males aged 15 to 64. %

	1991	1992	1993	1994	1995	1996	1997	1998	1999	2000	2001	
EU-15	74.3	72.5	70.7	70.1	70.2	70.1	70.3	71.0	71.7	72.5	73.0	EU-15
€-zone	73.2	71.7	69.9	69.1	69.0	68.8	68.9	69.6	70.4	71.3	61.9 *	€-zone
B	68.7	68.2	67.1	66.7	67.0	66.9	67.1	67.1	68.1	69.5	:	B
DK	78.4	77.4	75.8	77.5	79.9	80.1	80.5	79.9	80.8	80.8	80.2	DK
D	:	76.7	74.9	74.1	73.7	72.6	71.9	71.9	72.4	72.7	:	D
EL	72.6	72.4	72.1	72.4	72.5	72.7	72.1	71.6	70.8	71.1	70.8	EL
E	67.7	65.1	61.2	60.1	60.9	61.6	63.0	65.3	67.9	69.7	70.9	E
F	69.7	68.7	67.3	66.8	67.2	67.0	66.9	67.2	67.9	69.1	:	F
IRL	66.5	65.1	64.8	65.9	67.1	67.5	69.0	72.0	74.5	76.2	76.4	IRL
I	:	:	68.7	67.2	66.4	66.4	66.2	66.6	67.1	67.9	68.5	I
L	77.1	76.5	76.4	74.9	74.4	74.3	74.3	74.5	74.5	75.0	:	L
NL	75.7	75.9	74.9	74.6	75.2	76.3	78.3	79.8	80.5	82.1	82.8	NL
A	:	:	:	77.8	78.4	77.3	77.1	77.0	77.5	77.3	76.7	A
P	79.9	77.6	74.9	73.1	71.6	71.5	72.5	75.6	75.8	76.5	76.9	P
FIN	72.6	66.9	62.8	62.2	64.4	65.6	66.3	67.9	69.2	70.2	70.9	FIN
S	79.1	75.0	70.2	69.4	70.5	70.3	69.6	70.8	71.6	72.3	73.0	S
UK	78.5	75.9	74.5	74.7	75.2	75.6	76.7	77.4	77.7	78.1	78.3	UK
IS	:	:	:	:	85.4 *	86.3 *	85.7 *	87.8 *	89.3 *	90.4 *	:	IS
NO	:	:	:	:	76.0 *	78.9 *	81.0 *	82.4 *	81.7 *	81.8 *	81.1 *	NO
JP	:	:	:	:	:	:	:	:	:	:	:	JP
US	:	:	:	:	:	:	:	:	:	:	:	US

Total unemployment rate. Unemployed persons as a share of the total active population. %.
Annual average

	1991	1992	1993	1994	1995	1996	1997	1998	1999	2000	2001	
EU-15	:	:	10.1	10.5	10.1	10.2	10.0	9.4	8.7	7.8	7.3	EU-15
€-zone	:	:	10.2	10.9	10.6	10.9	10.9	10.2	9.3	8.4	8.0	€-zone
B	6.4	7.1	8.6	9.8	9.7	9.5	9.2	9.3	8.6	6.9	6.6	B
DK	7.9	8.6	9.5	7.7	6.7	6.3	5.2	4.9	4.8	4.4	4.3	DK
D	:	6.4	7.7	8.2	8.0	8.7	9.7	9.1	8.4	7.8	7.7	D
EL	7.1	7.9	8.6	8.9	9.2	9.6	9.8	10.9	11.9	11.1	10.5	EL
E	13.2	14.9	18.6	19.8	18.8	18.1	17.0	15.2	12.8	11.3	10.6	E
F	9.1	10.0	11.3	11.8	11.3	11.9	11.8	11.4	10.7	9.3	8.5	F
IRL	14.7	15.4	15.6	14.3	12.3	11.7	9.9	7.5	5.6	4.2	3.8	IRL
I	8.5	8.7	10.1	11.0	11.5	11.5	11.6	11.7	11.3	10.4	9.4	I
L	1.6	2.1	2.6	3.2	2.9	2.9	2.7	2.7	2.4	2.3	2.0	L
NL	5.5	5.3	6.2	6.8	6.6	6.0	4.9	3.8	3.2	2.8	2.4	NL
A	:	:	3.9	3.8	3.9	4.4	4.4	4.5	3.9	3.7	3.6	A
P	4.2	4.3	5.6	6.9	7.3	7.3	6.8	5.1	4.5	4.1	4.1	P
FIN	6.6	11.7	16.3	16.6	15.4	14.6	12.7	11.4	10.2	9.8	9.1	FIN
S	3.1	5.6	9.1	9.4	8.8	9.6	9.9	8.3	7.1	5.8	4.9	S
UK	8.6	9.8	10.2	9.4	8.5	8.0	6.9	6.2	5.8	5.4	5.0	UK
JP	2.1	2.2	2.5	2.9	3.1	3.4	3.4	4.1	4.7	4.7	5.0	JP
US	6.7	7.4	6.8	6.1	5.6	5.4	4.9	4.5	4.2	4.0	4.8	US

Long-term unemployment rate. Long-term unemployed (over 12 months) as % of the total active population

	1991	1992	1993	1994	1995	1996	1997	1998	1999	2000	2001	
EU-15	3.2	3.7	4.6	5.2	5.2	5.2	5.1	4.7	4.2	3.7	3.2	EU-15
€-zone	3.5	3.8	4.7	5.5	5.6	5.7	5.8	5.4	4.8	4.2	4.7 *	€-zone
B	4.2	4.0	4.5	5.6	5.8	5.7	5.5	5.6	4.9	3.8	:	B
DK	3.2	2.9	3.1	2.9	2.3	2.1	1.7	1.5	1.2	1.0	0.9	DK
D	:	2.3	3.2	3.8	4.0	4.3	4.9	4.9	4.4	4.0	:	D
EL	3.5	3.8	4.2	4.4	4.6	5.2	5.3	5.9	6.5	6.1	5.4	EL
E	7.9	8.1	10.7	12.9	12.3	11.7	10.8	9.4	7.3	5.9	5.1	E
F	3.5	3.6	4.1	4.7	4.7	4.8	5.0	4.9	4.4	3.7	:	F
IRL	9.9	9.4	9.7	9.4	7.8	7.1	6.1	3.9	2.6	1.6	1.3	IRL
I	:	:	5.8	6.7	7.3	7.5	7.5	7.0	6.9	6.4	5.9	I
L	0.4	0.4	0.7	0.9	0.7	0.9	0.9	0.8	0.7	0.5	:	L
NL	2.9	2.5	2.9	3.1	3.1	2.8	2.3	1.7	1.3	1.1	0.8	NL
A	:	:	:	1.0	1.0	1.1	1.2	1.3	1.1	1.0	0.9	A
P	1.6	1.2	1.8	2.6	3.1	3.3	3.2	2.1	1.7	1.6	1.5	P
FIN	2.5	4.3	6.0	6.1	5.7	5.4	4.7	4.0	3.0	2.8	2.5	FIN
S	0.2	0.6	1.5	2.5	2.5	2.9	3.4	3.1	2.2	1.7	1.2	S
UK	2.5	3.5	4.3	4.2	3.7	3.2	2.6	1.9	1.7	1.5	1.3	UK
IS	:	:	:	:	0.6 *	0.4 *	0.4 *	0.4 *	0.1 *	0.1 *	:	IS
NO	:	:	:	:	2.0 *	1.1 *	0.8 *	0.5 *	0.5 *	0.5 *	0.5 *	NO

Dispersion of regional unemployment rates. Coefficient of variation of unemployment rates across regions (NUTS 2 level) within countries

	1991	1992	1993	1994	1995	1996	1997	1998	1999	2000	2001	
EU-15	60.1	60.3	58.5	56.5	58.1	57.1	55.9	58.4	60.7	63.6	64.9	EU-15
B	40.4	40.8	37.7	34.3	37.8	37.6	40.6	45.6	48.7	54.2	55.9	B
DK	.	.	.	.	.	.	.	.	.	.	.	DK
D	51.6	68.7	50.4	40.0	39.2	39.1	42.9	47.9	47.0	48.8	47.6	D
EL	27.3	26.9	28.4	27.2	24.3	28.0	24.7	18.3	17.5	17.3	17.9	EL
E	32.8	30.2	25.1	22.2	24.1	23.7	26.5	29.8	35.7	41.3	37.8	E
F	19.3	20.2	17.5	16.9	18.1	19.6	20.6	20.7	22.3	24.4	27.2	F
IRL	.	.	.	.	.	.	.	.	.	.	.	IRL
I	67.7	52.8	51.9	55.5	57.9	61.6	60.8	63.3	66.3	71.5	75.7	I
L	.	.	.	.	.	.	.	.	.	.	.	L
NL	10.7	12.5	12.1	10.8	10.6	14.5	15.8	20.0	24.9	21.8	26.8	NL
A	:	:	:	:	26.2	23.8	25.5	27.2	28.3	28.8	28.4	A
P	42.7	32.0	25.9	26.8	30.3	27.7	27.3	30.0	29.2	32.6	28.6	P
FIN	:	:	12.5	9.4	11.0	16.3	19.0	23.1	27.0	30.3	32.7	FIN
S	:	:	6.1	9.0	14.0	14.0	18.3	18.1	21.2	28.7	30.6	S
UK	30.0	19.6	19.0	19.6	34.6	32.3	37.6	42.8	43.4	45.1	46.0	UK

Keeping oneself up-to-date: continuing vocational training in enterprises

Comparable statistical data on enterprise training are a key tool in analysing, among other things, the discrepancies between skills supply and demand, between training needs on the one hand, and the forms, fields and volume of training offered on the other hand, between the enterprises own resources and the use of external providers. Last but not least, one has to reflect on the training costs that originate both for the enterprises and the State, as well as on new methods of funding.

The European Commission launched a new survey on continuing vocational training after an initial survey was carried out in 1994 in the then 12 EU Member States. The second survey was conducted in 2000–01. It was not only implemented in all Member States and Norway but also in nine candidate countries (Bulgaria, the Czech Republic, Estonia, Hungary, Latvia, Lithuania, Poland — region Pomorovski —, Romania and Slovenia).

Enterprises in northern Europe provide more continuing vocational training

The percentage of enterprises in the EU Member States and Norway that provided continuing vocational training in 1999 ranged from 22 % in Portugal to 96 % in Denmark. In the Nordic countries, the Netherlands and the United Kingdom, the proportion was over 80 %. In contrast, in Greece, only 18 % of all enterprises provided continuing vocational training.

Preference given to external courses

In the EU Member States and Norway, enterprises providing continuing vocational training courses organised considerably more external than internal courses in 1999. In the Netherlands, nearly all of these enterprises (97 %) organised external courses, but only about one in three provided internal courses.

Different training habits in 'small' and 'big' enterprises?

No uniform relationship can be found between training intensity and the size of enterprise. In six countries, the training intensity (measured by hours in continuing vocational training courses per participant) was highest in large enterprises, while in four it was highest in small enterprises. The lowest number of course hours per participant was found mostly in medium-sized enterprises.

Training costs

Total expenditure per employee on continuing vocational training courses in 1999 ranged from 410 PPS in Austria to 1 169 PPS in Denmark. While enterprises in Norway, the Netherlands and Sweden also had high expenditure per employee, Germany, Portugal and Spain were at the bottom of the scale.

Further reading:

Statistics in Focus — Theme 3
— No 3 Continuing vocational training in enterprises in the European Union and Norway

Do you need more information?
— Ask your Data Shop (see last page)
— http://www.europa.eu.int/comm/eurostat
— Eurostat's data serves the political discussion in
Europe. Have a look at the website of the "DG Employment and Social Affairs" :
http://europa.eu.int/comm/dgs/employment_social/index_en.htm

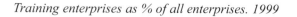

Training enterprises as % of all enterprises. 1999

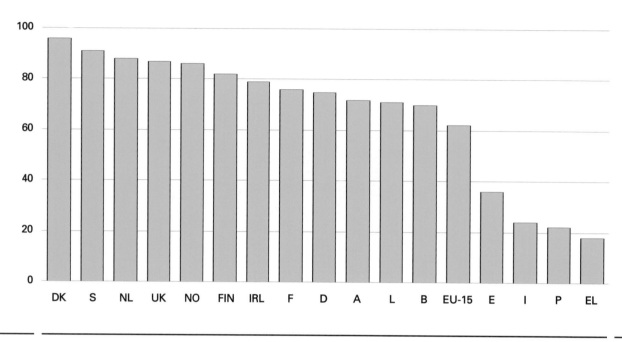

Source: CVTS2, Eurostat.

Percentage of employees (all enterprises) participating in CVT courses. 1999

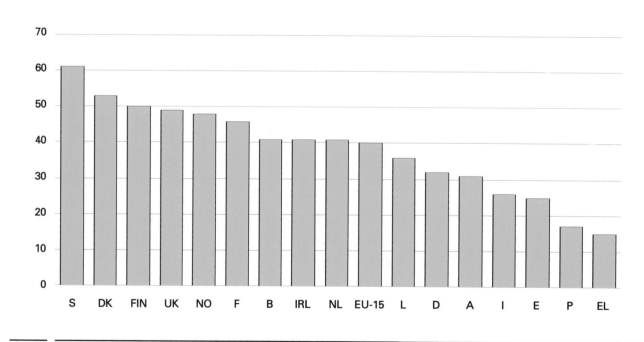

Source: CVTS2, Eurostat.

Percentage of employees (all enterprises) participating in CVT courses by sex. 1999

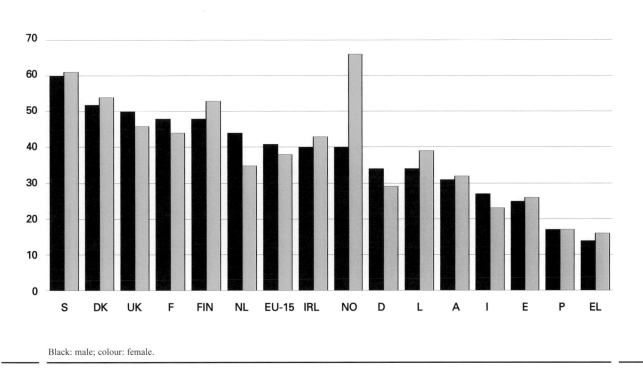

Black: male; colour: female.

B: no data available by sex. *Source:* CVTS2, Eurostat.

Hours in CVT courses per participant in small and large enterprises. 1999

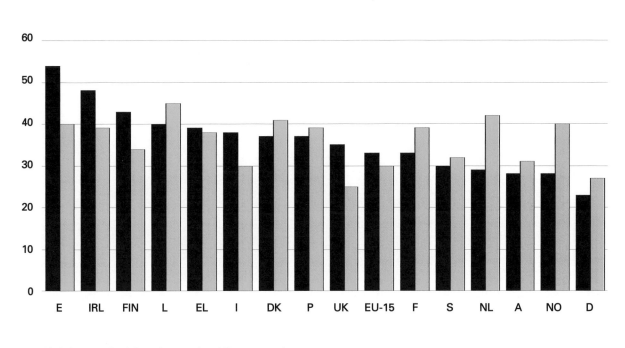

Black: between 10 and 49 employees; colour: 250 or more employees.

Source: CVTS2, Eurostat.

2

Percentage of enterprises providing CVT courses by type of course. 1999

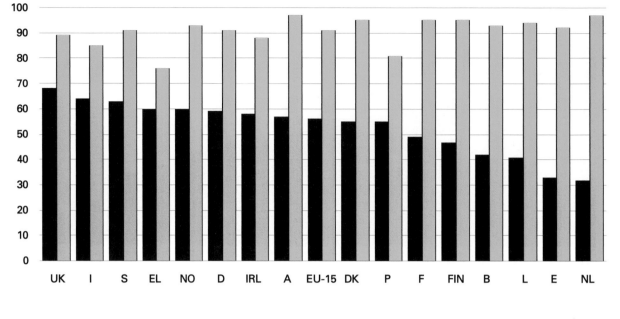

Black: internal course; colour: external course.

Source: CVTS2, Eurostat.

Total costs of CVT courses per employee in enterprises with CVT courses. PPS

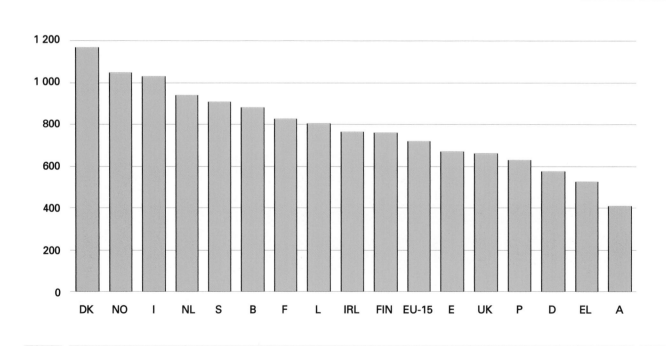

Source: CVTS2, Eurostat.

Targeting problems in the labour market

The labour market policy (LMP) database is based on a comprehensive methodology that has been developed over the past few years by Eurostat, in close cooperation with the Directorate-General for Employment and Social Affairs, all EU Member States and Norway, as well as the OECD. The LMP database is an instrument for the follow-up of the targeted employment policies developed and implemented by EU countries. These policies are a result of the agreement reached in November 1997 to launch the European employment strategy, to provide more jobs and to combat and reduce unemployment (Employment Summit in Luxembourg).

The EU LMP database has two main advances compared with previously existing sources of information: firstly, a detailed and comparable description of each labour market policy measure is collected, stored and published, and, secondly, detailed information on participants, stocks and flows are collected and published at the European level.

The scope of the LMP database

The LMP database refers to public interventions in the labour market aimed at reaching its efficient functioning and to correct disequilibria. These interventions can be distinguished from other general employment policy measures in that they act selectively to favour particular groups in the labour market.

The **classification by type of action** includes one base category of general public employment services and nine categories of LMP measures, most with two or more sub-categories.

0. General public employment services (PES): services of the public employment services which facilitate the job-search process and which are generally available to all jobseekers.

1. Intensive counselling and job-search assistance: programmes which assist the job-search process through intensive, individualised counselling and which are targeted at persons registered as unemployed jobseekers experiencing special difficulties in getting a job, or at other groups with difficult access to the labour market.

2. Training: programmes which aim to improve the employability of the unemployed and other target groups through training, and which are financed by public bodies. Measures here should include some evidence of classroom teaching, or, if in the workplace, supervision specifically for the purpose of instruction.

3. Job rotation and job sharing: programmes which facilitate the insertion of an unemployed person or a person from another target group into a work placement by substituting hours worked by an existing employee.

4. Employment incentives: programmes which facilitate the recruitment of unemployed persons and other target groups, or help to ensure the continued employment of persons at risk of involuntary job loss. The majority of the labour cost is normally covered by the employer.

5. Integration of the disabled: programmes which aim to promote integration of disabled persons into the labour market.

6. Direct job creation: programmes which create additional jobs, usually of community benefit or socially useful, in order to find employment for the long-term unemployed or persons otherwise difficult to place. The majority of the labour cost is normally covered by public finance.

7. Start-up incentives: programmes which promote entrepreneurship by encouraging the unemployed and target groups to start their own businesses or to become self-employed.

8. Out-of-work income maintenance: programmes which aim to compensate individuals for loss of wage or salary through the provision of cash benefits when:

— a person is capable of working and available for work but is unable to find suitable employment;

— a person is on lay-off or on enforced short-time work or is otherwise temporarily idle for economic or other reasons (including seasonal effects);

— a person has lost his/her job due to restructuring or similar (redundancy compensation).

9. Early retirement: programmes which facilitate the full or partial early retirement of older workers who are assumed to have little chance of finding a job or whose retirement facilitates the placement of an unemployed person or a person from another target group.

The **classification by type of expenditure** refers firstly to the direct recipient (individuals, employers or service providers) and secondly to the type of expenditure involved (either cash payments or through a reduction in obligatory levies).

Three variables are requested in order to evaluate the **numbers of participants** in these measures: stock, entrants and exits. 'Stock' refers to the number of participants in a measure at a given moment. 'Entrants' refers to the number of participants joining the measure during the year (inflow). 'Exits' refers to the number of participants leaving the measure during the year (outflow). As with entrants, the observation refers to participations and not individuals so that any given individual may be counted more than once in a year.

The LMP database includes data on participants broken down by sex, age, duration of unemployment, previous employment status of entrants, completions and drop-outs, and destination of exits.

Further reading:

Eurostat publications
— **Labour Market Policy Database — Methodology, April 2000**
— **European Social Statistics — Labour Market Policy — Expenditure and Participants —**
     Data 2000 — Detailed Tables

Statistics in Focus — Theme 3
— **N° 12/2002 Public expenditure on Labour Market Policies in 1999 varied greatly among**
                 Member States

Do you need more information?
— **Ask your Data Shop (see last page)**
— **http://www.europa.eu.int/comm/eurostat**
— **Eurostat's data serves the political discussion in**
     Europe. Have a look at the website of the "DG Employment and Social Affairs" :
     http://europa.eu.int/comm/dgs/employment_social/index_en.htm

Public expenditure on labour market policy measures in % of GDP. 2000

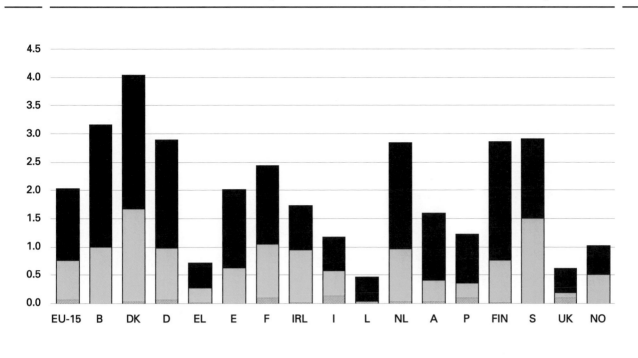

Black: out-of-work income maintenance and support — early retirement; colour: training — job rotation and job sharing — employment incentives — integration of the disabled — direct job creation — start-up incentives; grey: special support for apprenticeship.

Public expenditure on labour market policy measures for training, job rotation and job sharing, employment incentives, integration of the disabled, direct job creation and start-up incentives in % of GDP

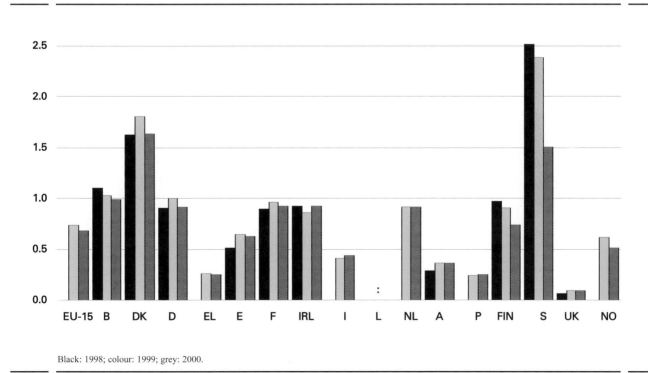

Black: 1998; colour: 1999; grey: 2000.

Public expenditure on labour market policy measures for out-of-work income maintenance and support and for early retirement in % of GDP

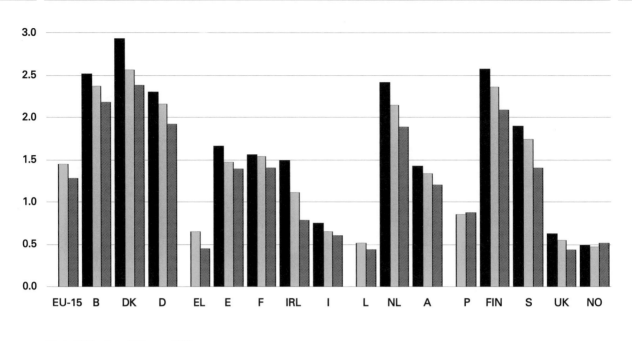

Black: 1998; colour: 1999; grey: 2000.

Labour market policy expenditure in active measures by type. EU-15. 2000

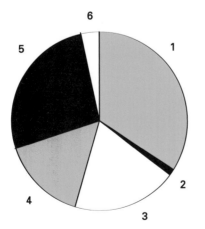

1. Training excluding special support for apprenticeship; 2. Job rotation and job sharing; 3. Employment incentives; 4. Integration of the disabled; 5. Direct job creation; 6. Start-up incentives.

Labour market policy expenditure in passive measures by type. EU-15. 2000

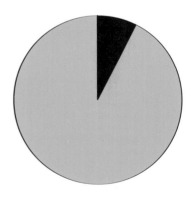

Black: early retirement; colour: out-of-work income maintenance and support.

Making consumer markets transparent

For everyone who wants to know more about consumer markets in the EU, this is a fundamental question: How do the volumes and the proportions of the markets develop?

The Eurostat yearbook answers this question. It presents data on household consumption expenditure for so-called 'consumption purposes' (markets). The yearbook presents data on the two-digit level of the 'classification of individual consumption by purpose' (Coicop), i.e. it provides a breakdown of consumption by 12 consumption purposes. Additionally, some subaggregates from the Coicop's three-digit level are presented.

Data on all consumption purposes are available in NewCronos, Theme 2, Domain breakdowns, collections coicop2 and coicop3. If you would like to benefit from the NewCronos database, please contact your Eurostat Data Shop. The addresses of the Data Shops can be found at the end of the yearbook.

Reliable source, harmonised definitions

Statistics on final consumption expenditure of households come from Eurostat's national accounts statistics.

Consumption is the value of goods and services used for directly meeting human requirements. It covers the purchases of goods and services, the consumption of own production (such as garden produce) and the imputed rents of owner-occupied dwellings.

The word 'expenditure' added in ESA 95 explicitly relates to direct spending by households; it excludes the proportion of consumption financed by general government or by NPISHs (non-profit-making institutions serving households). When this proportion is included, the sum is said to be, in the context of national accounts, 'actual' final consumption.

The nomenclature for consumption, as well as others, are accessible on the web site http://europa.eu.int/comm/eurostat/ramon/ (option 'classifications'), line 17 'Coicop'. It offers a two-digit and a more detailed three-digit level.

Some results

— **Food, drinks and tobacco** traditionally used to account for the biggest share of consumption almost everywhere. With few exceptions, they have gradually been overtaken by 'housing' and 'transport and communications' in the Member States, but not yet in the candidate countries. Their share of consumption is greater in the Mediterranean countries than in northern ones.

In the Member States, food and non-alcoholic beverages make up between 9.8 % (United Kingdom, 2000) and 18.5 % (Portugal, 2000) of the total consumption expenditure. In the candidate countries, they make up between 18.9 % (Slovenia, 1999) and 31.5 % (Lithuania, 1999).

More data on food and non-alcoholic beverages are available on the Eurostat dissemination database NewCronos, Theme 2, Domain brkdowns, collection coicop3, where 'food and non-alcoholic beverages' bear the code cp01 and subdivisions.

The consumption purpose 'food, drinks and tobacco' includes all purchases for consumption at home of: (a) food excluding specific pet foods; (b) non-alcoholic beverages (coffee, tea and cocoa, mineral waters, soft drinks, fruit and vegetable juices, etc.). It excludes: (a) all catering services in (or from) hotels, restaurants, cafes, catering contractors, etc., whether collected by the customer or delivered to the customer's home; (b) alcoholic beverages, tobacco, narcotics and medical products.

— The share of **housing**, varying greatly from one country to another, has increased in almost all candidate countries. With few exceptions, housing has the current biggest share in the Member States (with the Scandinavian countries on top) but not in the candidate countries.

In the Member States, housing makes up between 10.6 % (Portugal, 2000) and 30.6 % (Sweden, 1999) of the total consumption expenditure. In the candidate countries, it makes up between 15.0 % (Lithuania, 1999) and 23.9 % (Poland, 2000).

More data on housing are available on NewCronos, Theme 2, Domain brkdowns, collection coicop3, where 'housing' bears the code cp04 and subdivisions.

— The development of **transport and communications** went along with price decreases in this field (cheaper air fares, cheaper hardware, etc.). With few exceptions, the share of transport and communications in consumption is bigger than that of food and beverages in the Member States, but not in the candidate countries.

In the Member States, transport makes up between 8.6 % (Greece, 2000) and 17.4 % (Portugal, 2000) of the total consumption expenditure. In the candidate countries, it makes up between 9.2 % (Latvia, 1999) and 17.3 % (Slovenia, 1999).

More data on transport are available on NewCronos, Theme 2, Domain brkdowns, collection coicop3, where 'transport' bears the code cp07 and subdivisions.

— The share of **health** expenses has been globally stable in the Member States but has risen slightly in the candidate countries. The national health services' share of consumption varies greatly. Denmark, Ireland, Sweden and the United Kingdom have low shares (below 3 %) due to their public health services — not included here.

— Expenditure on **recreation and culture** varies considerably from one country to another, due partly to public spending patterns. Its share in consumption has risen in a majority of countries.

Further reading:

Eurostat publications
— **Household final consumption expenditure in the European Union, 1995–1999**
— **Consumption expenditures of private households in the European Union (CD-ROM)**
— **Income and living conditions**
— **Living conditions in Europe — Statistical pocketbook**

Do you need more information?
— **Ask your Data Shop (see last page)**
— **http://www.europa.eu.int/comm/eurostat**

Food and non-alcoholic beverages, at current prices. % of total household consumption expenditure

	1991	1992	1993	1994	1995	1996	1997	1998	1999	2000	2001	
B	:	:	:	:	14.5	14.1	14.0	13.8	13.1	13.0	:	B
DK	14.4	14.5	14.0	13.8	14.0	13.5	13.4	13.1	12.8	12.8	12.9	DK
D	14.0	13.5	13.1	12.7	12.5	12.3	12.2	12.1	11.9	11.9	12.3	D
EL	:	:	:	:	18.2	17.8	17.4	17.0	16.8	16.9	:	EL
E	:	:	:	:	17.7	17.4	16.7	15.8	15.2	15.2	:	E
F	16.1	15.6	15.4	15.1	15.1	14.7	14.8	14.7	14.3	14.2	14.4	F
IRL	17.7	18.0	17.5	16.4	15.5	15.0	13.7	12.7	11.5	10.9	10.7	IRL
I	18.8	18.5	18.1	17.4	16.8	16.4	15.8	15.3	14.7	14.4	14.4	I
L	:	:	:	:	:	:	:	:	:	:	:	L
NL	:	:	:	:	13.0	12.6	12.4	12.1	11.6	:	:	NL
A	14.9	14.7	14.4	14.0	13.4	13.1	13.2	13.1	12.9	12.7	12.6	A
P	21.9	21.1	21.5	21.6	20.5	19.9	19.2	19.0	18.7	18.5	:	P
FIN	17.0	17.0	16.6	16.3	14.8	14.0	13.7	13.3	13.0	12.7	12.8	FIN
S	:	:	:	:	14.4	13.4	13.2	12.9	12.6	12.5	12.8	S
UK	12.4	12.1	11.8	11.4	11.2	11.2	10.7	10.3	10.0	9.7	9.7	UK
IS	21.4	22.1	22.3	21.4	20.7	20.7	20.5	19.8	19.0	18.3	:	IS
NO	17.1	17.1	16.6	16.6	16.2	15.8	15.5	:	:	:	:	NO
JP	19.0	18.6	18.2	17.8	17.3	16.3	16.3	16.5	:	:	:	JP
US	8.8	8.4	8.2	8.1	7.9	7.8	7.5	7.3	7.1	:	:	US

2

Actual rents, at current prices. % of total household consumption expenditure

	1991	1992	1993	1994	1995	1996	1997	1998	1999	2000	2001	
B	:	:	:	:	5.3	5.3	5.2	5.0	4.9	4.7	:	B
DK	6.6	6.6	6.7	6.3	6.4	6.5	6.4	6.4	6.4	6.5	6.5	DK
D	6.2	6.6	7.2	7.5	7.8	8.0	8.1	8.2	8.1	8.1	8.1	D
EL	:	:	:	:	3.2	3.3	3.2	3.1	3.0	2.9	:	EL
E	:	:	:	:	1.1	1.1	1.2	1.1	1.1	:	:	E
F	4.2	4.5	4.6	4.6	4.7	4.8	4.8	4.8	4.7	4.7	4.6	F
IRL	1.2	1.3	1.3	1.3	1.4	1.5	1.6	1.7	1.8	1.8	2.0	IRL
I	1.9	2.0	2.2	2.3	2.3	2.5	2.4	2.4	2.4	2.4	2.5	I
L	:	:	:	:	:	:	:	:	:	:	:	L
NL	:	:	:	:	6.5	6.5	6.3	6.1	5.9	:	:	NL
A	1.4	1.5	1.5	1.9	1.9	2.0	2.2	3.0	2.9	2.8	2.8	A
P	0.8	0.8	0.8	0.8	1.1	1.1	1.1	1.1	:	:	:	P
FIN	3.8	4.4	4.8	4.8	5.2	5.2	5.5	5.6	5.8	5.9	6.0	FIN
S	:	:	:	:	10.1	10.2	10.3	10.1	9.7	9.5	9.1	S
UK	3.4	3.8	4.0	4.1	4.0	4.0	3.9	4.0	4.0	4.1	4.1	UK
NO	2.9	2.9	3.1	2.8	2.7	2.7	2.6	:	:	:	:	NO
US	3.9	3.8	3.6	3.6	3.5	3.4	3.4	3.3	3.2	:	:	US

Health, at current prices. % of total household consumption expenditure

	1991	1992	1993	1994	1995	1996	1997	1998	1999	2000	2001	
B	:	:	:	:	3.8	3.7	3.8	3.8	3.8	3.8	:	B
DK	2.4	2.5	2.6	2.5	2.4	2.4	2.4	2.5	2.5	2.6	2.7	DK
D	3.1	3.3	3.6	3.7	4.0	3.9	4.1	4.1	4.0	4.1	4.1	D
EL	:	:	:	:	5.7	5.5	5.4	5.5	5.6	5.0	:	EL
E	:	:	:	:	3.3	3.3	3.2	3.3	3.4	3.4	:	E
F	3.4	3.5	3.6	3.6	3.7	3.7	3.7	3.6	3.6	3.5	3.5	F
IRL	3.0	3.1	3.1	3.1	3.1	2.9	2.9	2.7	2.7	2.7	2.7	IRL
I	2.3	2.5	2.8	3.0	3.1	3.2	3.3	3.3	3.2	3.1	2.9	I
L	:	:	:	:	:	:	:	:	:	:	:	L
NL	:	:	:	:	3.5	4.1	4.0	3.8	4.0	:	:	NL
A	2.6	2.9	2.9	3.1	3.2	3.3	3.1	3.2	3.3	3.3	3.4	A
P	6.6	7.1	7.4	7.4	5.1	4.9	4.9	4.7	4.7	4.7	:	P
FIN	3.2	3.5	3.7	3.6	3.5	3.5	3.5	3.4	3.6	3.7	3.8	FIN
S	:	:	:	:	2.1	2.2	2.3	2.4	2.4	2.5	2.4	S
UK	1.5	1.5	1.5	1.6	1.5	1.5	1.5	1.5	1.5	1.5	1.5	UK
IS	1.9	2.2	2.6	2.5	2.5	2.6	2.6	2.9	2.8	2.9	:	IS
NO	2.6	2.6	2.6	2.5	2.6	2.7	2.7	:	:	:	:	NO
JP	9.6	9.8	10.1	10.4	10.8	11.0	11.1	11.1	:	:	:	JP
US	16.0	16.5	16.6	16.5	16.6	16.6	16.7	16.7	16.5	:	:	US

Education, at current prices. % of total household consumption expenditure

	1991	1992	1993	1994	1995	1996	1997	1998	1999	2000	2001	
B	:	:	:	:	0.4	0.4	0.4	0.4	0.4	0.4	:	B
DK	0.8	0.8	0.7	0.8	0.7	0.8	0.7	0.8	0.8	0.8	0.8	DK
D	0.6	0.7	0.7	0.7	0.7	0.7	0.7	0.7	0.7	0.7	0.7	D
EL	:	:	:	:	2.0	1.9	1.8	1.7	1.8	1.8	:	EL
E	:	:	:	:	1.7	1.8	1.8	1.8	1.7	1.7	:	E
F	0.6	0.6	0.6	0.6	0.6	0.6	0.7	0.7	0.6	0.6	0.6	F
IRL	0.9	0.9	1.0	1.0	1.2	1.4	1.0	0.8	0.8	0.9	1.0	IRL
I	1.0	1.0	1.0	1.0	1.0	1.0	1.0	1.0	1.0	1.0	1.0	I
L	:	:	:	:	:	:	:	:	:	:	:	L
NL	:	:	:	:	0.6	0.6	0.6	0.6	0.6	:	:	NL
A	0.6	0.6	0.6	0.6	0.6	0.6	0.6	0.6	0.7	0.7	0.7	A
P	1.2	1.3	1.4	1.4	1.5	1.5	1.5	1.4	1.4	1.4	:	P
FIN	0.3	0.3	0.5	0.5	0.5	0.5	0.6	0.6	0.5	0.5	0.5	FIN
S	:	:	:	:	0.1	0.2	0.2	0.2	0.2	0.2	0.2	S
UK	1.1	1.3	1.3	1.3	1.4	1.4	1.5	1.5	1.6	1.6	1.6	UK
IS	1.8	1.8	2.0	2.0	1.9	1.8	1.8	1.7	1.7	1.7	:	IS
NO	0.6	0.6	0.5	0.5	0.5	0.5	0.5	:	:	:	:	NO
US	2.2	2.3	2.3	2.3	2.3	2.3	2.4	2.4	2.4	:	:	US

eurostat

Income, poverty and social exclusion: statistics answer many questions

What is the average income level? Are some components more important than others? Is there a divide between the 'haves' and the 'have-nots', and, if so, how big is it? Are certain groups more at risk of poverty than others? Are they less involved in society? Do they have lower education attainment levels? Or worse health? Or larger families? Are their incomes less secure? Do they have access to a full range of goods and services? Is the situation stable over time? Are there differences between countries?

The demand for such information has received a new impetus in recent years following the social chapter in the Amsterdam Treaty (1997) which became the driving force for EU social statistics generally. This impetus was reinforced by the European Councils at Lisbon (March 2000), Nice (December 2000), Stockholm (March 2001) and Laeken (December 2001), keeping the social dimension high on the political agenda. Effective monitoring is an essential element in making operational the strategies agreed under the open method of coordination.

The statistical indicators

Income, poverty and social exclusion are multidimensional problems. To monitor them effectively at European level, a subset of so-called 'social cohesion indicators' has been developed within the structural indicators which are produced for the Commission's annual synthesis report to the Council. After a lengthy process of consultation and negotiation, the list of indicators for the 2002 annual synthesis report was finalised and adopted at Laeken in December 2001, and data were supplied for publication at Barcelona in March 2002.

Also presented at Laeken was the work by the Social Protection Committee subgroup on indicators, in which Eurostat and the Directorate-General for Employment and Social Affairs have played a leading role. A list of detailed indicators was established that sets a reference framework for reporting on income, poverty and social exclusion. It includes all the social cohesion indicators in the current set of structural indicators, and provides additional analytical information.

A hierarchy was agreed: 'primary' indicators (the most important elements identified as leading to social exclusion), 'secondary' indicators (other dimensions), and supplementary 'tertiary' indicators (specific national circumstances, which help to interpret the primary and secondary indicators; tertiary indicators are not necessarily harmonised at EU level).

Some key Laeken indicators on income, poverty and social exclusion are presented in tables of the Eurostat yearbook. To find out about other social indicators or additional breakdowns, please contact your Data Shop the address of which can be found at the end of the yearbook.

Where do the data come from?

To calculate indicators for EU Member States in recent years, Eurostat has principally used microdata from the European Community household panel (ECHP). However, after eight years of using this data source, it will be replaced with effect from 2003 by a new instrument, the EU statistics on income and living conditions (EU-SILC). One of the main reasons for this change is the need to adapt the content and timeliness of data production to reflect current political needs.

EU-SILC aspires to become the EU reference source for comparative income distribution and social exclusion statistics, with the two main goals of high quality, especially regarding comparability and timeliness, and flexibility. It will comprise both a cross-sectional dimension — the first priority — and a longitudinal dimension. Greater reliance will be placed on existing national data sources in an attempt to harmonise outcomes rather than inputs and improve timeliness.

The ECHP is a pioneering data collection instrument, which is currently the sole source of reliable harmonised information on income and related social issues. This 'longitudinal' survey involves annual interviews with participant households (around 80 000 across the EU: samples are designed to be nationally representative). This makes it possible to follow up the same individuals over consecutive years and to provide information on social dynamics (for example, transition from education to working life; from working life to retirement) which are not possible from more typical cross-sectional surveys (separate sample each year).

The ECHP is a cooperative exercise between Eurostat and the Member States. The end product is a user database (UDB) which is produced after a lengthy process of bilateral and multilateral validation. After final approval, the UDB is made available for publication (under strict confidentiality conditions), and is used by Eurostat for the calculation and publication of statistical indicators. The UDB for ECHP, wave 5, includes data for the years 1994 to 1998. It was issued in December 2001.

Due to an ongoing data collection the results presented in this Yearbook should be treated as provisional and interpreted with some caution.

Brief methodological details

In the ECHP, household income is established by summing all monetary income received from any source by each member of the household (including income from work, investment and social benefits) net of taxes and social contributions paid. In order to reflect differences in household size and composition, this total is divided by the number of 'equivalent adults' using a standard scale (the so-called 'modified OECD' scale), and the resulting figure is attributed to each member of the household. EU-15 estimates are calculated as population weighted averages of available national values.

Including the candidate countries

Eurostat has begun collaboration with the candidate countries to include a first subset of indicators relating to income and social exclusion in the Commission's synthesis report which will be presented at Thessaloniki in spring 2003.

Further reading:

Eurostat publications
— **European Community household panel (ECHP) — Selected indicators from the 1995 wave (PDF)**
— **European social statistics — Income, poverty and social exclusion**
— **Income, Poverty and Social Exclusion in the European Union**
— **The Social Situation in the European Union**
— **Social cohesion indicators adopted at the Laeken European Council**

Statistics in Focus — Theme 3
— **No 14 The EC household panel 'Newsletter'**

Do you need more information?
— **Ask your Data Shop (see last page)**
— **http://www.europa.eu.int/comm/eurostat**
— **Eurostat's data serves the political discussion in Europe. Have a look at the website of the "DG Employment and Social Affairs" :**
   http://europa.eu.int/comm/dgs/employment_social/index_en.htm

Average number of persons per private household

	1991	1992	1993	1994	1995	1996	1997	1998	1999	2000	2001	
EU-15	2.6	2.5	2.5	2.5	2.5	2.5	2.5	2.4	2.4	2.4	2.4	**EU-15**
B	2.6	2.5	2.5	2.5	2.5	2.5	2.5	2.4	2.4	2.4	2.4	**B**
DK	2.2	2.2	2.2	2.2	2.2	2.2	2.2	2.2	2.2	2.2	2.2	**DK**
D	2.3	2.3	2.2	2.2	2.2	2.2	2.2	2.2	2.2	2.2	2.1	**D**
EL	2.8	2.8	2.8	2.8	2.7	2.7	2.6	2.7	2.7	2.7	2.6	**EL**
E	3.3	3.3	3.3	3.2	3.2	3.2	3.2	3.1	3.1	3.0	3.0	**E**
F	2.5	2.5	2.5	2.5	2.4	2.4	2.4	2.4	2.4	2.4	2.4	**F**
IRL	3.3	3.2	3.2	3.1	3.1	3.1	3.0	3.0	3.0	3.0	3.0	**IRL**
I	2.8	2.8	2.8	2.8	2.8	2.8	2.8	2.7	2.7	2.6	2.6	**I**
L	2.7	2.7	2.6	2.6	2.8	2.5	2.6	2.6	2.6	2.6	2.5	**L**
NL	2.4	2.4	2.4	2.3	2.4	2.4	2.3	2.3	2.3	2.3	2.3	**NL**
A	2.6	2.6	2.6	2.5	2.5	2.5	2.5	2.5	2.4	2.4	2.4	**A**
P	3.1	3.1	3.0	3.0	3.0	2.9	2.9	3.0	3.0	2.9	2.9	**P**
FIN	2.3	2.3	2.2	2.2	2.2	2.2	2.2	2.2	2.2	2.2	2.1 *	**FIN**
S	2.1 *	2.1 *	2.1 *	2.1 *	2.1 *	2.0	2.0	2.0	2.0	2.0	2.0	**S**
UK	2.5	2.4	2.4	2.4	2.4	2.3	2.3	2.3	2.3	2.3	2.3	**UK**

Source: European Union labour force survey. DK, IRL: 1998–2001. A: 1991–94. FIN, S: data from national sources.

2

Percentage of persons living in private households by type of household. One adult living alone

Percentage of persons living in private households by type of household. Lone parent with dependent children

	1994	1995	1996	1997	1998	1994	1995	1996	1997	1998	
EU-15	11	11	11	11	11	3	3	3	3	3	**EU-15**
B	12	12	13	13	13	4	4	4	3	3	**B**
DK	18	17	17	17	17	5	3	2	3	2	**DK**
D	16	15	16	15	16	3	3	3	3	3	**D**
EL	7	8	7	8	8	1	2	2	2	1	**EL**
E	4	4	4	4	4	1	1	1	1	1	**E**
F	12	12	12	12	12	4	3	3	3	3	**F**
IRL	7	7	7	7	7	4	4	3	3	3	**IRL**
I	8	7	8	7	8	2	2	2	2	2	**I**
L	10	10	11	:	:	2	3	3	:	:	**L**
NL	14	14	14	14	15	3	3	3	3	2	**NL**
A	:	11	12	11	12	:	2	3	3	3	**A**
P	4	4	5	4	5	2	3	2	2	2	**P**
FIN	:	:	17	17	:	:	:	6	6	:	**FIN**
S	:	:	:	:	:	:	:	:	:	:	**S**
UK	13	13	13	13	13	6	6	6	6	6	**UK**

Source: ECHP-UDB, Eurostat, version December 2001.

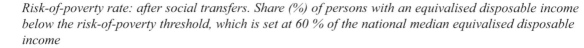

Risk-of-poverty rate: after social transfers. Share (%) of persons with an equivalised disposable income below the risk-of-poverty threshold, which is set at 60 % of the national median equivalised disposable income

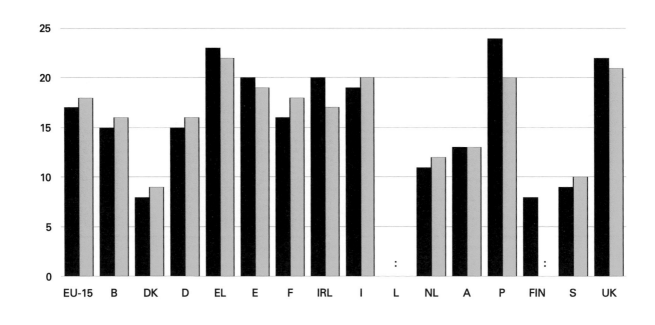

Black: 1997; colour: 1998.

Source: ECHP-UDB, Eurostat, version December 2001. EU-15: weighted average of national values estimated without missing countries. B, UK: provisional data. F, FIN: data only permit adjustment for social transfers on a gross basis, which may affect accuracy.

Risk-of-poverty rate: before social transfers([¹]). Share (%) of persons with an equivalised disposable income below the risk-of-poverty threshold, which is set at 60 % of the national median equivalised disposable income

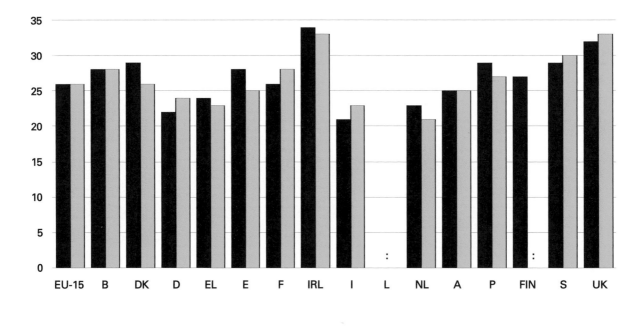

Black: 1997; colour: 1998.

([1]) Calculated using income before social transfers ('original income'). Original income includes pensions but excludes all other social transfers.
Source: ECHP-UDB, Eurostat, version December 2001. EU-15: weighted average of national values estimated without missing countries. B, UK: provisional data. F, FIN: data only permit adjustment for social transfers on a gross basis, which may affect the accuracy of this indicator.

Is the type of accommodation or the tenure status an indicator for the welfare of households?

Two different trends concerning the type of housing of European households are revealed. In southern countries, low-income households (household income less than 60 % compared with median actual current income) seem to live predominantly in houses, compared with higher-income households (household income greater than 140 % compared with median actual current income) that live predominantly in flats. An opposite trend is observed for northern countries.

It is very difficult to pinpoint the reasons for such differences. The distribution of households in individual houses or flats is related to the degree of urbanisation in each country and to the quality of accommodation. In Greece, Spain and Portugal, most low-income households live in a single house, while the opposite is observed in Denmark, Germany, Italy and Finland.

Within one's own four walls

Ownership of accommodation is higher in southern than in northern countries where income level determines the tenure status of the households. However, many southern low-income households live in poor housing conditions. In Greece, Spain and particularly in Portugal, more than 60 % of these households declare a lack of one of the basic amenities (bath or shower in the dwelling, toilet in the dwelling or central heating).

Does having children influence the ownership behaviour of the households?

When it comes to the ownership of accommodation, there is generally no significant gap between households with and without children; exceptions are Belgium, Denmark, Germany, the Netherlands and Austria where having children does influence the tenure status of the households.

Overcrowding: southern households seem to be more vulnerable

Nearly one in three low-income households and one in five high-income households in Greece seem to be overcrowded (more than one person per room). Considering the fact that ownership of accommodation is more important in southern countries, most owners there can be expected to have small accommodation.

The disparity between income groups is great in Italy, Portugal, Ireland and Spain. In all countries, low-income households are more vulnerable to overcrowding.

Further reading:

Statistics in Focus — Theme 3
— Living conditions in Europe
— Key indicators
— Statistical pocketbook
— Housing conditions of the elderly in the EU

Do you need more information?
— Ask your Data Shop (see last page)
— http://www.europa.eu.int/comm/eurostat

Percentage of households living in a house by median income group. 1998

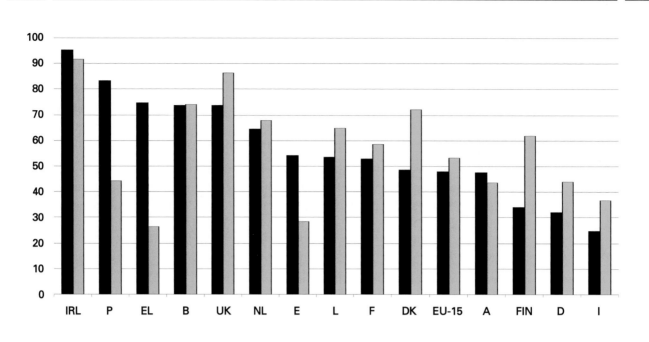

Black: household income lower than 60 % compared with median actual current income; colour: household income higher than 140 % compared with median actual current income.

L: 1996 data. FIN: 1997 data. S: data not reliable. *Source:* ECHP-UDB, Eurostat, version December 2001.

Percentage of households owning their accommodation by median income group. 1998

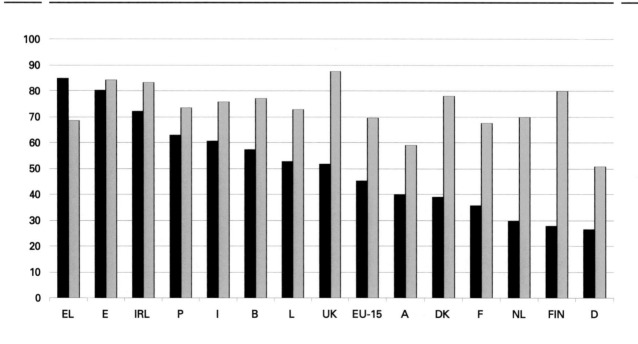

Black: household income lower than 60 % compared with median actual current income; colour: household income higher than 140 % compared with median actual current income.

L: 1996 data. FIN: 1997 data. S: data not reliable. *Source:* ECHP-UDB, Eurostat, version December 2001.

Percentage of persons living in overcrowded houses by median income group. 1998

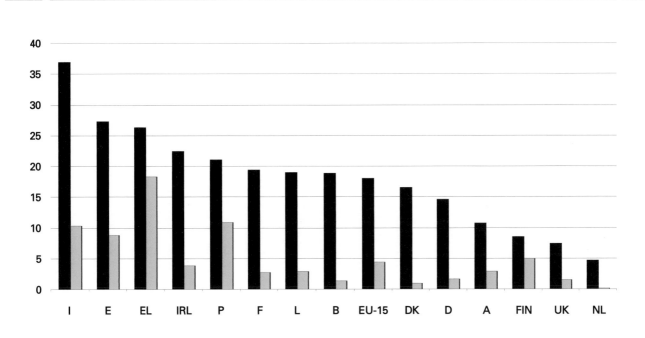

Black: household income lower than 60 % compared with median actual current income; colour: household income higher than 140 % compared with median actual current income.

L: 1996 data. FIN: 1997 data. S: data not reliable. Overcrowded households: more than one person per room. *Source:* ECHP-UDB, Eurostat, version December 2001.

Rooms per person by tenure status of the household. 1998

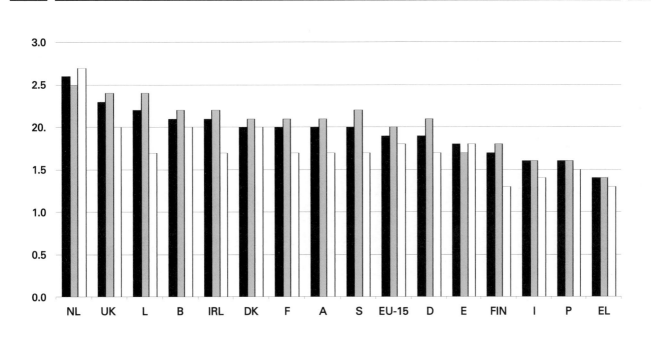

Black: total; colour: owner; white: rent.

L: 1996 data. FIN: 1997 data. *Source:* ECHP-UDB, Eurostat, version December 2001.

Percentage of households that cannot afford a car. 1998

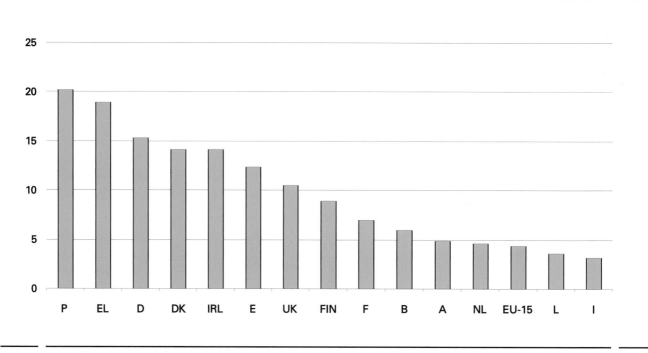

D, L, UK: 1996 data. FIN: 1997 data. Source: ECHP-UDB, Eurostat, version December 2001.

Percentage of households with/without financial burden due to housing costs. 1998

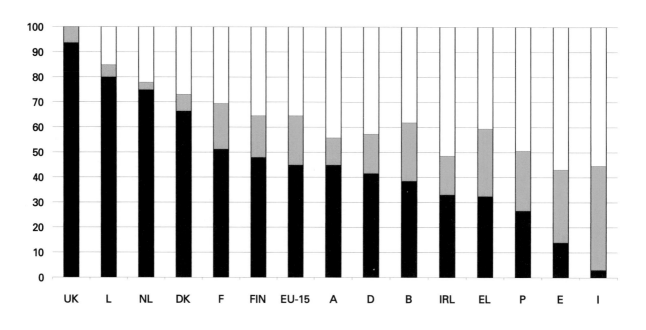

Black: households without financial burden due to housing costs; colour: households with heavy financial burden due to housing costs; white: house-holds with financial burden due to housing costs.

L: 1996 data. FIN: 1997 data. *Source:* ECHP-UDB, Eurostat, version December 2001.

Please find the complete information of the Eurostat Yearbook on the annexed CD-ROM.

The EU population

- Population increase per 1 000 people
- Natural population increase per 1 000 inhabitants
- Net migration, including corrections, per 1 000 people
- People aged under 15 as % of total population
- People aged under 15. EU-15. Millions
- People aged 15 to 24 as % of total population
- People aged 15 to 24. EU-15. Millions
- People aged 25 to 49 as % of total population
- People aged 25 to 49. EU-15. Millions
- People aged 50 to 64 as % of total population
- People aged 50 to 64. EU-15. Millions
- People aged 65 to 79 as % of total population
- People aged 65 to 79. EU-15. Millions
- People aged 80 or over as % of total population
- People aged 80 or over. EU-15. Millions
- Women per 100 men

Families and births

- Marriages and divorces per 1 000 people. EU-15
- Total fertility and completed fertility. EU-15

International migration

- Immigration of nationals
- Immigration of other EU nationals
- Immigration of non-EU nationals
- Emigration of nationals
- Emigration of other EU nationals
- Emigration of non-EU nationals
- Grants of refugee status
- Population by citizenship. Nationals
- Population by citizenship. Other EU nationals
- Acquisition of citizenship

Life expectancy and mortality

- Life expectancy at birth: difference between females and males. 2000
- Life expectancy at 60: difference between females and males. 1999

Health and safety

- Hampered in daily activities because of chronic conditions (15+ years). % (non-standardised). 1998
- Average number of calories per person/day. kcal
- Average amount of pure alcohol available on the market per person (older than 15) per year. Litres
- Average number of cigarettes available on the market per person per year
- Percentage of population (aged over 15) who are cigarette smokers. 1999
- AIDS incidence rates per million population by year of diagnosis, with adjustments for reporting delays
- Death (SDR) from cancer: women per 100 000 women
- Death (SDR) from cancer: men per 100 000 men
- Incidence of all types of cancer by age and sex in 1997. Age standardised rate using a standard world population
- Incidence of breast cancer by age in 1997. Age standardised rate per 100 000 females using a standard world population
- Incidence of prostate cancer by age in 1997. Age standardised rate per 100 000 males using a standard world population
- Death (SDR) from ischaemic heart diseases: women per 100 000 women
- Death (SDR) from ischaemic heart diseases: men per 100 000 men
- Death (SDR) by suicide: women per 100 000 women
- Death (SDR) by suicide: men per 100 000 men
- Deaths (SDR) in motor-vehicle traffic accidents: women per 100 000 women

2

- Deaths (SDR) in motor-vehicle traffic accidents: men per 100 000 men
- Incidence of malaria per 100 000 persons
- Incidence of legionellosis per 100 000 persons
- Incidence of pertussis per 100 000 persons
- Incidence of tuberculosis per 100 000 persons
- Incidence of salmonellosis per 100 000 persons
- Estimated number of people with Alzheimer's disease and other dementias in 2000 per 100 000 inhabitants
- Accidents at work: serious. Index of the number of serious accidents at work per 100 000 persons in employment. 1998 = 100
- Accidents at work: fatal. Index of the number of fatal accidents at work per 100 000 persons in employment. 1998 = 100
- Standardised incidence rate of accidents at work with more than three days' absence per 100 000 persons employed. 18 to 24 years
- Incidence rate of accidents at work with more than three days' absence per 100 000 persons employed. Agriculture, hunting and forestry
- Incidence rate of accidents at work with more than three days' absence per 100 000 persons employed. Manufacturing
- Incidence rate of accidents at work with more than three days' absence per 100 000 persons employed. Construction
- Incidence rate of accidents at work with more than three days' absence per 100 000 persons employed. Transport, storage and communication
- Number of fatal accidents at work. Manufacturing
- Number of fatal accidents at work. Construction
- Number of fatal accidents at work. Transport, storage and communication
- Total health expenditure per head of population in PPS
- Total health expenditure as a proportion of GDP
- Total number of dentists (practising or licensed) per 100 000 inhabitants

- Beds in psychiatric hospitals per 100 000 inhabitants
- Percentage of persons hospitalised during the last 12 months (15+ years). 2000 (% non-standardised)
- Solid organ transplants in Europe per million population: heart
- Solid organ transplants in Europe per million population: kidney
- Solid organ transplants in Europe per million population: liver
- Solid organ transplants in Europe per million population: lungs

Education

- School expectancy. 1999/2000
- Participation rate of four-year-olds in education
- Duration of compulsory schooling (age). 2000/01
- Pupil/teacher ratio in primary education. 1999/2000
- Percentage of pupils in upper secondary education enrolled in vocational stream, by gender. 1999/2000
- Percentage of pupils in upper secondary general education learning English
- Percentage of pupils in upper secondary general education learning French
- Percentage of pupils in upper secondary general education learning German
- Median age in tertiary education. 1999/2000
- Women among students in tertiary education. 1988/89 and 1999/2000. %
- Women among tertiary students in mathematics, science and computing. 2000. %
- Women among students in engineering, manufacturing and construction. 2000. %
- Flow of EU/EEA students in EU/EEA countries. Tertiary education. 1999/2000. 1 000s
- Science and technology graduates. Females. Tertiary graduates in science and technology per 1 000 female population aged 20 to 29
- Science and technology graduates. Males. Tertiary graduates in science and technology per 1 000 male population aged 20 to 29

- Early school-leavers not in further education or training. Females. Share of the population aged 18 to 24 with only lower secondary education and not in education or training
- Early school-leavers not in further education or training. Males. Share of the population aged 18 to 24 with only lower secondary education and not in education or training
- Lifelong learning (adult participation in education and training). Percentage of population aged 25 to 64 participating in education and training over the four weeks prior to the LFS
- Lifelong learning (adult participation in education and training). Females. Percentage of the female population aged 25 to 64 participating in education and training over the four weeks prior to the LFS
- Lifelong learning (adult participation in education and training). Males. Percentage of the male population aged 25 to 64 participating in education and training over the four weeks prior to the LFS
- Unemployment rates for total population aged 25 to 59 having completed no more than lower secondary education
- Unemployment rates for total population aged 25 to 59 having completed upper secondary education
- Unemployment rates for total population aged 25 to 59 having completed tertiary education
- Public expenditure on education by level of education as % of GDP. 1999
- Spending on human resources (public expenditure on education) as % of GDP

People in the labour market

- Employment growth: females. Annual percentage change in female employed population
- Employment growth: males. Annual percentage change in male employed population
- Persons in employment: women. Annual average. 1 000s

- Persons in employment: men. Annual average. 1 000s
- Employment rate of men and women (15 to 64). Annual average. 2001
- Total employment rate of older workers. Employed persons aged 55 to 64 as a share of the total population aged 55 to 64
- Employment rate of men and women aged 25 to 54 years. Annual average
- Employment rate of men and women aged 15 to 24 years. Annual average
- Employment rate of older workers: females. Employed persons aged 55 to 64 as a share of the females aged 55 to 64
- Employment rate of older workers: males. Employed persons aged 55 to 64 as a share of the males aged 55 to 64
- Employment rate of women aged 15 to 24 years. Annual average
- Employment rate of men aged 15 to 24 years. Annual average
- Employment rate of women aged 25 to 54 years. Annual average
- Employment rate of men aged 25 to 54 years. Annual average
- Persons employed in agriculture as % of total employment: men and women. Annual average
- Persons employed in industry as % of total employment: men and women. Annual average
- Persons employed in services as % of total employment: men and women. Annual average
- Average hours usually worked per week of part-time employed. Spring
- Average hours usually worked per week of full-time employed. Spring
- Men and women employed part-time as % of total employment. Spring
- Percentage of involuntary part-time employed. Spring
- Women employed part-time as % of all employed women. Spring
- Men employed part-time as % of all employed men. Spring
- Percentage of employees with contract of limited duration. Spring 2001
- Percentage of employed population with a second job. Spring 2001

2

- Percentage of persons usually working on Saturdays. Spring
- Percentage of persons usually working on Sundays. Spring
- Percentage of persons usually doing shift work. Spring
- Percentage of persons usually working at night. Spring
- Unemployment: men and women. Annual average. 1 000s
- Unemployment rate: females. Unemployed persons as a share of the female active population
- Unemployment rate: males. Unemployed persons as a share of the male active population
- Unemployment: women. Annual average. 1 000s
- Unemployment: men. Annual average. 1 000s
- Unemployment rate of population aged less than 25 years. Annual average
- Unemployment: persons aged less than 25 years. Annual average. 1 000s
- Long-term unemployment rate. Long-term unemployed (over 12 months) as % of the total active population
- Long-term unemployed as % of the active population. Annual average. 2001
- Long-term unemployment rate: females. Long-term unemployed (over 12 months) as % of the female active population
- Long-term unemployment rate: males. Long-term unemployed (over 12 months) as % of the male active population
- Population in jobless households. Persons aged 0 to 65 living in households with no member in employment as % of all persons living in those households where members are neither in education nor in retirement
- Population in jobless households. Persons aged 0 to 60 living in households with no member in employment as % of all persons living in those households where members are neither in education nor in retirement
- Percentage of population not in the labour force by age and sex. Spring 2001. EU-15
- Percentage of population not in the labour force: men and women aged 15 years and over. Spring

- Percentage of women aged 15 years and over not in the labour force. Spring
- Percentage of men aged 15 years and over not in the labour force. Spring

Continuing vocational training in enterprises

- Percentage of employees in small and large enterprises participating in CVT courses. 1999
- Total costs of CVT courses as % of total labour cost (all enterprises). 1999
- Hours in CVT courses per employee (all enterprises). 1999
- Hours in CVT courses per employee (all enterprises) by sex. 1999

Household consumption expenditure

- Food (without beverages), at current prices. % of total household consumption expenditure
- Alcoholic beverages, tobacco and narcotics, at current prices. % of total household consumption expenditure
- Alcoholic beverages, at current prices. % of total household consumption expenditure
- Tobacco, at current prices. % of total household consumption expenditure
- Clothing and footwear, at current prices. % of total household consumption expenditure
- Housing, water, electricity, gas and other fuels, at current prices. % of total household consumption expenditure
- Imputed rentals for housing, at current prices. % of total household consumption expenditure
- Electricity, gas and other fuels, at current prices. % of total household consumption expenditure
- Furnishings, household equipment and routine maintenance of the house, at current prices. % of total household consumption expediture
- Communications, at current prices. % of total household consumption expenditure
- Transport, at current prices. % of total household consumption expenditure

- Recreation and culture, at current prices. % of total household consumption expenditure
- Restaurants and hotels, at current prices. % of total household consumption expenditure
- Insurance, at current prices. % of total household consumption expenditure
- Miscellaneous goods and services, at current prices. % of total household consumption expenditure

Income and living conditions

- Percentage of persons living in private households by type of household. Two adults without dependent children
- Percentage of persons living in private households by type of household. Two adults with dependent children
- Percentage of persons living in private households by type of household. Three or more adults without dependent children
- Percentage of persons living in private households by type of household. Three or more adults with dependent children
- Inequality of income distribution (S80/S20 quintile share ratio)
- Persistent-risk-of-poverty rate. Share of persons with an equivalised disposable income below the risk-of-poverty threshold in the current year and in at least two of the preceding three years. The threshold is set at 60 % of the national median equivalised disposable income

2

3

Economy and ecology

National accounts

Prices, wages and finance

International trade

The environment

National accounts: a high-quality standard environment

Eurostat's national accounts data are measured with accuracy and exhaustiveness. They are a high-quality basis for economic and social analysis. Their main component is the gross domestic product (GDP), which principally covers all goods and services produced by a country in a given period.

The national accounts are grouped into three domains: economy (including employment), money and finance.

They are established based on a common official methodology, the European system of national and regional accounts (ESA 95). The data collected under ESA 95 are accurate and widely exhaustive and comparable, and hence suitable for economic analysis.

ESA 95 is the european version of the United Nations' SNA 93 (system of national accounts) with which it is compatible.

ESA 95 is available on the following free web sites:

— in English (http://www.cc.cec/home/eurostat/esa/en/een00sum.htm);

— in French (http://www.cc.cec/home/eurostat/esa/fr/efr00sum.htm);

— in German (http://www.cc.cec/home/eurostat/esa/de/esa95de.htm).

Breakdown of the economy: sectors and branches

The economy is usually divided in two ways for the purpose of analysis.

— By institutional sector, i.e. legal entities such as households, government, companies, etc.

  The sectors follow the nomenclature shown in ESA 95, Attachment IV.

— By branch of activity, i.e. homogeneous units of production like agriculture, fishing, chemicals, etc.

  The branches follow NACE Rev. 1, the new version of the NACE classification, the statistical classification of economic activities in the European Community (the European Union since 1994). The acronym NACE comes from the French 'nomenclature des activités économiques dans la Communauté européenne'.

  NACE breaks down the economy by branch of activity into various levels (= number of branches): A3, A6, A17, A31, A60. NACE Rev. 1 is accessible in English, French and German on the free web site http://europa.eu.int/comm/eurostat/ramon/, option 'Classifications', line 89. On this web site, you can also consult Coicop (classification of individual consumption by purpose) for final consumption expenditure of households and COFOG for consumption functions of government.

Better quality through increased accuracy and exhaustiveness

In the year 2000, the national accounts were improved concerning the following updated features.

(a) The new national accounts system ESA 95, which has been gradually introduced since 1999 as an expanded and fuller version of the earlier ESA 79.

Compared with ESA 79, ESA 95 provides:

— greater exhaustiveness: new activities (leasing, stock options, etc.) and inclusion or official acceptance of certain concepts (purchasing power parity and purchasing power standard, active population, unemployment, balance sheets, etc.);

3

— new concepts (actual final consumption, real disposable national income, holding gains, household subsectors, basic price evaluation, more detailed treatment of trade and transport margins, etc.);

— new statistical tools (recording methods and thresholds);

— characteristics relating to the European institutions.

As a result of the changeover from ESA 79 to ESA 95, the figures for gross domestic product have increased slightly. Generally, the data for final consumption in 1995 have equally increased.

In this issue of the yearbook, the national accounts' time series are completely based on ESA 95. Therefore, the series do not have a break in 2000.

(b) The new (versions of) related nomenclatures: NACE Rev. 1 for economic activities, Coicop for final consumption expenditure of households and COFOG for consumption functions of government. They improve the breakdowns of the economy to provide a better response to the changing needs of statistical users.

Economic output

GDP: the result of all production activity

Gross domestic product (GDP) at market prices is the final result of the production activity of resident producer units. It can be defined in three ways.

— GDP is the sum of gross value added of the various institutional sectors or the various industries, plus taxes and less subsidies on products (which are not allocated to sectors and industries). It is also the balancing item in the total economy production account (production approach).

— GDP is the sum of final uses of goods and services by resident institutional units (actual final consumption and gross capital formation), plus exports and minus imports of goods and services (expenditure approach).

— GDP is the sum of uses in the total economy generation of income account (compensation of employees, taxes on production and imports less subsidies, gross operating surplus and mixed income of the total economy) (income approach) (ESA 95, 8.89).

In these tables, GDP corresponds to the economy's output of goods and services less intermediate consumption, plus VAT on products and net taxes (i.e. taxes less subsidies) linked to imports. Valuation at constant prices means valuing the flows and stocks in an accounting period at the prices of the reference period (ESA 95, 1.56).

GDP per person: comparing economies' relative strengths

GDP, and in particular GDP per capita, is one of the main indicators for economic analysis as well as spatial and/or temporal international comparisons.

In order to facilitate these international comparisons, the GDP in national currency of each Member State is converted into a common currency (ecu until 1998, euro from the beginning of 1999) by means of its official exchange rate. However, this does not necessarily reflect the actual purchasing power of each national currency on its economic territory, because the converted GDP is a function not only of the level of goods and services produced on the economic territory, but also of the general price level. Therefore, the simple use of the GDP converted into a common currency does not provide, in most cases, a correct indication of the volume of goods and services.

In order to remove the distortions due to price-level differences, transitive purchasing power parities (PPPs) are calculated and used as a factor of conversion (exchange rate from national currency to PPS). These parities are obtained as a weighted average of relative price ratios regarding a homogeneous basket of goods and services, comparable and representative for each Member State.

The 'comparable volume' values of GDP obtained in this way are hence expressed in terms of purchasing power standards (PPS), a unit that is independent of any national currency.

Gross value added: 'producing' the GDP

The GDP is overwhelmingly composed of gross value added at basic prices, usually around 85–90 %.

Gross value added is recorded at basic prices. It is the net result of output valued at basic prices less intermediate consumption valued at purchasers' prices (ESA 95, 9.23). The basic price is the price receivable by the producers from the purchaser for a unit of a good or service produced as output minus any tax payable on that unit as a consequence of its production or sale (i.e. taxes on products), plus any subsidy receivable on that unit as a consequence of its production or sale (i.e. subsidies on products). It excludes any transport charges invoiced separately by the producer. It includes any transport margins charged by the producer on the same invoice, even when they are included as a separate item on the invoice (ESA 95, 3.48).

Who adds value to the GDP?

The contribution to gross value added of the nine main branches of industry, with manufacturing as a single branch, can be seen in the tables of this section.

The contribution of each branch is presented as a percentage in the total gross value added.

3

Further reading:

Eurostat publications
— **Economic Portrait of the European Union 2002**
— **Regions: Statistical yearbook 2002**

Statistics in Focus — Theme 2
— **Quarterly national accounts ESA**

Do you need more information?
— **Ask your Data Shop (see last page)**
— **http://www.europa.eu.int/comm/eurostat**
— **Eurostat's data serves the political discussion in Europe. Have a look at the website of the "Economic and Financial Affairs DG":**
   http://europa.eu.int/comm/dgs/economy_finance/index_en.htm

Gross value added at current basic prices and current exchange rates. Agriculture, hunting and forestry.
% of all branches

	1991	1992	1993	1994	1995	1996	1997	1998	1999	2000	2001	
B	:	:	:	:	1.6	1.6	1.6	1.5	1.3	1.3	1.4	**B**
DK	3.7	3.5	3.3	3.2	3.5	3.4	3.2	2.6	2.3	2.3	2.5	**DK**
D	1.4	1.3	1.3	1.3	1.3	1.3	1.3	1.2	1.2	1.2	:	**D**
EL	11.0	9.6	8.8	9.4	9.5	8.7	8.2	7.9	7.5	7.0	:	**EL**
E	:	:	:	:	4.1	4.5	4.3	:	:	:	:	**E**
F	:	:	:	:	:	:	:	:	:	:	:	**F**
IRL	:	:	:	:	:	:	:	:	:	:	:	**IRL**
I	3.4	3.2	3.1	3.1	3.1	3.1	3.0	2.9	2.9	2.7	2.6	**I**
L	:	:	:	:	1.1	1.0	0.8	0.7	0.8	0.7	:	**L**
NL	4.1	3.9	3.4	3.5	3.4	3.3	3.0	3.0	2.7	2.6	2.6	**NL**
A	3.1	2.9	2.7	2.7	2.5	2.5	2.4	2.4	2.3	2.2	2.3	**A**
P	7.1	5.8	5.6	5.3	5.0	4.7	4.0	3.7	3.7	:	:	**P**
FIN	5.5	4.9	4.9	5.3	4.6	4.1	4.1	3.7	3.6	3.5	3.3	**FIN**
S	:	:	2.5	2.6	2.5	2.1	2.1	2.0	1.9	:	:	**S**
UK	1.7	1.8	1.8	1.7	1.8	1.7	1.3	1.2	1.1	1.0	0.9	**UK**
NO	2.4	2.1	2.1	1.9	1.8	1.6	1.4	:	:	:	:	**NO**
JP	1.8	1.7	1.6	1.7	1.5	1.5	1.3	1.3	1.2	:	:	**JP**

IRL will supply these data from 2005 onwards.

3

Gross value added at current basic prices and current exchange rates. Fishing. % of all branches

	1991	1992	1993	1994	1995	1996	1997	1998	1999	2000	2001	
B	:	:	:	:	0.0	0.0	0.0	0.0	0.0	0.0	0.0	**B**
DK	0.4	0.4	0.3	0.3	0.3	0.2	0.3	0.3	0.3	0.2	0.2	**DK**
D	0.0	0.0	0.0	0.0	0.0	0.0	0.0	0.0	0.0	0.0	:	**D**
EL	0.4	0.4	0.4	0.4	0.3	0.4	0.3	0.3	0.3	0.3	:	**EL**
E	:	:	:	:	0.3	0.3	0.3	:	:	:	:	**E**
F	0.1	0.1	0.1	0.1	0.1	0.1	0.1	0.1	0.1	:	:	**F**
IRL	:	:	:	:	:	:	:	:	:	:	:	**IRL**
I	0.1	0.1	0.1	0.1	0.1	0.1	0.1	0.1	0.1	0.1	0.1	**I**
L	:	:	:	:	0.0	0.0	0.0	0.0	0.0	0.0	:	**L**
NL	0.1	0.1	0.1	0.1	0.1	0.1	0.1	0.1	0.1	0.1	0.1	**NL**
A	0.0	0.0	0.0	0.0	0.0	0.0	0.0	0.0	0.0	0.0	0.0	**A**
P	0.7	0.7	0.6	0.5	0.5	0.5	0.4	0.4	0.4	:	:	**P**
FIN	0.1	0.2	0.2	0.1	0.1	0.1	0.1	0.1	0.1	0.1	0.1	**FIN**
S	:	:	0.0	0.0	0.0	0.0	0.0	0.0	0.0	:	:	**S**
UK	0.1	0.1	0.1	0.1	0.1	0.1	0.1	0.1	0.1	0.1	0.1	**UK**
NO	0.7	0.7	0.8	1.0	1.0	0.8	0.8	:	:	:	:	**NO**
JP	0.4	0.4	0.4	0.3	0.3	0.3	0.3	0.2	0.2	:	:	**JP**

IRL will supply these data from 2005 onwards.

Gross value added at current basic prices and current exchange rates. Mining and quarrying. % of all branches

	1991	1992	1993	1994	1995	1996	1997	1998	1999	2000	2001	
B	:	:	:	:	0.2	0.2	0.2	0.2	0.2	0.2	0.1	**B**
DK	1.0	1.1	1.0	0.9	0.9	1.3	1.4	1.1	1.5	3.1	2.2	**DK**
D	0.8	0.7	0.7	0.6	0.6	0.3	0.3	0.3	0.3	0.3	0.3	**D**
EL	0.8	0.7	0.7	0.7	0.6	0.7	0.6	0.6	0.6	0.6	:	**EL**
E	:	:	:	:	0.6	0.5	0.4	:	:	:	:	**E**
F	0.3	0.3	0.2	0.3	0.2	0.2	0.2	0.2	0.2	:	:	**F**
IRL	:	:	:	:	:	:	:	:	:	:	:	**IRL**
I	0.5	0.5	0.5	0.5	0.5	0.5	0.5	0.4	0.4	0.5	0.5	**I**
L	:	:	:	:	0.2	0.1	0.1	0.1	0.1	0.1	:	**L**
NL	3.6	3.0	2.8	2.6	2.6	3.0	2.9	2.4	1.9	2.6	3.0	**NL**
A	0.5	0.5	0.5	0.4	0.4	0.4	0.4	0.3	0.3	0.4	0.4	**A**
P	0.5	0.4	0.4	0.4	0.5	0.4	0.5	0.4	0.4	:	:	**P**
FIN	0.4	0.4	0.4	0.4	0.4	0.3	0.3	0.3	0.3	0.2	0.2	**FIN**
S	:	:	0.4	0.4	0.4	0.3	0.4	0.3	0.3	:	:	**S**
UK	2.6	2.5	2.4	2.4	2.6	2.9	2.5	2.1	2.2	3.0	2.9	**UK**
NO	13.4	13.1	13.2	13.2	13.4	17.2	17.7	:	:	:	:	**NO**
JP	0.2	0.2	0.2	0.2	0.2	0.2	0.1	0.1	0.1	:	:	**JP**

IRL will supply these data from 2005 onwards.

3

Gross value added at current basic prices and current exchange rates. Manufacturing. % of all branches

	1991	1992	1993	1994	1995	1996	1997	1998	1999	2000	2001	
B	:	:	:	:	20.0	19.7	19.8	19.5	19.0	19.0	18.3	**B**
DK	17.8	17.9	17.2	17.4	17.7	17.0	17.4	16.7	16.4	16.3	16.5	**DK**
D	27.4	25.7	23.6	23.1	22.6	22.2	22.3	22.5	22.0	22.2	22.2	**D**
EL	15.2	15.0	14.3	13.2	13.0	13.1	11.7	11.8	11.0	11.1	:	**EL**
E	:	:	:	:	18.6	18.6	18.8	:	:	:	:	**E**
F	19.6	19.1	18.1	18.1	18.5	18.1	18.4	18.4	18.4	:	:	**F**
IRL	:	:	:	:	:	:	:	:	:	:	:	**IRL**
I	22.5	21.9	21.4	21.7	22.2	21.3	21.1	21.2	20.7	20.6	20.2	**I**
L	:	:	:	:	14.1	13.0	12.8	12.5	11.8	11.8	:	**L**
NL	18.2	17.8	17.3	17.7	17.9	17.3	17.1	16.8	16.3	16.3	15.6	**NL**
A	21.6	20.6	19.4	19.4	19.8	19.5	19.9	20.1	20.4	20.7	20.6	**A**
P	20.3	20.3	19.4	20.3	20.7	20.7	20.4	20.0	19.3	:	:	**P**
FIN	19.6	20.8	22.5	23.6	25.2	23.7	24.3	24.9	24.5	25.8	25.0	**FIN**
S	:	:	19.8	21.4	22.1	21.3	22.0	22.0	21.5	:	:	**S**
UK	21.6	21.2	21.0	21.5	21.8	21.5	21.1	20.1	19.1	18.3	17.5	**UK**
NO	12.1	12.2	12.5	12.8	13.4	12.3	12.4	:	:	:	:	**NO**
JP	25.6	24.6	23.2	22.1	22.1	22.1	22.0	21.1	20.7	:	:	**JP**

IRL will supply these data from 2005 onwards.

Gross value added at current basic prices and current exchange rates. Wholesale and retail trade including repairs. % of all branches

	1990	1991	1992	1993	1994	1995	1996	1997	1998	1999	2000	
B	:	:	:	:	:	12.0	11.7	11.7	11.6	11.7	11.5	B
DK	13.2	13.7	13.7	13.1	13.4	13.6	13.7	13.3	12.8	13.0	12.6	DK
D	10.0	10.5	10.3	10.3	10.6	10.7	10.5	10.4	10.5	10.7	11.3	D
EL	14.6	14.1	14.9	15.2	14.9	13.6	14.5	14.4	13.6	13.6	14.5	EL
E	:	:	:	:	:	11.4	11.4	11.4	:	:	:	E
F	10.9	10.9	10.3	10.5	10.4	10.5	10.0	10.2	10.3	10.0	:	F
IRL	:	:	:	:	:	:	:	:	:	:	:	IRL
I	13.7	13.9	13.7	13.5	13.8	13.8	13.6	13.4	13.4	13.3	13.1	I
L	:	:	:	:	:	10.8	10.6	11.0	10.5	10.3	10.5	L
NL	13.7	13.6	13.6	13.4	13.3	13.2	12.9	12.9	13.2	13.5	13.2	NL
A	13.9	13.8	13.6	13.0	12.8	12.8	12.7	12.8	12.7	12.7	12.8	A
P	17.0	16.8	16.8	16.8	16.7	15.6	15.7	15.7	15.5	15.6	:	P
FIN	11.1	10.5	9.9	9.7	10.0	9.9	10.1	10.7	10.4	10.4	9.6	FIN
S	:	:	:	10.3	10.7	10.4	10.3	10.4	10.4	10.6	:	S
UK	11.4	11.6	11.8	11.9	11.8	11.7	11.7	12.0	12.3	12.5	12.2	UK

IRL will supply these data from 2005 onwards.

Gross value added at current basic prices and current exchange rates. Real estate, renting and business activities. % of all branches

	1991	1992	1993	1994	1995	1996	1997	1998	1999	2000	2001	
B	:	:	:	:	19.7	20.2	20.5	21.1	21.5	22.2	22.6	B
DK	18.7	18.5	19.0	18.8	18.5	18.0	18.5	17.8	18.0	17.7	17.9	DK
D	19.2	20.1	21.4	21.6	22.3	23.4	23.8	24.2	24.7	25.1	25.5	D
EL	15.4	15.4	16.0	16.5	17.0	17.3	17.4	17.3	17.0	17.0	:	EL
E	:	:	:	:	13.1	13.4	13.7	:	:	:	:	E
F	21.8	22.4	22.5	22.5	22.6	23.4	23.6	24.0	24.6	:	:	F
IRL	:	:	:	:	:	:	:	:	:	:	:	IRL
I	15.1	15.8	16.4	16.7	17.3	18.1	18.8	18.7	19.6	19.9	20.4	I
L	:	:	:	:	18.0	18.2	17.7	18.2	17.8	17.7	:	L
NL	15.7	16.3	16.9	17.2	17.3	18.4	19.0	19.5	20.1	20.0	20.0	NL
A	11.6	12.1	12.5	13.0	13.9	14.4	14.9	15.4	15.8	16.1	16.9	A
P	:	:	:	:	12.2	12.0	12.2	12.2	12.0	:	:	P
FIN	14.4	15.3	15.8	15.8	15.7	16.3	16.6	16.8	17.5	17.4	17.9	FIN
S	:	:	21.2	20.8	19.6	20.4	21.5	21.6	21.9	:	:	S
UK	17.3	17.6	17.8	18.2	18.6	18.9	19.9	21.4	22.4	23.1	24.0	UK
NO	13.4	13.8	14.1	14.0	13.9	13.4	13.7	:	:	:	:	NO
JP	10.2	10.6	11.2	11.5	11.5	11.6	11.6	11.9	12.2	:	:	JP

IRL will supply these data from 2005 onwards.

Gross value added at current basic prices and current exchange rates. Education. % of all branches

	1991	1992	1993	1994	1995	1996	1997	1998	1999	2000	2001	
B	:	:	:	:	6.7	6.6	6.5	6.5	6.4	6.4	6.4	B
DK	5.5	5.5	5.8	5.7	5.4	5.5	5.4	5.3	5.2	5.0	5.0	DK
D	4.0	4.1	4.3	4.2	4.2	4.2	4.2	4.1	4.2	4.1	4.0	D
EL	4.6	4.6	4.6	4.6	4.5	4.3	4.8	4.8	4.9	4.9	:	EL
E	:	:	:	:	4.8	4.8	4.7	:	:	:	:	E
F	4.5	4.6	4.8	4.8	5.0	4.9	5.0	5.0	5.0	:	:	F
IRL	:	:	:	:	:	:	:	:	:	:	:	IRL
I	5.5	5.5	5.4	5.2	5.0	5.1	5.1	5.0	5.1	5.0	5.0	I
L	:	:	:	:	4.1	4.1	3.8	3.8	4.0	3.9	:	L
NL	4.4	4.5	4.5	4.5	4.4	4.3	4.2	4.2	4.2	4.1	4.2	NL
A	5.6	5.6	5.6	5.5	5.4	5.3	5.3	5.2	5.3	5.2	5.2	A
P	:	:	:	:	6.9	7.0	7.1	7.1	7.3	:	:	P
FIN	5.6	5.8	5.6	5.4	5.3	5.3	5.0	4.9	4.9	4.7	4.8	FIN
S	:	:	3.5	3.4	4.3	4.3	3.5	3.7	3.9	:	:	S
UK	5.4	5.5	5.5	5.4	5.3	5.4	5.4	5.4	5.7	5.9	6.0	UK
NO	4.7	4.9	4.8	4.8	4.7	4.6	4.5	:	:	:	:	NO
JP	0.7	0.8	0.8	0.8	0.8	0.9	0.9	0.9	0.9	:	:	JP

IRL will supply these data from 2005 onwards.

Gross value added at current basic prices and current exchange rates. Health and social work. % of all branches

	1991	1992	1993	1994	1995	1996	1997	1998	1999	2000	2001	
B	:	:	:	:	6.2	6.2	6.1	6.0	6.4	6.6	6.9	B
DK	10.5	10.5	10.7	10.2	10.1	10.2	10.3	10.4	10.2	9.8	9.8	DK
D	5.3	5.6	5.7	5.9	6.1	6.1	6.1	6.1	6.1	6.1	6.2	D
EL	4.5	4.6	4.8	5.5	5.2	5.1	5.3	5.4	5.5	5.0	:	EL
E	:	:	:	:	5.4	5.4	5.3	:	:	:	:	E
F	5.9	5.9	6.4	6.5	6.6	6.7	6.7	6.6	6.5	:	:	F
IRL	:	:	:	:	:	:	:	:	:	:	:	IRL
I	4.6	4.6	4.6	4.5	4.3	4.4	4.6	4.5	4.5	4.6	4.6	I
L	:	:	:	:	3.9	4.2	4.2	3.9	3.8	3.6	:	L
NL	7.2	7.4	7.5	7.4	7.3	7.2	7.2	7.1	7.3	7.3	7.6	NL
A	5.1	5.4	5.7	5.9	5.8	5.9	4.8	4.8	4.6	4.6	4.7	A
P	:	:	:	:	5.5	5.5	5.4	5.6	6.1	:	:	P
FIN	9.3	9.7	9.0	8.5	8.4	8.5	8.1	7.8	7.8	7.5	7.8	FIN
S	:	:	10.5	10.3	10.3	10.8	10.3	10.3	10.5	:	:	S
UK	6.2	6.3	6.4	6.5	6.6	6.6	6.5	6.5	6.6	6.7	7.0	UK
NO	8.0	8.3	8.3	8.4	8.4	8.4	8.4	:	:	:	:	NO

IRL will supply these data from 2005 onwards.

Gross domestic product at market prices. Current series in million ECU/EUR

	1991	1992	1993	1994	1995	1996	1997	1998	1999	2000	2001	
EU-15	5 779 191	6 023 484	6 043 394	6 336 297	6 588 159	6 919 468	7 287 354	7 630 393	8 029 646	8 552 861	8 827 067	**EU-15**
€-zone	4 561 385	4 807 506	4 857 384	5 071 595	5 309 137	5 534 454	5 648 718	5 883 181	6 150 836	6 447 980	6 824 167	**€-zone**
B	163 487	174 275	184 466	198 401	211 551	212 474	216 137	223 687	235 632	247 469	254 283	**B**
DK	108 446	113 694	118 541	128 024	137 793	144 155	149 169	154 069	163 216	173 889	180 418	**DK**
D	1 432 662	1 561 713	1 670 811	1 763 730	1 880 207	1 878 151	1 863 458	1 916 370	1 978 600	2 030 000	2 071 200	**D**
EL	73 081	77 024	79 771	84 353	89 888	97 972	107 103	108 978	118 000	123 121	130 927	**EL**
E	443 715	463 263	425 936	425 089	446 881	480 535	495 627	525 454	565 199	609 319	651 641	**E**
F	987 210	1 040 541	1 089 369	1 139 319	1 188 101	1 224 606	1 241 129	1 297 574	1 355 102	1 416 877	1 463 722	**F**
IRL	38 648	41 447	42 570	46 148	50 836	57 649	70 693	77 699	89 770	102 910	114 479	**IRL**
I	939 612	951 165	849 037	863 368	839 042	971 065	1 029 991	1 068 947	1 108 497	1 164 767	1 216 694	**I**
L	9 702	10 402	11 805	12 951	13 828	14 299	15 422	16 892	18 586	20 815	21 510	**L**
NL	244 411	258 416	277 679	293 807	317 323	324 479	332 654	351 648	374 070	402 599	429 172	**NL**
A	136 573	146 955	158 511	168 108	179 840	182 364	181 645	189 333	197 154	207 037	211 857	**A**
P	65 534	75 479	73 635	76 303	82 631	88 310	93 890	100 320	107 741	115 042	122 705	**P**
FIN	99 829	83 851	73 565	84 369	98 898	100 523	108 072	115 256	120 485	131 145	135 976	**FIN**
S	200 132	197 151	164 188	174 216	183 597	206 273	210 815	213 702	227 607	248 479	234 162	**S**
UK	836 147	828 109	823 509	878 109	867 743	936 614	1 171 548	1 270 463	1 369 988	1 559 392	1 588 320	**UK**
IS	5 469	5 369	5 052	5 280	5 330	5 717	6 516	7 269	8 077	9 281	8 487 *	**IS**
NO	96 019	98 274	99 935	104 298	113 139	125 287	138 596	133 729	148 373	180 589	187 722	**NO**
CH	188 248	188 344	202 173	220 482	235 052	233 328	225 895	234 268	242 771	260 313	274 662	**CH**
CA	482 716	446 556	481 356	474 472	451 533	483 327	562 536	549 514	619 020	777 037	787 841	**CA**
JP	2 818 309	2 932 493	3 738 214	4 053 971	4 046 254	3 699 223	3 807 082	3 523 112	4 219 003	5 162 452	4 665 807	**JP**
US	4 830 880	4 867 832	5 672 359	5 930 383	5 657 888	6 153 332	7 335 177	7 833 012	8 701 946	10 637 193	11 257 048	**US**

3

Gross domestic product at market prices. Current series in PPS per head

	1991	1992	1993	1994	1995	1996	1997	1998	1999	2000	2001	
EU-15	15 720 *	16 300 *	16 280 *	17 010 *	17 640	18 470	19 400	20 270	21 270	22 570	23 180	**EU-15**
€-zone	15 970 *	16 560 *	16 480 *	17 220 *	17 910	18 600	19 460	20 290	21 400	22 750	23 110	**€-zone**
B	16 840	17 880	18 500	19 390	19 860	20 580	21 630	22 440	22 650	24 090	24 690	**B**
DK	17 350	17 590	18 410	19 820	20 840	22 340	23 300	23 930	25 390	26 920	27 530	**DK**
D	16 770	17 740	17 670	18 730	19 420	19 910	20 920	21 520	22 630	23 800	24 140	**D**
EL	9 530	10 150	10 440	11 040	11 640	12 310	12 790	13 560	14 520	15 310	15 780	**EL**
E	12 680 *	12 840 *	12 950 *	13 220 *	13 800	14 650	15 510	16 070	17 470	18 460	19 100	**E**
F	17 290	17 690	17 370	17 780	18 320	18 700	19 210	20 050	21 200	22 690	23 620	**F**
IRL	12 070	13 040	13 610	14 940	16 450	17 290	20 130	21 520	23 890	25 990	27 470	**IRL**
I	16 590	17 130	16 660	17 530	18 250	19 300	19 800	20 980	21 980	23 580	24 270	**I**
L	25 620	26 540	28 240	29 560	30 140	31 180	33 690	36 250	39 820	44 510	45 750 *	**L**
NL	16 410	16 980	17 260	18 050	19 280	20 160	21 820	23 380	24 340	25 560	26 020	**NL**
A	17 020	17 680	18 180	18 940	19 460	20 640	21 540	22 290	23 650	25 710	26 320	**A**
P	10 210 *	10 720	11 090	11 830	12 310	12 950	14 240	14 630	15 310	16 190	16 920	**P**
FIN	15 060	14 230	14 900	15 530	17 110	17 900	19 270	20 520	21 490	23 500	24 280	**FIN**
S	16 700	16 370	16 290	17 080	18 100	18 920	19 830	20 580	21 550	22 790	23 130	**S**
UK	15 260	16 010	16 150	16 810	17 020	18 550	19 890	20 970	21 400	22 540	23 160 *	**UK**
IS	17 480	17 110	17 210	18 250	20 190	21 610	22 740	23 900	25 420	27 020	27 810 *	**IS**
NO	17 910	18 330	20 540	20 530	21 340	23 710	25 500	25 140	27 430	33 090	33 820	**NO**
CH	21 020	21 540	22 040	22 660	23 280	23 240	24 830	25 690	26 460	27 320 *	28 030 *	**CH**
CA	18 090	18 460	18 590	19 870	20 750	21 960	22 890	24 020	24 820	27 750 *	28 520 *	**CA**
JP	18 740	19 380	19 860	20 720	21 280	22 580	23 090	23 680	22 890	24 120	24 290 *	**JP**
US	22 690	23 660	23 810	25 340	26 110	26 720	27 930	29 960	30 500	32 270	32 400	**US**

Gross domestic product per capita in purchasing power standards (PPS). EU-15 = 100

	1991	1992	1993	1994	1995	1996	1997	1998	1999	2000	2001	
EU-15	100.0 *	100.0 *	100.0 *	100.0 *	100.0	100.0	100.0	100.0	100.0	100.0	100.0	EU-15
€-zone	101.6 *	101.6 *	101.2 *	101.2 *	101.5	100.7	100.3	100.1	100.6	100.8	99.7	€-zone
B	107.2 *	109.7 *	113.6 *	114.0 *	112.6	111.4	111.5	110.7	106.5	106.7	106.5	B
DK	110.4 *	107.9 *	113.1 *	116.5 *	118.2	120.9	120.1	118.1	119.4	119.3	118.7	DK
D	106.7 *	108.8 *	108.5 *	110.1 *	110.1	107.8	107.8	106.2	106.4	105.4	104.1	D
EL	60.6 *	62.2 *	64.1 *	64.9 *	66.0	66.7	65.9	66.9	68.3	67.8	68.1	EL
E	80.7 *	78.8 *	79.6 *	77.7 *	78.2	79.3	79.9	79.3	82.1	81.8	82.4	E
F	110.0 *	108.5 *	106.7 *	104.5 *	103.9	101.2	99.0	98.9	99.7	100.5	101.9	F
IRL	76.8 *	80.0 *	83.6 *	87.8 *	93.3	93.6	103.8	106.2	112.3	115.1	118.5	IRL
I	105.6 *	105.1 *	102.3 *	103.0 *	103.5	104.5	102.0	103.5	103.4	104.5	104.7	I
L	163.0 *	162.8 *	173.5 *	173.7 *	170.9	168.8	173.6	178.9	187.2	197.2	197.4 *	L
NL	104.4 *	104.1 *	106.0 *	106.1 *	109.3	109.1	112.5	115.3	114.4	113.3	112.3	NL
A	108.3 *	108.5 *	111.6 *	111.3 *	110.3	111.7	111.0	110.0	111.2	113.9	113.6	A
P	65.0 *	65.8 *	68.1 *	69.5 *	69.8	70.1	73.4	72.2	72.0	71.7	73.0	P
FIN	95.8 *	87.3 *	91.5 *	91.2 *	97.0	96.9	99.3	101.2	101.0	104.1	104.7	FIN
S	106.2 *	100.4 *	100.0 *	100.4 *	102.6	102.4	102.2	101.5	101.3	101.0	99.8	S
UK	97.1 *	98.2 *	99.2 *	98.8 *	96.5	100.4	102.5	103.4	100.6	99.9	99.9 *	UK
IS	111.2 *	104.9 *	105.6 *	107.2 *	114.4	116.9	117.1	117.8	119.5	119.8	120.0 *	IS
NO	114.0 *	112.4 *	126.1 *	120.7 *	121.0	128.3	131.4	124.0	129.0	146.6	145.9	NO
JP	119.2 *	118.9 *	122.0 *	121.8 *	120.6	122.2	119.0	116.8	107.6	106.9	104.8 *	JP
US	144.4 *	145.1 *	146.2 *	148.9 *	148.0	144.6	143.9	147.8	143.4	143.0	139.8	US

Growth rate of GDP at constant prices (base year 1995). Percentage change on previous year

	1991	1992	1993	1994	1995	1996	1997	1998	1999	2000	2001	
EU-15	:	1.3	- 0.4	2.8	2.4	1.6	2.5	2.9	2.8	3.4	1.5	EU-15
€-zone	:	1.6	- 0.8	2.4	2.2	1.4	2.3	2.9	2.8	3.5	1.4	€-zone
B	1.8	1.5	- 1.0	3.2	2.4	1.2	3.6	2.0	3.2	3.7	0.8	B
DK	1.1	0.6	0.0	5.5	2.8	2.5	3.0	2.5	2.3	3.0	1.0	DK
D	:	2.2	- 1.1	2.3	1.7	0.8	1.4	2.0	2.0	2.9	0.6	D
EL	3.1	0.7	- 1.6	2.0	2.1	2.4	3.6	3.4	3.6	4.2	4.1	EL
E	2.5	0.9	- 1.0	2.4	2.8	2.4	4.0	4.3	4.2	4.2	2.7	E
F	1.0	1.5	- 0.9	2.1	1.7	1.1	1.9	3.4	3.2	3.8	1.8	F
IRL	1.9	3.3	2.7	5.8	9.9	8.1	10.9	8.8	11.1	10.0	5.7	IRL
I	1.4	0.8	- 0.9	2.2	2.9	1.1	2.0	1.8	1.6	2.9	1.8	I
L	8.6	1.8	4.2	3.8	1.3	3.7	7.7	7.5	6.0	8.9	1.0	L
NL	2.5	1.7	0.9	2.6	3.0	3.0	3.8	4.3	4.0	3.3	1.3	NL
A	3.3	2.3	0.4	2.6	1.6	2.0	1.6	3.9	2.7	3.5	0.7	A
P	4.4	1.1	- 2.0	1.0	4.3	3.5	3.9	4.5	3.5	3.5	1.7	P
FIN	- 6.3	- 3.3	- 1.1	4.0	3.8	4.0	6.3	5.3	4.1	6.1	0.7	FIN
S	- 1.1	- 1.7	- 1.8	4.1	3.7	1.1	2.1	3.6	4.5	3.6	1.2	S
UK	- 1.4	0.2	2.5	4.7	2.9	2.6	3.4	2.9	2.4	3.1	2.0	UK
IS	0.7	- 3.3	0.6	4.5	0.1	5.2	4.6	5.3	3.9	5.0	1.5 *	IS
NO	3.8	3.3	2.7	5.3	4.4	5.3	5.2	2.6	2.1	2.4	1.4	NO
JP	3.1	0.9	0.4	1.0	1.6	3.5	1.8	- 1.1	0.7	2.4	0.1	JP
US	- 0.5	3.1	2.7	4.0	2.7	3.6	4.4	4.3	4.1	3.8	0.3	US

Consumption and spending

Final consumption: 'spending' the GDP

Following the 'expenditure approach', the GDP is the sum of final uses of goods and services. In simpler words: the tables in this section on 'final consumption expenditure' show for what purpose the goods and services (whose production has been recorded in the section 'Economic output') have been used.

According to the ESA regulation, final consumption expenditure consists of expenditure incurred by resident institutional units on goods or services that are used for the direct satisfaction of individual needs or wants or the collective needs of members of the community (ESA 95, 3.75). The acquisition of these goods and services is financed from the disposable income of households.

— The **private final consumption expenditure** includes households' and NPISHs' final consumption expenditure. Households consist of employers, employees, recipients of property incomes, recipients of pensions and recipients of other transfer incomes. NPISHs consist of non-profit-making institutions which are separate legal entities, which serve households and which are private non-market producers. Their principal resources, apart from those derived from occasional sales, are derived from voluntary contributions in cash or in kind from households in their capacity as consumers, from payments made by general governments and from property income.

— **Government final consumption expenditure** (ESA 95, 3.79) includes two categories of expenditure: the value of goods and services produced by general government itself other than own-account capital formation, and sales and purchases by general government of goods and services produced by market producers that are supplied to households — without any transformation — as social transfers in kind.

— **Gross fixed capital formation** (ESA 95, 3.102) consists of resident producers' acquisitions, less disposals, of fixed assets during a given period plus certain additions to the value of non-produced assets realised by the productive activity of producers or institutional units. Fixed assets are tangible or intangible assets produced as outputs from processes of production that are themselves used repeatedly, or continuously, in processes of production for more than one year.

— **Changes in inventories** (ESA 95, 3.117) are measured by the value of the entries into inventories less the value of withdrawals and the value of any recurrent losses of goods held in inventories.

— **External balance** (ESA 95, 8.68): imports of goods and services are recorded on the resources side of the account and exports of goods and services on the uses side. The difference between resources and uses is the balancing item in the account, called 'external balance of goods and services'. If it is positive, there is a surplus for the rest of the world and a deficit for the total economy, and vice versa if it is negative.

3

Final consumption expenditure of households and non-profit institutions serving households. Current series in % of GDP

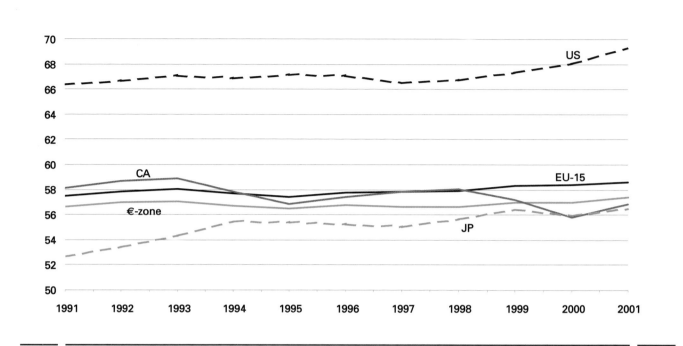

3

Gross fixed capital formation (investments). Current series in % of GDP

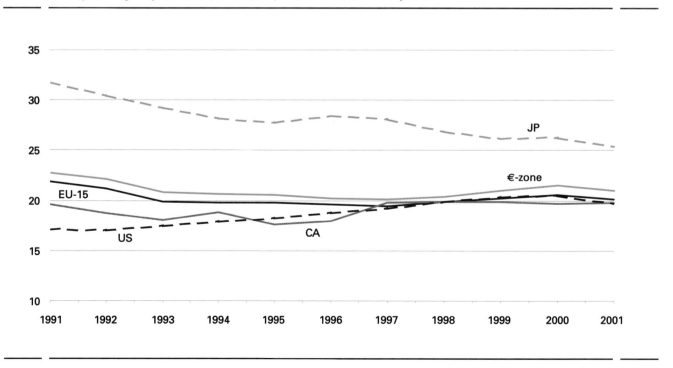

Income of the input factors

Factor income: 'earning' the GDP

Producing the GDP requires 'input factors' like the work of employees and capital. These income factors have to be paid for. The income side approach shows GDP as it is distributed among different participants in the production process. It is therefore represented as the sum of:

— **the compensation of employees:** this is defined as the total remuneration, in cash or in kind, payable by an employer to an employee in return for work done by the latter during the accounting period (ESA 95, 4.02). The compensation of employees is broken down into: (i) wages and salaries (wages and salaries in cash, wages and salaries in kind); (ii) employers' social contributions (employers' actual social contributions, employers' imputed social contributions);

— **the gross operating surplus of the total economy:** this is the surplus (or deficit) on production activities before account has been taken of the interest, rents or charges paid or received for the use of assets.

— the **mixed income of the total economy:** this is the remuneration for the work carried out by the owner (or by members of his/her family) of an unincorporated enterprise. This is referred to as 'mixed income' since it cannot be distinguished from the entrepreneurial profit of the owner.

— **taxes on production and imports less subsidies:** this consists of compulsory, unrequited payments to general government or institutions of the European Union, in respect of the production or import of goods and services, the employment of labour, and the ownership or use of land, buildings or other assets used in production.

Compensation of employees. Current series in % of GDP

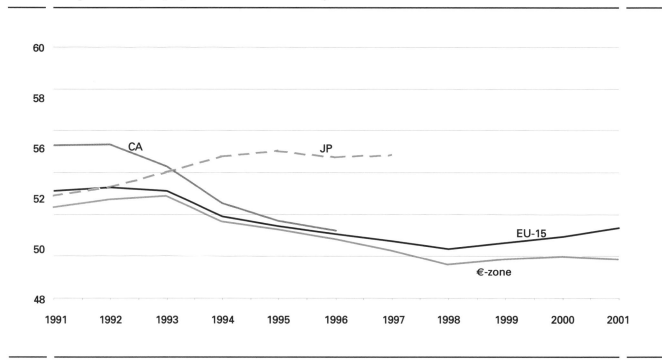

Gross operating surplus and mixed income: total economy. Current series in % of GDP

	1991	1992	1993	1994	1995	1996	1997	1998	1999	2000	2001	
EU-15	36.0	35.8	35.8	36.7	37.1	37.4	37.4	37.2	36.7	36.4	36.3	**EU-15**
€-zone	37.2	36.7	36.4	37.2	37.5	37.9	38.2	38.3	37.8	37.8	38.1	**€-zone**
B	36.5	36.3	35.7	36.1	36.7	36.5	36.6	36.8	36.3	36.5	35.8	**B**
DK	31.3	32.3	32.4	33.6	33.5	33.1	32.7	30.6	31.1	32.9	32.0	**DK**
D	34.3	33.4	33.2	34.3	34.8	35.3	36.0	36.4	35.8	35.2	35.3	**D**
EL	:	:	:	:	57.1	56.8	55.4	54.8	53.9	53.9	54.7	**EL**
E	39.7	38.5	39.4	40.4	41.4	41.4	41.0	40.5	39.8	39.7	39.9	**E**
F	34.1	34.3	34.1	34.3	33.9	33.4	33.6	34.0	33.7	33.8	33.3	**F**
IRL	41.9	40.8	41.8	41.1	44.2	45.0	46.3	48.6	48.5	48.4	48.6	**IRL**
I	44.2	44.1	43.9	45.3	46.6	47.0	46.1	45.3	45.3	45.4	45.6	**I**
L	36.6	34.5	34.5	35.2	34.9	35.6	37.8	39.3	38.3	38.4	35.6	**L**
NL	39.5	38.6	37.7	39.2	39.0	38.9	39.2	38.5	37.4	37.7	36.9	**NL**
A	34.0	33.7	33.0	33.2	33.5	34.7	34.3	35.1	34.6	35.7	35.9	**A**
P	:	:	:	:	39.4	39.3	39.2	42.3	:	:	:	**P**
FIN	29.8	32.0	35.9	37.9	39.1	38.5	39.1	39.7	39.1	41.0	40.0	**FIN**
S	:	:	31.6	33.4	34.9	31.8	31.5	30.4	29.8	28.8	27.4	**S**
UK	29.8	30.1	31.7	33.1	33.2	34.0	33.5	32.7	31.8	31.1	30.2	**UK**

eurostat

Government finances

Measuring government finances in the EU and the euro zone ...

The EU Member States that participate in the euro zone acknowledge the need for solid and sustainable government finances. Member States are to avoid situations of 'excessive government deficits': their ratio of planned or actual government deficit to gross domestic product (GDP) should be no more than 3 %, and their ratio of government debt to GDP should be no more than 60 % (unless the excess over the reference value is only exceptional or temporary, or unless the ratios have declined substantially and continuously). The rules on budgetary discipline were clarified and tightened under the Stability and Growth Pact (Amsterdam, 1997).

In the framework of the European statistical system, the criterion 'excessive deficit' is measured comparably for all EU Member States. The EU Member States notify their government deficit and debt statistics to the European Commission on 1 March and 1 September of each year under the 'excessive deficit procedure'.

Eurostat collects the data and ensures that the data from all Member States are in accordance with the relevant regulations.

... more than just about the surplus or deficit

Government finance statistics offer much more information on the general government sector, for example on:

— general government output;

— current taxes on income and wealth;

— social contributions;

— total general government revenue;

— gross fixed capital formation;

— total general government expenditure;

— final consumption expenditure;

— taxes on production and imports;

— subsidies;

— social benefits (other than social transfers in kind).

Further reading:

— ESA 95 manual on government deficit and debt
— Money, finance and the euro: statistics

Do you need more information?
— Ask your Data Shop (see last page)
— http://www.europa.eu.int/comm/eurostat
— Eurostat's data serves the political discussion in Europe. Have a look at the website of the "Economic and Financial Affairs DG":
  http://europa.eu.int/comm/dgs/economy_finance/index_en.htm

General government output as % of GDP

		1995	1996	1997	1998	1999	2000	2001	
EU-15		18.7	18.8	18.4	18.1	18.2	18.1	:	EU-15
€-zone		17.8	17.9	17.6	17.3	17.3	17.1	:	€-zone
B		16.5	16.5	16.3	16.2	16.2	16.0	16.2	B
DK		27.6	27.7	27.3	27.8	27.6	26.8	27.3	DK
D		14.7	14.5	14.1	13.8	13.7	13.5	13.3	D
EL		16.7	15.9	16.6	16.8	16.8	17.1	16.9	EL
E		17.0	16.8	16.5	16.2	16.1	16.1	16.0	E
F		21.9	22.4	22.5	21.7	21.6	21.4	21.3	F
IRL		16.6	15.8	15.2	14.5	14.0	13.6	:	IRL
I		17.2	17.5	17.6	17.4	17.5	17.6	17.6	I
L		16.6	16.7	15.8	15.0	14.5	13.7	14.6	L
NL		19.8	19.5	19.1	18.9	19.1	18.8	19.1	NL
A		21.4	21.2	18.0	17.8	17.8	17.3	16.4	A
P		19.0	19.4	19.5	19.5	20.5	21.4	21.3	P
FIN		27.5	28.0	26.8	25.7	25.5	24.4	24.8	FIN
S		29.5	29.8	29.3	29.3	29.2	28.1	28.5	S
UK		20.7	20.3	19.3	18.9	19.4	19.7	20.3	UK

3

Total general government revenue as % of GDP

		1995	1996	1997	1998	1999	2000	2001	
EU-15		:	46.8	46.9	46.6	47.0	46.8	:	EU-15
€-zone		:	47.4	47.7	47.2	47.7	47.3	:	€-zone
B		48.5	49.0	49.4	49.8	49.7	49.4	49.3	B
DK		:	58.8	58.3	58.7	59.1	56.5	57.0	DK
D		46.1	46.9	46.6	46.6	47.3	47.0	45.5	D
EL		40.3	41.8	43.4	45.0	46.0	48.1	46.9	EL
E		38.4	38.8	39.0	39.1	39.7	39.6	39.8	E
F		49.7	51.4	51.9	51.2	51.8	51.4	51.3	F
IRL		:	39.4	38.6	37.3	36.9	36.7	:	IRL
I		45.8 *	46.1	48.4	46.8	47.1	46.3	46.2	I
L		47.7	47.5	46.6	45.2	45.2	45.4	46.5	L
NL		47.3	47.8	47.1	46.4	47.6	47.4	46.5	NL
A		52.0	52.8	52.1	51.7	51.7	50.8	52.3	A
P		40.6	41.8	41.8	41.6	43.0	42.5	42.2	P
FIN		56.2 *	56.8	55.3	54.5	54.1	55.7	54.1	FIN
S		60.0	62.2	61.6	62.9	61.6	61.4	62.3	S
UK		38.9	38.6	38.9	40.1	40.3	40.9	41.4	UK

eurostat

General government gross fixed capital formation as % of GDP

	1995	1996	1997	1998	1999	2000	2001	
EU-15	2.6	2.4	2.2	2.2	2.3	2.3	:	**EU-15**
€-zone	2.7	2.6	2.4	2.4	2.5	2.5	:	**€-zone**
B	1.8	1.6	1.6	1.5	1.8	1.8	1.5	**B**
DK	1.8	2.0	1.9	1.7	1.7	1.7	1.7	**DK**
D	2.3	2.1	1.9	1.9	1.9	1.8	1.7	**D**
EL	3.2	3.2	3.4	3.6	3.6	3.8	3.8	**EL**
E	3.7	3.1	3.1	3.3	3.4	3.2	3.3	**E**
F	3.3	3.2	3.0	2.9	3.0	3.2	3.3	**F**
IRL	2.3	2.4	2.5	2.7	3.1	3.8	:	**IRL**
I	2.1	2.2	2.2	2.4	2.4	2.4	2.5	**I**
L	4.6	4.7	4.2	4.5	4.6	4.1	4.4	**L**
NL	3.0	3.1	2.9	2.9	3.0	3.2	3.4	**NL**
A	3.1	2.8	2.0	1.8	1.7	1.5	1.2	**A**
P	3.7	4.2	4.4	3.9	4.2	3.9	4.1	**P**
FIN	2.8	2.9	3.2	2.9	2.9	2.5	2.6	**FIN**
S	3.4	3.0	2.7	2.7	2.7	2.5	2.6	**S**
UK	2.0	1.5	1.2	1.2	1.1	1.1	1.3	**UK**

Total general government expenditure as % of GDP

	1995	1996	1997	1998	1999	2000	2001	
EU-15	:	51.0	49.3	48.3	47.8	46.2	:	**EU-15**
€-zone	:	51.6	50.3	49.4	49.0	47.1	:	**€-zone**
B	52.8	52.8	51.3	50.6	50.2	49.3	49.0	**B**
DK	:	59.8	58.0	57.6	56.0	54.0	54.2	**DK**
D	56.1	50.3	49.3	48.8	48.8	45.9	48.3	**D**
EL	50.5	49.2	47.4	47.4	47.9	48.9	46.9	**EL**
E	45.0	43.7	42.2	41.7	40.9	40.2	39.9	**E**
F	55.2	55.5	55.0	53.9	53.4	52.8	52.7	**F**
IRL	:	39.6	37.4	35.0	34.5	32.2	:	**IRL**
I	53.4 *	53.2	51.1	49.9	48.9	46.9	48.4	**I**
L	45.1	45.5	43.8	42.1	41.7	39.8	40.4	**L**
NL	56.4	49.6	48.2	47.2	46.9	45.3	46.4	**NL**
A	57.3	56.8	54.1	54.2	54.1	52.5	52.3	**A**
P	45.0	45.8	44.8	44.1	45.4	45.4	46.4	**P**
FIN	59.9 *	59.9	56.8	53.2	52.2	48.7	49.1	**FIN**
S	67.6	65.3	63.2	60.8	60.3	57.7	57.4	**S**
UK	44.6	43.0	41.1	39.8	39.1	39.3	40.5	**UK**

Public balance. Net borrowing/lending of consolidated general government sector as % of GDP

	1991	1992	1993	1994	1995	1996	1997	1998	1999	2000	2001	
EU-15	:	:	:	:	:	- 4.2	- 2.4	- 1.6 #	- 0.7 #	1.0 #	- 0.8 #	EU-15
€-zone	:	:	:	:	:	- 4.2	- 2.6	- 2.2 #	- 1.3 #	0.2 #	- 1.5 #	€-zone
B	- 7.4	- 8.0	- 7.3	- 5.0	- 4.3	- 3.7	- 2.0	- 0.7 #	- 0.5 #	0.1 #	0.4 #	B
DK	- 2.4	- 2.2	- 2.9	- 2.4	- 2.3	- 1.0	0.4	1.1	3.1	2.5	3.1 #	DK
D	- 3.0	- 2.5	- 3.1	- 2.4	- 3.3	- 3.4	- 2.7	- 2.2 #	- 1.5 #	1.1 #	- 2.8 #	D
EL	- 11.4	- 11.1	- 13.4	- 9.4	- 10.2	- 7.4	- 4.0	- 2.5 #	- 1.9 #	- 1.8 #	- 1.2 #	EL
E	:	:	:	:	:	- 4.9	- 3.2	- 2.7 #	- 1.1 #	- 0.6 #	- 0.1 #	E
F	- 2.4	- 4.2	- 6.0	- 5.5	- 5.5	- 4.1	- 3.0	- 2.7	- 1.6 #	- 1.3 #	- 1.4 #	F
IRL	- 2.9	- 3.0	- 2.7	- 2.0	- 2.2	- 0.2	1.2	2.4 #	2.2 #	4.4 #	1.5 #	IRL
I	- 11.7	- 10.7	- 10.3	- 9.3	- 7.6	- 7.1	- 2.7	- 2.8	- 1.8 #	- 0.5 #	- 2.2 #	I
L	1.3	2.5	4.8	4.5	2.3	2.6	3.4	3.1 #	3.6 #	5.6 #	6.1 #	L
NL	- 2.7	- 4.2	- 2.8	- 3.5	- 4.2	- 1.8	- 1.1	- 0.8	0.7 #	2.2 #	0.1 #	NL
A	- 3.0	- 2.0	- 4.2	- 5.0	- 5.2	- 3.8	- 1.9	- 2.4	- 2.3 #	- 1.5 #	0.2 #	A
P	- 8.1	- 6.0	- 8.9	- 6.6	- 4.5	- 4.0	- 2.7	- 2.6 #	- 2.4 #	- 2.9 #	- 4.1 #	P
FIN	- 1.1	- 5.6	- 7.3	- 5.7	- 3.7	- 3.2	- 1.5	1.3	1.9	7.0 #	4.9 #	FIN
S	:	:	- 11.9	- 10.8	- 7.9	- 3.4	- 1.5	1.9	1.5	3.7	4.8 #	S
UK	- 2.8	- 6.5	- 8.0	- 6.7	- 5.7	- 4.3	- 2.0	0.2 #	1.1 #	3.9 #	0.8 #	UK
IS	- 2.9	- 2.8	- 4.6	- 4.7	- 3.0	- 1.6	0.0	0.5	2.1	2.3	- 0.2 *	IS
NO	:	:	:	0.4	3.5	6.6	7.9	3.6	6.4	17.2	15.7	NO
JP	1.8	0.8	- 2.4	- 2.8	- 4.2	- 4.9	- 3.7	- 5.5	- 7.0	- 6.6	- 6.4 *	JP
US	- 5.0	- 5.9	- 5.0	- 3.6	- 3.1	- 2.2	- 0.9	0.3	0.8	1.7	0.6 *	US

3

General government consolidated gross debt as % of GDP

	1991	1992	1993	1994	1995	1996	1997	1998	1999	2000	2001	
EU-15	:	:	:	66.2	70.6	72.5	71.0 #	68.8 #	67.7 #	63.8 #	63.1 #	EU-15
€-zone	58.2	60.0	65.5	68.2	73.0	74.5	74.3 #	73.5 #	71.9 #	69.4 #	69.2 #	€-zone
B	130.9	132.5	138.2	135.9	134.0	130.2	124.8	119.2 #	114.9 #	109.2 #	107.6 #	B
DK	62.5	66.3	78.0	73.5	69.3	65.1	61.2	56.2	52.7	46.8	44.7 #	DK
D	40.4	42.9	46.9	49.3	57.0	59.8	61.0	60.9	61.2	60.2	59.5 #	D
EL	82.2	87.8	110.1	107.9	108.7	111.3	108.2	105.8 #	105.1 #	106.2 #	107.0 #	EL
E	44.3	46.8	58.4	61.1	63.9	68.1	66.6	64.6 #	63.1 #	60.5 #	57.1 #	E
F	35.8	39.6	45.3	48.4	54.6	57.1	59.3	59.5	58.5	57.3	57.3	F
IRL	102.8	100.1	96.2	90.4	82.7	74.1	65.0	55.2 #	49.7 #	39.1 #	36.4 #	IRL
I	100.6	107.7	118.1	123.8	123.2	122.1	120.2 #	116.3 #	114.5 #	110.5 #	109.8 #	I
L	3.8	4.7	5.7	5.4	5.6	6.2	6.1	6.3	6.0	5.6	5.6	L
NL	76.9	77.8	79.0	76.3	77.2	75.2	69.9	66.8	63.1 #	55.8 #	52.8 #	NL
A	57.5	57.2	61.8	64.7	69.2	69.1	64.7	63.9	64.9	63.6 #	63.2 #	A
P	60.7	54.4	59.1	62.1	64.3	62.9	59.1	55.0	54.4 #	53.3 #	55.5 #	P
FIN	22.6	40.6	56.0	58.0	57.2	57.1	54.1	48.8	46.8	44.0 #	43.4 #	FIN
S	:	:	:	76.2	76.2	76.0	73.1	70.5 #	65.0 #	55.3 #	56.6 #	S
UK	34.4	39.2	45.4	48.5	51.8	52.3	50.8	47.7	45.1	42.1	39.1 #	UK
IS	38.6	46.4	55.0	55.8	59.3	56.7	53.3	48.4	43.5	41.2	46.6 *	IS
NO	:	:	:	:	:	:	27.9	27.1	29.9	36.7	31.4	NO
JP	61.1	63.5	69.0	73.9	80.4	86.5	92.0	103.0	115.5	122.8	131.2 *	JP
US	71.4	74.1	75.8	75.0	74.5	73.9	71.4	68.3	65.3	59.4	57.5 *	US

Social protection

Social protection: relieving the burden

Social protection encompasses all action by public or private bodies to relieve households and individuals of the burden of a defined set of risks or needs associated with old age, sickness, childbearing and family, disability, unemployment, etc.

The data on social protection expenditure and receipts are harmonised according to the European system of integrated social protection statistics (Esspros).

Eurostat provides more detailed information on social protection in the NewCronos domain 'sespros'. If you wish to benefit from this, please contact your Data Shop. The addresses of the Data Shops can be found at the end of the yearbook.

The eight 'functions' to classify social protection benefits

Social protection expenditure includes provision of social benefits, administration costs and other expenditure (for example, interest paid to banks). Benefits provision represents the core of social protection expenditure. Expenditure on education is excluded.

Social benefits are direct transfers in cash or kind by social protection schemes to households and individuals to relieve them of the burden of distinct risks or needs. Benefits via the fiscal system are excluded.

Benefits are classified according to eight social protection 'functions':

1. sickness and healthcare;

2. disability;

3. old age;

4. survivors;

5. family and children;

6. unemployment;

7. housing;

8. social exclusion not elsewhere classified.

The following are brief explanations of the above functions.

— **Sickness/healthcare benefits** include mainly paid sick leave, medical care and provision of pharmaceutical products.

— **Disability benefits** include mainly disability pensions and the provision of goods and services (other than medical care) to the disabled.

— **Old-age benefits** include mainly old-age pensions and the provision of goods and services (other than medical care) to the elderly.

— **Survivors' benefits** include income maintenance and support in connection with the death of a family member, such as survivors' pensions.

— **Family/children benefits** include support (except healthcare) in connection with the costs of pregnancy, childbirth, childbearing and caring for other family members.

— **Unemployment benefits** also include vocational training financed by public agencies.

— **Housing benefits** include interventions by public authorities to help households meet the cost of housing.

— **Social exclusion benefits** include income support, rehabilitation of alcohol and drug abusers and other miscellaneous benefits (except healthcare).

Financing social protection

Units responsible for providing social protection are financed in different ways. Their receipts comprise social contributions paid by employers and by protected persons, contributions by general government and other receipts. Other receipts come from a variety of sources, for example interest, dividends, rent and claims against third parties.

Social contributions are paid by employers and by the protected persons.

Social contributions by employers are all costs incurred by employers to secure employees' entitlement to social benefits. These include all payments by employers to social protection institutions (actual contributions) and social benefits paid directly by employers to employees (imputed contributions). Social contributions by protected persons comprise contributions paid by employees, by the self-employed and by pensioners and other persons.

Social benefits are recorded without any deduction of taxes or other compulsory levies payable on them by beneficiaries. 'Tax benefits' (tax reductions granted to households for social protection purposes) are generally excluded.

Further reading:

Eurostat publications
— **The social situation in the European Union**
— **European social statistics — Social protection — Expenditure and receipts**

Statistics in Focus — Theme 3
— **No 1   Social protection in Europe**

Do you need more information?
— **Ask your Data Shop (see last page)**
— **http://www.europa.eu.int/comm/eurostat— Eurostat's data serves the political discussion in Europe. Have a look at the website of the "DG Employment and Social Affairs": http://europa.eu.int/comm/dgs/employment_social/index_en.htm**

Total expenditure on social protection at current prices as % of GDP

	1991	1992	1993	1994	1995	1996	1997	1998	1999	2000	
EU-15	26.4	27.7	28.8	28.5	28.2	28.4	28.0	27.6 *	27.5 *	:	EU-15
B	27.1	27.4	29.3	28.7	28.1	28.6	27.9	27.6 *	27.4 *	26.7 *	B
DK	29.7	30.3	31.9	32.8	32.2	31.4	30.4	30.2	29.8	28.8	DK
D	26.1	27.6	28.4	28.3	28.9	29.9	29.5	29.3	29.6	29.5 *	D
EL	21.6	21.2	22.1	22.1	22.3	22.9	23.3	24.2	25.5	26.4 *	EL
E	21.2	22.4	24.0	22.8	22.1	21.9	21.2	20.6 *	20.2 *	20.1 *	E
F	28.4	29.3	30.7	30.5	30.7	31.0	30.8	30.5	30.2	:	F
IRL	19.6	20.3	20.2	19.7	18.9	17.8	16.7	15.5	14.8	14.1	IRL
I	25.2	26.2	26.4	26.0	24.8	24.8	25.5	25.0	25.3 *	25.2 *	I
L	22.5	22.6	23.7	23.0	23.7	24.0	22.6	21.7	21.8	21.0	L
NL	32.6	33.2	33.6	31.7	30.9	30.1	29.4	28.4	28.0	27.4 *	NL
A	27.0	27.6	28.9	29.8	29.6	29.5	28.8	28.4	28.8	28.7	A
P	16.5	18.2	20.7	20.8	20.8	21.4	21.6	22.2	22.7	:	P
FIN	29.8	33.6	34.6	33.8	31.8	31.6	29.3	27.3	26.7	25.2 *	FIN
S	34.3	37.1	39.0	37.6	35.5	34.7	33.8	33.4	32.9	32.3 *	S
UK	25.7	27.9	29.0	28.6	28.2	28.1	27.5	26.9	26.6	:	UK
IS	17.7	18.3	19.4	18.4	19.0	18.8	18.6	18.5	19.1	19.5	IS
NO	27.3	28.4	28.3	27.6	26.8	26.1	25.4	27.3	27.7	25.1	NO
EEA	26.4	27.7	28.7	28.4	28.2	28.4	28.0	27.6	27.5 *	:	EEA
CH	21.3	23.3	24.8	25.2	25.8	26.9	28.0	28.0	28.3	28.7	CH

Total expenditure on social protection per head of population in ECU/EUR. 1999

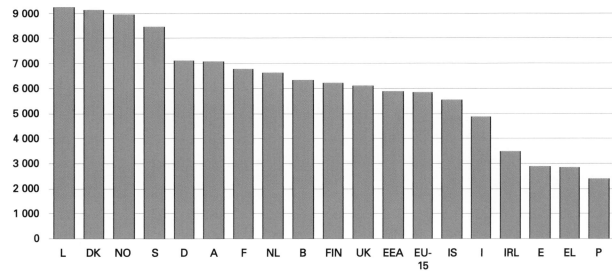

Social benefits by functions as % of total benefits. 1999. EU-15

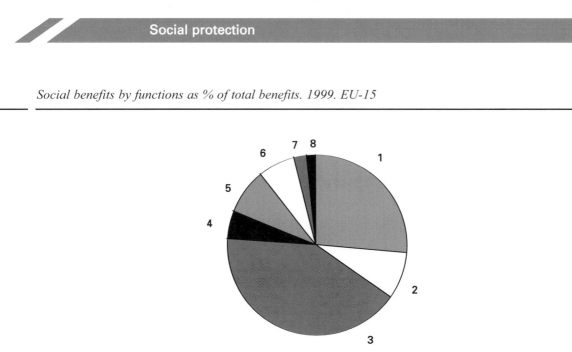

1. Sickness/healthcare; 2. Disability; 3. Old age; 4. Survivors; 5. Family/children; 6. Unemployment; 7. Housing; 8. Social exclusion n.e.c.

Social protection receipts by type as % of total receipts. 1999

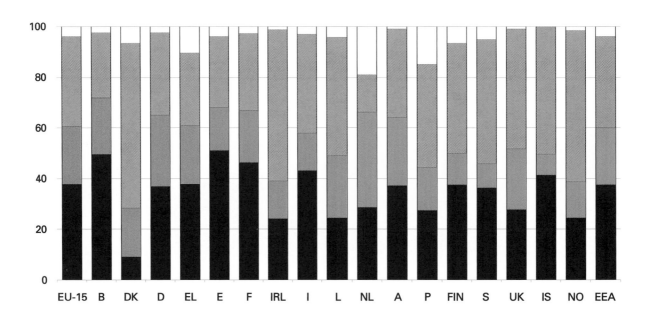

Black: employers' social contributions; colour: social contributions paid by protected persons; grey: general government contributions; white: other receipts.

Protected persons include employees, the self-employed, pensioners and other people.

Consumer prices

HICPs: a comparable measure of inflation in the EU

The harmonised indices of consumer prices (HICPs) provide the best statistical basis for comparisons of consumer price inflation within the EU. The methodology ensures comparability between Member States. Eurostat publishes the HICPs monthly, about 18 days after the end of the reporting month. The HICP series starts with the index for January 1995. For ease of comparison, they are presented with a common base year, 1996 = 100.

HICP coverage

HICPs cover virtually all forms of household expenditure on goods and services (household final monetary consumption expenditure — HFMCE). HICP coverage follows the international classification Coicop (classification of individual consumption by purpose), adapted to the needs of HICPs.

HICP aggregate indices

There are three aggregate indices of the HICPs: the monetary union index of consumer prices (MUICP) for the euro zone; the European index of consumer prices (EICP) for EU-15; the European Economic Area index of consumer prices (EEAICP), which additionally covers Iceland and Norway.

The HICP methodology allows country weights to change each year: for the MUICP, a Member State's weight is its share of HFMCE in the EMU total; for the EICP and the EEAICP, a Member State's weight is its share of HFMCE expressed in euro in the EU and EEA totals. For the latter two indices, expenditure in national currencies is converted using purchasing power parities. The HICP is computed as an annual chain index. Starting in 1999, the MUICP is treated as a single entity within the EICP.

Price stability in the euro zone

With the launch of the euro in January 1999, the MUICP is used for the monitoring of inflation in the EMU and for assessment of inflation convergence. As price stability is the primary objective of the European System of Central Banks, the MUICP is used by the European Central Bank (ECB) as a prime indicator for monetary policy management for the euro zone. The ECB has defined price stability as a year-on-year increase in the HICP for the euro zone of below 2 %.

General inflation trends

The annual rate of change as measured by the harmonised index of consumer prices for EU-15 (EICP) shows a downward trend from the beginning of 1996 to the end of 1998, followed by a general upward trend. This upward trend can broadly be attributed to rising energy prices. The EICP then increased, peaking in mid-2001 and at the beginning of 2002, before falling back to an annual rate of 1.8 % by June 2002. The harmonised index for the euro zone (MUICP) shows a similar pattern.

3

Harmonised annual average consumer price indices. Index 1996 = 100

	1995	1996	1997	1998	1999	2000	2001	
EU-15	97.7 *	100.0 *	101.7	103.0	104.3	106.2	108.6 #	EU-15
€-zone	97.9 *	100.0 *	101.6	102.7	103.8	106.0	108.5 #	€-zone
B	98.3	100.0	101.5	102.4	103.6	106.4	109.0	B
DK	98.0	100.0	101.9	103.3	105.4	108.3	110.7	DK
D	98.8	100.0	101.5	102.1	102.8	104.2 #	106.2 #	D
EL	92.7	100.0	105.4	110.2	112.6	115.8	120.1	EL
E	96.6	100.0	101.9	103.7	106.0	109.7	112.8	E
F	98.0	100.0	101.3	102.0	102.5	104.4	106.3	F
IRL	97.9 *	100.0 *	101.2	103.4	106.0	111.5	116.0	IRL
I	96.2	100.0	101.9	103.9	105.7	108.4	110.9	I
L	98.8	100.0	101.4	102.4	103.4	107.3	109.9	L
NL	98.6	100.0	101.9	103.7	105.8	108.2	113.8	NL
A	98.3	100.0	101.2	102.0	102.5	104.5	106.9	A
P	97.2	100.0	101.9	104.2	106.4	109.4	114.2	P
FIN	98.9	100.0	101.2	102.6	103.9	107.0	109.8	FIN
S	99.2	100.0	101.9	102.9	103.4	104.8	107.6	S
UK	97.6	100.0	101.8	103.4	104.8	105.6	106.9	UK
IS	97.9	100.0	101.8	103.2	105.4	110.0	117.3	IS
NO	99.3	100.0	102.6	104.6	106.8	110.0	113.0	NO
EEA	97.7 *	100.0 *	101.7	103.1	104.3	106.3	108.6 #	EEA

3

Inflation rate. Annual average rate of change in harmonised indices of consumer prices (HICPs)

	1996	1997	1998	1999	2000	2001	
EU-15	2.4 *	1.7 *	1.3	1.2	2.1	2.3	EU-15
€-zone	2.2 *	1.6 *	1.1	1.1	2.3	2.5	€-zone
B	1.8	1.5	0.9	1.1	2.7	2.4	B
DK	2.1	1.9	1.3	2.1	2.7	2.3	DK
D	1.2	1.5	0.6	0.6	2.1	2.4	D
EL	7.9	5.4	4.5	2.1	2.9	3.7	EL
E	3.6	1.9	1.8	2.2	3.5	2.8	E
F	2.1	1.3	0.7	0.6	1.8	1.8	F
IRL	2.2 *	1.2 *	2.1	2.5	5.3	4.0	IRL
I	4.0	1.9	2.0	1.7	2.6	2.3	I
L	1.2	1.4	1.0	1.0	3.8	2.4	L
NL	1.4	1.9	1.8	2.0	2.3	5.1	NL
A	1.8	1.2	0.8	0.5	2.0	2.3	A
P	2.9	1.9	2.2	2.2	2.8	4.4	P
FIN	1.1	1.2	1.4	1.3	3.0	2.7	FIN
S	0.8	1.8	1.0	0.6	1.3	2.7	S
UK	2.5	1.8	1.6	1.3	0.8	1.2	UK
IS	2.2	1.8	1.3	2.1	4.4	6.6	IS
NO	0.7	2.6	2.0	2.1	3.0	2.7	NO
JP	0.2	:	0.7	- 0.3	- 0.7	- 0.7	JP
US	2.9	:	1.5	2.2	3.4	2.8	US

US, JP: data on the national consumer price indices are given, which are not strictly comparable with the HICPs.

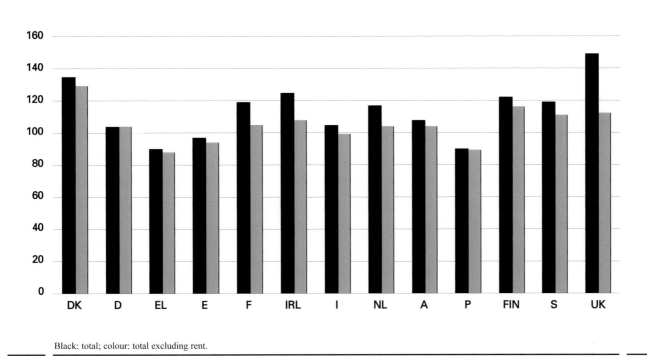

Cost-of-living comparisons in the European Union. 2002. B = 100

Black: total; colour: total excluding rent.

Country codes refer to the capital of the countries.

Cost-of-living comparisons in the European Union. B = 100

		1995	1996	1997	1998	1999	2000	2001	2002	
DK		123	125	129	129	132	132	133	135	DK
D		111	111	110	108	108	107	105	104	D
EL		80	86	88	84	87	85	87	90	EL
E		85	91	91	91	92	94	95	97	E
F		111	116	118	120	119	118	118	119	F
IRL		89	92	105	104	110	116	122	125	IRL
I		82	97	100	101	101	102	103	105	I
NL		103	105	108	112	114	114	115	117	NL
A		114	115	115	111	110	111	109	108	A
P		81	84	86	85	85	87	89	90	P
FIN		119	117	117	117	118	120	122	122	FIN
S		97	118	117	120	120	126	117	119	S
UK		101	115	142	157	157	160	164	149	UK

Country codes refer to the capital of the countries.

Relative price levels. Relative price levels of private final consumption including indirect taxes. EU-15 = 100.

	1991	1992	1993	1994	1995	1996	1997	1998	1999	2000	2001	
EU-15	100.0	100.0	100.0	100.0	100.0	100.0	100.0	100.0	100.0	100.0	100.0	**EU-15**
€-zone	:	:	:	:	:	:	:	:	:	:	:	**€-zone**
B	102.0	100.0	102.0	105.0	109.0	103.0	99.0	99.0	102.0	100.1	98.4	**B**
DK	131.0	133.0	133.0	130.0	133.0	126.0	126.0	124.0	122.0	121.3	125.7	**DK**
D	107.0	109.0	115.0	112.0	115.0	112.0	106.0	106.0	104.0	99.6	101.9	**D**
EL	77.0	77.0	78.0	78.0	78.0	81.0	83.0	80.0	82.0	79.3	81.4	**EL**
E	95.0	95.0	86.0	84.0	83.0	83.0	82.0	84.0	83.0	83.0	82.5	**E**
F	101.0	103.0	109.0	110.0	111.0	113.0	106.0	104.0	105.0	101.9	98.8	**F**
IRL	95.0	95.0	91.0	90.0	86.0	94.0	97.0	99.0	103.0	107.8	112.8	**IRL**
I	99.0	98.0	98.0	86.0	80.0	87.0	89.0	88.0	86.0	88.6	91.6	**I**
L	92.0	93.0	97.0	100.0	106.0	101.0	100.0	101.0	98.0	96.4	99.4	**L**
NL	99.0	100.0	105.0	106.0	107.0	103.0	96.0	95.0	97.0	99.8	99.0	**NL**
A	105.0	105.0	110.0	110.0	115.0	109.0	106.0	106.0	101.0	96.9	98.0	**A**
P	68.0	75.0	73.0	69.0	73.0	74.0	73.0	72.0	73.0	72.3	73.9	**P**
FIN	:	129.0	108.0	116.0	123.0	117.0	119.0	118.0	120.0	116.1	116.7	**FIN**
S	148.0	146.0	121.0	120.0	118.0	127.0	126.0	122.0	125.0	127.8	121.7	**S**
UK	96.0	91.0	90.0	90.0	88.0	88.0	104.0	108.0	112.0	118.3	115.3	**UK**
IS	:	:	122.0	113.0	111.0	108.0	117.0	122.0	123.0	131.2	122.2	**IS**
NO	:	:	123.0	124.0	130.0	126.0	132.0	126.0	127.0	128.9	134.8	**NO**
JP	85.0	82.0	90.0	90.0	:	:	:	:	:	111.0	:	**JP**
US	122.0	122.0	150.0	159.0	:	:	:	:	:	162.0	:	**US**

3

 Price convergence between EU Member States

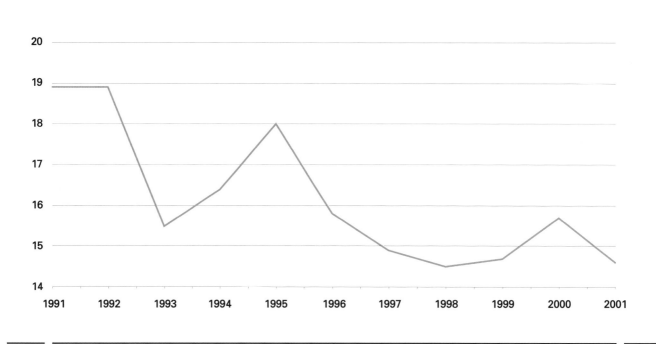

Price convergence — coefficient of variation of relative price levels of private final consumption including indirect taxes. If this coefficient becomes smaller, the relative prices of private final consumption in the individual Member States come closer together; in the opposite case, price levels deviate from each other. See also PPPs and PPS in the glossary.

Wages and labour costs

Results of the labour costs survey 2000

Information on labour costs is of major importance for employers' associations, trade unions, political parties, economists and other users who are interested in the level and structure of labour costs. The term 'labour costs' refers to the expenditure necessarily incurred by employers in order to employ workers. The results of the four-yearly European labour costs survey (LCS) for the year 2000 have recently become available. The results permit the comparison of total labour costs between different countries and between different industries within a country. Aggregate labour cost figures for 2000 are presented here in euro.

The 2000 LCS provides different breakdowns of total labour costs. Detailed descriptions are given in the glossary.

By far the largest component of total labour costs is accounted for by the gross annual earnings of employees. Data is presented for full-time employees for 'industry and services', broken down by gender; the ratio of female to male earnings is also portrayed. As for labour costs, the aggregate gross earnings are given in euro.

Tax rates on low-wage earners

In connection with low pay, one of the Commission's structural indicators is the 'tax rate on low-wage earners' which relates to a single person without children on 67 % of the average earning of a production worker in manufacturing. Tax rates differ markedly between the countries, but the trend across Europe in recent years is downwards. For information and for comparison, tax rates are also presented for a married couple with two children and with one spouse on 100 % of the average earning of a production worker in manufacturing.

3

Further reading:

Statistics in Focus — Theme 3
— No 3   Minimum wages in the European Union

Do you need more information?
— Ask your Data Shop (see last page)
— http://www.europa.eu.int/comm/eurostat
— Eurostat's data serves the political discussion in Europe. Have a look at the website of the
   "DG Employment and Social Affairs":
   http://europa.eu.int/comm/dgs/employment_social/index_en.htm

Gender pay gap. Average gross hourly earnings of females as % of average gross hourly earnings of males

	1994	1995	1996	1997	1998	1999	
EU-15	84 *	83 *	84 *	84 *	84 *	84 *	EU-15
€-zone	:	:	:	:	:	:	€-zone
B	87	88	90	90	91	89	B
DK	89	85	85	87	88	86	DK
D	79	79	79	79	78	81	D
EL	87	83	85	87	88	87	EL
E	90	87 *	86 *	86 *	84 *	86 *	E
F	87	87	87	88	88	88	F
IRL	81	80	79	81	80	78	IRL
I	92	92	92	93	93	91	I
L	83	81	82	:	:	:	L
NL	77	77	77	78	79	79	NL
A	:	78	80	78	79	79	A
P	90	95	94	93	94	95	P
FIN	:	:	83	82	81	81	FIN
S	84	85	83	83	82	83	S
UK	72	74	76	79	76	78	UK

3

Tax rate on low-wage earners. %. Single person without children on 67 % of the average earnings of a production worker in manufacturing. 1996–2001

	1996	1997	1998	1999	2000	2001	
EU-15	40.6	40.8	40.3	39.1	38.6	37.7	EU-15
B	50.5	49.5	51.1	51.0	49.9	49.1	B
DK	41.3	41.7	40.4	41.3	41.2	40.6	DK
D	46.5	47.7	47.5	47.0	46.5	45.5	D
EL	34.9	35.0	35.1	34.3	34.3	34.3	EL
E	34.4	34.8	35.1	32.6	32.8	33.3	E
F	44.3	41.6	42.5	40.3	39.6	38.4	F
IRL	26.5	24.9	23.4	21.5	18.1	17.4	IRL
I	48.3	48.8	44.4	44.1	43.3	42.8	I
L	29.1	29.7	28.9	29.5	30.4	28.8	L
NL	39.3	38.8	39.2	40.2	40.6	36.8	NL
A	41.0	41.1	41.5	41.6	40.1	39.7	A
P	30.6	30.8	30.7	30.2	30.4	29.5	P
FIN	44.4	44.2	44.0	42.6	42.4	41.0	FIN
S	48.6	49.2	49.3	48.7	47.9	46.8	S
UK	26.8	28.4	28.5	25.8	25.3	24.5	UK
IS	15.2	15.9	17.2	16.9	18.0	18.9	IS
NO	34.4	34.3	34.5	34.4	34.2	33.8	NO
JP	29.2	29.2	29.1	29.2	29.0	27.7	JP
US	18.4	19.4	17.7	23.1	23.1	23.2	US

eurostat

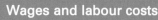

Tax rate on low wage earners. %. Single person without children on 67% of the average earnings of a production worker in manufacturing

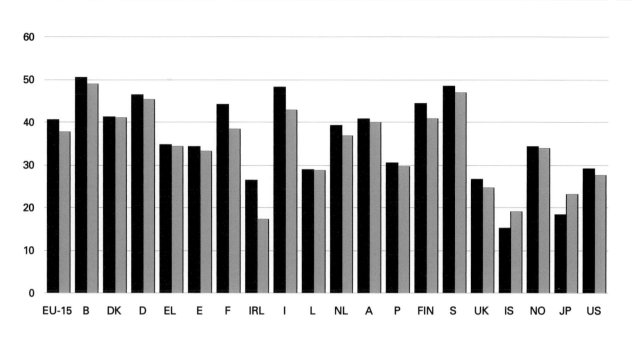

Black: 1996; colour: 2001.

3

Tax rate on low-wage earners. %. Married couple with two children with one working spouse on 100 % of the average earnings of a full-time production worker in manufacturing

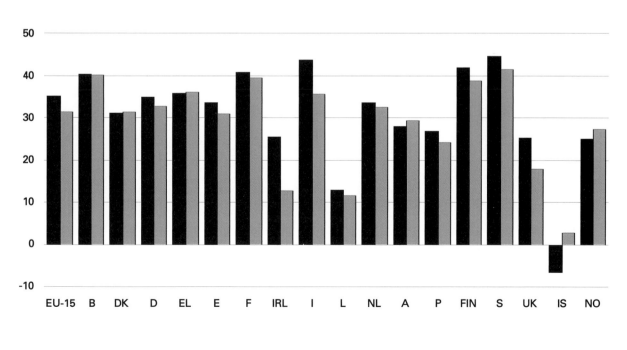

Black: 1996; colour: 2001.

eurostat

Financial market indicators

A wide range of financial market indicators

The NewCronos database contains a wide range of financial market data: Exchange rates, interest rates, stock and bond market information, data on banking transactions and money supply and other financial data are available.

For more information, please contact your Data Shop. The addresses of the Data Shops can be found at the end of the yearbook.

Financial market indicators in the Eurostat yearbook

The following financial market indicators are presented in this edition of the Eurostat yearbook.

— Nominal exchange rates of various currencies against the euro/ecu as well as the evolution of five leading currencies against the US dollar on an index basis (1995 = 100).

— Two short-term interest rates: the day-to-day money rate is the rate at which banks lend and borrow among themselves overnight on the interbank market. This rate averaged over a year is a good indicator of the state of monetary policy in that year. Since January 1999, the EONIA rate has replaced the national day-to-day money market rates for the 11 countries of the euro zone (since 2001 also for Greece).

Additionally, the three-month interbank rate for four leading economies is shown in a graph. Since the beginning of monetary union, Euribor has been the interbank offer rate for the Member States of the euro zone.

— Yields on 10-year government bonds are used as a measure for the long-term interest rates, one of the four convergence criteria which decide if a Member State is eligible for monetary union. The four convergence criteria are explained in detail in the glossary.

— Share price indices, which show the trend in share values on various stock exchanges. These indices have been re-based for the graph to 1995 = 100. For the European aggregates, Dow Jones Stoxx share price indices are used.

3

Further reading:

Eurostat publications
— **Money, finance and the euro: statistics (Monthly)**

Do you need more information?
— **Ask your Data Shop (see last page)**
— **http://www.europa.eu.int/comm/eurostat**
— **Eurostat's data serves the political discussion in Europe. Have a look at the website of the "Economic and Financial Affairs DG":**
    http://europa.eu.int/comm/dgs/economy_finance/index_en.htm

Exchange rates. Annual average. One unit of national currency = USD. 1995 = 100

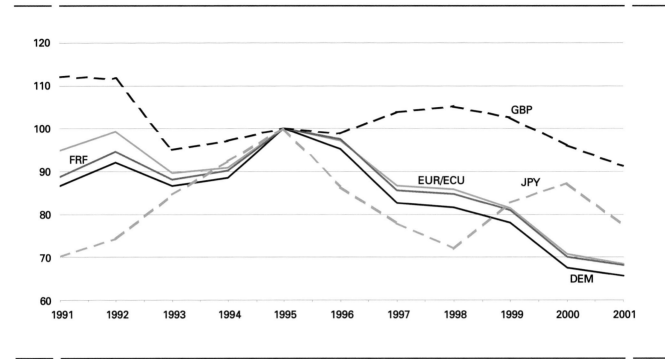

Ecu/euro exchange rates. Annual average. ECU/EUR 1 = ...

	1991	1992	1993	1994	1995	1996	1997	1998	1999	2000	2001	
B/L	42.2233	41.5932	40.4713	39.6565	38.5519	39.2986	40.5332	40.6207	40.3399	40.3399	40.3399	**B/L**
DK	7.90859	7.80925	7.59359	7.54328	7.32804	7.35934	7.48361	7.4993	7.43552	7.45382	7.45207	**DK**
D	2.05076	2.02031	1.93639	1.92453	1.87375	1.90954	1.96438	1.96913	1.95583	1.95583	1.95583	**D**
EL	225.216	247.026	268.568	288.026	302.989	305.546	309.355	330.731	325.82	336.678	340.75	**EL**
E	128.469	132.526	149.124	158.918	163	160.748	165.887	167.184	166.386	166.386	166.386	**E**
F	6.97332	6.84839	6.63368	6.58262	6.52506	6.493	6.6126	6.60141	6.55957	6.55957	6.55957	**F**
IRL	0.767809	0.760718	0.799952	0.793618	0.815525	0.793448	0.747516	0.786245	0.787564	0.787564	0.787564	**IRL**
I	1533.24	1595.52	1841.23	1915.06	2130.14	1958.96	1929.3	1943.65	1936.27	1936.27	1936.27	**I**
L	42.2233	41.5932	40.4713	39.6565	38.5519	39.2986	40.5332	40.6207	40.3399	40.3399	40.3399	**L**
NL	2.31098	2.27482	2.17521	2.15827	2.09891	2.13973	2.21081	2.21967	2.20371	2.20371	2.20371	**NL**
A	14.4309	14.2169	13.6238	13.5396	13.1824	13.4345	13.824	13.8545	13.7603	13.7603	13.7603	**A**
P	178.614	174.714	188.37	196.896	196.105	195.761	198.589	201.695	200.482	200.482	200.482	**P**
FIN	5.00211	5.80703	6.69628	6.19077	5.70855	5.82817	5.88064	5.98251	5.94573	5.94573	5.94573	**FIN**
S	7.47927	7.53295	9.12151	9.16308	9.33192	8.51472	8.65117	8.91593	8.80752	8.44519	9.25511	**S**
UK	0.701012	0.73765	0.779988	0.775903	0.828789	0.813798	0.692304	0.676434	0.658735	0.609478	0.621874	**UK**

eurostat

Short-term interest rates: day-to-day money rates. Annual average. %

	1991	1992	1993	1994	1995	1996	1997	1998	1999	2000	2001	
EU-15	:	:	8.71	6.25	6.45	5.12	4.67	4.54	3.26	4.46	4.50	EU-15
€-zone	:	:	:	:	:	:	:	:	2.74	4.12	4.38	€-zone
B	:	9.27	8.68	5.51	4.60	3.21	3.36	3.51 |	-	-	-	B
DK	9.54	10.97	12.10	5.80	5.96	3.89	3.53	4.11	3.11	4.37	4.70	DK
D	8.84	9.42	7.49	5.35	4.50	3.27	3.18	3.41 |	-	-	-	D
EL	22.73	23.48	23.47	23.69	15.83	13.31	12.93	12.58	10.41	8.24 |	-	EL
E	13.20	13.01	12.25	7.81	8.98	7.65	5.49	4.34 |	-	-	-	E
F	9.48	10.35	8.75	5.70	6.35	3.73	3.24	3.36 |	-	-	-	F
IRL	10.46	15.70	14.86	5.33	5.61	5.22	6.08	5.78 |	-	-	-	IRL
I	11.83	14.39	10.25	8.20	10.07	9.10	7.02	5.23 |	-	-	-	I
L	:	9.27	8.68	5.51	4.60	3.21	3.36	3.51 |	-	-	-	L
NL	9.01	9.27	7.10	5.14	4.22	2.89	3.07	3.21 |	-	-	-	NL
A	9.10	9.32	7.21	5.02	4.36	3.19	3.27	3.36 |	-	-	-	A
P	15.81	17.56	13.25	10.85	8.91	7.38	5.83	4.34 |	-	-	-	P
FIN	14.91	13.32	7.74	4.39	5.25	3.63	2.86	3.26 |	-	-	-	FIN
S	11.81	16.53	9.08	7.36	8.54	6.29	4.21	4.24	3.14	3.81	4.09	S
UK	11.83	9.61	5.94	4.95	6.25	5.88	6.52 |	7.22	5.23	5.85	5.04	UK
IS	:	:	:	:	:	:	:	:	7.98	11.97	13.44	IS
NO	10.59	14.10	7.70	5.54	5.59	5.05	3.66	5.82	6.97	6.60	7.33	NO
CH	7.71	7.70	4.98	3.91	2.76	1.69	1.25	1.22	0.95	2.79	2.85	CH
CA	:	:	:	:	6.91	4.45	3.24	4.87	4.74	5.52	4.11	CA
JP	7.46	4.65	3.06	2.20	1.21	0.47	0.48	0.37	0.06	0.11	0.06	JP
US	5.69	3.52	3.02	4.20	5.82	5.30	5.46	5.35	4.97	6.24	3.89	US

Euro zone: EONIA (Euro overnight interest average) rate replaced from January 1999 the national day-to-day money rates of the countries of the euro zone. EU-15: weighted average using GDP, end year.

3

Short-term interest rates: three-month interbank rates. Annual average. %

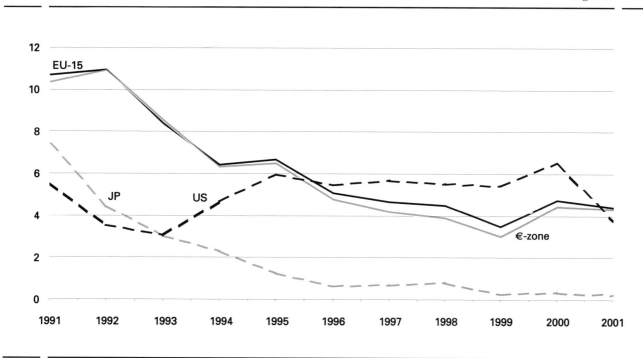

Long-term interest rates: 10-year government bond yields, secondary market. Annual average. %

	1991	1992	1993	1994	1995	1996	1997	1998	1999	2000	2001	
EU-15	10.20	9.75	8.27	8.44	8.85	7.50	6.27	4.93	4.73	5.43	5.00	**EU-15**
€-zone	10.22	9.79	8.08	8.18	8.73	7.23	5.99	4.71	4.66	5.44	5.03	**€-zone**
B	9.29	8.65	7.23	7.75	7.48	6.49	5.75	4.75	4.75	5.59	5.13	**B**
DK	9.23	8.91	7.30	7.83	8.27	7.19	6.26	4.94	4.91	5.64	5.08	**DK**
D	8.47	7.85	6.51	6.87	6.85	6.22	5.64	4.57	4.49	5.26	4.80	**D**
EL	:	:	23.29	20.72	17.02	14.46	9.92	8.48	6.30	6.10	5.30	**EL**
E	12.31	11.70	10.22	9.99	11.27	8.74	6.40	4.83	4.73	5.53	5.12	**E**
F	9.04	8.59	6.78	7.22	7.54	6.31	5.58	4.64	4.61	5.39	4.94	**F**
IRL	9.30	9.32	7.69	7.92	8.25	7.29	6.29	4.80	4.71	5.51	5.01	**IRL**
I	13.12	13.27	11.18	10.52	12.21	9.40	6.86	4.88	4.73	5.58	5.19	**I**
L	8.11	7.86	6.85	7.15	7.23	6.32	5.60	4.73	4.66	5.52	4.86	**L**
NL	8.74	8.10	6.36	6.86	6.90	6.15	5.58	4.63	4.63	5.40	4.96	**NL**
A	8.62	8.27	6.71	7.03	7.14	6.32	5.68	4.71	4.68	5.56	5.07	**A**
P	14.23	11.68	11.19	10.48	11.47	8.56	6.36	4.88	4.78	5.60	5.16	**P**
FIN	:	11.97	8.83	9.04	8.79	7.08	5.96	4.79	4.72	5.48	5.04	**FIN**
S	10.79	9.98	8.53	9.70	10.24	8.03	6.62	4.99	4.98	5.37	5.11	**S**
UK	9.87	9.08	7.55	8.15	8.32	7.94	7.13	5.60	5.01	5.33	5.01	**UK**
NO	9.99	9.61	6.87	7.44	7.45	6.76	5.89	5.40	5.51	6.21	6.24	**NO**
CH	6.23	6.40	4.58	5.06	4.71	4.24	3.52	3.04	3.04	3.93	3.38	**CH**
JP	6.50	5.19	4.09	4.24	3.32	3.03	2.15	1.30	1.75	1.76	1.34	**JP**
US	8.01	7.13	5.97	7.21	6.69	6.54	6.45	5.33	5.64	6.03	5.01	**US**

For EU Member States data refer to the rates used in the context of the convergence criteria. In this respect, data may refer in specific cases to bonds with a shorter maturity or to primary market rates.

3

Share price indices. Annual average

	1991	1992	1993	1994	1995	1996	1997	1998	1999	2000	2001	
EU-15	978.8	1 024.1	1 195.2	1 321.5	1 375.0	1 643.0	2 349.0	3 109.5	3 747.7	4 871.2	3 911.4	**EU-15**
€-zone	982.3	1 028.6	1 206.0	1 363.6	1 388.1	1 658.1	2 321.4	3 071.3	3 786.8	5 077.7	4 048.9	**€-zone**
B	1 117.7	1 153.7	1 284.7	1 452.1	1 424.1	1 740.1	2 295.0	3 110.0	3 214.7	2 965.7	2 807.1	**B**
DK	102.6	87.5	91.0	102.8	98.6	118.1	172.6	221.0	215.9	301.6	294.8	**DK**
D	1 579.6	1 635.8	1 809.0	2 121.0	2 138.5	2 567.8	3 721.1	5 020.4	5 340.9	7 116.3	5 619.5	**D**
EL	530.1	416.8	436.7	486.9	474.9	504.3	794.6	1 458.9	2 490.0	2 374.2	1 605.2	**EL**
E	2 673.9	2 481.9	2 945.8	3 419.7	3 251.4	4 108.9	6 324.5	9 245.5	10 068.8	10 974.6	8 815.9	**E**
F	1 766.5	1 850.5	2 021.2	2 058.1	1 869.8	2 078.8	2 759.9	3 692.9	4 550.8	6 269.9	5 014.1	**F**
IRL	1 386.1	1 303.1	1 594.6	1 856.3	2 014.1	2 507.3	3 392.7	4 783.8	5 010.3	5 343.4	5 724.7	**IRL**
I	:	:	10 000.0	10 867.8	9 927.1	9 961.7	13 639.9	21 842.8	24 322.9	31 445.5	25 593.1	**I**
L	326.3	311.5	428.9	617.0	557.4	655.1	852.4	1 073.6	1 071.3	1 542.9	1 231.5	**L**
NL	122.5	133.3	152.9	186.5	199.0	252.1	378.0	495.6	563.9	664.4	544.9	**NL**
A	1 092.8	887.3	904.3	1 097.8	989.5	1 072.5	1 293.8	1 335.0	1 176.6	1 124.4	1 157.0	**A**
P	:	:	1 258.4	1 703.6	1 643.3	1 899.9	3 095.9	5 016.6	4 609.6	5 398.6	4 058.4	**P**
FIN	966.9	771.7	1 240.2	1 847.6	1 918.4	2 032.1	3 206.7	4 528.0	7 800.0	14 845.9	8 560.4	**FIN**
S	54.1	50.8	66.8	84.6	94.4	115.0	169.0	198.7	244.3	346.2	259.6	**S**
UK	2 466.4	2 559.4	2 962.1	3 140.5	3 351.2	3 828.3	4 696.6	5 628.4	6 282.6	6 361.5	5 560.4	**UK**
NO	475.6	391.2	503.8	632.4	686.9	112.5	159.5	154.2	148.7	191.5	172.6	**NO**
CH	1 640.7	1 855.0	2 379.9	2 714.3	2 832.6	3 621.1	5 227.8	7 094.0	7 130.9	7 669.9	6 947.2	**CH**
JP	24 295.6	18 108.6	19 100.2	19 935.9	17 329.7	21 088.4	18 397.5	15 356.0	16 817.9	17 118.9	12 122.2	**JP**
US	2 929.0	3 284.1	3 524.9	3 794.2	4 494.3	5 739.6	7 447.0	8 630.8	10 493.4	10 733.0	10 208.9	**US**

Indices for EU-15 and the euro zone do not cover L. Index for EU-15 also covers NO and CH. Base year varying according to countries. NO: series break end 1995.

Balance of payments

Gauging a country's economic position in the world

Like any company or household, a country needs to keep track of its credit and debit transactions. The balance of payments records all economic transactions between a country (i.e. its residents) and foreign countries or international organisations (i.e. the non-residents of that country) during a given period.

More specifically, the EU balance of payments is compiled by aggregating cross-border transactions of EU residents vis-à-vis non-EU residents as reported by the 15 Member States. The balance of payments of the EU institutions is added to the EU aggregate.

The balance of payments is divided into two sub-balances:

— the **current account** which takes care of real resources;

— the **capital and financial account** which covers financial items.

Eurostat calculates the balance of payments not only for the EU, but also for the euro-zone. The European Central Bank (ECB) is responsible for the compilation and dissemination of the euro-zone balance of payments. The data which Eurostat publishes for the euro-zone are validated by the ECB. However, these data do not match up exactly with those released by the ECB because Eurostat and the ECB have different cut-off dates for receiving the data from the Member States. Revisions can take place between the different cut-off dates. Another reason is that some minor methodological differences remain between the data transmitted to Eurostat and the ECB by some Member States.

Until 1991, the data are following the methodological framework of the fourth IMF balance-of-payments manual, and, from 1992 onwards, that of the fifth IMF balance-of-payments manual. This switch appears as a break in the data series.

The current account: dealing with real resources ...

Since the current international transactions implicate a large variety of real resources, the current account is subdivided into a number of accounts. The broadest categorisation differentiates:

— the **trade in goods:** it generally forms the biggest category of the current account.

  Please refer to the section 'Trade in goods' to learn more about it;

— the **trade in services:** it forms the second major category of the current account.

  For more information, please consult the section 'Trade in services';

— **income:** it covers the compensation of employees for work performed for economic units whose place of residence is different from their own, and investment income;

— **current transfers:** these consist of all transfers that are not transfers of capital. With the use of the fifth IMF balance-of-payments manual, capital transfers are included in the capital and financial account.

... and with money: the financial account

The financial account records financial transactions. It includes foreign direct investment, portfolio investment, and other investment and reserve assets flows.

The annual European Union **foreign direct investment** statistics give a detailed presentation of foreign direct investment (FDI) flows and stocks, showing which Member State invests in which countries and in which sectors.

A firm wishing to sell overseas can choose between a variety of methods: exporting, licensing and using agents are some examples, with straightforward exporting up to now being the most common. FDI (producing and selling directly in the chosen country) is being increasingly adopted. There are two kinds of FDI:

— the creation of productive assets by foreigners (greenfield investment);

— the purchase of existing assets by foreigners (acquisitions, mergers, takeovers, etc.).

FDI differs from portfolio investments because it is made with the purpose of having control or an effective voice in management and a lasting interest in the enterprise. Direct investment does not only include the initial acquisition of equity capital, but also subsequent capital transactions between the foreign investor and domestic and affiliated enterprises.

Eurostat collects FDI statistics for quarterly and annual flows as well as for stocks at the end of the year. The FDI stocks (assets and liabilities) are a part of the international investment position of an economy at the end of the year.

In the Eurostat yearbook, the sign convention adopted for the different sets of data (flows and stocks) is as follows: an investment is always recorded with a positive sign and a disinvestment with a negative sign.

3

Further reading:

Eurostat publications
— **European Union foreign direct investment yearbook 2001**
— **EU international transactions — Data 1991–2001**
— **International trade in services**

Statistics in Focus — Theme 2
— **No 15/2002**   **EU current transactions in 2000, detailed results**
— **No 34/2002**   **EU current account preliminary annual results: deficit with extra-EU contracted to EUR -14.6 bn in 2001**
— **No 30/2002**   **EU FDI with extra-EU down by nearly 40% in 2001 - First results FDI 2001**

Do you need more information?
— **Ask your Data Shop (see last page)**
— **http://www.europa.eu.int/comm/eurostat**
— **Eurostat's data serves the political discussion in Europe. Have a look at the website of the "DG Trade": http://trade-info.cec.eu.int/europa/index_en.php**

Evolution of EU current transactions with the extra-EU: credits and debits. 1 000 million ECU/EUR

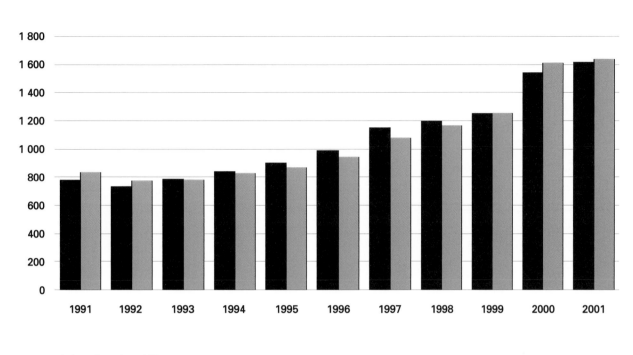

Black: credits; colour: debits.

From 1992 onwards, data for A, FIN and S are included in EU. Before 1992 the current account includes the capital account.

3

EU current account, goods, services, income and current transfers balances with the extra-EU.
1 000 million ECU/EUR

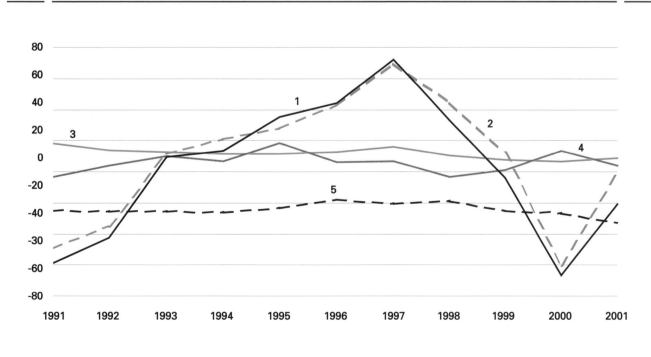

1. Current account; 2. Goods; 3. Services; 4. Income; 5. Current transfers.

From 1992 onwards, data for A, FIN and S are included in EU. Before 1992 the current account includes the capital account and the current transfers includes the capital transfers.

EU foreign direct investment flows: extra-EU, intra-EU and net as % of GDP

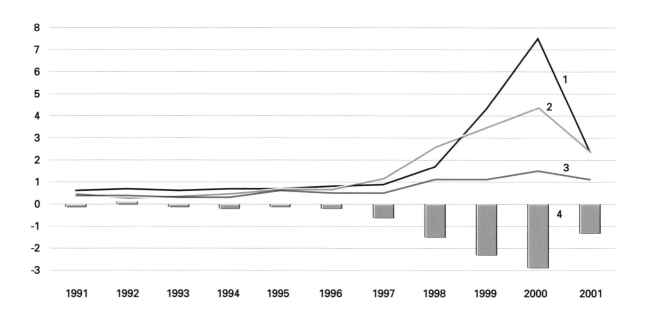

1. Intra-EU flows; 2. EU outward flows to non-EU countries; 3. EU inward flows from non-EU countries; 4. Net inflows.

EU-12 in 1991 and EU-15 from 1992; figures exclude reinvested earnings.

3

EU foreign direct investment stocks. 1996-2000. Million ECU/EUR

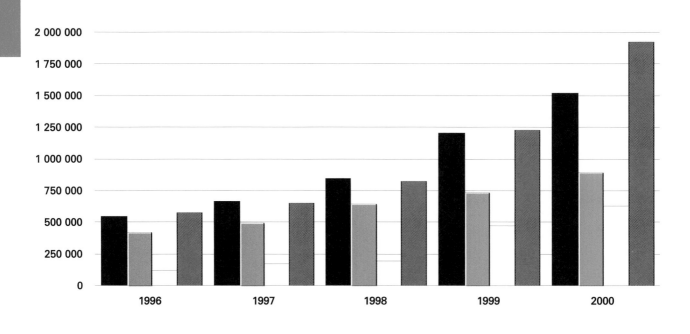

Black: assets; colour: liabilities; white: net; grey: intra-EU.

Trade in goods

Essential information in a more and more open world economy

The need for statistics on the trading of goods is self-evident. International trade forms an increasing part of the world economy and, as such, must be measured reliably. The relevant data must be widely available and understood.

International trade statistics are an important primary source for most public and private sector decision-makers. For example, they help European companies carry out market research and define their commercial strategy. They enable Community authorities to prepare for multilateral and bilateral negotiations within the framework of the common commercial policy and to evaluate the progress of the single market or the integration of the European economies. Moreover, they constitute an essential source for balance-of-payments statistics, national accounts and studies of economic cycles.

Harmonised statistics on international trade in goods ...

The compilation of trade figures is founded on a legal basis which is set out in a series of Council and Commission regulations. The concrete work is based on a cooperative effort between Eurostat and the appropriate bodies in the Member States which are responsible for collecting and processing the basic information.

Eurostat is responsible for harmonising Community legislation in the field of statistics on the trading of goods and for ensuring that the legislation is applied correctly. The statistics provided to Eurostat are therefore based on precise legal texts directly applicable in the Member States and on definitions and procedures which have to a large extent been harmonised.

... which cover all physical movements of goods across frontiers

In broad terms, the aim of international trade statistics is to record all goods that add to or subtract from the stock of material resources of a country by entering or leaving its territory. By their nature, international trade statistics are concerned with transportable goods.

The most important component of the international trade statistics is related to transactions involving actual or intended transfer of ownership against compensation. Nevertheless, trade statistics also cover movements of goods without a transfer of ownership such as operations following, or with a view of, processing under contract or repair.

Some methodological notes

— Export and import valuation

In external trade statistics, exports are recorded at their fob value (fob — free on board) and imports at their cif value (cif — cost, insurance, freight). Therefore, and contrary to the balance-of-payments statistics, import value includes charges, such as transport and insurance, relating to that part of the journey which takes place outside the statistical territory of the importing country. Export value corresponds to the value of goods at the time and place where they leave the statistical territory of the exporting country.

— Trade of country groups

EU-15, the euro zone and the European Economic Area (EEA) are calculated as total trade less intra-EU-15, intra-euro zone and intra-EEA trade respectively.

— Indices

The indices, which are linked from year to year, relate to EU-12 up to 1995 and to EU-15 thereafter.

— Trade by product

Agrifood products are food products obtained from agriculture. They are determined according to Sections 0 and 1 of the standard international trade classification (SITC), Revision 3. Trade in fuel products refers to products determined according to Section 3 of the SITC. Trade in chemicals refers to products determined according to Section 5 of the SITC. Machinery and transport equipment refers to products determined according to Section 7 of the SITC.

Would you like to know more about international trade concepts and definitions?

Please refer to the publications *Statistics on the trading of goods — User guide or Geonomenclature* which can be downloaded from the Eurostat web site (theme 'External trade', collection 'Methods and nomenclatures').

Are you interested in more statistics on trading in goods?

You can consult our paper publications — the monthly bulletin or the statistical yearbook — or our CD-ROM. Please contact your Data Shop to have a complete overview of our supply. The addresses of the Data Shops can be found at the end of the yearbook.

Free publications can also be downloaded from our web site. *Statistics in Focus* (SIF) publications analyse EU trading in specific goods such as high-technology or agricultural products, or exchanges of goods of the EU with particular trading partners such as China, the ACP or candidate countries.

3

Further reading:

Eurostat publications
— **Statistics on the trading of goods — User guide**
— **Geonomenclature**
— **External and intra-European Union trade — Monthly statistics**
— **External and intra-European Union trade — Statistical yearbook**
— **Intra- and extra-EU trade — Monthly data — 11 CD-ROMs and 2 supplements on CD-ROM**

Statistics in Focus — Theme 6
— **No 5/2001 An enlarged EU — A trade heavyweight**
— **No 7/2001 EU-15 and the 12 Mediterranean partners: solid trade links**
— **No 8/2001 The 13 candidate countries' trade with the EU in 2000**
— **No 2/2002 EU trade with OPEC**
— **No 3/2002 EU trade with ACP countries**
— **No 4/2002 EU trade with China and Russia**

Do you need more information?
— **Ask your Data Shop (see last page)**
— **http://www.europa.eu.int/comm/eurostat**
— **Eurostat's data serves the political discussion in Europe. Have a look at the website of the "DG Trade": http://trade-info.cec.eu.int/europa/index_en.php**

Exports (fob) at current prices. 1 000 million ECU/EUR

	1991	1992	1993	1994	1995	1996	1997	1998	1999	2000	2001	
EU-15	403.4	415.3	468.1	523.8	573.3	626.3	721.1	733.4	760.2	942.0	985.3	**EU-15**
€-zone	440.7	456.5	498.5	559.6	622.5	669.6	762.9	797.1	832.8	1 011.1	1 059.4	**€-zone**
B	95.1	95.4	106.7	119.1	136.3	139.7	153.9	162.3	168.1	204.0	207.1	**B**
DK	29.5	31.2	32.2	35.6	38.9	40.5	43.5	43.7	47.2	55.5	57.8	**DK**
D	323.8	331.3	324.6	358.9	400.2	413.2	452.3	485.0	510.0	597.5	638.2	**D**
EL	7.0	7.6	7.2	7.9	8.5	9.2	10.0	9.7	10.4	11.9	11.4	**EL**
E	51.0	53.0	55.2	64.5	74.8	84.5	88.9	99.9	98.0	124.8	130.3	**E**
F	184.8	192.5	189.3	210.7	230.2	240.6	266.4	286.0	305.4	354.7	361.1	**F**
IRL	19.5	21.8	24.8	28.6	34.2	38.1	47.0	57.4	66.8	83.8	92.3	**IRL**
I	136.8	137.6	144.5	160.9	178.7	198.7	212.0	219.3	221.0	260.4	269.2	**I**
L	:	:	:	:	:	:	:	:	:	7.7	9.1	11.6	**L**
NL	107.8	108.6	106.3	128.9	155.3	164.6	183.3	190.9	205.1	252.4	257.8	**NL**
A	33.2	34.2	34.3	37.9	44.1	45.9	52.7	57.2	62.0	73.3	79.0	**A**
P	13.2	14.2	13.2	15.1	17.4	19.4	21.1	22.1	23.0	26.4	27.3	**P**
FIN	18.6	18.5	20.1	25.0	31.0	32.4	36.6	39.0	39.6	49.9	48.3	**FIN**
S	44.5	43.2	42.6	51.5	61.5	66.9	73.0	75.6	79.7	94.3	84.4	**S**
UK	147.3	144.6	154.9	172.4	181.9	203.6	247.3	244.4	255.4	309.0	304.5	**UK**
IS	1.3	1.2	1.2	1.4	1.4	1.5	1.6	1.7	1.9	2.0	2.3	**IS**
NO	27.5	27.1	27.2	29.2	31.9	38.5	42.1	36.0	42.2	63.0	64.8	**NO**
EEA	394.2	406.1	459.1	513.5	562.2	614.3	706.5	714.9	746.3	929.0	972.2	**EEA**
CH	49.7	50.6	54.0	59.2	62.4	63.7	67.2	70.3	75.3	88.4	91.7	**CH**
CA	102.3	103.6	123.5	139.8	146.1	159.3	190.5	191.4	224.0	300.6	290.2	**CA**
JP	253.8	261.7	308.2	332.6	338.6	323.6	371.2	346.2	391.8	519.8	450.4	**JP**
US	340.2	344.6	396.9	430.7	445.7	490.5	606.3	606.9	650.0	846.4	816.2	**US**

B: includes L up to 1998.

Imports (cif) at current prices. 1 000 million ECU/EUR

	1991	1992	1993	1994	1995	1996	1997	1998	1999	2000	2001	
EU-15	471.6	465.4	464.7	514.3	545.3	581.0	672.6	710.5	779.8	1 033.4	1 028.0	**EU-15**
€-zone	482.1	478.0	462.6	519.4	562.7	592.4	675.4	711.4	781.2	1 008.8	1 010.5	**€-zone**
B	102.5	101.9	98.3	107.1	126.1	132.2	142.8	150.7	154.6	192.2	194.1	**B**
DK	26.8	26.8	26.7	30.9	35.1	35.7	39.6	41.8	42.9	49.3	50.9	**DK**
D	314.0	315.6	292.6	320.6	354.6	361.6	393.1	420.6	444.8	538.3	549.9	**D**
EL	17.4	18.4	18.8	18.1	19.8	22.2	23.7	27.0	28.6	32.2	31.5	**EL**
E	72.5	74.9	66.2	74.7	86.8	95.5	102.0	121.9	127.0	169.1	172.7	**E**
F	200.1	199.4	185.6	206.8	221.2	232.0	251.3	274.5	296.3	367.0	366.9	**F**
IRL	16.8	16.8	18.1	21.5	24.7	27.0	33.3	38.5	43.9	55.3	56.5	**IRL**
I	147.3	145.6	126.5	142.2	157.5	164.0	185.3	194.9	207.0	258.5	260.1	**I**
L	:	:	:	:	:	:	:	:	10.5	12.2	13.5	**L**
NL	110.7	113.5	95.8	120.1	141.6	150.4	168.2	174.5	193.4	236.3	233.0	**NL**
A	40.9	41.7	41.5	46.5	50.6	54.0	58.0	62.0	66.9	78.4	83.3	**A**
P	21.3	23.4	20.7	22.8	24.9	27.7	30.9	34.3	37.5	43.3	44.1	**P**
FIN	17.6	16.3	15.4	19.6	22.5	24.8	27.9	29.4	30.1	37.3	36.4	**FIN**
S	40.2	38.4	36.4	43.5	49.7	52.7	57.8	61.0	64.4	78.9	70.4	**S**
UK	169.5	171.3	178.8	196.8	204.3	226.3	271.2	286.5	304.8	372.2	371.8	**UK**
IS	1.4	1.3	1.2	1.2	1.3	1.6	1.8	2.2	2.4	2.8	2.5	**IS**
NO	20.6	20.1	20.5	23.0	25.0	27.0	31.2	32.6	31.7	36.6	36.3	**NO**
EEA	456.3	450.4	449.8	497.2	526.0	560.0	647.2	691.2	758.8	999.4	993.2	**EEA**
CH	53.7	50.7	52.0	57.2	61.3	62.4	67.0	71.4	74.9	90.7	93.9	**CH**
CA	95.3	94.3	112.2	124.6	125.7	134.4	173.7	179.6	202.3	260.4	247.4	**CA**
JP	191.1	179.5	205.5	231.0	257.0	275.0	298.8	250.3	290.9	411.8	390.0	**JP**
US	410.7	426.4	515.1	579.3	589.3	643.9	791.9	842.4	993.9	1 364.6	1 317.6	**US**

B: includes L up to 1998.

3

3

Trade balance at current prices. 1 000 million ECU/EUR

	1991	1992	1993	1994	1995	1996	1997	1998	1999	2000	2001	
EU-15	- 68.2	- 50.1	3.4	9.4	28.0	45.3	48.6	22.9	- 19.6	- 91.4	- 42.7	**EU-15**
€-zone	- 41.4	- 21.5	35.9	40.2	59.7	77.2	87.5	85.7	51.6	2.3	48.9	**€-zone**
B	- 7.4	- 6.5	8.3	12.0	10.2	7.4	11.1	11.5	13.5	11.8	13.0	**B**
DK	2.7	4.4	5.5	4.8	3.8	4.8	3.9	1.9	4.3	6.2	6.9	**DK**
D	9.8	15.7	32.0	38.3	45.6	51.6	59.2	64.5	65.2	59.1	88.2	**D**
EL	- 10.4	- 10.8	- 11.6	- 10.2	- 11.4	- 13.0	- 13.8	- 17.3	- 18.3	- 20.3	- 20.1	**EL**
E	- 21.4	- 21.8	- 11.0	- 10.2	- 12.0	- 11.0	- 13.2	- 22.0	- 29.0	- 44.3	- 42.4	**E**
F	- 15.3	- 6.9	3.6	3.8	9.0	8.6	15.1	11.5	9.2	- 12.3	- 5.8	**F**
IRL	2.7	5.0	6.7	7.1	9.5	11.0	13.8	18.9	23.0	28.6	35.8	**IRL**
I	- 10.4	- 8.0	18.1	18.7	21.2	34.7	26.7	24.4	14.0	1.9	9.2	**I**
L	:	:	:	:	:	:	:	:	- 2.8	- 3.1	- 1.9	**L**
NL	- 2.9	- 4.9	10.5	8.8	13.7	14.2	15.1	16.4	11.7	16.1	24.8	**NL**
A	- 7.8	- 7.5	- 7.2	- 8.6	- 6.5	- 8.1	- 5.3	- 4.8	- 4.9	- 5.1	- 4.3	**A**
P	- 8.1	- 9.2	- 7.5	- 7.6	- 7.5	- 8.3	- 9.8	- 12.2	- 14.5	- 16.9	- 16.7	**P**
FIN	1.0	2.1	4.7	5.4	8.4	7.6	8.7	9.6	9.5	12.6	11.8	**FIN**
S	4.3	4.7	6.2	8.0	11.8	14.2	15.1	14.6	15.3	15.4	14.0	**S**
UK	- 22.2	- 26.7	- 23.9	- 24.4	- 22.4	- 22.7	- 23.9	- 42.2	- 49.5	- 63.2	- 67.3	**UK**
IS	- 0.1	- 0.1	0.0	0.1	0.0	- 0.1	- 0.2	- 0.5	- 0.5	- 0.8	- 0.3	**IS**
NO	6.9	7.0	6.7	6.3	6.9	11.5	10.8	3.4	10.4	26.4	28.5	**NO**
EEA	- 62.1	- 44.3	9.3	16.3	36.1	54.3	59.3	23.7	- 12.5	- 70.4	- 21.0	**EEA**
CH	- 4.0	- 0.1	2.0	2.0	1.1	1.2	0.2	- 1.1	0.4	- 2.2	- 2.2	**CH**
CA	7.0	9.3	11.4	15.2	20.5	24.9	16.8	11.8	21.8	40.2	42.8	**CA**
JP	62.8	82.1	102.7	101.6	81.7	48.6	72.5	95.9	101.0	108.0	60.4	**JP**
US	- 70.5	- 81.8	- 118.2	- 148.5	- 143.6	- 153.5	- 185.6	- 235.4	- 343.8	- 518.2	- 501.4	**US**

Extra-EU exports by main trading partners. 1 000 million ECU/EUR

	1991	1992	1993	1994	1995	1996	1997	1998	1999	2000	2001
Extra-EU-15	403.4	415.3	468.1	523.8	573.3	626.3	721.1	733.4	760.2	942.0	985.3
JP	23.9	22.2	24.7	29.0	32.9	35.8	36.1	31.6	35.4	44.9	44.9
US	76.8	79.3	91.4	103.4	103.3	114.9	141.4	161.6	183.0	232.5	239.9
CH	43.6	41.9	42.7	46.7	51.0	51.5	53.0	57.2	62.6	70.8	74.8
CN	6.3	7.6	12.4	14.0	14.7	14.8	16.5	17.4	19.4	25.5	30.1
NO	14.2	14.3	14.4	16.4	17.5	19.8	23.4	25.1	23.2	25.6	26.2
RU	:	7.1	13.2	14.4	16.1	19.1	25.5	21.2	14.7	19.9	28.0
PL	8.9	9.2	11.1	12.3	15.3	20.0	25.1	28.2	29.0	33.8	35.7
TR	8.6	8.8	12.4	9.3	8.7	10.0	13.6	16.9	18.4	23.0	23.9
CZ	:	:	7.1	9.2	11.7	14.0	15.9	17.2	18.4	24.0	27.7
HU	4.7	5.4	6.5	8.1	13.4	18.3	22.4	22.2	20.6	30.0	20.3
CCs	:	:	51.5	56.5	70.7	86.0	105.0	116.8	118.5	151.3	152.8
EFTA	58.7	57.0	57.9	63.8	69.8	72.7	78.1	84.2	87.8	99.0	103.3
DAEs	35.3	37.3	46.9	57.0	65.6	70.2	77.7	60.1	62.0	81.6	81.9
OPEC	41.0	43.2	42.1	37.8	39.0	41.9	51.1	47.1	43.9	54.0	63.9
ACP	22.6	23.6	23.2	23.0	26.5	27.5	30.2	32.7	31.5	38.4	40.2

Extra-EU imports by main trading partners. 1 000 million ECU/EUR

	1991	1992	1993	1994	1995	1996	1997	1998	1999	2000	2001
Extra-EU-15	471.6	465.4	464.7	514.3	545.3	581.0	672.6	710.5	779.8	1 033.4	1 028.0
JP	56.9	56.3	52.2	53.8	54.3	52.6	59.9	66.0	71.9	87.1	76.3
CH	37.3	37.7	38.5	41.8	43.2	42.8	45.1	49.5	52.9	60.0	60.8
US	97.0	92.8	90.6	99.9	103.7	113.1	137.9	152.0	160.6	199.0	195.6
CN	16.0	18.0	21.1	24.6	26.3	30.0	37.5	42.0	49.7	70.3	75.9
NO	21.4	20.6	21.1	23.7	25.5	27.9	33.7	28.1	29.6	45.8	45.1
RU	:	10.9	17.6	21.4	21.5	23.4	27.0	23.2	26.0	45.7	47.7
PL	7.1	8.0	8.4	10.1	12.3	12.3	14.2	16.2	17.6	23.3	26.6
TR	6.5	6.9	6.9	7.9	9.2	10.2	11.9	13.6	15.1	17.6	20.2
CZ	:	:	5.6	7.4	9.0	9.8	11.8	14.7	16.8	21.6	25.1
HU	4.6	5.0	4.9	6.1	7.6	8.9	11.7	14.7	17.6	22.1	24.8
CCs	:	:	36.6	45.6	55.5	58.8	69.9	82.7	92.8	117.8	134.1
EFTA	59.6	59.3	60.4	66.4	69.9	72.0	80.5	79.5	84.5	108.3	108.6
DAEs	43.2	43.0	46.0	50.6	54.4	57.9	68.1	77.9	85.2	109.4	98.1
OPEC	46.9	42.8	41.5	41.5	38.4	44.0	51.3	40.5	48.4	86.2	77.0
ACP	28.5	27.9	24.4	26.1	27.7	30.3	32.1	31.2	32.6	43.3	47.6

Exports to EU countries as % of total national exports (fob)

	1991	1992	1993	1994	1995	1996	1997	1998	1999	2000	2001	
EU-15	67.4	67.0	63.2	63.3	64.0	63.1	61.8	63.2	63.8	62.4	61.8	EU-15
€-zone	:	:	:	:	:	:	:	:	:	:	:	€-zone
B	79.9	79.7	76.8	75.8	77.1	76.7	74.6	76.3	76.4	74.4	74.8	B
DK	68.9	68.1	66.0	64.9	66.6	66.6	66.4	66.5	67.0	66.9	65.7	DK
D	63.2	63.4	58.5	58.0	58.2	57.4	55.6	56.5	57.5	56.5	55.1	D
EL	67.7	69.3	58.9	57.1	60.1	54.0	50.9	53.8	53.9	43.5	41.0	EL
E	69.3	68.5	64.3	66.6	67.9	67.8	68.3	71.1	71.2	70.3	71.4	E
F	65.8	65.3	62.2	63.4	63.0	62.5	62.0	62.4	62.5	61.8	60.8	F
IRL	78.0	77.6	72.4	73.5	74.0	71.2	68.9	69.3	66.0	63.2	63.0	IRL
I	63.4	61.8	57.1	57.5	57.3	55.4	55.0	56.9	58.2	55.5	53.8	I
L	:	:	:	:	:	:	:	:	85.4	84.2	86.9	L
NL	81.9	80.9	77.7	78.3	79.9	80.0	79.1	78.9	79.5	78.7	78.7	NL
A	68.0	68.1	65.5	64.8	65.8	64.1	62.0	64.2	62.9	61.4	61.5	A
P	82.4	81.4	79.9	80.0	80.1	80.6	80.8	82.0	83.2	80.3	80.1	P
FIN	64.7	65.5	57.3	56.8	57.5	54.5	53.2	56.1	57.8	55.7	53.7	FIN
S	62.0	62.3	59.0	55.5	59.6	57.1	55.6	58.0	58.4	55.9	54.6	S
UK	60.5	59.8	56.7	57.6	58.2	57.6	55.5	58.0	58.6	57.1	57.5	UK
IS	68.9	71.2	61.8	61.6	62.7	62.4	60.6	65.0	64.1	67.8	68.5	IS
NO	80.0	78.8	78.3	77.8	77.2	76.9	76.2	77.2	73.8	76.5	76.8	NO
EEA	67.7	67.2	63.5	63.6	64.3	63.4	62.1	63.4	64.0	62.8	62.2	EEA
CH	64.7	63.2	62.5	60.6	62.3	60.8	59.8	62.4	61.2	58.9	60.1	CH
CA	8.4	7.4	5.9	5.4	6.4	7.0	5.2	5.1	5.6	4.6	4.5	CA
JP	20.4	19.8	16.7	15.5	15.9	15.4	15.6	18.5	17.9	16.4	16.0	JP
US	25.7	24.1	21.8	21.0	21.2	20.5	20.6	22.0	21.9	21.1	21.8	US

B: includes L up to 1998.

Imports from EU countries as % of total national imports (cif)

	1991	1992	1993	1994	1995	1996	1997	1998	1999	2000	2001	
EU-15	63.8	64.5	62.4	62.8	64.1	63.8	62.3	63.0	62.0	59.0	59.5	EU-15
€-zone	:	:	:	:	:	:	:	:	:	:	:	€-zone
B	74.2	74.9	72.6	73.4	72.8	73.1	71.3	71.1	70.4	68.7	68.7	B
DK	68.8	69.8	69.3	69.2	71.8	70.6	70.2	70.4	69.8	68.3	68.4	DK
D	62.1	62.3	59.0	59.3	60.4	60.3	59.2	59.0	57.8	54.9	55.9	D
EL	64.0	66.7	63.0	67.9	70.1	64.4	65.0	65.6	66.9	56.0	54.0	EL
E	62.8	63.3	65.0	66.4	68.5	69.3	66.0	70.7	68.7	66.4	67.0	E
F	67.5	68.8	66.9	68.0	68.5	68.0	65.9	67.6	66.8	65.3	65.2	F
IRL	72.1	74.9	67.1	66.0	64.6	66.6	64.0	61.6	61.7	62.2	65.6	IRL
I	62.0	63.3	59.6	60.7	60.9	61.1	61.0	62.0	61.5	56.7	56.5	I
L	:	:	:	:	:	:	:	:	81.7	82.7	78.8	L
NL	62.6	62.7	64.3	61.6	63.2	61.6	58.6	58.1	55.1	51.1	51.7	NL
A	70.2	70.4	69.3	68.4	75.9	74.4	73.4	73.7	72.3	68.8	68.2	A
P	74.9	76.6	74.5	73.5	74.0	76.3	76.3	78.1	78.1	75.1	75.1	P
FIN	58.8	58.9	56.9	54.7	65.0	65.3	64.4	65.7	65.4	61.9	63.5	FIN
S	63.1	62.9	62.5	62.2	68.6	68.5	67.7	69.2	67.7	64.2	65.5	S
UK	55.1	55.6	53.3	54.5	54.6	54.2	53.7	53.4	53.2	49.5	50.0	UK
IS	62.5	57.8	58.0	58.3	59.8	56.4	58.1	56.2	55.9	57.1	54.9	IS
NO	67.9	69.0	67.2	68.9	71.4	70.8	69.5	69.3	68.6	63.6	66.6	NO
EEA	63.8	64.6	62.5	62.9	64.2	63.9	62.4	63.1	62.1	59.1	59.5	EEA
CH	76.6	78.5	78.8	79.2	79.8	79.0	77.1	76.8	77.8	74.5	76.2	CH
CA	11.8	10.7	9.6	9.7	10.0	10.1	9.9	9.5	10.2	10.3	11.2	CA
JP	14.5	14.5	13.7	14.1	14.5	14.1	13.3	13.9	13.8	12.3	12.8	JP
US	18.9	18.9	18.1	18.0	17.8	18.0	18.1	19.3	19.0	18.0	19.2	US

B: includes L up to 1998.

The services traded

What are the services exported and imported by the EU and its Member States, and in what quantity?

In the balance-of-payments statistics, the balance of trade in services is divided into three major components: transport, tourism, and other services. The categories transport services and other services are broken down into detailed sub-items such as passenger air transport or construction services.

— **Transport services** cover all transportation services that are performed by residents of one country for those of another. They comprise the transport of passengers, goods (freight), rentals (charters) of carriers with crew, or related supporting and auxiliary services. In the Eurostat classification, transport services are further broken down by mode of transportation (sea, air and other transport) and by kind of services (transport of passengers, transport of freight and auxiliary services).

— **Tourism** refers to all goods and services acquired by travellers for their own use from residents of the countries in which they are travelling. A traveller is an individual staying in a country of which he/she is not a resident for less than one year. The international carriage of travellers, which is covered in transport services, is excluded.

— **Other services** comprise all international service transactions other than tourism and transport. They cover highly varied services such as communications services, construction services, insurance services, financial services, computer and information services, royalties and licence fees, trade earnings, miscellaneous business services, audiovisual and recreational services, and government services.

Grasping the intangible

Due to its intangible nature, international trade in services is much more difficult to record than trade in goods. Three types of problems may arise: difficulty in defining the service; the value of the services is not specified separately; and practical difficulties for identifying gross flows (as many services can be paid for by means of an international offsetting mechanism). Such problems could lead to an underestimation of the service flows.

3

Further reading:

Eurostat publications
— **International trade in services, Geographical breakdown of the current account — EU —
   CD-ROM (2003 Edition)**

Statistics in Focus — Theme 2
— **Trade in transportation services**
— **Postal and courier services remained a significant mean of EU external communications in 1998**
— **EU remains world's top destination for tourists but external travel balance shows a deficit of ECU
   −1.3 bn in 1998**
— **The EU's external transactions in telecommunication services: a mirror of the dawning information
   society**
— **EU computer and information services surplus up to EUR 2.5 bn in 1999**
— **Miscellaneous business, professional and technical services: the European Union was the largest
   international trader over the period 1994–2000**

Breakdown of total EU external transactions in services (exports and imports) between transportation, travel and other services. 1 000 million ECU/EUR

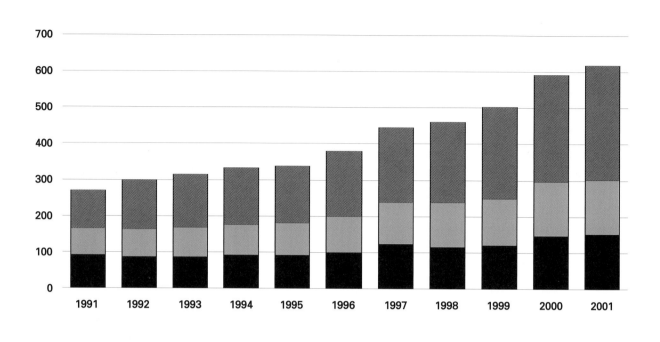

Black: transportation; colour: travel; grey: other services.

From 1992 onwards, data for A, FIN and S are included in EU.

3

Share of transportation, travel and other services in Member States' world total services transactions (exports and imports). 2001. %

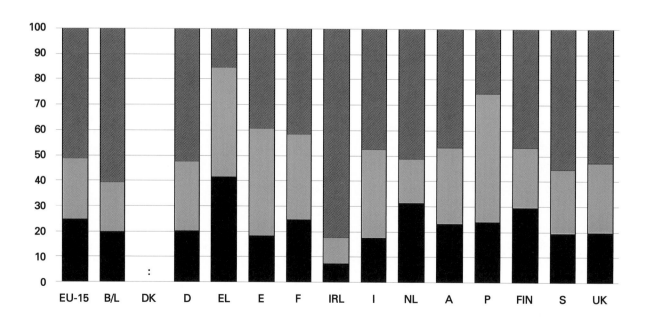

Black: transportation; colour: travel; grey: other services.

Trading partners

Europe's trading partners in the world

Eurostat provides detailed information on the geographical breakdown of the current account of the European Union. The geographical breakdown distinguishes between:

— **intra-EU** transactions, corresponding to the sum of the transactions declared by EU Member States with other EU Member States; and

— **extra-EU** transactions, corresponding to the transactions declared by EU Member States with countries outside the European Union. Extra-EU transactions are further broken down into detailed partner zones: individual countries (e.g. Hungary, the United States, Japan), economic zones (e.g. OECD countries, ACP countries), and geographical zones (e.g. America, Asia).

World transactions are equal to the sum of intra-EU transactions and extra-EU transactions, plus a remainder that cannot be allocated.

Finding the residence

In the balance-of-payments statistics, the EU current account is geographically allocated according to the **residence** of the trading partner. However, precise information on residence is not always available. In this case, the currency in which transactions are recorded might be used to determine the origin or destination of the flows. The concept of residence thus corresponds to the concept of 'country of origin' (for imports) and 'country of destination' (for exports).

However, from 1997 onwards, the geographical allocation of imports of goods has changed. All goods imported by an EU Member State from outside the EU that transit through another EU Member State should be geographically allocated to the transit country and not the origin country.

3

Further reading:

Eurostat publications
— **Geographical breakdown of the EU current account & International trade in services – EU (CD-ROM)**
— **Geonomenclature (PDF)**

Statistics in Focus — Theme 2
— **No 19/2000 EU trade and investment with Mexico before the new trade agreement**
— **EU trade and investment with Mediterranean Partner Countries1: towards a better partnership? (MED)**

Do you need more information?
— **Ask your Data Shop (see last page)**
— **http://www.europa.eu.int/comm/eurostat**
— **Eurostat's data serves the political discussion in Europe. Have a look at the website of the "DG Trade": http://trade-info.cec.eu.int/europa/index_en.php**

EU current international credits: breakdown by partner zones. % of EU total credits

	1991	1992	1993	1994	1995	1996	1997	1998	1999	2000	2001
World	100.0	100.0	100.0	100.0	100.0	100.0	100.0	100.0	100.0	100.0	100.0
Intra-EU-15	57.8	62.5	61.8	62.3	63.1	62.4	61.2	62.1	62.7	61.1	61.1
Extra-EU-15	42.0	35.3	36.7	36.5	36.5	37.2	38.5	37.6	36.9	38.1	38.5
EFTA	9.4	5.0	4.9	4.9	4.9	4.7	4.5	4.7	4.7	4.6	4.7
Other Europe	:	3.9	4.3	4.3	4.8	5.4	5.9	6.0	5.6	5.9	6.2
CZ	:	0.3	0.4	0.5	0.6	0.6	0.6	0.6	0.7	0.7	0.8
HU	:	0.4	0.4	0.5	0.5	0.5	0.6	0.7	0.7	0.7	0.7
PL	:	0.6	0.6	0.6	0.7	0.9	0.9	1.1	1.0	1.0	1.0
RU	:	0.9	0.9	0.8	0.9	0.9	1.1	0.9	0.6	0.7	0.9
Africa	:	2.7	2.7	2.4	2.6	2.5	2.4	2.4	2.3	2.3	2.4
America	:	12.8	13.3	13.3	12.7	13.0	14.3	14.4	14.7	15.6	15.5
US	9.8	8.9	9.9	9.9	9.4	9.6	10.6	10.6	11.1	11.9	11.7
Asia	:	9.6	10.1	10.2	10.3	10.2	10.1	8.5	8.3	8.6	8.5
JP	3.3	2.6	2.5	2.5	2.5	2.4	2.2	1.9	2.0	2.0	1.9
Australia, Oceania	0.8	0.8	0.8	0.8	0.8	0.9	0.9	0.8	0.8	0.8	0.8
OECD	:	81.5	81.4	81.9	80.4	80.6	84.0	84.8	86.1	85.4	85.4
CEECs	:	1.9	2.3	2.5	2.8	3.1	3.4	3.7	3.6	3.7	3.9
NAFTA	:	10.2	11.2	11.2	10.5	10.7	11.8	11.9	12.4	13.2	13.1
ACP	1.5	1.3	1.3	1.0	1.1	1.3	1.2	1.5	1.5	1.5	1.5
OPEC	3.1	2.8	2.6	2.2	2.2	2.4	2.4	2.2	2.0	2.0	2.2
ASEAN	:	1.6	1.8	1.9	2.1	2.1	2.1	1.4	1.4	1.5	1.5
CIS	:	1.0	1.1	1.0	1.1	1.2	1.3	1.2	0.8	0.9	1.2
Mercosur	:	0.7	0.9	0.8	1.1	1.1	1.2	1.2	1.0	0.9	0.9

From 1992 onwards, data for A, FIN and S are included in EU.

3

EU current international debits: breakdown by partner zones. % of EU total debits

	1991	1992	1993	1994	1995	1996	1997	1998	1999	2000	2001
World	100.0	100.0	100.0	100.0	100.0	100.0	100.0	100.0	100.0	100.0	100.0
Intra-EU-15	56.0	61.5	61.7	62.3	63.7	62.8	62.0	61.8	62.0	59.6	60.4
Extra-EU-15	43.8	36.3	36.5	36.2	35.9	36.6	37.6	37.6	37.4	39.6	39.1
EFTA	9.8	5.8	5.7	5.4	5.4	5.4	5.2	4.8	4.8	4.9	4.8
Other Europe	:	3.8	3.9	4.2	4.6	4.9	5.1	5.4	5.3	5.7	6.1
CZ	:	0.2	0.4	0.4	0.5	0.5	0.5	0.6	0.6	0.6	0.7
HU	:	0.3	0.3	0.3	0.4	0.4	0.5	0.6	0.6	0.6	0.6
PL	:	0.5	0.5	0.6	0.6	0.6	0.7	0.8	0.7	0.7	0.8
RU	:	0.9	1.0	1.1	1.1	1.1	1.0	0.8	0.9	1.2	1.3
Africa	:	3.0	2.8	2.7	2.7	2.8	2.8	2.3	2.4	2.8	2.8
America	:	12.1	12.3	12.4	11.9	12.3	13.1	13.5	13.3	13.6	13.6
US	10.3	9.2	9.6	9.5	9.1	9.5	10.1	10.3	10.4	10.6	10.4
Asia	:	10.4	10.3	10.2	10.2	10.2	10.6	10.2	10.5	11.5	10.7
JP	4.0	3.7	3.4	3.3	3.1	3.0	2.9	2.8	2.9	3.1	2.7
Australia, Oceania	0.6	0.6	0.6	0.5	0.5	0.5	0.5	0.5	0.5	0.5	0.5
OECD	:	81.7	81.8	82.2	81.0	81.0	84.2	84.2	84.7	82.8	81.5
CEECs	:	1.7	1.9	2.1	2.5	2.5	2.7	3.1	3.1	3.1	3.4
NAFTA	:	10.1	10.4	10.4	10.0	10.4	11.0	11.2	11.3	11.6	11.4
ACP	1.8	1.4	1.3	1.3	1.3	1.4	1.4	1.5	1.5	1.6	1.6
OPEC	2.7	2.6	2.5	2.2	2.1	2.5	2.6	2.0	2.1	2.8	2.5
ASEAN	:	1.6	1.7	1.8	1.9	2.0	2.1	2.0	2.0	2.2	2.0
CIS	:	1.1	1.2	1.3	1.3	1.3	1.2	1.0	1.2	1.5	1.6
Mercosur	:	0.7	0.7	0.8	0.8	0.7	0.8	0.8	0.7	0.7	0.7

From 1992 onwards, data for A, FIN and S are included in EU.

Water

Water: essential and under strain

Water is a natural resource that both in terms of quality and availability is a major concern in many regions. Water resources are limited and water quality is affected by human activities such as industrial production, household discharges, animal husbandry, arable farming, etc.

At the same time, water is essential for human life and activities. Economic development and growing populations put increasing pressure on water quantity and quality. In many places on earth, freshwater resources are being consumed faster than nature can replenish them. The pollution of rivers, lakes and groundwater remains a concern all over the world.

A directive to protect water

Because the quality of the water available is deteriorating and its quantity is limited, there is a need to reconsider the use of different sources of water as well as the demand on water. This has been set out in the Water Framework Directive 2000/60/EC. It states that sustainable water resource management has to be based on the principle of integrated river basin management. The directive also promotes a 'combined approach' of emission limit values and quality standards, getting the prices right and getting citizens more closely involved in water problems.

Keeping a close eye on water

Water statistics are collected from all European countries through the 'Inland waters' section of the joint Eurostat/OECD questionnaire which has recently been revised to be adapted to the EU policy framework. It reports on the following.

— Water abstraction (in particular from groundwater) which is a major pressure on freshwater resources. A large part of the water abstracted for domestic, energy production, industrial or agricultural use is returned to the environment (to rivers, lakes or directly to the sea) as wastewater with impaired quality. The pollution of water bodies by wastewater through direct discharges or inadequate treatment increases the concentration of pollutants and undesirable changes in the composition of aquatic biota (bacterial concentration, oxygen deficiencies, etc.), but not all the uses described above cause the same pressure on the environment or require the same type of treatment.

— Public sewerage that collects domestic effluent, together with industrial wastewater and/or run-off water. Sewage treatment systems, when efficient, preserve the purity of water resources, the soil and human health.

3

Water abstracted by public water supply. Million m³

	1990	1995	1996	1997	1998	1999	2000	
B	:	747	740	746	730	:	:	B
DK	571	470	514	:	:	:	:	DK
D	:	5 810	:	:	5 557	:	:	D
EL	:	:	:	861	:	:	:	EL
E	:	4 296	:	5 393	:	:	:	E
F	6 091	:	:	5 890	5 863	5 898	:	F
IRL	:	:	:	:	:	:	:	IRL
I	:	:	:	:	10 116	:	:	I
L	:	33	:	:	:	38	:	L
NL	1 277 *	1 229	1 267	1 257	1 242	1 263	:	NL
A	613	611	609	604	:	:	:	A
P	:	:	:	:	:	:	:	P
FIN	424	412	419	416	404	404	:	FIN
S	977	937	937	923	923	923	923	S
UK	7 782	7 432	7 462	7 252	7 221	:	:	UK
IS	:	82	79	77	75	74	74	IS
NO	750	:	860	:	:	768	:	NO
CH	1 162	1 068	1 052	1 056	1 063	1 057	1 061	CH

3

Population connected to public sewerage treatment by type of treatment. %

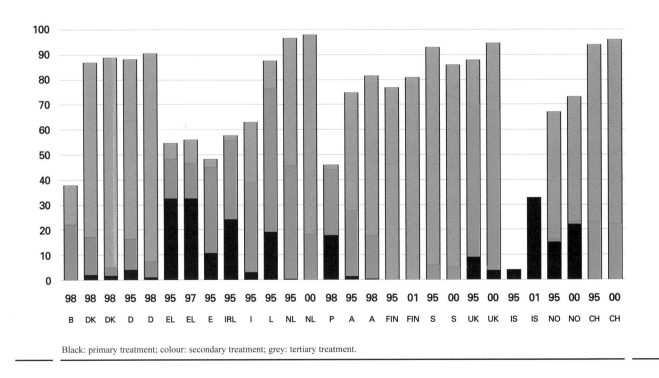

Black: primary treatment; colour: secondary treatment; grey: tertiary treatment.

Waste

Decoupling waste generation from economic growth

The generation of waste represents, on the one hand, a loss of materials and energy. On the other hand, its deposition contributes to major environmental problems such as climate change and an impaired quality of surface and groundwater bodies as well as landscapes. Waste generation might also lead to the deterioration of human health (through the release into the environment of hazardous substances that some types of waste contain).

The sixth environment action programme states the objective of decoupling the generation of waste from economic growth. A significant overall reduction in the volumes of waste generated shall be achieved through improved waste-prevention initiatives, better resource efficiency and a shift to more sustainable consumption patterns.

Who generates waste ...

Municipal waste constitutes approximately 15 % of total waste produced and is the most reliable indicator to make comparisons among countries.

The economic activities that are large contributors to the waste mountain are construction, agriculture, mining and manufacturing industry. Waste streams such as construction and demolition waste, sewage sludge (a residual product of the treatment of municipal and industrial wastewater) pose various types of management problems and environmental impacts.

... and what to do with it?

Landfilling, waste incineration (with or without energy recovery) and recycling are the most important treatment methods applied to municipal waste. Recycling is considered to be one of the most beneficial for the environment and is supported by several directives and policy measures in the EU.

Continuous improvement of statistics on waste

Waste statistics are collected from all European countries through the 'Waste' section of the joint Eurostat/OECD questionnaire.

It is generally recognised that differences in methods of data production among countries plus the variances in interpretation of definitions and/or waste categories make comparison of data among countries rather difficult.

The major piece of EU legislation for waste statistics is the regulation on waste statistics, which is about to be adopted (presently stands as the 'Amended proposal for a regulation of the European Parliament and of the Council on waste statistics'). It is expected that, once adopted and implemented, statistical data on waste will improve markedly.

3

Waste generated by economic sector. 1999. 1 000 t

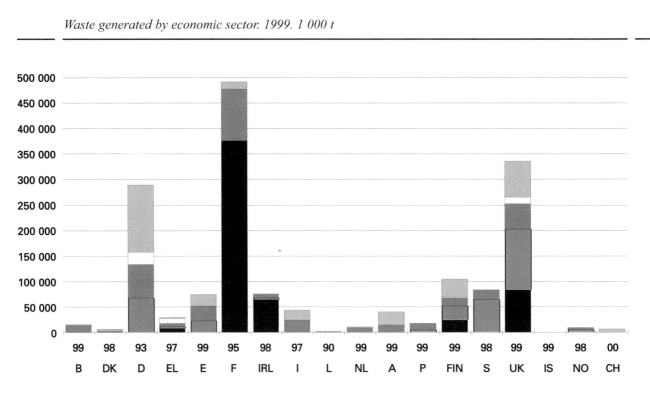

Black: agriculture and forestry; colour: mining and quarrying; grey: manufacturing industry; white: energy production; light grey: construction.

3

Treatment of municipal waste. 2000. 1 000 t

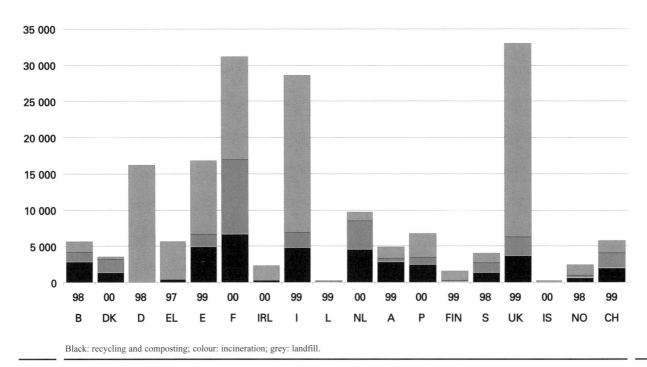

Black: recycling and composting; colour: incineration; grey: landfill.

DK: composting refers only to garden waste. P: landfill-controlled corresponds to final disposal (landfill + other disposal operations).

Environmental protection expenditure

About encouragement, regulations and 'the polluter shall pay'

The public has become increasingly aware of the need to protect the environment against pollution. Environmental protection is now being integrated into all policy fields with the general aim of ensuring sustainable development.

To encourage firms and private households to protect the environment, governments can use regulatory measures or levy taxes directly linked to pollution. The 'polluter pays' principle is another weapon in the fight against pollution. The data on environmental protection expenditure are an indicator of the response of society to reduce pollution.

Protecting the environment benefits the economy

Environmental protection measures cost money but can also generate revenues. Measures to protect the environment are increasingly being taken on a voluntary basis, for example, to meet the expectations of consumers or stakeholders, to increase market shares, or to improve company image. By the same token, environmental protection creates new markets for environmental goods and services, with benefits for exports and employment.

Spending on environmental protection occurs in all sectors of the economy. The public sector and industry are the sectors for which data are available for most Member States.

Statistical data on environmental protection expenditure

The legal framework for the statistical data on environmental protection expenditure by industry is Council Regulation (EC, Euratom) No 58/97 on structural business statistics which was adopted in December 1996. The regulation provides a tool for the development in the coming years of regular data collection on the variables and economic activities of the highest policy interest.

Total expenditure is the sum of investments and current expenditure. Effective interpretations need to take into account that:

— high levels of spending in one country could, for example, be the result of new stricter policies or the result of long periods of no spending;

— the proportion of public sector expenditure versus industry expenditure could vary between countries depending on the degree of privatisation of the basic environmental protection activities, i.e. waste collection, waste treatment and sewage treatment.

Environmental protection expenditure statistics are collected through the joint Eurostat/OECD questionnaire.

3

Total expenditure by public sector. Million ECU

	1996	1997	1998	1999	2000	
B	929.0	1 019.0	1 149.0	1 113.0	1 266.0	B
DK	1 808.0	1 882.0	1 946.0	2 101.0	2 189.0	DK
D	13 003.0	11 220.0	10 395.0	:	:	D
EL	665.0	681.0	702.0	730.0	:	EL
E	3 356.0	4 045.0	5 053.0	4 977.0	:	E
F	10 071.0	10 428.0	10 901.0	11 650.0	12 617.0	F
IRL	:	:	412.0	:	:	IRL
I	6 587.0	7 013.0	7 527.0	8 032.0	8 592.0	I
L	:	108.0	:	:	:	L
NL	:	4 072.0	:	:	:	NL
A	2 416.0	358.0	484.0	353.0	:	A
P	754.0	775.0	628.0	665.0	729.0	P
FIN	529.0	538.0	520.0	481.0	509.0	FIN
S	353.0	190.0	381.0	359.0	:	S
UK	:	5 542.0	5 967.0	6 624.0	7 576.0	UK
IS	18.0	22.0	24.0	30.0	31.0	IS
CH	2 154.0	1 943.0	2 028.0	2 043.0	:	CH

3

Total expenditure by industry. Million ECU

	1996	1997	1998	1999	2000	
B	:	:	:	1 165	:	B
DK	:	:	:	:	:	DK
D	9 222	11 082	:	:	:	D
EL	281	:	:	:	:	EL
E	:	681	824	1 000	1 455	E
F	:	:	:	:	:	F
IRL	:	:	166	:	:	IRL
I	:	1 392	:	:	:	I
L	:	:	:	:	:	L
NL	:	1 393	1 269	1 662	:	NL
A	1 230	1 317	1 208	1 142	:	A
P	219	180	261	340	444	P
FIN	577	554	525	490	:	FIN
S	:	975	:	1 073	:	S
UK	:	6 159	:	5 931	6 935	UK

Air emissions and air quality

Air pollution: complex but severe effects

The air we breathe is affected by emissions of substances to the atmosphere caused by fuel combustion, industrial processes and other activities. Atmospheric pollution contributes to various environmental problems such as climate change, acidification and eutrophication and to the formation of tropospheric ozone.

The greenhouse gas effect

There is a broad consensus in the scientific community that climate change is happening.

High concentrations of carbon dioxide (CO_2), methane (CH_4), nitrous oxide (N_2O) and halocarbons (hydrofluorocarbon (HFC), perfluorocarbon (PFC) and sulphur hexafluoride (SF_6)) change the composition of the air in the atmosphere. This leads to the known greenhouse gas effect that impacts on the earth's climate.

In the Kyoto Protocol (1997), under the UN Framework Convention on Climate Change (UNFCCC), the European Union agreed to reduce its greenhouse gas emissions by 8 % below 1990 levels by 2008 to 2012. The European climate change programme (ECCP) has been developed to identify common and coordinated policies and measures at Community level to meet the EU's Kyoto target.

Data on greenhouse gas emissions are submitted annually to the UNFCCC and to the European Commission under the monitoring mechanism (Council Decision 1999/296/EC). To estimate the emissions, countries apply common guidelines and a common reporting format. On behalf of the Commission, the European Environment Agency's European Topic Centre on Air and Climate Change (EEA/ETC-ACC) compiles data for the EU and regularly produces data and trend reports.

Acidification and eutrophication

The emissions of mainly sulphur dioxide (SO_2), nitrogen oxides (NO_X) and ammonia (NH_3) contribute to the acidification and eutrophication of the soil and water bodies and may damage materials. They affect air quality and pose threats to human health and ecosystems.

The EU has set a reduction target with the 2010 national emission ceilings directive (NECD) that is stricter than the corresponding 1999 Gothenburg Protocol under the UN/ECE Convention on Long-range Transboundary Air Pollution (CLRTAP).

Tropospheric ozone

The emissions of substances such as carbon monoxide (CO), non-methane volatile organic compounds (NMVOCs), methane (CH_4) and nitrogen oxides (NO_X), the so-called tropospheric ozone precursors, contribute to the formation of ground-level ozone, which has adverse effects on human health and ecosystems.

The data source for these groups of substances is the official national data, which are regularly reported according to the several protocols under the CLRTAP, and the corresponding EU directives and decisions. The EEA/ETC-ACC also compiles these data.

To estimate the emissions of these pollutants, countries apply methods and guidelines agreed upon by the parties to both conventions.

Special attention: urban areas

The air quality framework directive takes care of the fact that around 80 % of Europe's population live in urban areas. Human exposure to high concentrations of hazardous substances, fine particles and elevated ozone concentration levels can give rise to inflammatory responses and decreases in lung function. The observed symptoms are a cough, chest pain and difficulties in breathing, headache and eye irritation.

Data on air emissions and air quality

The European Environment Agency is the body that compiles data on air emissions and air quality for the EU and candidate countries. It receives the same data that are officially submitted by Member States and other countries in line with their commitments under the conventions and various EU directives and regulations. The EEA uses the data to produce reports and assessments.

The data is regularly published on its web site (http://www.eea.eu.int).

Further reading:

Eurostat publications
— **Environment statistics — Yearbook**
— **Regional environmental statistics — Initial data collection results**
— **Environmental protection expenditure in Europe**
— **Environmental pressure indicators for the EU**
— **Measuring Progress Towards a more sustainable Europe**
— **Environment Statistics Pocketbook**
— **Waste Generated in Europe**

Statistics in Focus — Theme 8
— **No 5 Organic farming**
— **No 6 Water resources, abstraction and use in European countries**
— **No 7 Environmental protection expenditure in Europe**
— **No 13 Water management in the regions of the European Union**
— **No 14 Waste water in European countries**

Do you need more information?
— **Ask your Data Shop (see last page)**
— **http://www.europa.eu.int/comm/eurostat**
— **Eurostat's data serves the political discussion in Europe. Have a look at the website of the "Environment Directorate-General": http://europa.eu.int/comm/dgs/environment/index_en.htm**

Emissions of acidifying pollutants. 1 000 t

	1991	1992	1993	1994	1995	1996	1997	1998	1999	2000	
EU-15	969	917	865	818	781	736	699	678	644	630	EU-15
B	23	23	22	21	20	20	19	19	18	18	B
DK	22	19	18	18	17	19	16	14	13	11	DK
D	219	192	177	159	142	122	111	103	98	98	D
EL	29	29	29	28	30	29	29	30	30	30	EL
E	125	124	117	118	113	108	113	109	111	109	E
F	133	126	118	115	113	113	107	108	102	98	F
IRL	15	15	14	15	15	14	15	16	15	14	IRL
I	118	113	111	106	107	102	96	93	87	87	I
L	1	1	1	1	1	1	1	1	1	1	L
NL	31	28	28	25	26	24	25	23	22	21	NL
A	12	11	11	10	10	10	10	10	9	9	A
P	24	27	25	24	25	24	24	26	26	26	P
FIN	15	13	12	12	11	11	11	11	10	9	FIN
S	15	14	14	13	12	13	12	11	11	10	S
UK	188	183	168	152	138	126	111	106	91	87	UK
IS	2	2	2	2	2	2	1	1	2	2	IS
NO	18	20	21	22	23	23	23	23	23	24	NO
CH	12	12	11	11	11	10	8	7	7	7	CH

3

Emissions of tropospheric ozone precursors. 1 000 t

	1990	1991	1992	1993	1994	1995	1996	1997	1998	1999	2000	
EU-15	36 988	36 198	35 100	33 563	32 434	31 402	30 291	29 126	28 251	27 069	26 473	EU-15
B	822	794	805	795	787	766	743	732	780	720	720	B
DK	592	644	581	578	577	551	605	544	506	473	461	DK
D	7 830	6 951	6 329	5 900	5 475	5 208	4 919	4 664	4 441	4 238	4 235	D
EL	886	902	904	908	930	932	976	989	1 041	1 036	1 036	EL
E	3 629	3 802	3 758	3 585	3 684	3 605	3 576	3 594	3 628	3 678	3 673	E
F	5 931	5 980	5 824	5 497	5 227	5 087	4 932	4 701	4 596	4 379	4 174	F
IRL	308	309	326	301	293	288	301	304	310	283	282	IRL
I	5 464	5 620	5 691	5 650	5 390	5 404	4 857	4 652	4 429	4 174	4 174	I
L	67	69	71	73	62	54	55	46	40	40	41	L
NL	1 350	1 286	1 242	1 181	1 129	1 074	1 089	982	928	897	885	NL
A	762	734	681	661	650	626	611	610	590	580	569	A
P	898	954	1 018	1 009	1 008	1 039	1 008	1 073	1 063	1 064	1 064	P
FIN	656	629	606	595	590	555	564	550	534	534	508	FIN
S	1 069	1 050	1 012	987	999	962	959	904	887	861	814	S
UK	6 724	6 476	6 249	5 844	5 634	5 251	5 096	4 781	4 478	4 112	3 837	UK
IS	64	67	68	69	72	69	61	49	48	56	64	IS
NO	701	668	685	712	724	739	753	747	723	721	712	NO
CH	547	518	485	453	429	406	388	371	353	336	325	CH

Urban air quality — Population exposure to air pollution by ozone — Percentage of urban population exposed to concentration levels exceeding target values

	1991	1992	1993	1994	1995	1996	1997	1998	1999	2000	2001	
EU-15	:	:	:	:	:	:	:	12.8	:	19.7	:	EU-15
B	:	:	:	:	:	:	:	-	:	-	:	B
DK	:	:	:	:	:	:	:	0.0	:	:	:	DK
D	:	:	:	:	:	:	:	18.0	:	9.6	:	D
EL	:	:	:	:	:	:	:	:	:	:	:	EL
E	:	:	:	:	:	:	:	46.4	:	41.2	:	E
F	:	:	:	:	:	:	:	:	:	18.3	:	F
IRL	:	:	:	:	:	:	:	:	:	:	:	IRL
I	:	:	:	:	:	:	:	:	:	69.9	:	I
L	:	:	:	:	:	:	:	:	:	:	:	L
NL	:	:	:	:	:	:	:	-	:	-	:	NL
A	:	:	:	:	:	:	:	89.8	:	95.4	:	A
P	:	:	:	:	:	:	:	:	:	-	:	P
FIN	:	:	:	:	:	:	:	0.0	:	0.0	:	FIN
S	:	:	:	:	:	:	:	-	:	-	:	S
UK	:	:	:	:	:	:	:	0.0	:	0.0	:	UK
IS	:	:	:	:	:	:	:	-	:	-	:	IS
NO	:	:	:	:	:	:	:	-	:	-	:	NO

Urban air quality — Population exposure to air pollution by particulate matter (PM10) — Percentage of urban population exposed to concentration levels exceeding limit values

	1991	1992	1993	1994	1995	1996	1997	1998	1999	2000	2001	
EU-15	:	:	:	:	:	:	:	17.0	:	36.2	:	EU-15
B	:	:	:	:	:	:	:	9.1	:	-	:	B
DK	:	:	:	:	:	:	:	:	:	:	:	DK
D	:	:	:	:	:	:	:	2.9	:	36.2	:	D
EL	:	:	:	:	:	:	:	:	:	:	:	EL
E	:	:	:	:	:	:	:	100.0	:	97.6	:	E
F	:	:	:	:	:	:	:	:	:	:	:	F
IRL	:	:	:	:	:	:	:	:	:	:	:	IRL
I	:	:	:	:	:	:	:	:	:	100.0	:	I
L	:	:	:	:	:	:	:	:	:	:	:	L
NL	:	:	:	:	:	:	:	100.0	:	95.6	:	NL
A	:	:	:	:	:	:	:	:	:	-	:	A
P	:	:	:	:	:	:	:	100.0	:	100.0	:	P
FIN	:	:	:	:	:	:	:	0.0	:	0.0	:	FIN
S	:	:	:	:	:	:	:	-	:	56.0	:	S
UK	:	:	:	:	:	:	:	0.0	:	0.0	:	UK
IS	:	:	:	:	:	:	:	-	:	1.0	:	IS
NO	:	:	:	:	:	:	:	:	:	:	:	NO

Transport

Ensuring sustainable transport

Transport plays an essential role in modern societies, providing supply and distribution chains for industry, facilitating trade and tourism, and providing mobility to individuals in their everyday lives. It is therefore not surprising to observe a strong relationship between the development of transport and GDP.

Transport also has social and environmental consequences. Most notable are pollutant emissions (responsible for health problems and premature death), greenhouse gas emissions (responsible for global warming and climate change), noise (responsible for annoyance and health problems), traffic accidents (responsible for injuries and deaths), and congestion (responsible for inconvenience and delays).

These impacts are fundamentally linked to how people travel and how goods are transported, as well as to measures taken to increase safety (e.g. safety belts, airbags, speed limits) and to reduce environmental impacts (e.g. catalytic converters, cleaner fuels). They are therefore amenable to improvement.

This is why the EU sustainable development strategy includes transport as one of its four priority areas. It aims to tackle rising volumes of traffic and levels of congestion, noise and pollution and encourage the use of environment-friendly forms of transport as well as to ensure that prices better reflect the real costs to society. It also aims to weaken (or 'decouple') the link between economic development and transport growth. This can be achieved through increased use of teleservices, shifting production away from heavy industry towards high-tech products, and moving towards a more service-oriented economy.

The structural indicators include indicators intended to follow the linkage between transport and economic growth, as well as dependence on road transport and the car. These indicators show that over the last decade:

— freight transport in the EU as a whole has grown slightly faster than GDP, and few Member States show signs of decoupling. In Norway, freight transport has grown at a substantially higher rate than GDP. On the other hand, there are some signs of decoupling in the United States and Japan;

— in the case of passenger transport, the progress of some EU countries in decoupling has been counterbalanced by the opposite tendency in others. Norway and the United States show some signs of decoupling, while Japan shows no real change;

— freight transport has slowly become more dependent on road in most countries, with few exceptions;

— in many countries, there has been no significant change in car dependency. The exceptions are Greece, Portugal and Japan, where car dependency has increased slowly.

About the indicators

The freight transport data upon which these indicators are based include road, rail and inland waterways. The unit is tonne-kilometres.

Sources

EU

— EU-wide surveys on goods transport by road, rail and inland waterways

— National statistical offices

— Eurostat/ECMT/UNECE common questionnaire for transport statistics

— Energy and Transport DG

Non EU

— National statistical offices

— Eurostat/ECMT/UNECE common questionnaire for transport statistics

Concepts

Transport is inherently difficult to quantify consistently across modes and geographical regions. Unlike other sectors, such as agriculture or industry, transport involves movement from place to place, often across borders. We are therefore faced with fundamental questions about the most appropriate concept to use. Whereas movements on national territory may be appropriate for rail and inland waterways, they would not be appropriate for air and sea. Transport by these modes takes place largely outside national territory, especially in the case of the small countries in Europe, and origin-destination is the preferred concept. In the case of road transport, surveys are usually carried out at the enterprise level, introducing yet another concept.

In the interests of comparability between the EU and the United States and Japan, the traditional concepts of transport are used for all modes. It should be borne in mind, however, that this decision introduces certain distortions. For example, Luxembourg road hauliers carry out much of their work outside Luxembourg, thus inflating the real road transport activity relative to other countries.

Volume of freight transport relative to GDP. Index of inland freight transport volume relative to GDP. Measured in tonne-km/GDP and indexed on 1995

	1991	1992	1993	1994	1995	1996	1997	1998	1999	2000	2001	
EU-15	95.4	94.3	93.7	97.2	100.0	99.9	105.8	106.5	108.1	105.6	:	EU-15
B	91.6	86.1	91.4	101.3	100.0	91.5	93.8	86.1	81.3	70.3	:	B
DK	91.1	94.6	96.7	99.6	100.0	92.3	91.2	88.8	93.2	93.6	85.9	DK
D	94.4	91.3	90.3	94.6	100.0	97.9	100.3	101.9	106.4	103.9	104.5	D
EL	110.5	98.7	122.3	121.3	100.0	99.2	106.4	94.1	104.3	90.3	:	EL
E	92.0	91.5	92.6	96.7	100.0	98.0	101.6	106.9	110.7	117.8	:	E
F	98.9	99.5	94.6	98.4	100.0	113.2	113.5	112.6	117.7	115.3	112.0	F
IRL	116.3	113.3	108.2	105.1	100.0	104.6	103.0	109.1	122.4	132.2	126.0	IRL
I	87.8	90.9	86.6	88.9	100.0	104.9	102.9	108.8	100.4	101.9	:	I
L	98.7	109.4	113.4	94.8	100.0	81.2	96.6	97.6	118.0	128.8	:	L
NL	98.3	99.0	97.7	100.8	100.0	99.0	105.6	102.5	103.6	96.9	95.3	NL
A	94.7	90.3	90.5	95.0	100.0	96.4	98.1	97.7	124.0	128.2	:	A
P	152.9	138.1	132.0	147.2	100.0	74.6	82.3	76.9	169.8	123.5	137.4	P
FIN	100.3	104.4	111.2	111.3	100.0	96.2	97.0	86.2	90.1	88.0	85.0	FIN
S	94.4	94.6	98.6	98.0	100.0	101.6	104.1	99.6	95.3	91.3	86.7	S
UK	96.9	94.9	96.8	98.6	100.0	92.3	124.7	126.9	116.4	111.1	:	UK
IS	:	:	:	:	100.0	98.3	98.7	96.9	100.2	100.4	101.7	IS
NO	103.3	100.9	97.6	95.2	100.0	105.0	110.2	113.5	112.6	114.1	:	NO
JP	98.0	:	:	:	100.0	99.9	98.2	97.1	98.3	97.7	:	JP
US	93.8	95.7	95.4	98.1	100.0	100.5	96.9	94.9	95.4	:	:	US

Volume of passenger transport relative to GDP. Index of inland passenger transport volume relative to GDP. Measured in passenger-km/GDP and indexed on 1995

	1991	1992	1993	1994	1995	1996	1997	1998	1999	2000	2001	
EU-15	:	:	:	:	100.0	99.9	99.2	99.2	98.2	95.1	:	EU-15
B	:	:	:	:	100.0	99.4	97.2	98.5	97.2	94.6	95.7	B
DK	103.0	104.0	104.1	100.1	100.0	100.3	100.0	99.2	99.4	96.5	95.0	DK
D	100.1	100.0	102.4	99.0	100.0	99.4	98.3	96.5	95.5	89.9	88.4	D
EL	83.4	85.1	90.0	96.5	100.0	106.1	107.9	109.2	111.7	106.7	:	EL
E	92.0	96.0	99.0	99.5	100.0	99.8	101.5	114.2	116.4	115.5	:	E
F	99.7	100.6	102.8	103.8	100.0	100.8	100.5	100.0	99.8	96.8	97.6	F
IRL	102.3	101.9	103.3	104.0	100.0	98.9	95.6	92.1	89.2	84.8	82.5	IRL
I	94.2	100.6	100.5	99.9	100.0	100.9	100.4	101.5	100.2	98.1	:	I
L	91.4	92.2	92.2	91.0	100.0	98.0	92.7	87.6	82.9	76.7	79.6	L
NL	104.5	106.2	103.0	101.6	100.0	97.9	96.7	93.3	92.0	89.1	88.4	NL
A	107.6	104.7	103.6	101.6	100.0	97.6	95.8	94.1	92.0	94.9	:	A
P	80.2	90.9	95.9	100.2	100.0	101.8	102.9	105.1	108.0	103.8	:	P
FIN	97.3	107.2	107.1	102.9	100.0	96.9	93.5	90.5	88.9	84.9	88.2	FIN
S	101.2	104.1	104.3	101.6	100.0	99.5	98.2	95.7	94.3	92.4	92.2	S
UK	108.9	108.5	105.8	101.9	100.0	99.2	97.4	95.5	93.0	90.1	:	UK
IS	:	:	:	:	100.0	99.6	101.0	101.6	101.7	98.5	97.8	IS
NO	112.5	109.5	108.3	104.4	100.0	99.0	94.7	94.9	94.1	92.9	:	NO
JP	:	:	:	100.5	100.0	99.4	98.5	100.5	100.2	98.4	:	JP
US	105.0	104.6	103.7	101.3	100.0	99.5	98.1	96.6	94.1	92.6	:	US

Modal split of freight transport. Percentage share of road transport in total inland freight transport, tonne-km

	1991	1992	1993	1994	1995	1996	1997	1998	1999	2000	2001	
EU-15	72.4	73.4	74.6	74.3	75.5	76.1	76.4	77.7	78.2	77.3	:	EU-15
B	71.9	71.0	73.6	75.0	75.6	74.5	75.3	73.0	72.2	67.8	:	B
DK	90.9	91.2	92.0	91.5	91.9	92.4	91.6	91.2	92.3	92.2	91.9	DK
D	58.6	60.6	61.6	61.4	63.8	64.4	64.4	65.0	68.2	66.3	67.5	D
EL	96.1	96.0	96.8	98.1	97.8	97.5	97.9	97.7	98.0	97.7	:	EL
E	89.3	90.7	92.1	91.4	90.2	90.1	89.7	93.1	91.7	92.4	:	E
F	68.5	69.1	70.4	70.5	73.5	76.4	74.8	76.6	76.8	75.6	77.7	F
IRL	89.5	89.1	89.9	90.2	90.1	91.8	93.1	94.6	95.1	96.2	96.0	IRL
I	87.1	88.0	88.1	87.1	88.0	89.2	88.2	89.3	89.0	88.9	:	I
L	75.1	78.8	81.2	77.6	81.1	77.7	81.2	82.3	86.0	87.6	:	L
NL	57.9	60.6	62.1	60.0	61.1	61.8	60.3	60.7	61.9	60.2	59.7	NL
A	49.6	51.3	52.7	50.8	50.7	49.3	48.2	47.8	59.3	58.1	:	A
P	91.9	90.6	90.4	91.7	85.5	82.7	81.8	83.0	92.0	89.4	90.8	P
FIN	76.4	75.9	73.0	72.1	69.8	72.4	71.3	79.4	73.0	73.1	73.0	FIN
S	57.4	55.8	58.2	58.6	60.2	62.3	63.3	63.0	63.2	61.0	60.5	S
UK	89.9	89.6	91.1	92.1	92.3	90.8	92.7	92.8	92.0	91.9	:	UK
IS	100.0	100.0	100.0	100.0	100.0	100.0	100.0	100.0	100.0	100.0	100.0	IS
NO	82.8	82.7	82.4	84.5	85.4	85.3	85.9	86.8	86.7	87.9	:	NO
JP	91.0	:	:	:	92.1	92.4	92.6	92.9	93.2	93.4	:	JP
US	35.4	36.2	37.3	36.8	35.7	36.2	36.8	37.2	37.8	:	:	US

3

Modal split of passenger transport. Percentage share of car transport in total inland passenger transport, passenger-km

	1991	1992	1993	1994	1995	1996	1997	1998	1999	2000	2001	
EU-15	:	:	:	:	84.1	84.1	84.2	84.5	84.5	84.0	:	EU-15
B	:	:	:	:	83.1	83.1	83.1	83.2	83.4	83.5	83.4	B
DK	82.3	82.3	82.0	81.8	81.4	81.1	81.3	81.5	82.0	81.7	81.4	DK
D	83.5	83.9	84.1	83.8	82.8	82.7	83.0	83.3	83.3	82.4	82.2	D
EL	73.5	73.7	75.9	77.7	78.1	79.2	79.6	81.2	81.5	81.6	:	EL
E	78.4	78.9	79.1	79.5	79.4	80.4	79.0	82.1	82.1	81.5	:	E
F	85.1	85.6	86.2	86.5	86.8	86.4	86.4	86.4	86.5	85.9	86.1	F
IRL	78.1	78.2	78.1	77.7	78.3	79.2	79.7	80.0	80.8	80.9	80.9	IRL
I	80.5	82.0	82.6	82.1	82.4	82.5	82.7	83.4	83.2	82.8	:	I
L	86.1	86.8	87.2	87.0	79.8	80.2	80.4	80.7	80.5	81.5	80.1	L
NL	84.2	84.4	84.3	85.1	85.7	85.8	86.0	85.8	86.3	86.0	86.0	NL
A	79.3	78.4	77.3	77.2	77.0	74.6	76.3	76.5	76.7	76.7	:	A
P	72.5	70.9	75.1	77.4	79.2	80.8	82.5	82.5	83.7	83.9	:	P
FIN	80.4	82.0	81.9	81.8	81.7	81.7	82.0	82.7	83.3	83.4	81.5	FIN
S	86.4	86.4	86.0	86.2	86.0	85.8	85.2	85.0	84.8	84.4	84.1	S
UK	88.2	88.5	88.6	89.0	88.9	88.8	88.6	88.3	88.0	87.9	:	UK
IS	:	:	:	:	88.6	88.6	88.6	88.6	88.8	88.8	88.8	IS
NO	87.7	87.6	787.7	87.6	88.1	87.7	87.3	87.2	87.0	87.2	:	NO
JP	:	:	:	56.3	56.7	57.9	59.1	60.2	60.8	61.1	:	JP
US	95.8	95.9	95.8	95.6	95.7	95.7	95.7	95.7	95.4	95.5	:	US

Please find the complete information of the Eurostat Yearbook on the annexed CD-ROM.

Economic output

- Gross domestic product at market prices. Current series in Million PPS
- Gross value added at basic prices. Yearly growth as % of previous year (real growth in volume)
- Gross value added at basic prices. Current series in million ECU/EUR
- Labour productivity. Gross domestic product in purchasing power standards (PPS) per person employed. EU-15 = 100
- Labour productivity. Gross domestic product in purchasing power standards (PPS) per hour worked relative to EU-15. EU-15 = 100
- Unit labour cost growth. Growth rate of the ratio compensation per employee in current prices divided by GDP (in current prices) per total employment
- Gross value added at current basic prices and current exchange rates. Mining and quarrying of energy-producing materials. % of all branches
- Gross value added at current basic prices and current exchange rates. Mining and quarrying, except of energy-producing materials. % of all branches
- Gross value added at current basic prices and current exchange rates. Manufacture of food products, beverages and tobacco. % of all branches
- Gross value added at current basic prices and current exchange rates. Manufacture of textiles and textile products. % of all branches
- Gross value added at current basic prices and current exchange rates. Manufacture of leather and leather products. % of all branches
- Gross value added at current basic prices and current exchange rates. Manufacture of wood and wood products. % of all branches
- Gross value added at current basic prices and current exchange rates. Manufacture of pulp, paper and paper products; publishing and printing. % of all branches
- Gross value added at current basic prices and current exchange rates. Manufacture of coke, refined petroleum products and nuclear fuel. % of all branches
- Gross value added at current basic prices and current exchange rates. Manufacture of chemicals, chemical products and man-made fibres. % of all branches
- Gross value added at current basic prices and current exchange rates. Manufacture of rubber and plastic products. % of all branches
- Gross value added at current basic prices and current exchange rates. Manufacture of other non-metallic mineral products. % of all branches
- Gross value added at current basic prices and current exchange rates. Manufacture of basic metals and fabricated metal products. % of all branches
- Gross value added at current basic prices and current exchange rates. Manufacture of machinery and equipment n.e.c. % of all branches
- Gross value added at current basic prices and current exchange rates. Manufacture of electrical and optical equipment. % of all branches
- Gross value added at current basic prices and current exchange rates. Manufacture of transport equipment. % of all branches
- Gross value added at current basic prices and current exchange rates. Manufacturing n.e.c. % of all branches
- Gross value added at current basic prices and current exchange rates. Electricity, gas and water supply. % of all branches
- Gross value added at current basic prices and current exchange rates. Construction. % of all branches
- Gross value added at current basic prices and current exchange rates. Wholesale and retail trade; repair of motor vehicles, motor-cycles and personal and household goods. % of all branches
- Gross value added at current basic prices and current exchange rates. Hotels and restaurants. % of all branches

3

- Gross value added at current basic prices and current exchange rates. Transport, storage and communication. % of all branches
- Gross value added at current basic prices and current exchange rates. Financial intermediation. % of all branches
- Gross value added at current basic prices and current exchange rates. Public administration and defence; compulsory social security. % of all branches
- Gross value added at current basic prices and current exchange rates. Other community, social and personal services. % of all branches
- Gross value added at current basic prices and current exchange rates. Private households with employed persons. % of all branches

Consumption and spending

- Final consumption expenditure of households and non-profit institutions serving households. Current series in million ECU/EUR
- Final consumption expenditure of general government. Current series in million ECU/EUR
- Final consumption expenditure of general government. Current series in % of GDP
- Gross fixed capital formation (investments). Current series in million ECU/EUR
- External balance of goods and services. Current series in million ECU/EUR
- External balance of goods and services. Current series in % of GDP
- Business investment. Gross fixed capital formation by the private sector as % of GDP

Income of the input factors

- Compensation of employees: total economy. Current series in million ECU/EUR
- Gross wages and salaries: total economy. Current series in million ECU/EUR
- Gross wages and salaries: total economy. Current series in % of GDP
- Gross operating surplus and mixed income: total economy. Current series in million ECU/EUR

Government finances

- General government output as % of GDP. 2001
- Current taxes on income, wealth, etc. as % of GDP
- Current taxes on income, wealth, etc. as % of GDP. 2001
- Social contributions as % of GDP
- Social contributions as % of GDP. 2001
- Taxes on production and imports as % of GDP
- Taxes on production and imports as % of GDP. 2001
- Total general government revenue as % of GDP. 2001
- General government gross fixed capital formation as % of GDP. 2001
- Total general government expenditure as % of GDP. 2001
- General government final consumption expenditure as % of GDP
- General government final consumption expenditure as % of GDP. 2001
- Subsidies paid by general government as % of GDP
- Subsidies paid by general government as % of GDP. 2001
- Social benefits (other than social transfers in kind) paid by general government as % of GDP
- Social benefits (other than social transfers in kind) paid by general government as % of GDP. 2001
- Public procurement. Value of public procurement which is openly advertised as % of GDP
- Sectoral and ad hoc State aid as % of GDP

Social protection

- Total expenditure on social protection at current prices as % of GDP. 1999
- Total expenditure on social protection per head of population in ECU/EUR
- Total expenditure on social protection per head of population in PPS. 1999
- Total expenditure on social protection per head of population at constant prices. 1990 = 100

- Total expenditure on social protection by type as % of total expenditure. 1999. EU-15
- Social benefits as % of total expenditure
- Administration costs as % of total expenditure
- Other expenditure as % of total expenditure
- Social benefits by functions at constant prices. 1990 = 100. EU-15
- Social benefits for the function 'sickness/healthcare' as % of total benefits
- Social benefits for the function 'disability' as % of total benefits
- Social benefits for the function 'old age' as % of total benefits
- Social benefits for the function 'survivors' as % of total benefits
- Social benefits for the function 'family/children' as % of total benefits
- Social benefits for the function 'unemployment' as % of total benefits
- Social benefits for the function 'housing' as % of total benefits
- Social benefits for the function 'social exclusion n.e.c.' as % of total benefits
- Social benefits per head of population in PPS. 1999
- Social benefits for the function 'sickness/healthcare' in PPS per head of population
- Social benefits for the function 'disability' in PPS per head of population
- Social benefits for the function 'old age' in PPS per head of population
- Social benefits for the function 'survivors' in PPS per head of population
- Social benefits for the function 'family/children' in PPS per head of population
- Social benefits for the function 'unemployment' in PPS per head of population
- Social benefits for the function 'housing' in PPS per head of population
- Social benefits for the function 'social exclusion n.e.c.' in PPS per head of population
- Social benefits for the function 'sickness/healthcare' at constant prices. 1990 = 100
- Social benefits for the function 'disability' at constant prices. 1990 = 100

- Social benefits for the function 'old age' at constant prices. 1990 = 100
- Social benefits for the function 'survivors' at constant prices. 1990 = 100
- Social benefits for the function 'family/children' at constant prices. 1990 = 100
- Social benefits for the function 'unemployment' at constant prices. 1990 = 100
- Social benefits for the function 'housing' at constant prices. 1990 = 100
- Social benefits for the function 'social exclusion n.e.c.' at constant prices. 1990 = 100
- Social protection receipts by type as % of total receipts. 1999. EU-15
- Social protection receipts for the type 'employers' social contributions' as % of total receipts
- Social protection receipts for the type 'social contributions paid by protected persons' as % of total receipts
- Social protection receipts for the type 'general government contributions' as % of total receipts
- Social protection receipts for the type 'other receipts' as % of total receipts
- Social protection receipts by type at constant prices. 1990 = 100, EU-15
- Social protection receipts at constant prices. 1990 = 100
- Social protection receipts for the type 'employers' social contributions' at constant prices. 1990 = 100
- Social protection receipts for the type 'social contributions paid by protected persons' at constant prices. 1990 = 100
- Social protection receipts for the type 'general government contributions' at constant prices. 1990 = 100
- Social protection receipts for the type 'other receipts' at constant prices. 1990 = 100

Wages and labour costs

- Average hourly labour cost in industry and services. Enterprises with 10 or more employees. 2000. EUR
- Average annual labour cost in industry and services. Enterprises with 10 or more employees. 2000. EUR

3

- Structure of labour costs as % of total costs. Industry and services. Enterprises with 10 or more employees. 2000. %
- Structure of labour costs as % of total costs. Industry. Enterprises with 10 or more employees. 2000. %
- Structure of labour costs as % of total costs. Services. Enterprises with 10 or more employees. 2000. %
- Average gross annual earnings in industry and services. Total. Full-time employees. Enterprises with 10 or more employees. 2000. EUR
- Average gross annual earnings for men in industry and services. Full-time employees. Enterprises with 10 or more employees. 2000. EUR
- Average gross annual earnings for women in industry and services. Full-time employees. Enterprises with 10 or more employees. 2000. EUR
- Earnings of women as % of men's in industry and services. Full-time employees. Enterprises with 10 or more employees. 2000

Financial market indicators

- Index of share prices. 1995 = 100. Annual average. %
- Capital raised on stock markets. Amount of new capital raised as % of GDP
- Venture capital: early stage. Venture capital investments as % of GDP. Breakdown by investment stages
- Venture capital: expansion. Venture capital investments as % of GDP. Breakdown by investment stages

Balance of payments

- International current transactions, cover rates. %
- Balance of the current account at current prices. % of GDP
- Balance of international trade in goods at current prices. % of GDP
- Balance of international trade in services at current prices. % of GDP

- Total trade in goods (exports-fob + imports-fob) as % of current account total flows
- International trade in goods, cover rates. %
- Balance in trade in goods of the EU, United States and Japan with the rest of the world. 1 000 million ECU/EUR
- Share of the EU, United States, Japan and the rest of the world in world total transactions in goods (exports and imports). 2001. %
- Total trade in services (exports and imports) as % of current account total flows
- International trade in services, cover rates. %
- Services balances of the EU, United States and Japan with the rest of the world. 1 000 million ECU/EUR
- Share of the EU, United States, Japan and the rest of the world in world total transactions in services (exports and imports). 2001. %
- Direct investment inflows: the EU, United States and Japan. Million ECU/EUR
- EU direct investment inflows from the extra-EU. Suppliers of direct investment to the EU. Million ECU/EUR
- EU direct investment inflows. Suppliers of direct investment to the EU. Million ECU/EUR
- EU direct investment inflows. Recipients of direct investment from the extra-EU. Million ECU/EUR
- EU direct investment inflows from the extra-EU. Million ECU/EUR
- Direct investment outflows: the EU, United States and Japan. Million ECU/EUR
- EU direct investment outflows to the extra-EU. Recipients of direct investment. Million ECU/EUR
- EU direct investment outflows. Recipients of direct investment. Million ECU/EUR
- EU direct investment outflows. Suppliers of direct investment to the extra-EU. Million ECU/EUR
- EU direct investment outflows to the extra-EU. Million ECU/EUR
- Suppliers of EU direct investment intra-flows. Million ECU/EUR
- Recipients of EU direct investment intra-flows. Million ECU/EUR

Trade in goods

- Exports (fob) volume indices. 2000 = 100
- Imports (cif) volume indices. 2000 = 100
- Volume ratio. 2000 = 100
- Exports of agrifood products at current prices. 1 000 million ECU/EUR
- Imports of agrifood products at current prices. 1 000 million ECU/EUR
- Trade balance in agrifood products at current prices. 1 000 million ECU/EUR
- Exports of mineral fuels, lubricants and related products at current prices. 1 000 million ECU/EUR
- Imports of mineral fuels, lubricants and related products at current prices. 1 000 million ECU/EUR
- Trade balance in mineral fuels, lubricants and related products at current prices. 1 000 million ECU/EUR
- Exports of chemicals and related products at current prices. 1 000 million ECU/EUR
- Imports of chemicals and related products at current prices. 1 000 million ECU/EUR
- Trade balance in chemicals and related products at current prices. 1 000 million ECU/EUR
- Exports of machinery and transport equipment at current prices. 1 000 million ECU/EUR
- Imports of machinery and transport equipment at current prices. 1 000 million ECU/EUR
- Trade balance in machinery and transport equipment at current prices. 1 000 million ECU/EUR
- Exports of manufactured products at current prices. 1 000 million ECU/EUR
- Imports of manufactured products at current prices. 1 000 million ECU/EUR
- Trade balance in manufactured products at current prices. 1 000 million ECU/EUR
- Extra-EU trade balance by main trading partners. 1 000 million ECU/EUR
- Extra-EU exports of agrifood products by main trading partners. 1 000 million ECU/EUR
- Extra-EU imports of agrifood products by main trading partners. 1 000 million ECU/EUR

- Extra-EU trade balance in agrifood products by main trading partners. 1 000 million ECU/EUR
- Extra-EU exports of mineral fuels, lubricants and related products by main trading partners. 1 000 million ECU/EUR
- Extra-EU imports of mineral fuels, lubricants and related products by main trading partners. 1 000 million ECU/EUR
- Extra-EU trade balance in mineral fuels, lubricants and related products by main trading partners. 1 000 million ECU/EUR
- Extra-EU exports of chemicals and related products by main trading partners. 1 000 million ECU/EUR
- Extra-EU imports of chemicals and related products by main trading partners. 1 000 million ECU/EUR
- Extra-EU trade balance in chemicals and related products by main trading partners. 1 000 million ECU/EUR
- Extra-EU exports of machinery and transport equipment by main trading partners. 1 000 million ECU/EUR
- Extra-EU imports of machinery and transport equipment by main trading partners. 1 000 million ECU/EUR
- Extra-EU trade balance in machinery and transport equipment by main trading partners. 1 000 million ECU/EUR
- Extra-EU exports of manufactured products by main trading partners. 1 000 million ECU/EUR
- Extra-EU imports of manufactured products by main trading partners. 1 000 million ECU/EUR
- Extra-EU trade balance in manufactured products by main trading partners. 1 000 million ECU/EUR
- Exports to EU countries at current prices. 1 000 million ECU/EUR
- Imports from EU countries at current prices. 1 000 million ECU/EUR
- Intra-EU exports of agrifood products at current prices. 1 000 million ECU/EUR
- Intra-EU exports of mineral fuels, lubricants and related products at current prices. 1 000 million ECU/EUR
- Intra-EU exports of chemicals and related products at current prices. 1 000 million ECU/EUR

- Intra-EU exports of machinery and transport equipment at current prices. 1 000 million ECU/EUR
- Intra-EU exports of manufactured products at current prices. 1 000 million ECU/EUR

Trade in services

- International transactions in transportation, cover rates. %
- Total EU transactions in transportation (exports and imports). 2001. Breakdown by type of transport
- International transactions in sea transport services, cover rates. %
- International transactions in air transport services, cover rates. %
- International transactions in travel, cover rates. %
- Geographical breakdown of EU travel transactions in 2001. 1 000 million EUR
- International transactions in other services in 2001, cover rates. %
- Breakdown of international transactions in other services in 2001. % of other services total transactions (exports and imports)
- EU external balances of other services items. Comparison 2000 and 2001. 1 000 million ECU/EUR
- EU external balances of other services items. Comparison 2000 and 2001. 1 000 million ECU/EUR

Trading partners

- EU current transactions by partner zone, cover rates. %
- EU current account balances with the United States, Japan and EFTA. 1 000 million ECU/EUR
- EU international exports of goods: breakdown by partner zones. % of EU total exports
- EU international imports of goods: breakdown by partner zones. % of EU total imports
- EU goods balance by partner zone: comparison 1995, 1998 and 2001. 1 000 million ECU/EUR

- EU goods balance by economic zone: comparison 1995, 1998 and 2001. 1 000 million ECU/EUR
- EU international exports of services: breakdown by partner zones. % of EU total exports
- EU international imports of services: breakdown by partner zones. % of EU total imports
- EU services balance by partner: comparison 1995, 1998 and 2001. 1 000 million ECU/EUR
- EU services balance by economic zone: comparison 1995, 1998 and 2001. 1 000 million ECU/EUR
- EU international receipts of income: breakdown by partner zones. % of EU total receipts
- EU international payments of income: breakdown by partner zones. % of EU total payments
- EU income balance by partner: comparison 1995, 1998 and 2001. 1 000 million ECU/EUR
- EU income balance by economic zone: comparison 1995, 1998 and 2001. 1 000 million ECU/EUR
- EU international credits of current transfers: breakdown by partner zones. % of EU total credits
- EU international debits of current transfers: breakdown by partner zones. % of EU total debits
- EU current transfers balance by partner: comparison 1995, 1998 and 2001. 1 000 million ECU/EUR
- EU current transfers balance by economic zone: comparison 1995, 1998 and 2001. 1 000 million ECU/EUR

Water

- Total freshwater abstractions (surface- and groundwater). Million m³
- Total freshwater abstractions (surface- and groundwater). m³/capita
- Water abstracted by main sectors. m³/capita
- Population connected to public sewerage system . % of total population

- Population connected to public sewerage system with treatment. % of total population

Waste

- Municipal waste collected. kg per person per year
- Municipal waste landfilled. kg per person per year

- Municipal waste incinerated. kg per person per year

Environmental protection expenditure

- Total environmental expenditure by public sector by domain. %.
- Total expenditure by industry by domain. %

3

4

Entrepreneurial activities

Business structures

Business sectors

Science and technology

Agriculture, forestry and fisheries

Business structures at a glance

The background for doing business

Eurostat draws a comprehensive picture of the structure of the European business world and thus of the framework for entrepreneurial activity. Its data on business structures show developments in specific activities as well as structural changes of the economy as a whole. Without this information, short-term data on the economic cycle would lack background and be hard to interpret. Enterprises that want to determine their opportunities in a new market or put their performance into perspective use these data, as do business associations, trade unions, market researchers, administrators and politicians.

If you would like more detailed information on the topics presented below, please contact your Eurostat Data Shop. The addresses of the Data Shops can be found at the end of the yearbook.

Production and labour

Structural business statistics describe the economy by observing the activity of units engaged in an economic activity. They answer questions like: How much wealth is created in an activity? How many workforces are needed to create this wealth? How is this activity developing? Is this activity participating in the growth of the economy? Are investments made in this activity?

Principally, the structural information presented in the Eurostat yearbook relates to production or to employment. Among a number of variables describing the input and output sides of business activity, a selection of basic indicators is presented.

— **Turnover** corresponds to the total of all sales (excluding VAT) of goods and services carried out by the enterprises of a sector during the reference year.

— **Gross value added** at factor cost corresponds to the difference between the value of what is produced and intermediate consumption entering the production, corrected for subsidies on production and costs, and assimilated taxes and levies. It can be interpreted as the wealth created by the enterprises of a sector and which is used to remunerate the production factors (capital in the form of the gross operating surplus, and labour in the form of the personnel costs).

— **Personnel costs** are defined as the total amounts paid by the enterprises of a sector to remunerate the work of the enterprises' employees during the reference year. They cover wages and salaries and the social contributions paid by the employers.

— The number of **persons employed** is defined as the total number of persons who work for the enterprises of the sector, whether or not they are paid. This total, however, excludes borrowed staff and agency workers.

The SBS database

The data are taken from the SBS database, Eurostat's reference database on structural business statistics (SBS). It presents the data in absolute values and in the form of some basic ratios that make it possible, for example, to compare levels between countries or to calculate the share of an industry in a total.

A harmonised legal framework

The Council regulation on structural business statistics provides a harmonised legal framework for the annual collection of structural data from businesses in the European Union. It defines the nomenclatures (NACE Rev. 1, NUTS) and the statistical units to be used, the coverage (without size threshold), the common deadlines and the quality criteria to be fulfilled.

The regulation covers all market activities (excluding agriculture) normally included in the industry, construction, distributive trades and service sectors (Sections C to K of NACE Rev. 1). In the SBS domain of NewCronos, a much higher level of detail is available than in the Eurostat yearbook.

Data collection is carried out by the national statistical institutes, and the aggregated data are transmitted to Eurostat, which calculates the European totals. EU totals (levels) are only calculated when all countries' data are available and their comparability assessed.

For the reference year 1998, EU totals cannot be calculated for all enterprises because, depending on the activity, the data from two or more countries are missing. This is due to the fact that the SBS regulation is still in a transition period during which Member States are granted derogations that make it easier for them to adapt their system to the harmonised requirements. The year 1999 is the first reference year for which all countries have to comply with the regulation, and thus for which a consistent EU data set is available.

Further reading:

Eurostat publications
— Monthly panorama of European business — Annual subscription

Statistics in Focus — Theme 4
— No 17 SME Regio — High density of SMEs in southern Europe
— No 20 Foreign-owned enterprises

Do you need more information?
— Ask your Data Shop (see last page)
— http://www.europa.eu.int/comm/eurostat
**— Eurostat's data serves the political discussion in Europe. Have a look at the website of the
    "Enterprise Directorate-General": http://europa.eu.int/comm/dgs/enterprise/index_en.htm**

Value added at factor cost of mining and quarrying. Million EUR

	1998	1999	
B	282	298	**B**
DK	:	1 707	**DK**
D	:	9 579	**D**
EL	:	:	**EL**
E	1 541	1 631	**E**
F	2 030	1 939	**F**
IRL	329 *	323	**IRL**
I	3 348	3 618	**I**
L	21 *	27 *	**L**
NL	:	:	**NL**
A	490	512	**A**
P	378	384	**P**
FIN	256	219	**FIN**
S	691	569	**S**
UK	20 727	23 137	**UK**

IRL: enterprises with three persons or more employed.

Value added at factor cost of manufacturing. Million EUR

	1998	1999	
B	39 344	40 981	**B**
DK	22 751	23 575	**DK**
D	:	417 187	**D**
EL	:	:	**EL**
E	85 602	92 719	**E**
F	191 337	200 706	**F**
IRL	21 364 *	27 464	**IRL**
I	191 090	186 530	**I**
L	2 156 *	2 137 *	**L**
NL	50 689	51 457	**NL**
A	32 656	33 899	**A**
P	16 894	17 735	**P**
FIN	25 124	26 064	**FIN**
S	43 211	45 093	**S**
UK	217 808	225 583	**UK**

Value added at factor cost of construction. Million EUR

	1998	1999	
B	7 752	8 253	**B**
DK	6 532	7 129	**DK**
D	:	77 859	**D**
EL	:	:	**EL**
E	:	38 062	**E**
F	41 350	43 999	**F**
IRL	:	:	**IRL**
I	34 061	36 988	**I**
L	912 *	995 *	**L**
NL	15 638	17 411	**NL**
A	10 488	10 006	**A**
P	5 612	5 695	**P**
FIN	:	4 399	**FIN**
S	8 079	9 326	**S**
UK	50 484	58 317	**UK**

IRL: enterprises with three persons or more employed.

Personnel costs of mining and quarrying. Million EUR

	1998	1999	
B	118	132	**B**
DK	:	103	**DK**
D	:	6 760	**D**
EL	:	:	**EL**
E	1 075	1 128	**E**
F	1 768	1 593	**F**
IRL	211 *	185	**IRL**
I	1 042	992	**I**
L	10 *	11 *	**L**
NL	:	:	**NL**
A	266	257	**A**
P	186	198	**P**
FIN	123	103	**FIN**
S	396	386	**S**
UK	3 842	3 701	**UK**

4

Value added at factor cost of wholesale and retail trade; repair of motor vehicles, motorcycles and personal and household goods. Million EUR

Value added at factor cost of hotels and restaurants. Million EUR

	1998	1999		1998	1999	
B	21 486	23 274		2 418	2 763	B
DK	:	17 277		:	1 926	DK
D	:	181 255		:	20 034	D
EL	:	:		:	:	EL
E	:	59 656		13 164	14 325	E
F	106 143	113 435		17 757	19 717	F
IRL	6 410 *	7 264		1 866 *	:	IRL
I	84 057	85 736		16 201	15 901	I
L	1 530 *	1 715 *		318 *	350 *	L
NL	:	45 900		5 074	5 536	NL
A	19 748	20 133		4 131	4 452	A
P	13 392	11 623		1 966	2 563	P
FIN	9 787	9 844		1 375	1 343	FIN
S	20 186	21 828		2 413	2 659	S
UK	150 752	166 131		26 470	28 879	UK

Value added at factor cost of transport, storage and communication. Million EUR

Value added at factor cost of real estate, renting and business activities. Million EUR

	1998	1999		1998	1999	
B	14 616	14 986		15 103	17 123	B
DK	:	12 754		:	15 288	DK
D	:	98 293		:	443 565	D
EL	:	:		:	:	EL
E	:	32 901		:	47 854	E
F	62 154	72 038		100 924	112 515	F
IRL	3 535 *	:		3 918 *	:	IRL
I	54 471	51 780		58 975	66 541	I
L	:	:		1 309 *	1 557 *	L
NL	22 515	22 281		:	:	NL
A	11 644	12 043		11 990	12 869	A
P	5 965	6 370		5 701	7 752	P
FIN	7 387	7 491		7 072	7 443	FIN
S	13 333	14 222		24 592	27 461	S
UK	:	88 925		:	193 566	UK

4

Industry and construction

Statistics on industry and construction: a long tradition of rich and high-quality data

In the Eurostat yearbook, several indicators are presented.

— **Labour productivity:** this aims at measuring the amount of wealth created within an industry by a given amount of labour. Apparent labour productivity relates value added at factor costs to the number of persons employed. It stands at rather different levels, depending on the activity: it is highest in the capital-intensive chemical industry and lowest in the labour-intensive textile industry.

— **Production index for industry:** after a general increase over the last seven years, culminating in an annual growth rate of 5.0 % in 2000, the production index for industry showed a slight slowdown for EU-15 in 2001, following the negative trend in the United States and Japan.

— **Employment index in industry:** in the European Union, the industrial sector (total industry without construction) shows a gradual decrease in employment and a consequent decrease in the number of hours worked.

— **Producer prices index:** the significant increase in the producer prices index recorded in 2000 (+ 4.9 %), mostly due to the impact of the drastic rise in energy prices, continued in 2001 (+ 1.9 %).

— **The share of the gross operating surplus in value added:** value added is used to remunerate the production factors: capital in the form of the gross operating surplus (GOS), and labour in the form of the personnel costs. The relative share of the GOS varies greatly from sector to sector. It is close to 45 % in the chemical industry, and less than 30 % in labour-intensive industries such as the textile industry. The more capital-intensive the industry, the higher the ratio share of gross operating surplus in value added.

— **Value added in production:** this relates the value added to the value of production. It is an indicator of the degree of integration of a sector's enterprises: a high ratio for one particular sector reflects a production process there that comprises an important share of total transformation of the products. This ratio is very stable over time but varies greatly from one activity to another.

— **The share of research and development expenditures in total turnover:** this indicates the efforts made by the industry towards innovation and technological progress. High-technology industries (by definition, those industries with significant research and development expenditures) grow much faster than other industries in Europe.

— **Recent developments in construction:** after having steadily increased since 1997, the production index in construction stagnated for EU-15 in 2001.

4

Production, total industry (excluding construction). Growth rates. %. Working days adjusted

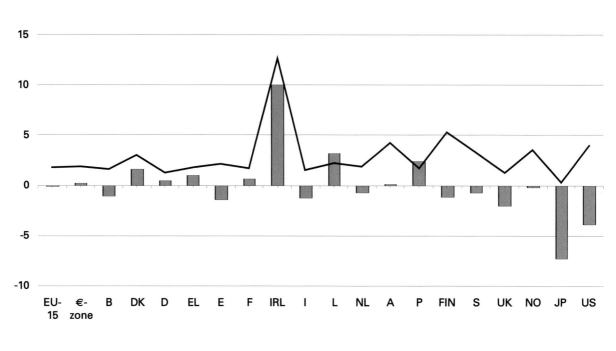

Bar: annual growth rate 2000/01; curve: average annual growth rates 1991–2000.

Industrial production index: main industrial groupings, trend series. 1995 = 100

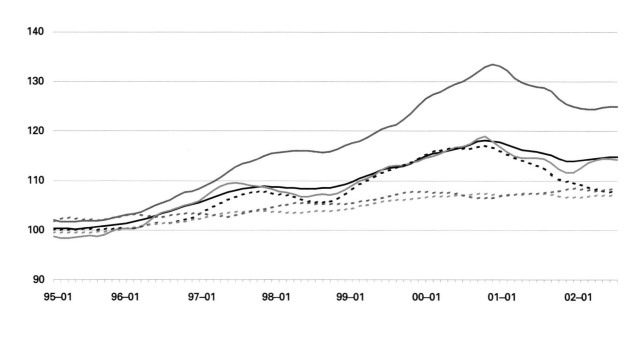

Black: total industry; colour: intermediate goods; grey: capital goods; dotted black: consumer durables; dotted colour: consumer non-durables; dotted grey: energy. EU-15

The scales for each country may be different.

Employment, total industry (excluding construction). Year on year growth rates. Gross. %

	1991	1992	1993	1994	1995	1996	1997	1998	1999	2000	2001	
EU-15	-	-	-	-	-	- 2.8	- 1.0	0.2	- 1.1	- 0.3	- 0.6	**EU-15**
€-zone	-	-	-	-	-	- 2.0	- 1.4	0.2	- 0.6	0.2	- 0.1	**€-zone**
B	-	-	-	-	-	- 1.5	- 1.1	1.6	0.5	0.9	- 0.1	**B**
DK	-	-	-	-	1.9	- 1.0	1.5	0.9	- 1.1	- 0.8	- 0.9	**DK**
D	1.4	- 10.2	- 8.7	- 6.5	- 4.0	- 3.8	- 3.2	- 0.3	- 0.7	- 0.2	0.1	**D**
EL	-	-	-	-	-	-	-	-	-	-	-	**EL**
E	- 2.4	- 2.8	- 9.3	- 2.6	- 0.1	0.6	3.7	5.8	3.5	4.4	3.1	**E**
F	- 1.7	- 3.3	- 4.6	- 2.0	0.1	- 1.2	- 0.8	0.1	- 0.2	1.2	1.0	**F**
IRL	0.7	- 0.1	- 0.1	2.4	5.3	4.1	6.0	2.2	-	-	-	**IRL**
I	- 2.8	- 5.5	- 6.0	- 2.9	- 1.6	- 1.5	- 2.3	- 2.0	- 3.1	- 2.1	- 3.0	**I**
L	- 0.9	- 0.8	- 5.1	- 3.2	- 0.7	- 0.3	- 0.3	1.2	1.5	1.4	0.6	**L**
NL	-	-	-	-	-	- 1.5	1.3	0.5	0.4	0.4	- 0.2	**NL**
A	0.1	- 2.9	- 6.1	- 2.9	- 1.1	- 4.3	- 2.1	1.5	- 1.6	- 0.2	0.9	**A**
P	- 1.7	- 3.1	- 6.5	- 0.5	- 1.4	- 1.5	- 1.6	- 2.1	- 2.9	- 2.8	- 3.9	**P**
FIN	- 9.2	- 9.7	- 6.5	0.3	6.8	0.9	0.5	2.4	2.7	1.2	0.7	**FIN**
S	-	-	-	-	-	-	-	-	-	-	-	**S**
UK	-	-	-	-	-	- 5.1	0.5	0.1	- 3.6	- 2.9	- 3.3	**UK**
JP	2.5	0.7	- 0.7	- 2.2	- 1.8	- 2.2	- 0.9	- 1.4	- 2.6	- 2.4	- 2.6	**JP**
US	-	-	-	-	-	-	-	-	-	-	-	**US**

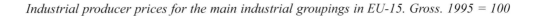

Industrial producer prices for the main industrial groupings in EU-15. Gross. 1995 = 100

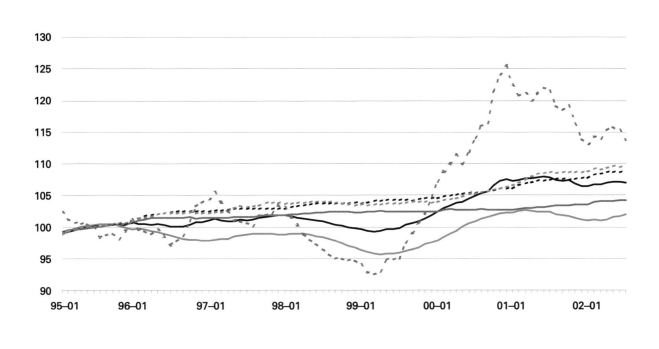

Black: total industry; colour: intermediate goods; grey: capital goods; dotted black: consumer durables; dotted colour: consumer non-durables; dotted grey: energy.

4

Building permits: dwellings authorised by 1 000 inhabitants

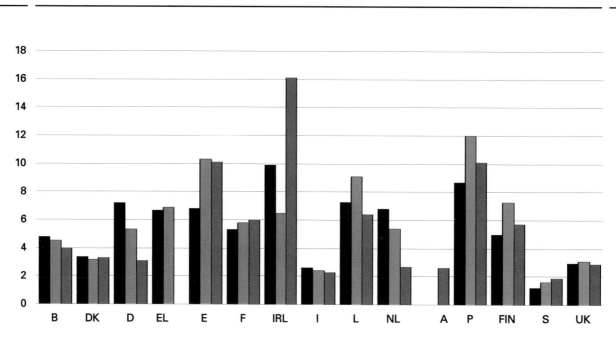

Black: 1996; colour: 1999; grey: 2001.

IRL and A: until September 2001.

EU-15 production indices for construction, seasonally adjusted. 1995 = 100

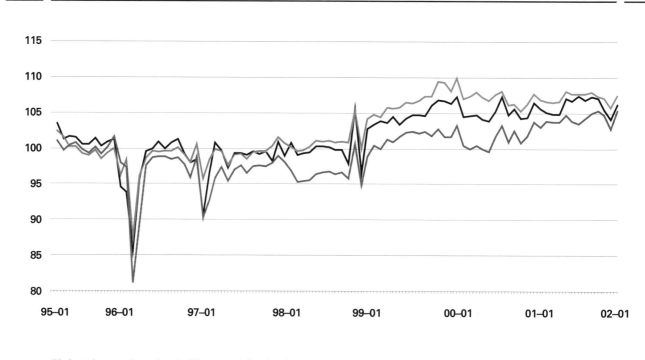

Black: total construction; colour: building; grey: civil engineering.

Distributive trades

Volume of sales in retail trade

Showing a positive economic climate, the volume of sales in retail trade has accelerated constantly from 1996 onwards; the annual growth for EU-15 attained a 2.2 % increase in 2001. At the individual level and since 1998, practically all Member States for which data are available, with the exception of Italy and Austria, have recorded a positive growth.

In 2001, growth was particularly strong in household goods.

Structural as well as short-term data

Since 1995, structural business statistics have been collected in the area of distributive trades according to the SBS regulation's harmonised framework. Short-term indicators have been collected at EU level in this area since reference year 1998.

One of the basic sets of information provided by structural business statistics is on the relative size of industries. This size is measured here in terms of both turnover and employment. The share of employment indicates which industries provide the most jobs.

While retail trade provides more than half of the jobs in distributive trades, it accounts for slightly less than one third of turnover. This shows that the turnover per capita is lower in retail trade than in distributive trades in general. The opposite situation is found in the highly concentrated productive activity of wholesale trade.

In all EU countries, the retail sale of food products constitutes a large share of total retail trade activities both in terms of total sales (turnover) and in terms of number of persons employed. This share ranges from approximately one third in Denmark, Austria and Portugal to close to one half in France and Ireland.

The retail sale of food is carried out either in specialised or non-specialised stores. In the EU as a whole, more than 80 % of food products are sold in non-specialised stores such as supermarkets. This turnover share is lowest in Spain (around 60 %) and highest in Finland (more than 90 %).

Further reading:

Eurostat publications
— **Monthly panorama of European business**
— **Business in Europe – Statistical pocketbook**
— **Economic portrait of the European Union 2002**

Statistics in Focus — Theme 4
— **No 19 Latest developments for the production index of total industry (excluding construction)**
— **No 20 Developments for construction in the fourth quarter of 2001**
— **No 22 Developments for output prices during the first quarter of 2002**
— **No 23 Developments for retail trade during the first quarter of 2002**
— **No 27 Developments for labour input indicators during the first quarter of 2002 — Industrial employment down by 0.9% in the EU & euro-zone**

Do you need more information?
— **Ask your Data Shop (see last page)**
— **http://www.europa.eu.int/comm/eurostat**

4

Breakdown of turnover in retail sale of food between specialised and non-specialised stores. %. 1999

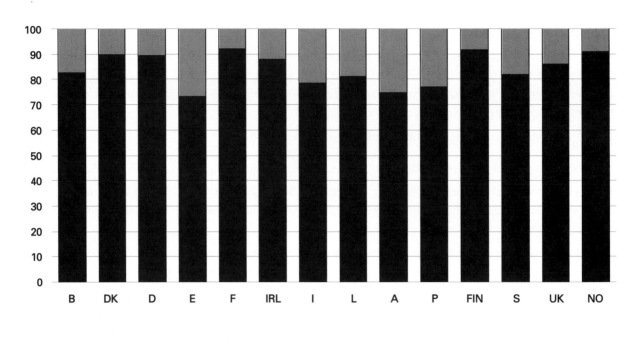

Black: retail sale of food in non-specialised stores; colour: retail sale of food in specialised stores.

Share of motor, wholesale and retail trades in EU-15 total distributive trades in terms of turnover. %. 2000 estimates

Share of motor, wholesale and retail trades in EU-15 total distributive trades in terms of employment. %. 2000 estimates

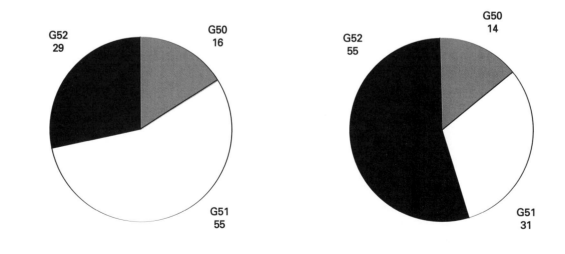

G50: Motor trade; G51: Wholesale trade except motor trade; G52: Retail trade except motor trade.

Services, including financial services

Structural business statistics cover market services activities in hotels and restaurants (NACE Rev. 1, Section H), transport, storage and communication (Section I), financial intermediation (Section J), and real estate, renting and business activities (Section K).

— The ratio of turnover to employment varies greatly from activity to activity. The EU-15 estimated average is lower than EUR 50 000 in labour-intensive activities such as industrial cleaning, labour recruitment, and hotels and restaurants, and reaches more than EUR 150 000 in renting activities and advertising.

— Unit labour costs relate personnel costs (including social charges) to the number of employees. They are lowest in activities employing less qualified personnel (such as industrial cleaning) and highest in activities employing highly qualified personnel (such as computer-related activities).

Transport services (covered by Divisions 60 to 63 of NACE Rev. 1) include activities related to providing passenger or freight transport, whether scheduled or not, by rail, pipeline, road, water or air as well as supporting activities and renting of transport equipment with driver or operator.

In EU-15 as a whole, freight transport by road is the largest transport activity with close to 45 % of the turnover in the sector, ahead of air transport (around 20 %) and water, railways and other land passenger transport (slightly more than 10 % each). However, the situation varies greatly from country to country.

In the EU, unit personnel costs are highest in air and rail transport (that employ highly qualified personnel) and lowest in road and other land transport.

Financial services: in the framework of structural business statistics, Eurostat also collects data on credit institutions, insurance services and pension funds. Detailed data on profit and loss accounts, balance-sheet items, geographical breakdowns and insurance products are available. The tables containing figures for the balance-sheet total of credit institutions and insurance services as well as the table on the total investments of pension funds give an idea of the relative importance of these institutions.

4

Turnover per persons employed in services. 1 000 ECU. EU-15 estimates. 1999

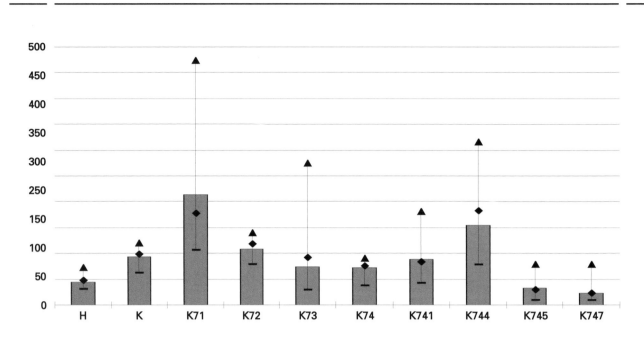

Column: EU-15 average; diamond: median; triangle: maximum; bar: minimum. H: Hotels and restaurants; K: Real estate, renting and business activities; K71: Renting of machinery without operator; K72: Computer and related activities; K73: Research and development; K74: Other business activities; K741: Legal, accounting and other consultancy activities; K744: Advertising; K745: Labour recruitment and provision of personnel; K747: Industrial cleaning.

Personnel cost per person employed in services. 1 000 ECU. EU-15 estimates. 1999

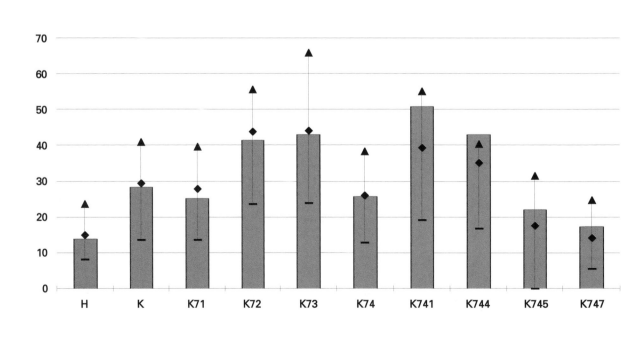

Column: EU-15 average; diamond: median; triangle: maximum; bar: minimum. H: Hotels and restaurants; K: Real estate, renting and business activities; K71: Renting of machinery without operator; K72: Computer and related activities; K73: Research and development; K74: Other business activities; K741: Legal, accounting and other consultancy activities; K744: Advertising; K745: Labour recruitment and provision of personnel; K747: Industrial cleaning.

4

eurostat

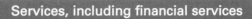

Personnel cost per person employed in transport activities. 1 000 ECU. EU-15 estimates. 1999

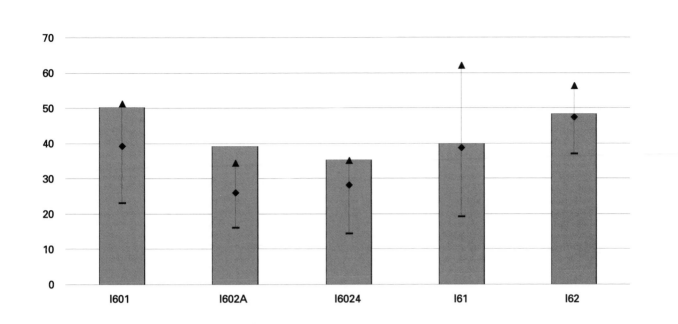

Column: EU-15 average; diamond: median; triangle: maximum; bar: minimum. l601: Transport via railways; l602A: Passenger transport by road; l6024: Freight transport by road; l61: Water transport; l62: Air transport.

Breakdown of turnover in rail, road, water and air transport. %. EU-15 estimates. 1999

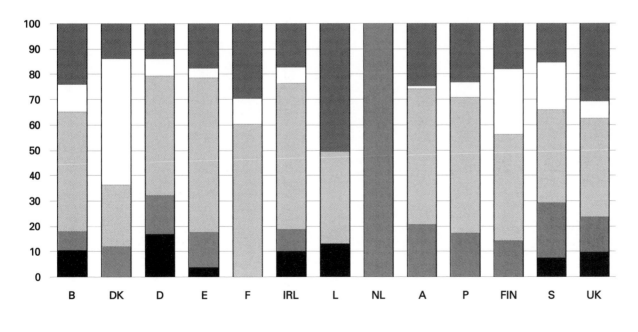

Black: transport via railways; colour: passenger transport by road; light grey: freight transport by road; white: water transport; dark grey: air transport.

4

Credit institutions: balance-sheet total. Million EUR

	1997	1998	1999	2000	
EU-15	17 356 527	18 905 100	:	23 432 587	**EU-15**
€-zone	12 960 857	14 012 661	:	16 915 866	**€-zone**
B	664 188	680 045	732 318	738 123	**B**
DK	322 562	357 841	384 534	429 775	**DK**
D	5 308 002	5 906 088	6 495 600	7 037 504	**D**
EL	107 811	108 841	133 257	152 402	**EL**
E	847 346	904 261	1 006 155	1 124 944	**E**
F	2 450 413	2 500 452	2 858 599	2 998 486	**F**
IRL	134 113	235 030	302 751	355 341	**IRL**
I	1 572 533	1 604 178	1 718 355	1 978 745	**I**
L	514 109	537 148	598 459	647 749	**L**
NL	689 698	766 543	904 862	1 018 788	**NL**
A	430 598	472 078	515 937	553 633	**A**
P	224 364	284 862	303 150	322 614	**P**
FIN	125 495	121 974	:	139 939	**FIN**
S	427 645 |	370 349	393 010	473 594	**S**
UK	3 537 651 |	4 055 409	4 231 053	5 460 950	**UK**
IS	:	:	:	13 568	**IS**
NO	165 123	174 485	194 554 *	224 564	**NO**
CH	1 113 085	1 302 809	1 441 658	1 387 079	**CH**

Data are delivered according to either the home- or the host-country principle.

Credit institutions: interest receivable and similar income. Million EUR

	1994	1995	1996	1997	1998	1999	2000	
EU-15	:	:	:	:	1 077 685	:	1 270 270	**EU-15**
€-zone	:	:	:	:	772 419	:	911 255	**€-zone**
B	49 234	53 703	51 230	53 942	55 264	53 448	69 908	**B**
DK	9 649	9 946	9 158	19 318	20 819	20 455	23 846	**DK**
D	:	:	:	279 201	300 660	315 065	358 962	**D**
EL	:	:	:	9 439	9 861	10 715	12 587	**EL**
E	60 459	63 841	64 585	43 484	46 817	41 350	49 394	**E**
F	146 382	157 457	144 792	142 918	147 397	146 268	173 882	**F**
IRL	:	6 755	7 669	:	15 781	15 761	22 032	**IRL**
I	:	:	:	96 318	85 733	69 006	83 772	**I**
L	29 346	34 812	33 172	33 007	37 129	36 593	49 893	**L**
NL	34 132	36 178	35 475	38 339	43 255	45 976	54 689	**NL**
A	23 250	24 345	22 448	22 212	22 511	22 138	27 204	**A**
P	11 038	12 893	12 643	12 162	12 110	11 566	15 052	**P**
FIN	:	:	:	5 717	5 764	:	6 466	**FIN**
S	27 931	29 642	29 967	28 179 |	22 818	20 410	24 479	**S**
UK	144 388	164 183	170 515	208 850 |	251 767	224 781	298 103	**UK**
IS	:	:	:	:	:	:	1 129	**IS**
NO	9 729	9 653	9 412	9 033	10 460	12 866 *	13 888	**NO**
CH	51 029	54 726	37 868	40 665	42 653	39 252	58 098	**CH**

Data are delivered according to either the home- or the host-country principle. B: including the positive results of derivatives. IRL: data refer to licensed banks only. UK: 1994–96: including NACE Rev. 1 class 65.11.

Insurance: balance-sheet total for all insurance enterprises. Million EUR

	1994	1995	1996	1997	1998	1999	2000	
EU-15	:	:	:	:	:	:	:	EU-15
€-zone	:	:	:	:	:	:	:	€-zone
B	59 221	65 015	70 052	75 488	86 005	98 759	:	B
DK	73 045	80 913	90 171	99 558	111 166	130 130	137 346	DK
D	545 880	619 678	667 756	726 062	835 256	927 161	987 746	D
EL	:	:	:	:	:	:	:	EL
E	:	53 105	62 869	70 808	82 366	98 934	114 871	E
F	:	:	571 612	654 426	721 225	832 337	907 805	F
IRL	:	17 744	20 799	29 266	33 921	43 888	:	IRL
I	:	:	160 919	188 926	213 394	254 147	297 461	I
L	:	:	17 241	23 931	27 982	34 803	40 676	L
NL	151 123	172 450	189 255	208 937	235 454	265 927	272 141	NL
A	35 134	39 553	42 876	45 310	47 477	50 607	53 952	A
P	7 236	10 110	13 165	15 862	18 724	22 340	25 548	P
FIN	11 055	13 339	15 273	17 760	20 187	27 510	34 444	FIN
S	:	:	134 367	155 439	174 267	214 421	236 157	S
UK	:	715 523	846 275	1 165 286	1 386 833	1 649 831	1 811 585	UK
IS	:	:	578	644	:	829	1 002	IS
NO	:	:	:	45 223	45 838	55 841	56 036	NO
CH	:	:	205 048	:	236 327	264 369	286 740	CH

Insurance: gross premiums written by life insurance enterprises. Million EUR

	1993	1994	1995	1996	1997	1998	1999	2000	
EU-15	:	:	210 795	224 771	255 609	:	:	:	EU-15
€-zone	116 992	:	147 320	151 341	156 756	145 557	171 489	:	€-zone
B	918	1 035	1 166	1 636	1 690	1 854	1 970	:	B
DK	3 107	3 903	4 424	5 314	5 827	6 818	6 614	7 326	DK
D	39 244	43 132	47 855	49 353	50 298	52 406	59 085	61 247	D
EL	:	:	685	791	770	:	:	:	EL
E	3 884	:	4 543	5 850	7 173	6 920	9 984	12 124	E
F	50 034	:	65 088	61 896	56 515	33 848	34 082	38 840	F
IRL	2 231	:	1 915	2 478	3 659	5 439	8 528	:	IRL
I	4 685	:	6 079	7 599	12 362	18 761	26 219	28 843	I
L	492	938	2 737	2 382	3 735	4 155	4 688	5 982	L
NL	11 743	12 726	14 872	15 785	17 280	19 625	21 193	23 022	NL
A	2 949	:	682	924	843	485	447	534	A
P	350	635	1 124	1 400	1 265	1 612	2 140	2 582	P
FIN	461	626	1 257	2 038	1 937	2 305	3 152	4 234	FIN
S	5 596	5 939	5 964	7 061	7 088	8 448	10 843	14 843	S
UK	66 012	60 321	52 403	60 265	85 168	115 162	142 899	199 807	UK
IS	6	6	6	7	7	10	13	20	IS
NO	1 905	2 301	2 273	2 407	3 147	3 133	3 138	3 379	NO
CH	14 867	:	19 497	21 540	22 955	26 372	24 513	24 833	CH

4

Pension funds: total investments. Million EUR

		1997	1998	1999	2000	
B		9 472	11 414	12 910	:	**B**
DK		4 840	4 794	5 637	5 639	**DK**
D		105 158	:	:	:	**D**
EL		:	:	:	:	**EL**
E		19 538	24 587	28 928	35 092	**E**
F		:	:	:	:	**F**
IRL		34 464	:	50 626	52 535	**IRL**
I		11 756	17 250	20 760	22 122	**I**
L		:	:	:	:	**L**
NL		361 625	373 468	440 534	453 820	**NL**
A		2 995	4 540	6 604	7 780	**A**
P		10 020	11 219	12 787	13 766	**P**
FIN		5 256	5 519	4 205	4 467	**FIN**
S		5 917	6 100	6 928	8 743	**S**
UK		909 459	986 973	1 148 248	1 027 934	**UK**
IS		4 305	4 995	6 597	7 702	**IS**
NO		9 235	9 213	10 923	12 182	**NO**
CH		182 740	262 059	:	296 032 *	**CH**

CH: 2000 data are provisional.

Transport

A short trip from the past to the future

'Victory is the beautiful bright coloured flower. Transport is the stem without which it could never have blossomed' (Sir Winston Churchill).

The quotation equally characterises the success achieved in increasing the standard of living in Europe and one of the major reasons behind this success: transport.

At the beginning of the 20th century, goods transport in Europe was dominated by waterways and railways. The railway network was larger then than it is today — which is impressive considering that the first railway was not opened until 1822. For passenger transport, water and rail were also predominant for long journeys, whereas, for short journeys, walking and horse transport were predominant.

During the last 100 years, the shares between the modes of transport have changed and the volumes have increased tremendously. Waterways and railways still play an important role, accounting for roughly 15 % of all tonnage transported, but the dominating mode of transport today is definitely road transport with its flexibility and individualism. There has been nearly a threefold increase since 1970 in road transport, while rail transport has declined by a quarter.

Today, about 80 % of all tonnage transported (about 45 % of all tonne-kilometres) and of all passenger-kilometres are by road. A passenger-kilometre represents the movement of a passenger over 1 kilometre, and a tonne-kilometre represents the movement of 1 tonne of goods over 1 kilometre. These indicators give a concept of the actual performance of transport.

In addition, the number of passenger cars has increased to more than 170 million. The disadvantage of this is there are more road accidents: even though fatalities are decreasing, around 40 000 people are still killed each year in the EU. Air transport is also increasing fast, and today more passenger-kilometres are by air than by rail.

It remains to be seen how environmental and safety issues will change the transport market in the future. The European Commission objectives for transport in the coming years can be found in the Directorate-General for Energy and Transport's White Paper 'European transport policy for 2010: Time to decide' (available online at http://europa.eu.int/comm/energy_transport/en/lb_en.html).

Transport statistics: spotting the movement

Eurostat's transport statistics describe the most important features of transport in the European Union not only in terms of the quantities of freight and passengers moved and the vehicles and infrastructure used, but also as part of the economy. Transport is not only a necessary support to personal life and economic activity, but also a major service industry: almost 5 million people are directly employed in the transport sector, which represents 4 % of the total EU workforce.

The data collection for this publication as well as for the other Eurostat publications on transport is supported by several legal acts obliging the Member States to report statistical data. In addition to this, there are voluntary agreements to supply additional data. In some cases, outside sources are used.

Eurostat provides information on:

— transport infrastructure;

— transport equipment;

— enterprises and employment in transport;

— passenger transport;

— transport of goods;

— energy consumption and emissions by transport;

— transport safety.

For more information on transport than is presented in the Eurostat yearbook, please contact your Eurostat Data Shop. The addresses of the Data Shops can be found at the end of the yearbook.

You might also have a look at the publications *Panorama of transport* and *EU energy and transport in figures*, available online (http://europa.eu.int/comm/energy_transport/etif/index.html), or the CARE, Community road accident database, available online (http://europa.eu.int/comm/transport/home/care/index_en.htm).

Further reading:

Eurostat publications
— **Panorama of transport**
— **International transport by air (intra- and extra-EU): 1999 data**
— **Road freight transport at regional level in the European Union**
— **Glossary for transport statistics — Second edition**

Statistics in Focus — Theme 7
— **No 1   Air transport: Passenger traffic 1993–1998**
— **No 2   EEA passenger transport by rail 1990–1998 — Some countries: huge increase — Some countries: large decrease**
— **No 4   Road freight cabotage 1991–1999**
— **No 5   Maritime goods transport 1990–1997**
— **No 6   International air transport — Passenger traffic 1998–1999**
— **No 1   Maritime transport of goods and passengers 1997–1999**
— **No 2   Trends in road freight transport 1990–1999**

Do you need more information?
— **Ask your Data Shop (see last page)**
— **http://www.europa.eu.int/comm/eurostat**
— **Eurostat's data serves the political discussion in Europe. Have a look at the website of the "DG Energy and Transport": http://europa.eu.int/comm/dgs/energy_transport/index_en.html**

4

Transport growth. EU-15. 1990 = 100

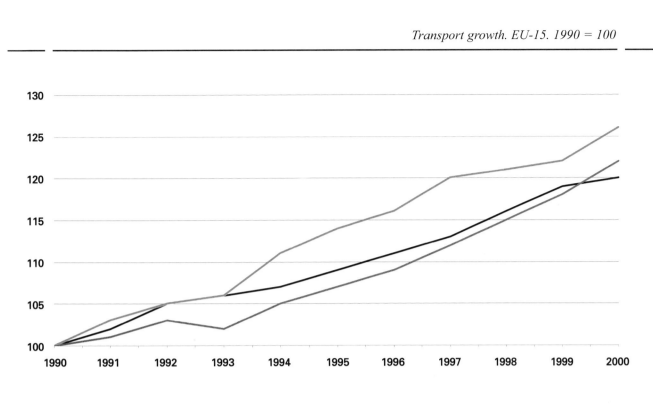

Black: passengers; colour: goods; grey: GDP.

Passengers: passenger cars, buses and coaches, tram and metro, railways and air. Goods: road, rail, inland waterways, pipelines and sea (intra-EU).
GDP: at constant prices.

Total inland transport per mode: EEA and Switzerland

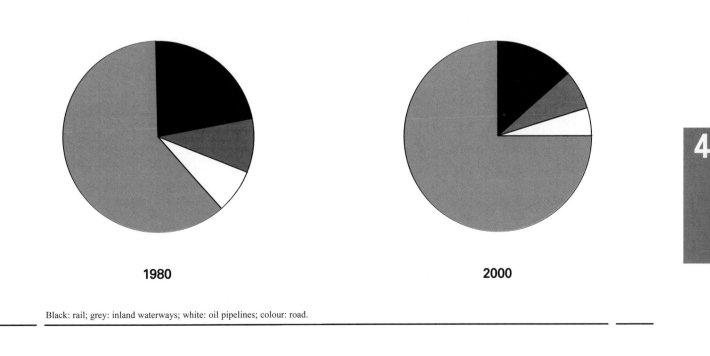

Black: rail; grey: inland waterways; white: oil pipelines; colour: road.

Total length of motorways in km

	1990	1991	1992	1993	1994	1995	1996	1997	1998	1999	2000	
EU-15	:	:	:	:	:	:	:	:	:	:	:	EU-15
€-zone	:	:	:	:	:	:	:	:	:	:	:	€-zone
B	:	1 650	1 667	1 686	1 666	1 666	1 674	1 679	1 682	1 691	1 702	B
DK	:	653	696	747	796	796	832	855	873	902	922	DK
D	:	10 955	11 013	11 080	11 143	11 190	11 246	11 309	11 427	11 515	11 712	D
EL	:	225	280	330	380	420	470	500 *	500 *	500		707	EL
E	:	5 235	6 486	6 577	6 497	6 962	7 295	7 750	8 269	8 893	9 049	E
F	:	7 080	7 408	7 614	7 956	8 275	8 596	8 864	9 303	9 626	9 766	F
IRL	:	32	32	53	72	72	80	94	103	103	103	IRL
I	:	6 301	6 289	6 401	6 401	6 435	6 465	6 469	6 478	6 478	6 478	I
L	:	78	95	100	121	123	115	118	115	115	115	L
NL	:	2 118	2 134	2 167	2 208	2 208	2 208	2 336	2 225	2 291	2 289	NL
A	:	1 532	1 554	1 557	1 559	1 596	1 607	1 613	1 613	1 634	1 633	A
P	:	474	520	579	587	687	710	797		1 252	1 441	1 482	P
FIN	:	249	318	337	388	394	431	444	473	512	549	FIN
S	:	968	1 005	1 061	1 125	1 262	1 350	1 423	1 439	1 484	1 506	S
UK	:	3 211	3 246	3 252	3 286	3 307	3 344	3 412	3 421		3 529	3 546	UK
NO	:	:	:	:	94	107	103	109	128	128	144	NO
CH	:	1 502	1 515	1 530	1 533	1 540	1 594	1 613	1 638	1 642	1 638	CH
CA	:	:	:	:	:	16 571	:	:	:	:	:	CA
JP	:	:	5 054	5 410	5 568	5 700	5 900	:	:	:	:	JP
US	:	85 258	86 818	87 447	87 814	88 035	88 588	88 704	88 892	89 232	89 426	US

JP: not including motorways constructed by local authorities.

Passenger cars per 1 000 inhabitants

	1990	1991	1992	1993	1994	1995	1996	1997	1998	1999	2000	
EU-15	393	401	408	415	422	425	434	441	450	461	469	EU-15
€-zone	394	404	414	420	427	432	438	445	455	465	473	€-zone
B	388	397	400	408	423	422	427	434	440	449	458	B
DK	309	309	310	312	310	319	331	337	343	346	347	DK
D	485	489	447	478	488	495	500	504	508	516	521	D
EL	171	173	177	189	199	211	223	238	254	275	304	EL
E	309	322	336	344	351	362	376	389	408	427	442	E
F	415	417	419	423	430	422	428	436	446	456	463	F
IRL	227	237	242	249	262	265	272	310	310	339	343	IRL
I	483	503	518	521	540	529	531	535	548	556	563	I
L	503	519	532	523	540	559	558	562	594	609	623	L
NL	368	370	373	376	383	364	370	378	382	401	411	NL
A	387	397	410	421	433	447	458	469	481	495	506	A
P	187	203	203	222	240	258	277	292	311	330	350	P
FIN	389	384	384	370	368	372	379	379	392	403	413	FIN
S	421	420	414	409	409	411	413	419	428	439	451	S
UK	375	383	382	371	376	374	388	398	403	414	419	UK
IS	468	467	458	439	436	445	463	487	510	542	565	IS
LI	582	590	593	586	596	609	620	636	639	652	:	LI
NO	380	379	378	379	381	387	379	399	403	407	412	NO
CH	445	450	450	448	453	459	462	469	476	485	493	CH
CA	:	:	:	:	:	445	:	:	:	:	:	CA
JP	:	:	313	327	341	356	375	:	:	:	:	JP
US	:	:	:	:	733	739	750	747	752	762	771	US

UK: GB only.

Tourism

Up and away

The definition of tourism is 'the activities of persons travelling to and staying in places outside their usual environment for not more than one consecutive year for leisure, business and other purposes'. Tourism can be measured following a demand-side or a supply-side approach.

Demand for tourism services

Tourism demand can be measured from different aspects.

— The number of tourists signifies visitors who stay at least one night in a collective or private accommodation in the place/country visited.

— The number of tourism trips means overnight trips made by tourists.

— There are two main reasons to travel: business or professional reasons on the one hand, holidays, recreation or leisure on the other. The latter also include visits to friends and relatives.

— The principal mode of transport used is the means of transport used for the longest part of the trip.

— Tourism expenditure for tourist trips is the total consumption expenditure made by a visitor or on behalf of a visitor for and during his/her trip and stay at his/her destination. Tourism expenditure encompasses a wide variety of items, ranging from the purchase of consumer goods and services inherent in travel and stays to the purchase of small durable goods for personal use.

Supply of tourism services

Tourist accommodation, i.e. the supply of tourism services, is measured by:

— the number of establishments that offer tourist accommodation; and

— the number of bed places in the establishments. This represents the number of people who can stay overnight in permanent beds, discounting any extra beds set up at the customers' request. The term 'bed place' applies to a single bed; a double bed is counted as two bed places.

Demand for accommodation by tourists includes all types of accommodation: hotels and similar establishments; camping sites; holiday dwellings; youth hostels and other collective accommodation.

Data from 1996 onwards are harmonised and comparable in the frame of Council Directive 95/57/EC on tourism statistics. Data before 1996 are not fully comparable between countries because the statistical unit (local unit or enterprise) and coverage vary. Trends, however, can be compared.

Further reading:

Eurostat publications
— **Methodological manual on the design and implementation of surveys on inbound tourism**
— **Tourism — Europe, central European countries, Mediterranean countries (MED)**
— **Yearbook on tourism statistics**

Statistics in Focus — Theme 4
— **No 14 Dynamic regional tourism**
— **No 15 How Europeans go on holiday**

Do you need more information?
— **Ask your Data Shop (see last page)**
— **http://www.europa.eu.int/comm/eurostat**

4

Tourist accommodation: hotels and similar establishments

	1994	1995	1996	1997	1998	1999	2000	2001	
EU-15	189 432	190 061	189 318	186 851	186 484	198 492	198 063	:	EU-15
€-zone	132 742	133 693	132 852	130 374	128 648	136 662	136 800	:	€-zone
B	1 946	2 038	2 062	2 000	1 998	2 015	1 998	2 034	B
DK	565	564	478	470	467	464	466	475	DK
D	37 307	38 172	38 565	38 971	38 914	38 701	38 551	38 529	D
EL	7 604	7 754	7 916	7 850	7 946	8 168	8 342	:	EL
E	10 063	10 422	9 482	7 520	7 539	16 229	16 287	16 369	E
F	20 664	20 819	20 590	20 272	19 555	19 379	19 315	19 309	F
IRL	5 034	5 039	5 274	5 164	5 460	5 692	5 449	5 222	IRL
I	34 549	34 296	34 080	33 828	33 540	33 341	33 361	33 421	I
L	372	369	368	344	342	325	319	314	L
NL	1 726	1 749	1 739	1 857	2 788	2 826	2 858	2 858	NL
A	18 402	18 120	17 990	17 692	15 780	15 378	15 865	15 293	A
P	1 728	1 733	1 744	1 768	1 754	1 772	1 786	1 781	P
FIN	951	936	958	958	978	1 004	1 011	989	FIN
S	1 855	1 829	1 851	1 905	1 891	1 898	1 906	1 979	S
UK	46 666	46 221	46 221	46 252	47 532	51 300	50 549	:	UK
IS	157	211	216	231	253	254	244	248	IS
NO	1 195	1 179	1 186	1 198	1 176	1 162	1 166	1 160	NO
CH	6 165	6 081	6 004	5 952	5 890	5 826	5 754 *	5 701 *	CH

New value : Hotels and similar establishments include hotels, apartment hotels, motels, roadside inns, beach hotels, residential clubs, rooming and boarding houses, tourist residences and similar accommodation. E: 1998/99 break in series due to incorporation of one-star hotels.

Tourist accommodation: other collective accommodation establishments

	1994	1995	1996	1997	1998	1999	2000	2001	
EU-15	206 365	203 954	:	:	:	:	311 323	:	EU-15
€-zone	181 285	191 903	:	:	:	:	297 832	:	€-zone
B	1 638	1 667	1 714	1 689	1 655	1 646	1 635	1 656	B
DK	524	623	635	633	627	621	622	624	DK
D	14 936	14 545	15 242	16 001	16 486	16 632	17 032	17 352	D
EL	319	320 *	334	335	340	344	344 *	:	EL
E	124 757	131 659	:	:	:	:	173 415	166 841	E
F	9 703	9 205	9 192	9 226	9 169	9 140	9 100	9 086	F
IRL	2 370	2 375	2 375	2 375	2 525	2 540	2 482	2 814	IRL
I	21 900	26 450	33 736	31 842	35 991	35 856	83 858	94 860	I
L	299	302	316	308	320	297	291	282	L
NL	1 901	1 947	1 973	2 212	3 502	3 595	3 651	3 651	NL
A	2 991	2 985	2 949	3 026	5 207	5 290	5 588	5 431	A
P	224	223	225	234	233	244	263	270	P
FIN	566	545	548	538	537	524	517	496	FIN
S	1 615	1 597	1 602	1 617	1 602	1 602	1 585	1 692	S
UK	22 622	9 511	9 518	9 432	11 237	10 938 *	10 940 *	:	UK
IS	391	421	:	296	294	469	378	402	IS
NO	:	:	:	:	1 235	1 212	1 213	1 197	NO
CH	:	:	3 837	93 945	94 073	94 081	94 055	94 045	CH

Other collective accommodation establishments include holiday dwellings, tourist campsites, youth hostels, tourist dormitories, group accommodation, school dormitories and other similar accommodation.

eurostat

Tourist accommodation: number of bed places in hotels and similar establishments

	1994	1995	1996	1997	1998	1999	2000	2001	
EU-15	8 684 558	8 613 208	8 938 626	8 962 682	9 015 320	9 521 175	9 362 098	:	EU-15
€-zone	6 858 768	6 733 047	7 079 047	7 091 314	7 089 685	7 501 347	7 313 444	:	€-zone
B	108 811	114 887	117 299	117 513	116 297	119 365	119 165	121 512	B
DK	99 275	98 991	60 080	59 339	59 772	60 513	62 107	63 994	DK
D	1 380 713	1 446 748	1 490 612	1 527 228	1 546 862	1 561 830	1 590 332	1 602 960	D
EL	508 408	557 188	571 656	577 259	584 834	597 855	607 614	:	EL
E	1 053 355	1 031 684	1 025 208	972 721	979 325	1 299 021	1 315 697	1 333 441	E
F	1 379 955	1 193 340	1 472 424	1 467 322	1 451 119	1 485 863	1 178 348	1 200 984	F
IRL	100 000	96 900	96 905	107 425	117 163	135 473	138 579	139 570	IRL
I	1 724 333	1 739 543	1 764 651	1 772 096	1 782 382	1 807 275	1 854 101	1 891 281	I
L	14 705	14 748	14 750	14 776	14 709	14 449	14 415	14 256	L
NL	138 060	142 516	142 800	157 926	169 078	169 749	174 314	174 314	NL
A	650 020	646 125	640 199	633 601	584 889	576 602	588 213	587 305	A
P	202 442	204 051	208 205	211 315	215 572	216 828	222 958	228 665	P
FIN	106 374	102 505	105 994	109 391	112 289	114 892	117 322	118 493	FIN
S	173 521	173 759	177 620	182 604	184 545	184 970	188 289	194 839	S
UK	1 044 586	1 050 223	1 050 223	1 052 166	1 096 484	1 176 490	1 190 644	:	UK
IS	8 130	9 752	10 209	10 713	12 030	12 471	12 471	12 632	IS
NO	129 199	131 217	133 521	135 605	137 188	137 653	140 580	143 804	NO
CH	264 824	264 983	262 471	261 482	260 290	260 592	259 721	260 122	CH

E: 1998/99 break in series due to incorporation of one-star hotels.

Number of bed places in other collective accommodation establishments

	1994	1995	1996	1997	1998	1999	2000	2001	
EU-15	:	:	:	:	:	:	:	:	EU-15
€-zone	:	:	:	:	:	:	10 053 399	:	€-zone
B	575 912	524 387	528 979	528 378	523 388	517 918	513 564	507 701	B
DK	1 303 500	316 869	315 349	314 945	317 760	318 249	319 756	319 581	DK
D	994 194	1 349 486	1 372 754	1 418 477	1 449 207	1 466 018	1 488 662	1 476 882	D
EL	98 838	90 217	95 904	97 233	97 280	93 941	:	:	EL
E	1 037 045	1 013 509	:	:	:	:	1 306 541	1 310 336	E
F	3 025 122	3 090 355	2 998 578	2 999 626	2 979 149	2 977 325	2 970 306	2 570 257	F
IRL	:	:	:	55 034	58 564	54 706	57 996	64 015	IRL
I	1 524 832	1 609 990	1 709 432	1 772 300	1 792 494	1 816 616	2 055 897	2 133 049	I
L	:	:	:	:	52 638	50 803	50 283	48 915	L
NL	662 049	664 024	676 338	713 226	957 271	965 322	968 469	968 469	NL
A	87 260	87 230	268 738	276 895	323 692	328 222	346 197	352 485	A
P	266 213	265 048	264 308	268 077	268 765	268 455	261 949	262 630	P
FIN	:	95 917	99 624	95 720	34 230	33 709	33 535	103 552	FIN
S	:	:	:	:	66 823	67 287	372 817	354 433	S
UK	1 744 231	1 739 921	1 739 921	1 712 766	1 759 673	:	:	:	UK
IS	:	:	:	:	:	:	:	:	IS
NO	:	:	:	:	371 220	364 397	360 280	356 494	NO
CH	:	:	813 081	806 024	811 399	812 241	811 610	808 668	CH

4

Nights spent by residents in hotels and similar establishments

	1994	1995	1996	1997	1998	1999	2000	2001	
EU-15	:	587 163 908	587 073 684	601 624 459	609 714 324	661 634 775	734 550 681	:	**EU-15**
€-zone	:	468 230 015	467 127 877	474 129 346	494 717 823	533 644 914	559 699 597	:	**€-zone**
B	2 861 389	3 053 572	3 139 997	3 337 966	3 497 946	3 651 528	4 045 372	4 057 418	**B**
DK	6 038 100	3 907 900	4 200 247	4 170 540	4 339 465	4 416 851	4 598 935	4 589 331	**DK**
D	141 306 629	145 147 374	144 746 699	144 496 967	147 273 906	154 418 733	163 429 396	159 363 124	**D**
EL	11 701 282	11 908 240	12 177 661	13 609 416	13 920 767	14 381 120	14 666 610	:	**EL**
E	56 876 372	58 281 364	58 043 148	61 298 203	66 552 436	81 503 641	83 381 971	85 060 810	**E**
F	89 500 785	90 348 833	90 720 671	92 665 842	96 696 040	108 774 202	114 059 371	115 575 150	**F**
IRL	:	6 698 000	5 647 000	5 583 000	6 667 000	6 938 000	6 786 000	:	**IRL**
I	124 943 061	123 466 900	122 918 051	122 223 434	126 178 391	128 237 924	136 391 687	138 559 383	**I**
L	97 019	89 177	90 740	82 953	80 936	66 789	68 344	73 867	**L**
NL	7 912 400	8 798 500	9 074 100	10 739 000	12 622 000	13 829 000	14 027 000	13 608 000	**NL**
A	16 089 705	16 302 434	15 891 821	16 088 223	16 490 829	17 241 283	18 031 455	18 467 691	**A**
P	7 361 178	7 579 637	8 100 911	8 499 088	9 163 983	9 397 225	9 693 160	9 985 020	**P**
FIN	7 943 362	8 464 224	8 754 739	9 114 670	9 494 356	9 586 589	9 785 841	9 882 208	**FIN**
S	13 898 042	14 771 326	14 667 899	14 815 157	15 643 369	16 191 890	16 585 539	16 736 713	**S**
UK	81 381 193	88 346 427	88 900 000	94 900 000	81 092 900	93 000 000	139 000 000	134 420 000	**UK**
IS	229 000	246 000	259 980	290 177	309 306	321 247	291 481	273 548	**IS**
NO	9 643 456	9 861 800	10 261 429	10 679 995	11 252 483	11 318 810	11 397 801	11 599 219	**NO**
CH	12 896 525	12 316 371	11 958 058	12 363 041	12 670 156	13 133 759	14 013 311	14 312 728	**CH**

E: 1998/99 break in series due to incorporation of one-star hotels.

Nights spent by non-residents in hotels and similar establishments

	1994	1995	1996	1997	1998	1999	2000	2001	
EU-15	494 067 162	477 499 594	481 892 270	500 541 903	520 475 039	572 074 503	587 505 500	:	**EU-15**
€-zone	365 962 073	376 451 324	380 872 778	393 418 352	413 575 317	462 139 072	478 448 781	:	**€-zone**
B	7 878 823	7 899 846	8 694 704	9 267 010	9 482 708	9 748 860	10 183 599	10 011 175	**B**
DK	5 932 200	4 145 870	4 473 482	4 504 919	4 462 299	4 349 793	4 610 620	4 550 986	**DK**
D	26 368 249	27 184 078	27 434 528	28 608 335	29 734 835	30 912 501	34 641 023	32 875 948	**D**
EL	40 331 166	37 473 643	35 101 968	40 220 443	42 163 769	45 489 939	46 636 293	:	**EL**
E	97 792 056	101 000 000	100 000 000	105 435 107	111 803 276	149 035 996	143 761 596	143 488 587	**E**
F	57 143 264	54 339 000	54 994 124	60 623 541	66 329 694	71 767 947	77 014 058	75 653 223	**F**
IRL	10 018 000	11 348 000	12 978 000	13 220 000	13 712 000	14 327 000	17 482 000	17 680 000	**IRL**
I	76 172 592	84 565 791	87 905 208	85 376 770	87 192 035	90 235 528	97 221 120	100 322 354	**I**
L	1 016 831	1 051 215	947 087	1 026 055	1 089 407	1 162 616	1 169 396	1 147 985	**L**
NL	8 732 900	9 581 400	9 923 000	12 444 000	14 262 000	15 224 000	15 695 000	14 955 000	**NL**
A	59 126 450	56 198 473	55 126 381	53 395 596	53 502 987	53 123 067	53 617 396	54 085 832	**A**
P	18 785 240	20 357 205	19 962 376	20 851 195	23 240 516	23 330 836	24 101 963	23 577 571	**P**
FIN	2 927 668	2 926 316	2 907 370	3 170 743	3 225 859	3 270 721	3 561 630	3 674 941	**FIN**
S	3 320 091	3 693 723	3 930 464	4 050 834	4 408 654	4 515 500	4 678 806	4 926 857	**S**
UK	78 521 632	55 735 034	57 513 578	58 347 355	55 865 000	55 580 199	53 131 000	49 780 996	**UK**
IS	516 000	598 000	635 986	701 506	791 412	862 433	894 974	907 029	**IS**
NO	5 041 322	4 985 458	5 050 277	5 039 279	5 168 217	5 207 568	4 966 857	4 816 725	**NO**
CH	19 669 524	18 386 194	17 283 592	18 034 307	18 712 433	18 544 486	19 914 293	19 273 175	**CH**

E: 1998/99 break in series due to incorporation of one-star hotels.

4

Energy

Powering everyday life

Energy is the 'force' behind industry, transport and heating. There is hardly an aspect of daily life which is not in one way or another accompanied by the use of energy. Energy shortages and fluctuations of its price have repercussions in the whole economy. How we use energy has a significant impact on the state of the environment. For these reasons, energy policy is one of the priorities of the European Union.

The major challenges with which the EU is confronted in the energy field are:

— the significant dependence on outside supplies, as the European Union is producing only about half of the energy it consumes (security of supplies);

— the growing need to ensure competitive energy prices in the context of the globalisation of economies, notably by means of liberalisation of the electricity and gas markets and the development of the trans-European energy networks (liberalisation of network industries);

— the pressing need to make the energy sector more compatible with environmental objectives, particularly in the light of the commitments made by the European Union under the Kyoto Protocol (climate change).

Energy monitoring

In order to meet the increasing requirements of energy monitoring and to quantify the components that are influencing energy policies, Eurostat has developed a coherent and harmonised system of energy statistics.

The Eurostat yearbook presents a representative selection of tables and graphs that give an insight into the broad spectrum of energy statistics.

Some of the basic items presented are as follows.

— **Production of primary energy** which comprises energy extracted from natural sources: coal, lignite, crude oil and natural gas. Renewable energies (hydro, biomass, geothermal, wind and solar energy) as well as nuclear energy are also considered primary energy sources. Nuclear energy is accounted for as the heat released during fission of uranium in a nuclear reactor.

Nuclear energy and natural gas represent the main energy sources in Europe, followed by crude oil. Solid fuels, despite the continued decline in their production, still account for about one sixth of EU primary energy production. The increase of the share of renewable energy sources in the EU energy balance is one of the main objectives of Community energy policy.

— **Gross inland consumption** is defined as primary production plus imports, recovered products and change in stocks, less exports and fuel supply to maritime bunkers (for seagoing ships of all flags). It therefore reflects the energy necessary to satisfy inland consumption within the limits of national territory.

The biggest share by far in total gross inland consumption is that of oil, followed by natural gas and nuclear energy.

— **Energy intensity** is defined as the ratio between gross inland consumption and GDP in kgoe/EUR 1 000.

— **Final energy consumption** includes all energy delivered to final consumers (in the transport, industry and other sectors), net of transformation and network losses. It also excludes consumption for non-energy purposes such as feedstocks in the petrochemical industry. Final use of petroleum products involves only refined products (e.g. motor spirit, gas oil, domestic fuel, kerosene and jet fuels). Final use of gas is mainly in the form of natural gas.

— **Gas and electricity prices** have been collected since 1991 on the basis of standard consumers and locations defined by Council Directive 90/377/EEC on Community procedure to improve the transparency of gas and electricity prices charged to industrial end-users.

Gas and electricity prices paid by domestic consumers are collected on the basis of a definition of standard consumers and locations. Final consumption of households varies greatly from country to country according to climatic conditions and standard of living.

Further reading:

Eurostat publications
— **Energy prices — Data 1990–2001**
— **Electricity prices — Data 1990–2001**
— **Gas prices — Data 1990–2001**
— **Energy balance sheets 1998–1999**

Statistics in Focus — Theme 8
— **No 1 Statistical aspects of the energy economy in 2000**
— **No 18 Unavailability of nuclear power stations, 1996–2000**
— **No 19 The European Union coal industry in 2000**
— **No 20 Statistical aspects of the oil economy in 2000**
— **No 21 Hard coal and coke imports 1998–2000**
— **No 22 Gas prices for EU households on 1 July 2001**
— **No 23 Gas prices for EU industry on 1 July 2001**
— **No 24 Electricity prices for EU households on 1 July 2001**
— **No 25 Electricity prices for EU industry on 1 July 2001**

Do you need more information?
— **Ask your Data Shop (see last page)**
— **http://www.europa.eu.int/comm/eurostat**
— **Eurostat's data serves the political discussion in Europe. Have a look at the website of the "DG Energy and Transport": http://europa.eu.int/comm/dgs/energy_transport/index_en.html**

Total production of primary energy. 1 000 toe

	1990	1991	1992	1993	1994	1995	1996	1997	1998	1999	2000	
EU-15	705 782	707 550	701 965	709 157	722 802	736 563	762 177	755 772	750 633	764 535 *	758 694 *	**EU-15**
€-zone	453 369	445 232	441 216	439 217	429 235	430 794	441 973	432 539	418 861	421 847 *	423 246 *	**€-zone**
B	11 971	11 753	11 531	11 015	10 780	11 025	11 360	12 642	12 112	13 376	13 155	**B**
DK	10 021	11 882	12 825	13 705	14 986	15 516	17 594	20 140	20 267	23 675	27 583	**DK**
D	185 829	164 933	159 663	148 089	141 286	140 155	138 175	138 163	131 743	134 632	131 719 *	**D**
EL	9 152	9 060	8 972	8 797	9 146	9 702	10 136	9 924	10 038	9 463	9 946	**EL**
E	33 353	33 339	32 615	32 483	32 234	31 408	32 169	30 855	31 460	30 305	31 154	**E**
F	108 069	114 592	114 987	122 049	119 458	122 775	125 670	123 859	120 637	122 779	130 092 *	**F**
IRL	3 495	3 291	3 082	3 470	3 628	4 256	3 614	2 843	2 479	2 611	2 281 *	**IRL**
I	27 243	27 780	28 777	29 986	31 252	30 687	31 545	31 548	32 446	31 435 *	30 505 *	**I**
L	47	46	48	47	51	47	40	47	50	46	57	**L**
NL	60 262	67 118	67 094	68 208	66 109	65 910	73 717	65 522	62 684	59 209	56 912	**NL**
A	8 707	8 577	8 899	9 029	8 409	8 738	9 039	9 113	9 099	9 311	9 436	**A**
P	2 659	2 653	2 396	2 851	2 944	2 607	3 261	3 213	3 036	2 656	3 131 *	**P**
FIN	11 735	11 150	12 123	11 991	13 083	13 187	13 382	14 733	13 116	15 487	14 805	**FIN**
S	29 606	31 359	29 060	29 004	30 800	31 138	31 257	31 728	32 710	32 719	29 601	**S**
UK	203 635	210 016	209 891	218 434	238 636	249 413	261 217	261 443	268 756	276 830	268 319	**UK**
IS	1 456	1 359	1 369	1 404	1 369	1 390	1 616	1 682	1 814	2 191	2 306	**IS**
NO	120 053	130 405	146 355	153 767	170 114	181 832	207 606	212 181	206 141	209 145	224 721	**NO**
EEA	827 290	839 314	849 689	864 329	894 285	919 784	971 399	969 635	958 588	975 870 *	985 721 *	**EEA**

Net imports of primary energy. 1 000 toe

	1990	1991	1992	1993	1994	1995	1996	1997	1998	1999	2000	
EU-15	644 017	666 861	677 998	650 638	631 293	650 890	678 620	692 437	723 404	705 941	740 124 *	**EU-15**
€-zone	595 740	615 464	628 034	608 453	619 045	642 148	666 286	683 318	717 129	717 910	745 446 *	**€-zone**
B	38 857	41 525	42 695	41 004	42 658	43 690	46 972	47 067	49 984	46 806	48 547	**B**
DK	7 745	7 230	6 492	5 721	5 939	7 529	5 623	3 913	1 544	- 3 270	- 7 099	**DK**
D	166 847	180 110	186 576	188 481	191 411	195 152	207 794	208 357	212 748	202 556	203 984	**D**
EL	15 374	15 617	17 743	17 236	15 799	18 207	18 834	19 196	21 106	19 744	21 982	**EL**
E	59 857	63 611	66 958	63 285	68 407	75 415	73 854	80 231	87 554	94 427	98 351	**E**
F	119 759	126 064	123 115	115 136	109 582	115 300	124 302	122 072	131 558	131 541	132 830 *	**F**
IRL	7 082	6 908	6 690	6 809	7 045	7 596	8 338	9 487	10 624	11 672	12 260	**IRL**
I	131 964	129 097	134 226	127 195	125 824	134 693	134 456	134 237	140 373	143 485	152 588	**I**
L	3 516	3 704	3 768	3 777	3 705	3 257	3 377	3 297	3 259	3 347	3 620	**L**
NL	17 388	14 474	14 088	13 367	17 182	16 340	14 029	22 712	23 466	25 889	34 271	**NL**
A	17 278	17 871	17 539	16 986	16 755	17 411	19 173	18 888	19 834	18 889	18 865	**A**
P	15 160	15 059	16 573	15 938	16 025	17 876	16 658	18 436	19 406	22 083	21 588	**P**
FIN	18 031	17 042	15 807	16 474	20 450	15 418	17 334	18 535	18 325	17 217	18 542	**FIN**
S	17 819	17 298	17 303	18 199	19 671	19 115	21 094	19 979	20 011	18 505	19 376	**S**
UK	7 339	11 252	8 426	1 029	- 29 162	- 36 108	- 33 217	- 33 968	- 36 385	- 46 948	- 39 581	**UK**
IS	786	679	776	761	798	798	863	868	929	967	1 030	**IS**
NO	- 96 177	- 108 285	- 122 890	- 128 926	- 145 668	- 156 756	- 182 103	- 186 942	- 180 144	- 181 591	- 197 826	**NO**
EEA	548 626	559 255	555 884	522 473	486 423	494 931	497 380	506 363	544 189	525 317	543 329 *	**EEA**

4

Final energy consumption. 1 000 toe

	1990	1991	1992	1993	1994	1995	1996	1997	1998	1999	2000	
EU-15	862 743	883 607	879 615	885 306	880 281	898 608	936 009	927 834	943 644 *	952 421 *	952 261 *	**EU-15**
€-zone	667 287	682 662	677 569	681 340	674 360	691 981	717 419	713 488	728 197 *	733 817 *	733 836 *	**€-zone**
B	31 299	33 084	33 829	33 153	33 927	34 462	36 360	36 438	36 818	36 895	36 944	**B**
DK	13 773	14 101	13 914	14 335	14 364	14 728	15 234	14 862	14 930	14 913	14 555	**DK**
D	227 287	224 318	217 887	220 029	216 406	221 338	228 609	224 004	223 898 *	221 316 *	213 789 *	**D**
EL	14 534	14 826	14 956	15 206	15 349	15 811	16 870	17 257	18 159	18 157	18 508	**EL**
E	56 524	60 104	59 940	59 217	62 256	63 461	65 184	67 681	71 673	74 297	79 288 *	**E**
F	136 068	142 580	143 209	143 501	137 505	141 380	148 539	145 475	150 522	150 611 *	150 096 *	**F**
IRL	7 135	7 107	7 170	7 154	7 694	7 827	8 261	8 726	9 306	9 856	10 399 *	**IRL**
I	110 415	113 294	113 413	113 571	111 815	116 629	117 287	118 025	121 443	126 025 *	125 981 *	**I**
L	3 325	3 561	3 552	3 618	3 551	3 148	3 235	3 224	3 183	3 341	3 544	**L**
NL	42 938	45 092	44 833	46 443	45 739	47 403	51 393	49 131	49 259	48 473	49 773	**NL**
A	19 940	20 996	20 547	20 680	20 301	21 216	22 209	22 901	22 608	22 121	22 558	**A**
P	11 059	11 527	12 139	12 393	12 884	13 047	13 968	14 718	15 364	15 976	16 929	**P**
FIN	21 295	20 999	21 051	21 582	22 282	22 070	22 374	23 165	24 123	24 904	24 535	**FIN**
S	30 432	30 629	30 579	32 218	33 190	33 671	34 117	33 439	33 365	32 942	32 897	**S**
UK	136 718	141 390	142 597	142 206	143 017	142 416	152 369	148 788	148 993	152 592	152 464	**UK**
IS	1 602	1 564	1 607	1 662	1 662	1 660	1 726	1 753	1 819	1 952	2 056	**IS**
NO	16 084	15 838	15 717	16 170	16 698	16 854	17 669	17 466	18 187	18 618	17 884	**NO**
EEA	880 429	901 009	896 939	903 138	898 640	917 122	955 404	947 053	963 650 *	972 991 *	972 201 *	**EEA**

Final energy consumption by households, trades, services, etc. 1 000 toe

	1990	1991	1992	1993	1994	1995	1996	1997	1998	1999	2000	
EU-15	343 426	369 453	360 804	366 767	356 123	363 626	391 869	376 064	382 429 *	381 922 *	371 491 *	**EU-15**
€-zone	263 620	283 382	275 429	279 110	270 569	277 227	298 861	287 559	292 597 *	292 780 *	281 779 *	**€-zone**
B	11 707	12 999	13 199	13 229	13 267	13 899	15 773	14 666	14 644	14 100	13 625	**B**
DK	6 992	7 061	6 890	7 245	6 977	7 159	7 668	7 182	7 215	7 154	6 906	**DK**
D	96 955	100 280	95 407	99 221	95 679	96 508	105 432	101 912	101 476 *	98 050 *	89 234 *	**D**
EL	4 764	5 077	4 979	5 030	5 154	5 267	5 995	6 192	6 446	6 549	6 880	**EL**
E	14 448	15 711	15 644	15 446	16 753	16 996	17 734	18 078	18 755	20 038	21 112	**E**
F	57 115	64 385	63 755	62 666	59 474	60 177	65 325	62 005	64 027	65 354 *	63 403 *	**F**
IRL	3 336	3 217	3 326	3 411	3 594	3 795	3 735	3 875	4 018	4 079	4 318 *	**IRL**
I	40 109	42 948	41 536	42 026	39 191	41 857	42 767	41 924	43 878	45 774 *	44 765 *	**I**
L	593	692	673	679	662	662	735	729	767	722	714	**L**
NL	19 434	22 309	21 084	21 652	21 478	22 327	25 088	22 402	22 519	21 904	22 172	**NL**
A	8 777	9 379	9 125	9 190	8 621	9 111	9 793	9 474	9 674	9 901	9 532	**A**
P	3 342	3 464	3 593	3 680	3 766	3 942	4 352	4 395	4 423	4 669	4 896	**P**
FIN	7 805	7 999	8 088	7 911	8 085	7 953	8 128	8 099	8 416	8 189	8 009	**FIN**
S	11 374	11 872	11 871	13 114	13 319	13 383	14 091	13 102	13 147	12 856	12 338	**S**
UK	56 675	62 061	61 635	62 269	60 103	60 590	65 254	62 029	63 024	62 583	63 589	**UK**
IS	941	937	975	1 014	977	991	971	983	975	1 039	1 045	**IS**
NO	5 864	6 286	6 217	6 303	6 494	6 509	6 990	6 764	6 894	6 964	6 666	**NO**
EEA	350 230	376 676	367 997	374 084	363 594	371 127	399 830	383 812	390 298 *	389 925 *	379 202 *	**EEA**

4

Renewable energy primary production: biomass, hydro, geothermal, wind and solar energy.
1 000 toe. EU-15

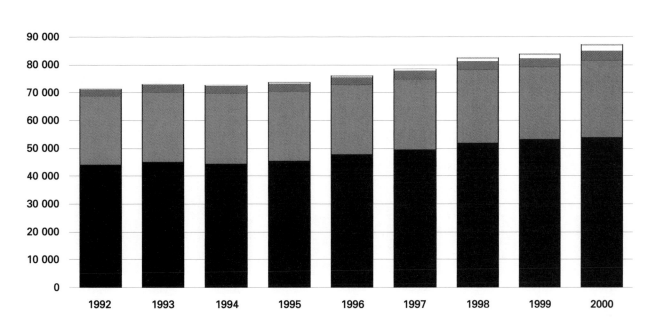

Black: biomass; colour: hydro; dark grey: geothermal; white: wind; light grey: solar.

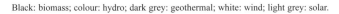

Energy intensity: gross inland consumption per unit of GDP in 1995 prices. kgoe per EUR 1 000

	1990	1991	1992	1993	1994	1995	1996	1997	1998	1999	2000	
EU-15	:	216.8	212.5	213.4	207.7	207.0	211.2	205.1	203.6	198.3	194.0 *	**EU-15**
B	:	248.5	248.6	244.2	240.7	238.3	251.9	248.4	247.8	243.3	235.1	**B**
DK	:	157.4	151.7	154.1	151.1	149.3	164.5	148.5	141.9	132.3	125.0	**DK**
D	:	194.4	186.5	187.7	181.8	179.3	184.1	179.7	176.0	168.6	165.1 *	**D**
EL	:	257.3	262.7	262.0	268.1	268.5	276.1	268.3	272.7	262.1	264.2	**EL**
E	:	221.4	222.4	215.9	224.0	228.9	220.4	222.8	223.6	227.1	227.6 *	**E**
F	:	207.2	201.7	206.1	194.0	198.4	207.5	198.6	198.1	191.9	189.5 *	**F**
IRL	:	248.5	238.5	234.7	236.7	216.6	213.1	201.5	197.6	189.5	172.0 *	**IRL**
I	:	196.3	197.2	195.9	189.1	193.9	191.5	190.5	193.6	193.5	190.8 *	**I**
L	:	315.4	305.5	297.7	280.1	241.1	237.4	214.6	198.1	196.4	192.7	**L**
NL	:	238.8	233.5	235.6	229.1	231.2	233.2	221.0	211.7	202.6	198.8	**NL**
A	:	160.9	149.8	148.7	145.0	146.6	152.9	152.8	149.2	143.1	139.1	**A**
P	:	215.1	230.1	232.0	236.1	237.4	229.8	235.1	239.2	249.2	242.3 *	**P**
FIN	:	301.7	301.6	316.4	321.9	291.7	300.7	297.7	287.4	275.8	257.8	**FIN**
S	:	275.4	266.4	273.4	276.7	271.9	278.8	265.8	258.0	247.6	223.7	**S**
UK	:	274.7	272.5	270.5	260.1	251.7	255.7	241.6	242.6	235.4	229.8	**UK**
IS	:	388.0	409.8	422.7	401.8	401.7	405.0	397.5	426.0	494.1	509.3	**IS**
NO	:	228.1	225.1	229.6	217.9	213.1	197.4	198.6	202.4	209.5	201.9	**NO**
JP	:	115.3	116.4	116.9	121.4	123.1	122.1	121.5	121.3	121.5	120.8	**JP**
US	:	387.7	384.0	381.5	374.2	369.1	365.3	353.5	341.8	338.4	332.4	**US**

Unit of GDP in 1995 prices and exchange rates to the euro.

4

Prices of premium unleaded gasoline 95 RON. EUR per 1 000 litres. January 2002

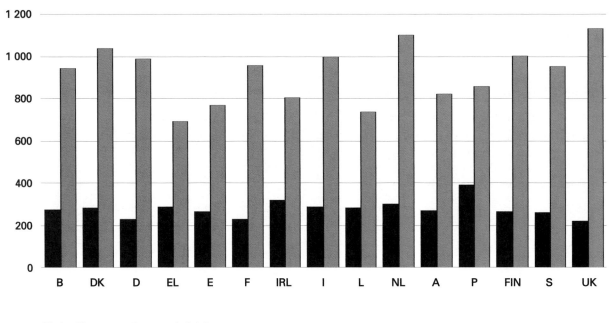

Black: without taxes; colour: taxes included.

National average prices.

Prices of diesel oil. EUR per 1 000 litres. January 2002

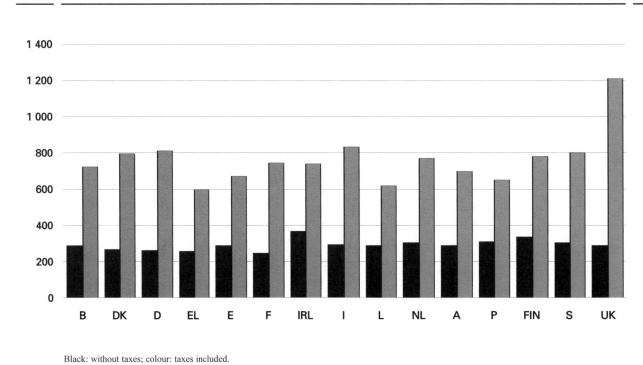

Black: without taxes; colour: taxes included.

National average prices.

Steel

A modern reporting system with a long tradition

Monitoring the production of iron, steel and steel products has a long tradition. In fact, it was there at the start of the European integration that began, in 1951, with the foundation of the European Coal and Steel Community. The ECSC Treaty was the first European Community Treaty ever ratified. Instigated for a period of 50 years, the Treaty expired on 23 July 2002.

Over that time, the production of steel as well as the steel products themselves have evolved considerably, and with it the statistical reporting system. This industry continues to be an important one, with a modern statistical reporting system.

Production of iron and steel

The steel industry encompasses all stages of production from raw material processing to finished steel products. There are two main ways of making steel: via pig iron made in blast furnaces from iron ore and other raw materials (57 % of EU-15 crude steel production in 2001); and by recycling steel scrap in electric furnaces.

Most finished products are made by hot rolling. The two main primary product classes are long products, such as rod and wire (39 % of EU-15 hot-rolled production in 2001), and flat products, such as sheet and plate (61 % of EU-15 hot-rolled production in 2001). There are various qualities of steel (ordinary, special and alloy) and nowadays a growing proportion of finished products is coated.

Trends ...

Between the mid-1970s and 1987, the steel industry in industrialised countries suffered serious setbacks. Restructuring after 1980 led to significant productivity gains by reducing capacity and cutting the labour force. Cyclical changes during the next decade resulted in a major recovery culminating in the record year 2000 with EU crude steel production of over 163 million tonnes; this figure went down slightly to 158 million tonnes in 2001. Hot-rolled production was 141 million tonnes in 2001.

... and trade

The EU is the world's largest steel producer, followed by China, Japan and the United States. It is also the largest steel exporter. Major markets for EU steel are North America, Asia (including Japan) and the EFTA countries. The collapse of domestic demand in eastern Europe in the early 1990s led to falling exports and rising imports. There was also intense competition from the region in third markets. The downturn in the Asian economies starting in the second half of 1997 directly and indirectly affected the EU trade balance in steel products, with the result that, for the first time, the EU became a net importer of steel products in 1998. This deficit continued in 1999, 2000 and 2001.

Further reading:

Eurostat publications
— **Iron and steel — Monthly statistics — Annual subscription 2002**
— **50 years of the ECSC Treaty — Coal and Steel Statistics**

Do you need more information?
— **Ask your Data Shop (see last page)**
— **http://www.europa.eu.int/comm/eurostat**
— **Eurostat's data serves the political discussion in Europe. Have a look at the website of the
   "DG Energy and Transport": http://europa.eu.int/comm/dgs/energy_transport/index_en.html**

4

Production of crude steel. 1 000 t

	1992	1993	1994	1995	1996	1997	1998	1999	2000	2001	
EU-15	132 224	132 278	139 001	155 758	146 602	159 798	159 582	155 081	163 211	158 498	EU-15
€-zone	121 665	121 392	127 862	131 590	122 041	134 359	135 469	132 008	140 827	:	€-zone
B	10 331	10 178	11 332	11 557	10 773	10 738	11 426	10 931	11 637	10 763	B
DK	592	604	722	653	737	787	792	730	800	751	DK
D	39 711	37 625	40 827	42 051	39 791	45 009	44 046	42 061	46 376	44 775	D
EL	923	980	846	940	848	1 016	1 108	951	1 088	1 281	EL
E	12 254	12 960	13 444	13 796	12 154	13 670	14 827	14 888	15 840	16 500	E
F	17 979	17 107	18 025	18 105	17 641	19 773	20 153	20 225	21 001	19 431	F
IRL	258	329	283	309	340	337	359	337	359	150	IRL
I	24 834	25 720	26 148	27 765	23 911	25 800	25 642	24 701	26 475	26 483	I
L	3 070	3 292	3 074	2 613	2 501	2 580	2 477	2 600	2 571	2 725	L
NL	5 437	6 001	6 173	6 409	6 325	6 640	6 377	6 075	5 666	6 037	NL
A	3 946	4 149	4 387	5 004	4 454	5 196	5 298	5 211	5 723	5 887	A
P	768	775	748	829	871	905	935	1 044	1 088	728	P
FIN	3 077	3 256	3 421	3 152	3 280	3 711	3 928	3 934	4 091	3 927	FIN
S	4 358	4 592	4 955	4 898	4 888	5 106	5 122	4 985	5 190	5 450	S
UK	16 067	16 707	17 379	17 677	18 088	18 530	17 090	16 407	15 305	13 610	UK

Further reading:

Eurostat publications
— **Iron and steel — Monthly statistics — Annual subscription 2002: PDF — last publication on that issue: April 2003**
— **Iron and steel — yearly statistics — edition 2002**
— **Iron and steel — Glossarium 1997**
— **50 years of the ECSC Treaty — Coal and Steel Statistics — data 1952–2000 — edition 2002, free of charge**

Production of hot-rolled steel products. 1 000 t

	1992	1993	1994	1995	1996	1997	1998	1999	2000	2001	
EU-15	115 140	111 597	119 469	134 721	128 386	140 623	139 873	140 771	146 825	141 242	EU-15
€-zone	:	:	:	112 908	106 482	117 842	118 318	119 883	126 757	:	€-zone
B	10 336	9 751	10 981	11 033	10 963	12 047	12 194	12 779	13 689	12 770	B
DK	541	527	638	631	621	706	661	689	559	635	DK
D	33 042	31 140	33 873	34 316	32 889	37 074	36 593	35 879	38 974	37 011	D
EL	1 566	1 354	1 298	1 436	1 244	1 381	1 195	1 368	1 646	1 734	EL
E	10 769	11 563	12 104	12 771	10 971	12 421	13 260	13 847	14 554	14 931	E
F	15 204	14 046	15 195	15 109	15 189	16 588	16 823	17 293	17 474	16 593	F
IRL	242	305	242	276	312	306	325	322	342	110	IRL
I	22 613	21 760	22 850	24 075	21 246	23 146	22 569	22 917	23 917	23 059	I
L	2 563	2 608	2 644	2 407	2 313	2 466	2 516	2 775	3 019	2 974	L
NL	4 185	4 119	4 554	4 702	4 810	5 175	4 964	4 786	4 956	5 335	NL
A	:	:	:	4 213	3 837	4 516	4 641	4 656	5 034	5 251	A
P	679	659	701	703	660	789	750	853	910	865	P
FIN	:	:	:	3 303	3 292	3 314	3 683	3 776	3 890	3 842	FIN
S	:	:	:	4 461	4 369	4 545	4 485	4 575	4 689	4 694	S
UK	13 400	13 765	14 389	15 285	15 670	16 149	15 214	14 255	13 173	11 440	UK

4

eurostat

Research and development

Research and development: an engine of growth

Research and development (R & D) is a driving force behind economic growth, job creation, innovation of new products and increasing quality of products in general, as well as improvements in healthcare and environmental protection. At the Lisbon Summit in March 2000, the European Council set a clear strategic objective for Europe in the next decade: to make the EU the most competitive and dynamic knowledge-based economy in the world.

Eurostat supports this ambitious goal with its reliable and relevant statistical information on R & D and innovation as well as on science and technology. Eurostat calculates a number of indicators and provides data for deeper analytical studies. Most indicators are calculated annually and are available at national and regional level (for most of the countries at NUTS 2 level). Depending on the indicator, data are available not only for the Member States of the European Union but also for other members of the European Economic Area, candidate countries, Japan or the United States. For more information, ask your Data Shop for the publications *Statistics on science and technology in Europe* and *Statistics on innovation in Europe*. The addresses of the Data Shops can be found at the end of the yearbook.

Inputs into R & D

Data on R & D expenditure and personnel as well as on government budget appropriations or outlays for research and development (GBAORD) are mainly collected every year from the national statistical offices.

R & D expenditure is a 'priority indicator' for the effort devoted to R & D. The basic measure is 'intramural expenditures', i.e. all expenditures for R & D performed within a statistical unit or sector of the economy, whatever the source of funds. Among the several indicators available, R & D intensity (i.e. R & D expenditure as a percentage of GDP) is the most recommended for international comparisons and is very significant for comparing the countries' R & D efforts.

R & D intensity for EU-15 showed a decreasing trend during the 1990s, but it stabilised towards the end of the decade at about 1.9 %. When compared with the United States (2.6 %) and Japan (3 %), the EU lags behind, but this is mainly due to the differences observed in the business enterprise sector. Within the EU, R & D intensity is highest in Finland and Sweden, which outperform countries with the highest R & D expenditure in terms of volume (Germany, France and the United Kingdom).

In terms of human resources, data on scientific and technical R & D personnel provide indicators for useful international comparisons of resources devoted to R & D. For statistical purposes, indicators on R & D personnel are compiled in terms of persons, i.e. head count (HC), in full-time equivalent (FTE) or person-years and by gender. At the EU level, R & D personnel in HC as a proportion of the labour force has seen a modest increase over the last decade, with the Nordic countries taking the lead.

GBAORD are the amount governments allocate towards R & D activities. Comparisons of GBAORD across countries give an impression of the relative importance attached to State-funded R & D. GBAORD statistics complement the ex post figures on 'government-financed' gross expenditure on research and development (GERD) and, when broken down by socioeconomic objective, underline the domains governments believe to be important for current and future policy action. When measured as a proportion of GDP, Japan has caught up with both the EU and the United States to a significant degree since the end of the 1980s. Data show that the efforts made by governments in R & D activities are clearly converging.

Outputs of R & D

Patents reflect part of a country's inventive activity and show the country's capacity to exploit knowledge and translate it into potential economic gains. In this context, indicators based on patent statistics are widely used as a measure of R & D output and serve to assess the inventive performance of the countries, regions or industries. Patent data published in the Eurostat yearbook are provided by the European Patent Office (EPO) and the United States Patent and Trademark Office (USPTO). The data from the EPO refer to patent applications filed under the European Patent Convention or under the Patent Cooperation Treaty and designating the EPO for protection. Although not all applications are granted, each one still represents technical effort by the inventor and so is regarded as an appropriate indicator of innovative potential. German regions have the highest patenting activities when measured relative to their labour force. Some regions of the Netherlands, Finland, Sweden Belgium and the United Kingdom are present in the top 15 leading regions. Finland and Sweden are leading in high-technology patenting and show a high specialisation in the communication technology field.

Human resources

The importance of high-technology sectors has increased considerably over the last few years and this has had a significant impact on the structure and organisation of employment in Europe. In order to permit analysis of knowledge- and technology-intensive sectors, Eurostat collects data on employment in high-technology and medium-high-technology manufacturing sectors, knowledge-intensive services (KIS), high-technology service sectors, other subsectors and reference sectors (for definitions, see glossary entry 'High-technology sectors'). Data on employment in high-technology and derived indicators are extracted and built up using data from the Community labour force survey (LFS). Data are available both at the national and regional levels. Within Europe, Germany's manufacturing sector shows high employment in high- and medium-high technology. In the service sector, UK regions appear to be the most dynamic regarding employment in KIS.

4

Further reading:

Eurostat publications
— **Statistics on science and technology in Europe**
— **Statistics on innovation in Europe**

Statistics in Focus — Theme 4
— **No 3 R & D expenditure and personnel in Europe and its reg**
— **No 4 Patent activities in the EU: international, national and regional perspect**
— **No 5 How much do governments budget for R & D activities? — Benchmarking Europe, the US and Japan**

Total research and development expenditure. Million current PPS. All sectors

	1991	1992	1993	1994	1995	1996	1997	1998	1999	2000	2001	
EU-15	107 995 *	111 709 *	112 801 *	116 009 *	118 807 *	124 534 *	131 163 *	137 888 *	148 921 *	158 671 *	165 873 *	EU-15
B	2 693	:	3 162 *	3 325 *	3 454 *#	3 771 *#	4 112 *#	4 347 *#	4 538 *#	:	:	B
DK	1 446	1 505 *	1 655	:	2 000	2 177 *	2 388	2 614 *|	2 820 #	3 011 *	:	DK
D	33 500		34 152	33 813	34 745	35 790	36 780 *		39 316	40 849 *	45 241 #	48 493 *	#	50 192 *		D
EL	347	:	505	:	592 *|	:	680	:	1 031 *	:	:	EL
E	4 086		4 347	4 418	4 201	4 390	4 777 *	4 989	5 660 *	6 118	6 974 *#	7 525 *		E
F	23 576		24 385	24 499	24 647	25 149	25 608	25 504	26 105	27 854	28 993 *	:	F
IRL	391 *	473 *	565 *	697 *	796 *	825 *	947 *	1 001 *|	1 074 *	:	:	IRL
I	11 361	11 376	10 644	10 544	10 453	11 155	11 969 #|	12 886 #	13 173 #	:	:	I
L	:	:	:	:	:	:	:	:	:	:	:	L
NL	4 790	4 840	5 058		5 465	5 929	6 361	6 946	7 119	7 778 #	:	:	NL
A	1 923 *	2 004 *	2 119	2 334 *	2 436 *	2 667 *	2 940 *	3 212	3 493 *	3 650 *	3 850 *|	A
P	:	643	:	:	703 #	:	891	:	1 178 #	:	:	P
FIN	1 515	1 511	1 637	1 806	1 999	2 331	2 691	3 059	3 573	4 052 #	4 485 *	FIN
S	3 952	:	4 357	:	5 538	:	6 453	6 824 *	7 220	:	:	S
UK	17 980	19 038	19 693	20 231	19 667	20 722	21 405	22 520	23 519	25 362 #	26 471 *#	UK
IS	51	58		62	67		83	88		113	133	164	:	:	IS
NO	1 227	:	1 512	:	1 579	:	1 839	:	2 017	:	:	NO
EEA	109 273 *	113 065 *	114 375 *	117 588 *	120 469 *	126 355 *	133 116 *	139 851 *	151 102 *	161 265 *	168 528 *	EEA
JP	66 876		68 516		69 353		70 647		76 228		78 770		83 952	87 533	85 149	90 976	:	JP
US	152 101		156 930		153 937		158 344		170 490		182 283		198 207		212 642		224 590		246 207 *|	:	US

FIN: forecasts for 2001. UK: forecasts for 2001 and 2002. US: provisional data for 2000. US, JP: *Source:* OECD.

Total research and development expenditure as % of GDP. All sectors (GERD)

	1991	1992	1993	1994	1995	1996	1997	1998	1999	2000	2001	
EU-15	1.94 *	1.92 *	1.95 *	1.91 *	1.89 *	1.88 *	1.87 *	1.87 *	1.93 *	1.93 *	1.94 *	EU-15
€-zone	1.89 *	1.86 *	1.89 *	1.84 *	1.83 *	1.82 *	1.81 *	1.82 *	1.87 *	1.87 *	1.89 *	€-zone
B	1.62	:	1.70 *	1.69 *	1.71 *#	1.80 *#	1.87 *#	1.89 *#	1.96 *#	:	:	B
DK	1.64	1.68 *	1.74	:	1.84	1.85 *	1.94	2.06 *	2.09 #	2.07 *	:	DK
D	2.54		2.42	2.37	2.28	2.26	2.26 *	2.29	2.31 *	2.44 #	2.48 *#	2.52 *	D
EL	0.36 *	:	0.47 *	:	0.49 *	:	0.51	:	0.67 *	:	:	EL
E	0.84		0.88	0.88	0.81	0.81	0.83 *	0.82	0.89 *	0.88	0.94 *#	0.97 *	E
F	2.37		2.38	2.40	2.34	2.31	2.30	2.22	2.17	2.18	2.13 *	:	F
IRL	0.93 *	1.04 *	1.17 *	1.31 *	1.34 *	1.32 *	1.29 *	1.26 *	1.21 *	:	:	IRL
I	1.23	1.18	1.13	1.05	1.00	1.01	1.05 #|	1.07 #	1.04 #	:	:	I
L	:	:	:	:	:	:	:	:	:	1.36 *	:	L
NL	1.97	1.90	1.93		1.97	1.99	2.03	2.04	1.94	2.02 #	:	:	NL
A	1.47 *	1.45 *	1.47	1.54 *	1.56 *	1.60 *	1.69 *	1.79	1.83 *	1.80 *	1.86 *	A
P	:	0.61	:	:	0.57 #	:	0.62	:	0.76 #	:	:	P
FIN	2.04	2.13	2.18	2.29	2.29	2.54	2.72	2.89	3.22	3.37 #	3.67 #	FIN
S	2.79	:	3.09	:	3.46	:	3.68	3.75 *	3.78	:	:	S
UK	2.07	2.08	2.11	2.06	1.97	1.90	1.82	1.81	1.85	1.85 #	1.86 #	UK
IS	1.16	1.33	1.33	1.38	1.54	1.51	1.84	2.04	2.32	:	:	IS
NO	1.64	:	1.72	:	1.70	:	1.64	:	1.65	:	1.62 *	NO
JP	2.93	2.89	2.82	2.76	2.89	2.77		2.83	2.94	2.94	2.98	:	JP
US	2.72	2.65	2.52	2.43	2.51	2.55	2.58	2.61	2.66	2.70 *	:	US

US, JP: *Source:* OECD.

Business research and development expenditure as % of GDP. Business enterprise sector (BERD)

	1991	1992	1993	1994	1995	1996	1997	1998	1999	2000	2001	
EU-15	1.24 *	1.22 *	1.22 *	1.20 *	1.19 *	1.18 *	1.19 *	1.19 *	1.25 *	1.26 *	1.28 *	**EU-15**
€-zone	1.19 *	1.16 *	1.16 *	1.13 *	1.13 *	1.12 *	1.13 *	1.13 *	1.19 *	1.21 *	1.23 *	**€-zone**
B	1.08	1.16 *	1.22 *	1.21 *	1.22 *	1.29 *	1.34 *	1.34 *#	1.40 *	1.45 *	:	**B**
DK	0.96	0.98 *	1.02	:	1.05	1.13 *	1.19	1.33	1.32 #	1.32 *	:	**DK**
D	1.76	1.66	1.58	1.51	1.50	1.49 *	1.54	1.57 *	1.70 #	1.76 *#	1.80 *	**D**
EL	0.09 *	:	0.13 *	:	0.14	0.12	0.13	:	0.19 #	:	:	**EL**
E	0.47	0.44	0.42	0.38	0.39	0.40 *	0.40	0.47	0.46	0.50 *#	0.52 *	**E**
F	1.46 |	1.49	1.48	1.45	1.41	1.41	1.39	1.35	1.38	1.36 *		**F**
IRL	0.59 *	0.67 *	0.80 *	0.91 *	0.96 *	0.93 *	0.91 *	0.91 *	0.88	:	:	**IRL**
I	0.68	0.66	0.60	0.56	0.53	0.54	0.52 #	0.52 #	0.51 #	0.51i #	0.53	**I**
L	:	:	:	:	:	:	:	:	:	1.19 *	:	**L**
NL	0.98	0.93	0.95 |	1.01	1.04	1.06	1.11	1.05	1.14 #	:	:	**NL**
A	:	:	0.82	:	:	:	:	1.14 #	:	:	:	**A**
P	:	0.13	:	:	0.12	:	0.14	:	0.17	:	:	**P**
FIN	1.16	1.21	1.27	1.42	1.45	1.68	1.79	1.94	2.19	2.39 #	2.68 *	**FIN**
S	1.91	:	2.23	:	2.57	:	2.75	2.85 *	2.84	:	:	**S**
UK	1.39	1.39	1.41	1.35	1.29	1.24	1.19	1.19	1.25	1.22 #	1.21 *#	**UK**
IS	0.25	0.29	0.42	0.43	0.49	0.47	0.75	0.75	1.08	:	:	**IS**
NO	0.89	:	0.92	:	0.96	:	0.93	:	0.92	:	0.97 *	**NO**
JP	2.08	1.99	1.86	1.83	1.89	1.97 |	2.04	2.09	2.08	2.11	:	**JP**
US	1.97	1.90	1.78	1.71	1.80	1.87	1.91	1.94	1.99	2.04 *	:	**US**

*Research and development personnel (head count), by sectors of the economy as % of the labour force.
1999*

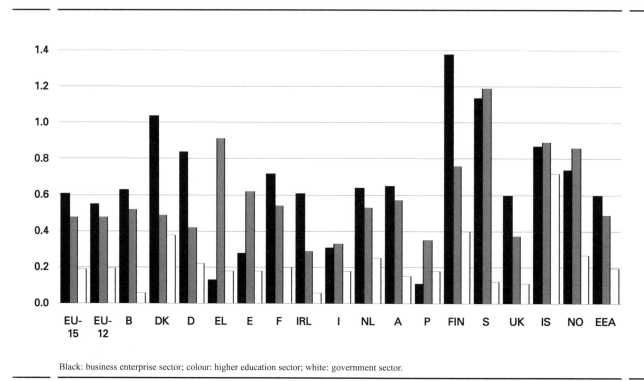

Black: business enterprise sector; colour: higher education sector; white: government sector.

Research and development personnel (head count) as % of the labour force. All sectors

	1991	1992	1993	1994	1995	1996	1997	1998	1999	2000	2001	
EU-15	1.25 *	1.26 *	1.25 *	1.28 *	1.28 *	1.28 *	1.30 *	1.34 *	1.36 *	1.38 *	1.41 *	**EU-15**
B	1.37 *	:	1.22 *	1.26 *	1.28 *	1.35 *	1.40 *	1.46 *	1.52 *	:	:	**B**
DK	1.43	:	1.53	:	1.81	:	1.85	:	1.89 #	:	:	**DK**
D	1.73 *	1.65 *	1.61 *	:	1.55 *	1.53 *	1.55 *	1.54 *	1.59 *	1.62 *	:	**D**
EL	0.56	:	0.75	:	0.87	:	0.77 #	:	1.28	:	:	**EL**
E	0.77	0.79	0.80	:	0.94	:	0.97	:	1.09	:	:	**E**
F	1.40		1.45	1.44	1.45	1.46	1.46	1.49	1.49	:	:	:	**F**
IRL	0.82 *	0.87 *	0.77 *	0.81 *	0.88 *	0.89 *	0.93 *	0.94 *	0.96 *	:	:	**IRL**
I	0.75	0.79	0.79	0.81	0.81	0.81	:	0.96	0.92	:	:	**I**
L	:	:	:	:	:	:	:	:	:	:	:	**L**
NL	1.42 *	1.41 *	1.43 *	1.47 *	1.45 *	1.45 *	1.46 *	1.46 *	1.54 *	:	:	**NL**
A	:	:	1.17 *	:	:	:	:	1.38	:	:	:	**A**
P	:	:	:	:	0.53	:	0.61	:	0.73 #	:	:	**P**
FIN	1.86 *	:	1.75 *	:	1.97	:	2.23	2.42	2.53	2.58	:	**FIN**
S	:	:	1.77 *	:	2.18	:	2.34	:	2.45	:	:	**S**
UK	:	:	:	:	:	:	:	:	:	:	:	**UK**
IS	1.57 *	:	1.89 *	:	1.97 *	:	2.51	2.56	2.70 #	:	:	**IS**
NO	1.47 *	:	1.59 *	:	1.87	:	1.93	:	1.88	:	:	**NO**
EEA	1.25 *	1.26 *	1.26 *	1.28 *	1.29 *	1.29 *	1.31 *	1.35 *	1.37 *	1.39 *	1.41 *	**EEA**

611AC

Total researchers (head count)

	1991	1992	1993	1994	1995	1996	1997	1998	1999	
B	24 777 *	:	28 424 *	30 999 *	31 592 *	32 766 *	34 283 *	37 604 *	40 484 *	**B**
DK	20 503	:	22 701	:	25 942	:	:	:	28 115	**DK**
D	327 450 *	:	316 461 *	:	316 407 *	:	322 711 *	325 201 *	346 122 *	**D**
EL	:	:	16 119	:	18 147	:	20 703	:	:	**EL**
E	:	77 430	80 113	70 508	100 070	:	103 905	:	116 595	**E**
F	:	177 634	181 181	186 387	189 000	190 904	197 032	198 484	:	**F**
IRL	7 729 *	8 388 *	9 787 *	:	:	:	:	:	11 392 *	**IRL**
I	:	:	:	:	:	:	:	:	98 217	**I**
L	:	:	:	:	:	:	:	:	:	**L**
NL	:	:	47 093 *	49 486 *	49 009 *	48 760 *	:	:	57 646 *	**NL**
A	:	:	:	:	:	:	:	31 404	:	**A**
P	:	:	:	:	18 697	:	22 217	:	28 375	**P**
FIN	25 397	:	25 784	:	29 939	:	35 317	39 623	43 163	**FIN**
S	:	:	:	:	:	:	:	:	:	**S**
UK	157 711 *	171 980 *	177 246 *	189 762 *	:	191 679 *	191 669	:	:	**UK**
IS	1 321	:	1 659	:	1 926	:	2 181	2 290	2 780	**IS**
NO	:	:	21 825	:	26 662	:	30 244	:	30 961	**NO**

611AX

4

eurostat

Total government research and development appropriations (GBAORD) as % of GDP. Comparison of the EEA with the United States and Japan

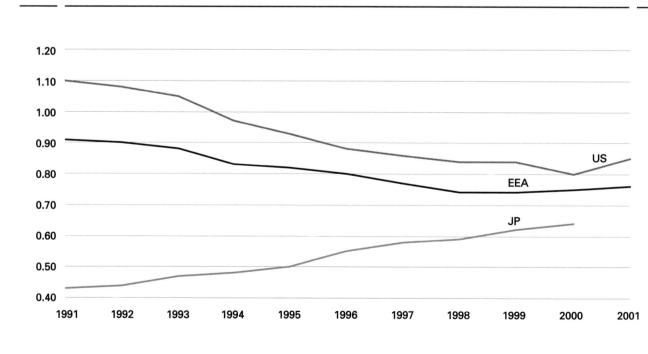

EEA: L and LI not included. US, JP: *Source:* OECD.

European high-technology patents per million inhabitants

	1990	1991	1992	1993	1994	1995	1996	1997	1998	1999	2000	
EU-15	7.5	8.0	8.9	8.7	10.4	11.7	14.2	19.5	23.2	29.3	31.6 *	**EU-15**
€-zone	7.0 *	7.8 *	8.3 *	8.0 *	9.6 *	10.6 *	12.9 *	18.0 *	21.7 *	27.2 *	28.5 *	**€-zone**
B	6.8	8.7	10.3	8.6	10.9	12.3	12.1	16.9	21.2	22.5	23.4 *	**B**
DK	8.4	9.5	10.0	11.3	13.8	12.9	21.1	24.8	28.9	38.4	42.1 *	**DK**
D	11.0	11.6	11.7	11.0	13.6	16.4	19.8 *	29.6	35.3	45.2	48.8 *	**D**
EL	0.2	0.6	0.4	0.2	0.5	0.3	0.4	0.6	0.9	0.8	2.1 *	**EL**
E	0.6	0.6	0.9	0.8	1.1	0.9	1.4	2.0	3.1 *	3.3 *	3.6 *	**E**
F	10.8	12.0	11.5	11.4	12.8	12.4	15.4	20.2	24.6	29.0	30.3 *	**F**
IRL	2.8	5.2	3.4	2.5	6.8	7.0	8.2	10.2	15.2 *	30.2 *	30.7 *	**IRL**
I	2.6	2.9	3.7	3.8	4.0	4.7	4.7	5.4	5.7	6.8	6.5 *	**I**
L	-	-	-	-	3.3	1.6	6.0	6.5	9.3 *	30.5 *	10.9 *	**L**
NL	13.9	17.1	19.0	18.7	20.5	23.0	32.3	38.4	48.0	61.2	68.8 *	**NL**
A	5.5	4.5	5.4	5.8	8.0	7.6	7.7	10.9	12.4	17.5	18.8 *	**A**
P	0.1	0.3	0.3	0.0	0.0	0.1	0.5	0.1	0.4	0.8	0.7 *	**P**
FIN	12.8	17.2	30.8	29.3	44.3	48.8	57.6 *	99.5	120.2	155.5	136.1 *	**FIN**
S	10.2	11.4	17.3	15.5	26.4	36.0	44.5	72.6	73.6	102.0	100.9 *	**S**
UK	9.6	8.4	10.4	10.8	12.1	13.6	15.8	18.5	22.9	28.7	35.6 *	**UK**
IS	5.2	-	3.8	1.9	15.7	1.9	14.8	17.1	26.4	53.9	31.0 *	**IS**
LI	91.6	:	11.0	76.9	32.6	:	80.3	63.9	8.1	154.2	:	**LI**
NO	1.9	2.8	2.9	2.9	4.0	5.1	8.9	17.0	11.8	15.7	49.6 *	**NO**
EEA	7.4	7.9	8.8	8.6	10.4	11.6	14.1	19.4	23.1	29.2	31.8 *	**EEA**
CA	3.1	3.2	3.3	4.9	6.3	8.0	11.1	14.0	16.2	22.2	25.9 *	**CA**
JP	26.0	23.1	19.0	19.8	19.6	22.2	27.0	29.2	32.4	40.1	44.9 *	**JP**
US	10.8	15.6	12.7	13.7	15.7	18.4	21.1	21.1	37.2	51.3	57.0 *	**US**

US, JP: 2000 population data; *Source:* UN. EEA 2000: excludes LI.

Patents (EPO): number of European patent applications at the European Patent Organisation per million inhabitants

	1991	1992	1993	1994	1995	1996	1997	1998	1999	2000	2001	
EU-15	79.8	83.7	83.4	86.1	92.1	97.1	108.2	130.0	141.0	158.7	161.1 *	**EU-15**
€-zone	78.5 *	83.7 *	82.7 *	85.1 *	91.0 *	95.9 *	106.4 *	130.3 *	141.4 *	158.0 *	159.6 *	**€-zone**
B	61.3	74.5	88.1	90.1	94.0	94.2	112.5	140.0	145.1	157.7	151.8 *	**B**
DK	90.0	91.4	103.5	113.6	120.0	130.1	144.2	139.7	168.5	199.3	211.0 *	**DK**
D	144.8	154.7	152.9	156.5	169.6	177.9	193.1 *	247.6	273.5	305.1	309.9 *	**D**
EL	3.3	4.2	4.3	3.4	4.1	4.6	5.3	7.1	8.1	6.1	7.7 *	**EL**
E	8.5	9.1	9.6	11.8	12.1	13.0	16.7	21.0	23.3 *	24.9 *	24.1 *	**E**
F	92.4	95.7	89.9	91.4	96.7	99.6	110.4	125.6	131.0	144.4	145.3 *	**F**
IRL	19.5	24.8	31.1	25.8	36.9	39.3	43.7	55.2	69.9 *	95.4 *	85.6 *	**IRL**
I	40.1	46.3	43.0	0.0	46.0	50.7	56.8	64.4	68.1	76.8	74.7 *	**I**
L	104.4	90.0	61.2	103.4	72.3	100.8	138.6	143.5	200.5 *	198.7 *	211.3 *	**L**
NL	108.2	108.9	109.7	112.9	117.3	136.1	165.0	178.3	197.3	228.8	242.7 *	**NL**
A	91.0	92.1	88.5	94.2	100.4	98.5	111.3	142.3	140.3	158.4	174.2 *	**A**
P	0.9	1.3	1.6	2.2	1.6	1.5	2.7	2.4	4.6	4.0	5.5 *	**P**
FIN	117.0	108.7	144.2	155.3	175.1	174.1	173.5 *	260.2	294.2	343.7	337.8 *	**FIN**
S	140.8	143.3	152.4	165.8	199.7	218.0	264.4	307.0	308.5	361.5	366.6 *	**S**
UK	75.9	74.4	75.2	76.9	78.8	82.3	90.4	0.1	111.2	128.4	133.5 *	**UK**
IS	27.5	42.0	19.1	26.4	31.9	30.1	62.8	84.8	109.6	0.1	117.2 *	**IS**
NO	51.7	64.7	67.6	59.4	70.2	87.1	104.7	118.1	121.5	136.2	288.8 *	**NO**
JP	106.0	96.6	89.0	89.7	88.3	100.7	115.1	122.9	131.7	159.5	174.7 *	**JP**
US	72.6	80.9	78.2	80.9	85.9	93.9	102.9	106.9	141.9	166.2	169.8 *	**US**

US, JP: 2000 population data; *Source:* UN. EEA 2000: excludes LI.

4

Information society

The information society: an opportunity for Europe ...

Information technology is developing vigorously day by day. However, the information society, a society whose wealth and growth is based on its ability to handle information efficiently, is not only a technical phenomenon: it is transforming the way we communicate, the way we do business, and the way we live. The information society holds enormous potential and opportunities for Europe and all of its citizens.

... and a challenge for statisticians

Monitoring the rapid change powered by the Internet and other new means of information and communication is a challenge statisticians are well aware of. They rethink their statistical tools and how best to use them to satisfy the new demands for data concerning all aspects of the information society. They cooperate with the different kinds of data users to identify and mediate the new demands.

The information society in the Eurostat yearbook

The Eurostat yearbook introduced a new section on the information society in its 2000 edition to present basic variables about the phenomenon, especially personal computers, Internet hosts, Internet users and mobile phones. If you would like more detailed information, please contact one of the Data Shops the addresses of which can be found at the end of the yearbook.

— Data on the number of personal computers (PCs) include PCs at home and PCs used at work. In spring 2000, 35 % of the EU population (15 years and older) had a desktop computer at home, while 29 % used such a computer at home. In all, 5 % of the population had a laptop computer and 3 % a palm computer at home.

In 2001, 26 million computers (of which 23 % portable and 77 % desktop) were sold in the EU. The number of personal computers in the EU, however, was estimated to have increased by only 8 million in the same year. The large number of old computers being dismantled reflects the technical progress and the growth of processing power of new computers.

— Internet hosts are computers connected to the Internet and providing data and services to other computers.

Automated host counts are in many statistics on a country level restricted to country code top-level domains (domain names like '.de', '.uk' or '.fr'). This is also the case for the figures which are shown in this section. Based on registrations, some statistics also attribute generic domain codes (examples are '.com' and '.org') to countries. This results in higher figures than the counting of the country code top-level domains only.

At the end of 2001, the number of Internet subscribers in the EU was about five times as high, and the number of users nine times as high, as the number of Internet hosts.

— Internet users: according to a *Eurobarometer* survey carried out in November 2001, 38 % of the EU population (15 years and older) or 120 million persons used the Internet. According to this survey, 69 % of users access the Internet at home (of which 98 % through a PC; 72 % accessed it via a normal telephone line, 16 % via an ISDN line, and about 15 % via a broadband connection) and 40 % access it at work.

In all, 41 % of Internet users go online every day, 83 % at least once a week and 92 % at least once a month. In many surveys carried out at a national level, using the Internet at least once a month is applied as a threshold for considering someone an Internet user.

— Mobile phones were first introduced in Europe in the early 1980s. Constrained by weight and power requirements, they were at the beginning mainly confined to cars. As mobile phones became lighter, cheaper and technically more advanced, the market started to take off, especially in the second half of the 1990s.

However mobile phone penetration is now approaching saturation. While in the year 2000 the number of mobile phone subscribers in the EU increased by 59 %, growth slowed down to 15 % in 2001. As with main telephone lines, there has been a switch from analogue to digital technology: in 2001, the share of digital mobile phones approached 100 % of the EU market.

The statistics available refer to the number of cellular mobile telephone subscriptions; the number of mobile phone sets in use roughly corresponds to the number of subscriptions.

Further reading:

Eurostat publications
— **Information society statistics — Pocketbook**

Statistics in Focus — Theme 4
— **No 23 Information society statistics — Rapid expansion of Internet and mobile phone usage in the European Union in 2000**
— **No 34 Information society statistics — 4 million persons employed in the information and communication technology sector in the EU**

Do you need more information?
— **Ask your Data Shop (see last page)**
— **http://www.europa.eu.int/comm/eurostat**
— **Eurostat's data serves the political discussion in Europe. Have a look at the website of the " DG Information Society": http://europa.eu.int/comm/dgs/information_society/index_en.htm**

4M1LL

Price of telecommunications: local calls. Price level and evolution in the telecommunications market.
EUR per 10 min call

	1997	1998	1999	2000	2001	
EU-15	0.37	0.41	0.41	0.41	0.41	EU-15
€-zone	:	:	:	:	:	€-zone
B	0.45	0.49	0.49	0.49	0.54	B
DK	0.45	0.45	0.41	0.41	0.41	DK
D	0.43	0.44	0.43	0.43	0.43	D
EL	0.16	0.18	0.21	0.31	0.36	EL
E	0.20	0.32	0.31	0.28	0.28	E
F	0.45	0.42	0.42	0.42	0.39	F
IRL	0.58	0.58	0.49	0.51	0.51	IRL
I	0.23	0.24	0.24	0.25	0.25	I
L	0.37	0.37	0.37	0.37	0.31	L
NL	0.34	0.32	0.32	0.30	0.31	NL
A	0.49	0.80	0.80	0.64	0.64	A
P	0.27	0.25	0.27	0.23	0.30	P
FIN	0.21	0.21	0.21	0.22	0.23	FIN
S	0.28	0.29	0.29	0.30	0.30	S
UK	0.65	0.64	0.64	0.64	0.64	UK
NO	0.36	0.35	0.31	0.34	0.34	NO
JP	0.42	0.38	0.38	0.38	0.41	JP
US	0.13	0.13	0.13	0.13	0.13	US

4M4LL

Market share of the incumbent in fixed telecommunications — local calls — as % of total market. 2001

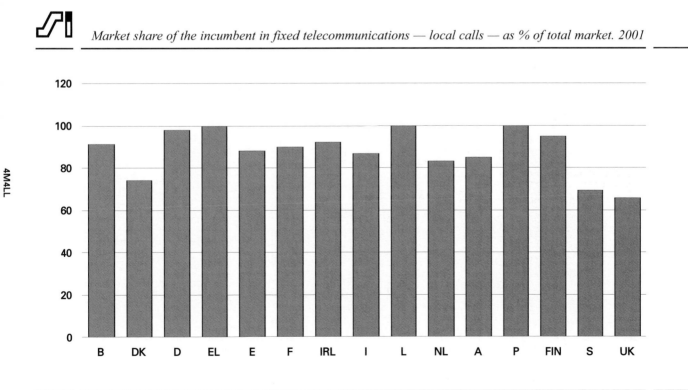

4

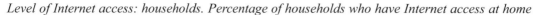

Level of Internet access: households. Percentage of households who have Internet access at home

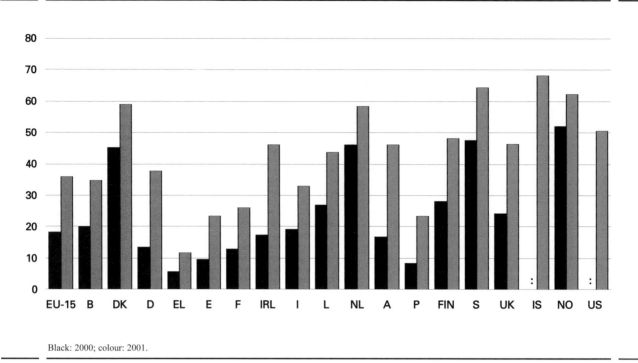

Black: 2000; colour: 2001.

Sources: Information Society DG and Press and Communication DG (Eurobarometer surveys).

Level of Internet access: enterprises. Percentage of enterprises who have Internet access. 2001

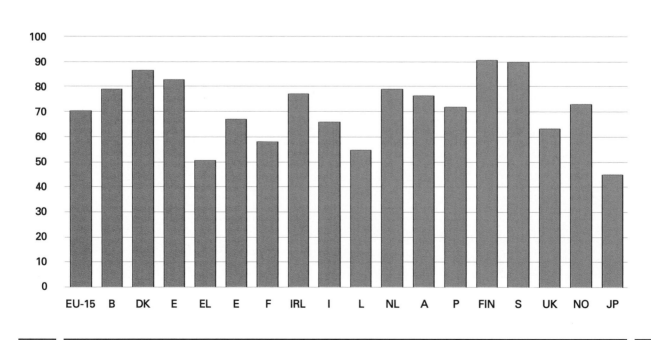

Includes only enterprises with more than nine persons employed. *Sources:* Eurostat e-commerce survey and estimates for 2000; Information Society DG and Eurostat for 2001.

4

ICT expenditure: IT expenditure. Expenditure on information technology as % of GDP

	1992	1993	1994	1995	1996	1997	1998	1999	2000	
EU-15	3.0	3.2	3.1	3.1	3.2	3.4	3.6	3.9	4.2	EU-15
B	3.4	3.5	3.4	3.2	3.3	3.7	4.0	4.3	4.5	B
DK	3.9	4.1	3.9	4.0	4.1	4.3	4.8	5.0	5.4	DK
D	2.9	3.0	3.0	2.8	3.0	3.3	3.6	4.0	4.3	D
EL	0.7	0.8	0.8	0.9	0.9	0.9	1.0	1.1	1.2	EL
E	1.6	1.7	1.6	1.5	1.6	1.7	1.8	1.9	2.0	E
F	3.6	3.8	3.6	3.7	3.7	4.1	4.1	4.3	4.7	F
IRL	2.4	2.4	2.3	2.3	2.2	2.0	2.4	2.5	2.4	IRL
I	1.8	1.9	1.9	1.9	1.8	1.9	2.0	2.2	2.4	I
L	:	:	:	3.9	4.2	4.9	5.4	5.3	5.5	L
NL	4.0	4.0	3.9	3.7	3.8	4.1	4.8	5.2	5.3	NL
A	2.7	2.8	2.8	2.8	2.8	3.1	3.3	3.5	3.8	A
P	1.2	1.3	1.3	1.5	1.5	1.5	1.7	1.9	2.0	P
FIN	2.9	3.3	2.1	3.2	3.4	3.5	3.9	4.3	4.5	FIN
S	4.4	5.2	5.0	4.8	4.7	5.3	6.2	6.5	6.9	S
UK	4.4	4.8	4.6	4.8	4.9	4.9	4.8	5.2	5.6	UK
NO	3.2	3.3	3.2	3.3	3.3	3.5	4.0	4.3	3.9	NO
JP	3.8	3.4	3.2	3.2	3.6	3.8	3.9	3.6	3.8	JP
US	4.5	4.5	4.6	4.7	4.9	5.0	5.2	5.3	5.5	US

Sources: OECD (1992–99); Eurostat (2000–01). Figures for 2000–01 are extrapolations of 1999 results using growth rates from the EITO 2002 report.

9H3DE

ICT expenditure: telecommunications expenditure. Expenditure on telecommunications technology as % of GDP

	1992	1993	1994	1995	1996	1997	1998	1999	2000	
EU-15	2.1	2.2	2.1	2.2	2.3	2.4	2.3	2.5	2.7	EU-15
B	1.8	1.9	1.9	2.0	2.2	2.4	2.3	2.5	2.7	B
DK	2.1	2.2	2.1	2.1	2.2	2.3	2.3	2.3	2.4	DK
D	2.2	2.3	2.1	2.2	2.2	2.2	2.2	2.3	2.6	D
EL	1.5	1.4	2.6	2.7	2.9	3.0	3.2	3.4	3.8	EL
E	2.0	2.0	2.0	2.0	2.2	2.3	2.2	2.3	2.5	E
F	2.0	2.1	1.9	2.0	2.1	2.2	2.2	2.3	2.5	F
IRL	2.7	2.6	3.1	3.1	3.3	3.2	3.0	3.0	3.0	IRL
I	1.7	1.8	2.1	2.1	2.2	2.3	2.3	2.5	2.7	I
L	:	:	:	2.2	2.8	2.4	2.6	2.7	2.5	L
NL	2.2	2.3	2.2	2.4	2.5	2.6	2.7	2.8	3.1	NL
A	2.1	2.2	1.7	1.7	1.8	2.0	2.0	2.1	2.4	A
P	1.2	1.3	2.8	2.9	3.1	3.3	3.2	3.3	3.5	P
FIN	1.6	1.7	2.3	2.3	2.4	2.4	2.3	2.4	2.3	FIN
S	2.9	3.0	2.5	2.5	2.6	2.6	2.6	2.7	2.9	S
UK	2.5	2.4	2.4	2.5	2.7	2.7	2.6	2.7	2.9	UK
NO	2.2	2.3	2.1	2.2	2.2	2.2	2.3	2.3	2.0	NO
JP	1.7	1.8	1.9	2.1	2.8	3.6	4.3	4.4	4.7	JP
US	2.7	2.7	2.8	2.8	2.7	2.7	2.6	2.6	2.8	US

Sources: OECD (1992–99); Eurostat. Data for 2000–01 are extrapolations of 1999 OECD data, using the growth rate in the EITO 2002 report.

9H4DE

4

Agriculture

Agricultural statistics have a long tradition

The common agricultural policy (CAP) has been one of the major policies of the European Union over the decades since the founding of the European Economic Community. Indeed, in 2002, the CAP absorbed about 47 % of the EU budget. An efficient use of these resources requires a rich system of EU agricultural statistics including those on farm structure and agricultural production as well as economic statistics.

Eurostat offers more detailed data on agriculture than are presented in the Eurostat yearbook. These can be taken from the respective domains of the NewCronos database: 'Eurofarm' for the farm structure survey, 'Zpa1' for the production of crop and animal products, 'Prag' for prices and price indices, and 'Cosa' for agricultural accounts. If you wish to benefit from these NewCronos domains, please ask one of the Eurostat Data Shops the addresses of which can be found at the end of the yearbook.

Farm structure survey

The farm structure survey, carried out about every two years throughout the EU, is devoted to measuring the size (both physical and economic) of holdings. The latest survey from which all figures are available was conducted in 2000. Between 1997 and 2000, the number of agricultural holdings in the EU decreased (– 3.1 %) while the average size of holdings in utilised agricultural area (UAA) increased (+ 1.7 %).

The survey also yields information which allows farms to be classified on their type of production. The standard gross margin (SGM) allows different agricultural products to be measured on a common basis. It is basically the difference between the production value and certain costs of production. It is measured for each type of crop and animal production. Specialised farms generate more than two thirds of their SGM from the main categories of field crops, horticulture, permanent crops, grazing livestock or granivores (pigs and poultry). Non-specialised farms or mixed farms generate less than two thirds of their SGM from one of the main categories.

Farm labour is measured in two ways. According to the survey of the structure of agriculture, the labour force includes total employment in agricultural holdings, including work by the farmer and his family. According to the European system of integrated economic accounts (ESA), farm labour is employment in agricultural activities. Between 1997 and 2000, the volume of agricultural labour in annual work units (AWUs) for the EU declined (– 9.8 %).

Production

Cereals are the main Community agricultural production in volume. Having achieved self-sufficiency, the EU exports a large part of its cereal harvest. From 1993, the reformed common agricultural policy has been bringing supply into line with demand, combining direct aids to cereal farmers with a compulsory set-aside scheme. The EU is the world's largest wine producer with more than one half of total world production. The main part of the production is consumed in Europe, although exchanges with other continents (particularly America and Asia) are increasing. In 2001, milk collection within the EU was nearly stable. In contrast, cheese production rose by 4.6 % from 1997 to 2001 confirming the change in consumer eating habits which are turning more to this type of product.

Since 1996, the overall trends in the meat markets in the European Union have been characterised by instability. In 1996, the first BSE crisis depressed the bovine sector. Gradually, consumer confidence returned and cattle production recovered. A second BSE crisis occurred in November 2000, followed

4

by a further recovery in 2002. Overall meat production in the EU in 1999 was 38 million tonnes, comprising pigmeat (46 %), poultry (24 %), beef and veal (19 %), sheepmeat and goatmeat (3 %), as well as other meat (8 %).

Prices

Producer price indices cover sales of crop and animal products (output) from agriculture to the rest of the economy. The share of crop and animal products in total agricultural sales differs between Member States. Purchase price indices cover purchases of means of agricultural production (input). Indices are calculated from farm-gate prices excluding VAT. The agricultural price indices may be deflated using the consumer price index. In 2001 relative to 2000, there was an increase (+ 2.2 %) in the deflated index of the prices of agricultural products; the deflated index of the prices of the means of agricultural production also rose (+ 1.1 %).

Economic accounts for agriculture

Under the new methodology of the economic accounts for agriculture (EAA 97), agricultural output comprises all (agricultural) output sold by agricultural units, held in stock on the farms, or used for further processing by agricultural producers. Furthermore, it includes the intra-unit consumption of crop products used in animal feed, as well as output accounted for by own-account production of fixed capital goods and own final consumption of agricultural units.

Gross value added at basic prices is calculated by deducting intermediate consumption from the output of the agricultural industry (which includes, besides agricultural output, the output of non-agricultural secondary activities which are inseparable from the principal agricultural activity). The agricultural income indicator A is defined as the index of the real income of factors in agriculture, per annual work unit. This indicator corresponds to the real net value added at factor cost of agriculture, per total annual work unit. Net value added at factor cost is calculated by subtracting from gross value added at basic prices the consumption of fixed capital, and adding the value of the (other) subsidies less taxes on production. Income from agricultural activity in the EU is estimated to have increased (+ 6.5 %) in 2001 relative to 2000.

Further reading:

Eurostat publications
— **Agricultural prices — Price indices and absolute prices**
— **Agriculture — Statistical yearbook 2001**

Statistics in Focus — Theme 5
— **No 1   Agricultural price trends in the EU**
— **No 7   Agriculture in Europe: the spotlight on women**
— **No 8   Increase in EU-15 agricultural income in 2000 confirmed: +1.9 % in real terms**
— **No 10 Survey of bovine animals, November/December 2000**

Do you need more information?
— **Ask your Data Shop (see last page)**
— **http://www.europa.eu.int/comm/eurostat**
— **Eurostat's data serves the political discussion in Europe. Have a look at the website of the "Agriculture Directorate-General": http://europa.eu.int/comm/dgs/agriculture/index_en.htm**

Number of holdings. 1 000s   *Holders being a natural person. 1 000 persons*

	1990	1993	1995	1997	2000	1990	1993	1995	1997	2000	
EU-15	:	:	7 370	6 989	6 766	:	:	7 269	6 869	:	EU-15
B	85	76	71	67	62	85	75	70	65	59	B
DK	81	74	69	63	58	81	73	68	63	57	DK
D	654	606	567	534	472	646	600	561	518	440	D
EL	850	819	802	821	814	850	819	802	821	813	EL
E	1 594	1 384	1 278	1 208	1 287	1 568	1 354	1 241	1 168	1 236	E
F	924	801	735	680	664	910	786	718	662	538	F
IRL	171	159	153	148	142	170	159	153	148	141	IRL
I	2 665	2 488	2 482	2 315	2 152	2 647	2 475	2 471	2 302	:	I
L	4	3	3	3	3	4	3	3	3	3	L
NL	125	120	113	108	102	122	116	110	104	95	NL
A	:	:	222	210	199	:	:	217	206	195	A
P	599	489	451	417	416	594	484	445	411	409	P
FIN	:	:	101	91	81	:	:	101	91	76	FIN
S	:	:	89	90	81	:	:	83	84	76	S
UK	243	243	235	233	233	227	228	225	223	206	UK

1990: 1989/90 survey; 2000: 1999/2000 survey.

Holders < 35 years old. 1 000 persons   *Holders > = 65 years old. 1 000 persons*

	1990	1993	1995	1997	2000	1990	1993	1995	1997	2000	
EU-15	:	:	571	522	:	:	:	2 022	1 950	:	EU-15
B	10	9	11	9	7	17	16	12	12	12	B
DK	9	7	7	7	5	16	16	16	13	11	DK
D	101	103	98	86	73	47	42	42	41	26	D
EL	74	59	49	44	71	216	241	249	281	252	EL
E	113	88	77	69	111	384	364	371	368	347	E
F	121	104	92	79	53	126	116	110	106	97	F
IRL	22	24	21	18	18	39	32	33	32	28	IRL
I	138	133	110	119	:	851	851	912	828	:	I
L	0	0	0	0	0	1	1	1	1	1	L
NL	11	12	10	7	6	19	19	19	20	18	NL
A	:	:	40	35	31	:	:	21	21	19	A
P	40	23	19	15	17	171	161	157	155	155	P
FIN	:	:	16	13	9	:	:	7	5	5	FIN
S	:	:	7	6	5	:	:	18	18	16	S
UK	17	15	14	13	11	50	51	55	50	52	UK

1990: 1989/90 survey; 2000: 1999/2000 survey.

4

Number of holdings with dairy cows. 1 000s *Number of dairy cows. 1 000s*

	1990	1993	1995	1997	2000		1990	1993	1995	1997	2000	
EU-15	:	:	986	882	730		:	:	22 535	21 983	20 579	EU-15
B	31	25	22	20	18		842	698	688	633	616	B
DK	23	18	16	13	11		762	714	702	670	640	DK
D	276	229	203	182	153		6 058	5 324	5 217	5 149	4 765	D
EL	38	31	28	19	12		205	171	184	148	154	EL
E	207	144	123	102	78		1 598	1 404	1 357	1 339	1 242	E
F	227	178	161	148	128		5 304	4 698	4 624	4 411	4 193	F
IRL	49	47	42	40	32		1 331	1 343	1 312	1 316	1 177	IRL
I	206	143	115	104	82		2 642	2 298	2 173	2 179	1 895	I
L	2	2	1	1	1		61	50	49	46	45	L
NL	47	41	37	37	35		1 878	1 747	1 708	1 643	1 650	NL
A	:	:	90	87	77		:	:	706	730	697	A
P	99	67	58	47	33		406	372	382	381	356	P
FIN	:	:	33	31	24		:	:	396	392	364	FIN
S	:	:	18	16	14		:	:	481	468	449	S
UK	45	41	38	36	32		2 845	2 661	2 555	2 476	2 335	UK

1990: 1989/90 survey; 2000: 1999/2000 survey.

Share of holdings with organic farming. 2000. %

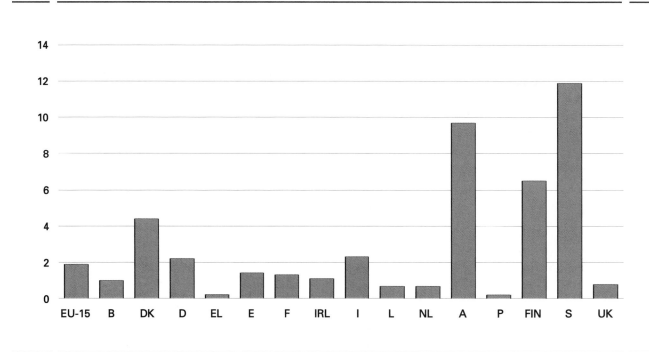

Holding managers. 1 000 persons   *Female managers. 1 000 persons*

	1990	1993	1995	1997	2000	1990	1993	1995	1997	2000	
EU-15	:	:	7 370	6 989	:	:	:	1 315	1 322	:	EU-15
B	85	76	71	67	62	12	11	10	10	9	B
DK	81	74	69	63	58	5	4	4	5	5	DK
D	654	606	567	534	445	51	48	46	47	36	D
EL	850	819	802	821	814	143	136	134	164	192	EL
E	1 594	1 384	1 278	1 208	1 287	264	218	196	192	272	E
F	924	801	735	680	618	156	158	153	143	142	F
IRL	171	159	153	148	142	15	14	14	13	14	IRL
I	2 665	2 488	2 482	2 315	:	640	559	566	560	:	I
L	4	3	3	3	3	1	1	0	0	0	L
NL	125	120	113	108	100	5	5	6	6	8	NL
A	:	:	222	210	199	:	:	61	61	61	A
P	599	489	451	417	416	98	83	80	78	95	P
FIN	:	:	101	91	77	:	:	10	9	8	FIN
S	:	:	89	90	81	:	:	7	9	8	S
UK	243	243	235	233	212	34	29	28	27	32	UK

1990: 1989/90 survey; 2000: 1999/2000 survey.

Regular labour force. 1 000 persons   *Female regular labour force. 1 000 persons*

	1990	1993	1995	1997	2000	1990	1993	1995	1997	2000	
EU-15	:	:	15 244	14 757	:	:	:	5 601	5 436	:	EU-15
B	141	132	122	117	107	48	48	44	41	37	B
DK	139	142	141	130	103	41	40	38	37	22	DK
D	1 776	1 478	1 325	1 231	1 161	647	534	466	429	419	D
EL	1 543	1 774	1 567	1 596	1 426	648	810	678	698	591	EL
E	2 839	2 571	2 543	2 497	2 439	900	786	769	757	784	E
F	1 859	1 610	1 507	1 404	1 428	658	560	520	476	459	F
IRL	313	320	293	282	258	93	99	87	81	70	IRL
I	5 287	4 762	4 773	4 601	:	2 101	1 808	1 838	1 802	:	I
L	9	8	7	7	7	4	3	3	2	2	L
NL	289	290	276	282	280	86	89	87	94	93	NL
A	:	:	547	513	527	:	:	230	214	229	A
P	1 561	1 263	1 173	1 070	1 064	728	588	548	502	499	P
FIN	:	:	232	224	194	:	:	87	82	68	FIN
S	:	:	164	169	157	:	:	54	55	51	S
UK	659	651	572	636	551	199	193	153	168	163	UK

1990: 1989/90 survey; 2000: 1999/2000 survey.

4

Number of pigs. 1 000s

	1990	1993	1995	1997	2000	
EU-15	:	:	111 963	115 751	122 626	EU-15
B	6 657	7 122	7 241	7 313	7 369	B
DK	9 197	11 568	11 084	11 383	11 626	DK
D	27 354	26 040	24 298	23 719	26 101	D
EL	934	808	848	877	969	EL
E	11 841	13 064	12 700	14 226	22 015	E
F	12 203	13 929	14 162	15 080	14 870	F
IRL	1 304	1 570	1 501	1 700	1 722	IRL
I	8 392	8 396	8 061	8 293	8 603	I
L	77	72	73	77	86	L
NL	13 846	14 964	14 397	15 189	13 567	NL
A	:	:	3 695	3 670	3 425	A
P	2 439	2 618	2 368	2 419	2 418	P
FIN	:	:	1 400	1 476	1 296	FIN
S	:	:	2 313	2 359	2 115	S
UK	7 550	7 763	7 823	7 969	6 443	UK

1990: 1989/90 survey; 2000: 1999/2000 survey.

Number of poultry. Millions

	1990	1993	1995	1997	2000	
EU-15	:	:	1 013	1 035	1 234	EU-15
B	27	29	33	38	41	B
DK	16	20	20	19	21	DK
D	98	86	96	99	118	D
EL	34	32	27	35	39	EL
E	118	104	109	100	181	E
F	245	264	281	277	289	F
IRL	12	13	12	14	14	IRL
I	172	150	138	133	171	I
L	0	0	0	0	0	L
NL	95	98	92	96	108	NL
A	:	:	14	15	14	A
P	31	33	30	32	43	P
FIN	:	:	10	11	13	FIN
S	:	:	13	13	14	S
UK	138	145	138	153	168	UK

1990: 1989/90 survey; 2000: 1999/2000 survey.

Production of cereals. 1 000 t

	1991	1992	1993	1994	1995	1996	1997	1998	1999	2000	2001	
EU-15	:	:	:	:	177 413	206 283	205 527	210 444	200 831	213 609	199 901	**EU-15**
€-zone	:	:	140 777	136 608	137 391	161 855	161 723	168 436	160 717	170 479	161 673	**€-zone**
B	2 068	1 996	2 139	2 091	2 212	2 535	2 394	2 536	2 407	2 513	2 359	**B**
DK	9 231	6 954	8 198	7 825	9 150	9 217	9 530	9 356	8 775	9 413	9 755	**DK**
D	39 268	34 758	35 547	36 329	39 864	42 136	45 486	44 575	44 452	45 271	49 709	**D**
EL	6 056	4 946	4 275	5 318	4 213	4 669	4 755	4 419	4 288	4 062	4 091	**EL**
E	18 885	13 945	17 156	14 833	11 241	21 644	18 563	21 778	17 321	23 740	17 053	**E**
F	60 122	60 327	55 262	53 039	53 143	62 120	62 887	67 808	64 136	65 582	60 229	**F**
IRL	1 964	2 018	1 626	1 609	1 796	2 142	1 943	1 865	2 011	1 963	2 156	**IRL**
I	17 984	18 629	18 464	17 826	18 338	19 483	18 464	19 317	19 639	19 392	18 649	**I**
L	156	152	152	134	148	176	162	167	154	153	144	**L**
NL	1 249	1 378	1 512	1 406	1 549	1 711	1 623	1 569	1 416	1 819	1 742	**NL**
A	5 045	4 323	4 206	4 436	4 452	4 709	5 009	4 772	4 806	4 490	4 827	**A**
P	1 620	1 228	1 380	1 513	1 321	1 500	1 395	1 279	1 506	1 466	1 145	**P**
FIN	:	:	3 332	3 391	3 328	3 700	3 799	2 769	2 868	4 089	3 661	**FIN**
S	5 207	:	:	:	4 791	5 954	5 986	5 618	4 931	5 670	5 391	**S**
UK	22 640	22 068	19 500	19 955	21 868	24 587	23 533	22 616	22 119	23 985	18 991	**UK**

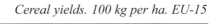

Cereal yields. 100 kg per ha. EU-15

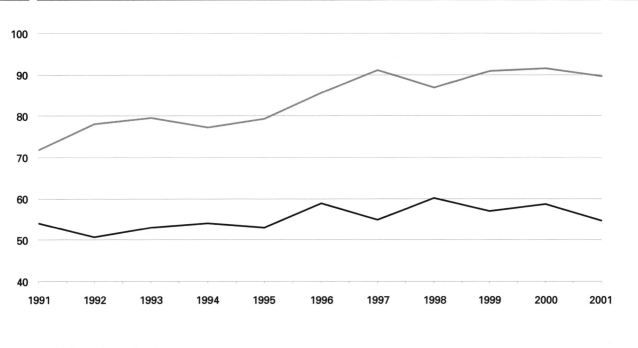

Black: wheat; colour: grain maize.

Collection of cow's milk. 1 000 t

	1991	1992	1993	1994	1995	1996	1997	1998	1999	2000	2001	
EU-15	:	:	:	:	113 668	113 641	113 576	113 696	114 946	114 282	:	EU-15
€-zone	:	:	:	:	91 234	91 222	90 989	91 239	92 080	91 865	:	€-zone
B	2 961	2 914	2 878	2 916	2 972	3 022	2 944	3 287	3 264	3 124	3 088	B
DK	4 440	4 405	4 461	4 441	4 473	4 495	4 433	4 468	4 456	4 519	4 418	DK
D	26 409	25 440	25 829	25 862	26 774	26 991	26 986	26 752	26 783	26 984	26 883	D
EL	533	549	602	639	644	608	617	648	656	670	706	EL
E	5 829	5 438	5 352	4 926	5 602	5 547	5 463	5 482	5 664	5 413	5 763	E
F	23 332	23 045	22 854	23 278	23 413	23 208	23 045	23 032	23 109	23 303	23 225	F
IRL	5 212	5 257	5 202	5 280	5 288	5 297	5 256	5 091	5 121	5 160	5 338	IRL
I	9 894	9 746	9 501	9 540	9 911	10 133	10 130	10 292	10 325	10 084	10 006	I
L	193	187	193	187	190	187	255	255	258	256	261	L
NL	10 536	10 431	10 500	10 496	10 825	10 535	10 458	10 541	10 777	10 545	10 828	NL
A	2 208	2 210	2 200	2 207	2 292	2 342	2 419	2 448	2 540	2 661	2 654	A
P	1 551	1 531	1 451	1 497	1 600	1 632	1 662	1 696	1 844	1 893	1 821	P
FIN	:	:	:	:	2 365	2 329	2 370	2 363	2 394	2 442	:	FIN
S	3 130	3 133	3 287	3 357	3 243	3 258	3 276	3 278	3 299	3 297	3 290	S
UK	14 138	14 046	14 130	14 378	14 075	14 058	14 261	14 063	14 456	13 932	14 160	UK
IS	:	:	:	:	106	105	105	109	:	:	110	IS
NO	:	:	:	:	1 709	1 686	:	:	:	:	:	NO

Production and utilisation of milk on the farm. Annual data. 1 000 t milk

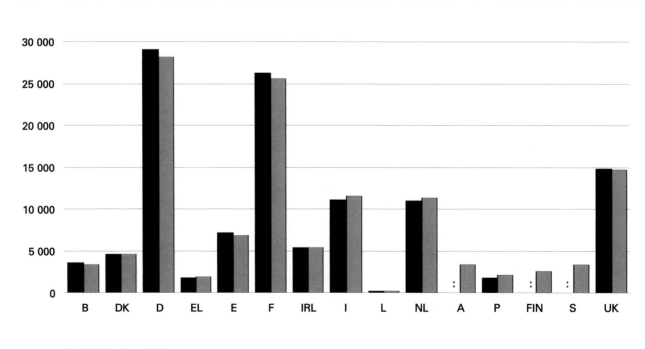

Black: 1991; colour: 2001.

Eurostat estimation including confidential data.

eurostat

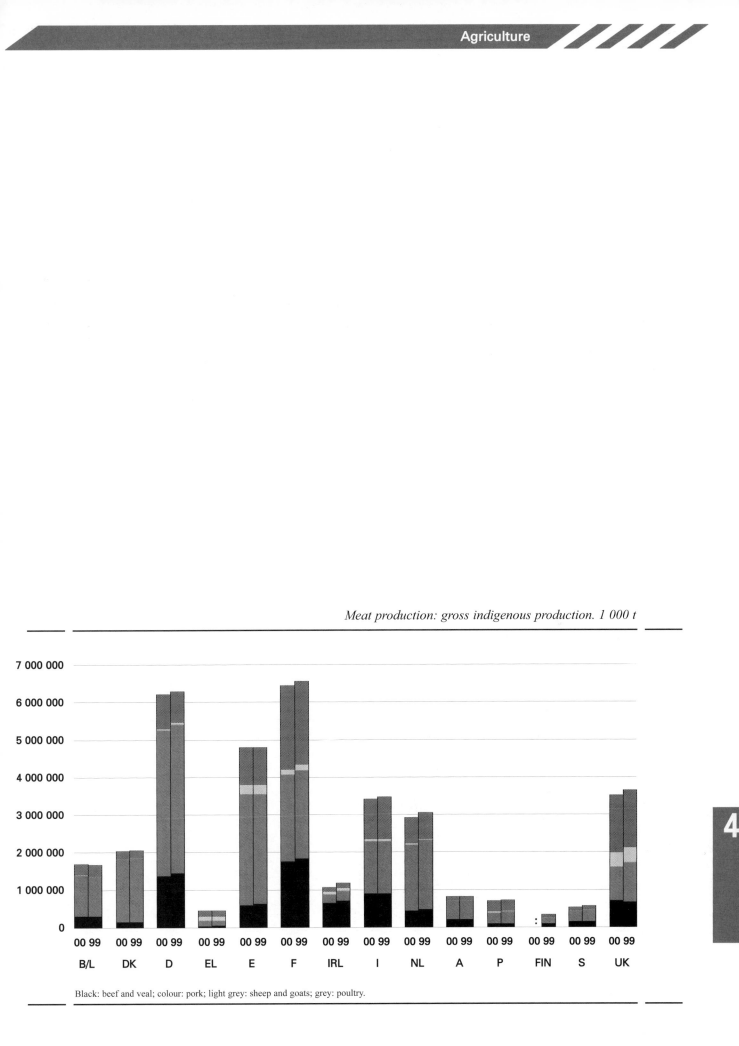

Meat production: gross indigenous production. 1 000 t

Black: beef and veal; colour: pork; light grey: sheep and goats; grey: poultry.

eurostat

Production of meat: pigs. 1 000 t

	1991	1992	1993	1994	1995	1996	1997	1998	1999	2000	2001	
EU-15	:	:	:	:	15 976	16 317	16 250	17 637	17 980	17 577	17 532	EU-15
B	908	944	995	1 012	1 035	1 061	1 006	1 077	993	1 055	1 072	B
DK	1 265	1 372	1 490	1 519	1 475	1 457	1 523	1 631	1 642	1 624	1 714	DK
D	3 918	3 684	3 747	3 604	3 602	3 635	3 564	3 834	4 103	3 982	4 074	D
EL	153	153	147	142	142	142	142	143	138	141	137	EL
E	1 869	1 912	2 081	2 102	2 175	2 316	2 401	2 744	2 892	2 912	2 993	E
F	1 831	1 903	2 034	2 126	2 144	2 183	2 220	2 313	2 349	2 312	2 315	F
IRL	180	202	212	215	211	211	220	242	250	226	238	IRL
I	1 333	1 328	1 370	1 347	1 346	1 410	1 396	1 412	1 472	1 488	1 510	I
L	7	7	8	8	8	9	9	9	12	10	10	L
NL	1 591	1 585	1 747	1 673	1 622	1 624	1 376	1 725	1 711	1 623	1 432	NL
A	:	:	:	:	466	481	489	508	520	502	488	A
P	216	237	288	292	282	299	303	330	344	327	315	P
FIN	:	:	:	:	166	171	179	184	182	172	176	FIN
S	:	:	:	:	309	320	329	330	325	277	276	S
UK	979	971	999	1 035	992	998	1 094	1 155	1 047	923	782	UK

Production of meat: cattle. 1 000 t

	1991	1992	1993	1994	1995	1996	1997	1998	1999	2000	2001	
EU-15	:	:	:	:	7 966	7 954	7 889	7 651	7 691	7 404	7 266	EU-15
B	373	352	367	349	349	353	331	296	273	275	285	B
DK	212	217	203	190	185	182	175	163	157	154	153	DK
D	2 181	1 829	1 604	1 420	1 408	1 482	1 448	1 366	1 374	1 304	1 361	D
EL	81	80	76	74	70	71	69	68	65	63	60	EL
E	504	535	485	472	508	565	592	651	678	632	642	E
F	1 860	1 877	1 704	1 627	1 683	1 735	1 718	1 630	1 609	1 514	1 566	F
IRL	557	568	528	448	481	538	570	595	644	577	489	IRL
I	1 182	1 218	1 188	1 173	1 181	1 182	1 160	1 113	1 164	1 154	1 133	I
L	8	7	7	7	7	8	8	8	9	8	11	L
NL	623	635	611	604	580	580	565	534	508	471	372	NL
A	:	:	:	:	196	222	206	198	203	204	215	A
P	126	123	115	94	104	100	104	90	96	100	94	P
FIN	:	:	:	:	96	96	99	93	90	90	89	FIN
S	:	:	:	:	143	137	149	142	144	150	143	S
UK	1 019	960	859	916	974	702	696	705	678	708	652	UK

4

Producer price indices, deflated; total agricultural production. 1995 = 100

	1996	1997	1998	1999	2000	2001	
EU-15	99.0	96.3	91.5	86.4	87.6	89.6	**EU-15**
B	101.4	101.2	94.2	85.4	91.8	91.6	**B**
DK	101.7	99.8	86.6	81.7	87.7	92.2	**DK**
D	98.3	97.8	92.5	86.3	89.8	93.0	**D**
EL	99.0	96.0	91.1	89.6	90.6	92.8	**EL**
E	98.8	93.9	89.8	85.0	85.9	86.7	**E**
F	97.7	96.7	96.0	92.3	92.2	93.7	**F**
IRL	93.5	86.6	84.1	78.6	79.5	80.0	**IRL**
I	100.4	99.0	93.9	88.1	87.9	89.9	**I**
L	94.3	95.2	94.2	91.2	88.7	88.4	**L**
NL	101.5	105.9	98.7	91.2	96.0	96.6	**NL**
A	99.9	101.2	93.3	87.1	91.4	95.1	**A**
P	99.1	97.9	96.9	90.4	92.2	94.0	**P**
FIN	95.8	93.7	91.6	88.8	89.9	91.7	**FIN**
S	94.7	91.3	89.2	87.3	85.1	87.2	**S**
UK	97.4	83.0	73.7	69.7	67.9	72.3	**UK**

Purchase price indices, deflated; total means of agricultural production. 1995 = 100

	1996	1997	1998	1999	2000	2001	
EU-15	102.0	101.4	97.2	94.1	96.2	97.1	**EU-15**
B	102.2	102.8	98.0	96.1	100.0	98.7	**B**
DK	100.9	101.9	99.1	95.5	95.6	99.9	**DK**
D	101.6	101.5	98.1	96.9	100.5	101.2	**D**
EL	99.7	96.8	94.4	94.1	96.5	95.2	**EL**
E	100.9	101.7	99.4	96.0	97.7	96.1	**E**
F	101.3	101.5	98.7	97.3	99.6	100.5	**F**
IRL	101.6	99.3	96.0	95.1	95.6	96.5	**IRL**
I	104.6	105.2	97.1	91.4	92.5	93.6	**I**
L	100.4	100.2	99.0	104.5	105.3	106.6	**L**
NL	103.7	102.3	98.1	95.8	99.2	101.1	**NL**
A	100.6	100.8	97.9	97.2	98.3	98.1	**A**
P	100.1	97.0	92.3	90.4	91.3	93.9	**P**
FIN	100.4	101.0	98.4	96.9	99.5	98.1	**FIN**
S	104.3	103.5	100.8	100.3	102.8	105.9	**S**
UK	98.9	93.6	86.6	84.0	85.7	88.3	**UK**

4

Indicator A of the income from agricultural activity. 1995 = 100

	1991	1992	1993	1994	1995	1996	1997	1998	1999	2000	2001	
EU-15	:	:	:	:	:	:	:	:	:	:	:	EU-15
B	116.9	113.6	109.9	111.6	100.0	109.6	114.0	107.7	92.6	103.0	:	B
DK	83.1	72.8	74.4	83.7	100.0	100.4	97.7	77.8	73.8	93.2	:	DK
D	91.6	95.8	90.7	94.4	100.0	110.9	116.1	105.9	96.5	129.6	:	D
EL	:	:	:	:	100.0	95.2	95.5	97.4	101.7	100.4	:	EL
E	:	:	:	:	100.0	112.3	113.7	111.1	108.0	119.9	:	E
F	77.3	83.9	83.4	94.4	100.0	100.2	103.5	108.0	105.7	105.8	:	F
IRL	77.3	86.1	87.6	88.9	100.0	100.6	97.8	93.9	86.6	91.2	:	IRL
I	83.6	83.0	85.3	91.1	100.0	105.7	108.3	108.5	118.1	113.5	:	I
L	87.8	88.2	91.1	87.1	100.0	103.6	95.7	104.5	94.5	96.7	95.0	L
NL	112.1	103.4	86.1	96.7	100.0	97.0	104.8	94.1	82.9	80.2	:	NL
A	92.7	85.9	75.6	89.0	100.0	89.7	83.1	82.6	79.3	81.4	:	A
P	93.8	70.1	67.9	91.1	100.0	109.6	104.6	103.0	117.7	106.8	:	P
FIN	91.6	81.0	81.4	87.6	100.0	82.6	82.2	74.0	81.2	93.8	:	FIN
S	:	:	85.1	84.6	100.0	92.1	98.1	107.8	98.1	107.9	:	S
UK	66.4	72.5	85.4	90.5	100.0	93.7	72.6	62.3	61.1	55.3	:	UK

Indicator A corresponds to the real (i.e. deflated) net value added at factor cost of agriculture, per total annual work unit.

Forestry

Different (statistical) views on forests

Forests have many benefits, two of them being their economic use and their worth to the environment.

Forests and wooded land cover more than 40 % of the EU's territory. This is approximately equal to the EU's agricultural area. However, the share of the gross value added contributed by forestry in the gross domestic product was just 0.17 % in 1997 (calculated for the Member States for which data were available). About 2 % of the EU's total value added was produced by the wood-based products and paper industries (excluding the furniture industry). Around 300 000 persons work in silviculture and approximately 1.7 million in the wood-based products and paper industries.

Not all the wooded area is used for wood production: some of it might serve for land protection; other parts might simply not be accessible for wood harvesting. Furthermore, wooded land cannot be harvested regularly every year: according to the forest's age class and density, it is only possible to harvest a certain amount of wood in a particular year. The cutting age for trees varies for different species and regions; the average is around 100 years.

Global data on forests need further local analysis

Even though forests in the European Union vary widely (different structures of their biological and economic resources), the figures available are suitable especially for overall descriptions of the production and environmental aspects of forests. They might show problems that do not play a role at the local level. On the other hand, they might hide problems that could be essential from a regional viewpoint. An example is the evaluation of the potential (natural or man-made) damage to forests. Although the economic consequences of the damage may, for the moment, be of minor importance at the global level, the environmental consequences may be serious in the affected regions.

Data on forestry come from different sources

The data on forests (e.g. structure, areas) are provided by the forest resources assessment (FRA) managed by the Food and Agriculture Organisation (FAO). To meet the requirements at the European level, the United Nations Economic Commission for Europe (UN/ECE) in Geneva manages a temperate and boreal forest resources assessment (TBFRA) which covers all the members of the UN/ECE, including all candidate countries. The Commission is involved in the preparation of this TBFRA.

The data on wood and wood-based products come from the joint questionnaire managed by the Intersecretariat Working Group on the Forestry Sector including the FAO, UN/ECE, ITTO (International Tropical Timber Organisation) and Eurostat. Each organisation is fully responsible for the management of data of a group of countries (Eurostat for the data for EU and EFTA countries).

4

Further reading:

Eurostat publications
— Economic accounts for agriculture and forestry and agricultural labour input statistics —
  1973–2001 data

Statistics in Focus — Theme 5
— No 9   **Forestry: wood and wood-based products**
— No 17   **Forest and environment**
— N° 01/2003 Agricultural statistics — Quarterly bulletin

Total roundwood production. 1 000 m³

	1991	1992	1993	1994	1995	1996	1997	1998	1999	2000	2001	
EU-15	232 310	226 734	226 283	248 647	263 928	247 749	259 930	261 314	261 813	286 271	259 735	**EU-15**
€-zone	169 683	162 561	161 648	181 581	189 667	180 263	188 648	190 230	191 878	210 039	186 936	**€-zone**
B	4 360	3 868	3 938	3 930	4 340	4 185	4 470	4 400	4 400	5 410	4 190	**B**
DK	2 309	1 915	1 777	1 853	1 926	1 876	1 817	1 538	1 538	3 280	2 370	**DK**
D	33 618	27 759	27 958	34 618	39 343	37 011	38 207	39 053	37 634	53 710	39 483	**D**
EL	2 546	2 193	2 096	2 091	1 961	2 117	1 783	1 692	2 215	2 171	2 171	**EL**
E	15 188	13 822	13 756	15 305	16 074	15 631	15 631	14 875	14 810	14 321	14 321	**E**
F	43 554	42 418	39 363	42 240	43 371	40 472	41 962	42 527	43 301	45 828	38 805	**F**
IRL	1 670	1 960	1 861	2 018	2 204	2 291	2 180	2 266	2 593	2 673	2 455	**IRL**
I	8 327	9 067	9 042	9 452	9 730	9 018	9 146	9 550	11 138	9 329	7 447	**I**
L	599	372	302	411	477	443	450	450	260	260	260	**L**
NL	1 123	1 086	1 045	1 018	1 079	951	1 109	1 023	1 044	1 039	865	**NL**
A	15 572	12 249	12 256	14 360	13 805	15 011	14 725	14 033	14 083	13 276	13 467	**A**
P	10 809	10 278	10 207	9 819	9 350	8 978	8 970	8 548	8 978	10 831	11 262	**P**
FIN	34 863	39 682	41 920	48 410	49 894	46 272	51 798	53 660	53 637	54 262	52 210	**FIN**
S	51 400	53 520	54 000	55 900	62 900	56 400	60 200	60 600	58 700	63 300	62 820	**S**
UK	6 372	6 545	6 762	7 222	7 474	7 093	7 482	7 254	7 482	7 481	7 609	**UK**
NO	11 279	10 134	9 710	8 744	9 365	8 485	8 346	8 172	8 424	8 156	8 379	**NO**
CH	4 607	4 483	4 337	4 609	4 978	3 996	2 690	3 260	4 737	9 238	5 000	**CH**
CA	160 168	169 895	176 193	183 224	188 432	189 778	191 178	176 994	193 165	178 071	176 692	**CA**
US	478 600	493 400	488 792	498 438	499 310	478 830	485 880	494 016	497 641	500 173	481 092	**US**

Fisheries

Fisheries: a common policy for resources, production and markets

The common fisheries policy (CFP) is one of the major EU policies and comprises a number of elements including structural policy, market management policy and resource management policy.

Although in global economic terms fisheries are relatively unimportant (contributing less than 1 % to the GDP of EU Member States), regionally they can be of significant social and economic importance.

Furthermore, very few fishery resources can be managed on a local basis. The EU thus has a major role to play internationally both in the deliberations within international organisations and in negotiations with third countries.

A statistical telescope on fisheries

Eurostat's database on fishery statistics is designed to give statistical support to the various aspects of the common fisheries policy and includes data on the following topics:

— catches by fishing regions for all countries in the world;

— aquaculture production of all countries in the world;

— summary foreign trade in fishery products for all countries;

— supply balance sheets for fishery products;

— landings of fishery products in EEA countries;

— fishing fleet statistics for EEA countries;

— employment in the fisheries sector.

Standard concepts, definitions and formats

The data are derived from official national sources either directly by Eurostat for the EEA member countries or indirectly through other international organisations for other countries.

The data use internationally agreed concepts and definitions developed by the Coordinating Working Party on Fishery Statistics, comprising Eurostat and 12 other international organisations with responsibilities in fishery statistics.

Profit from the advantages of Eurostat's fisheries database

With the use of the standard concepts, definitions and formats covering a wide range of fishery topics, Eurostat's fisheries database is among the most comprehensive and user-friendly available.

Your Eurostat Data Shop will help you to obtain more information from the fisheries database. The addresses of the Data Shops can be found at the end of the yearbook.

Some results

— The EEA catch of fishery products has remained relatively stable at between 9 and 12 million tonnes per year in the last decade, a reflection of the state of the limited resources and the strict management regimes for most of the fisheries.

— The major EEA fishing countries are Norway, Iceland and Denmark, with 25, 18 and 14 % of the total EEA catch in 2000.

— The north-east Atlantic is the major fishing region for EEA countries, contributing 87 % to the total in 2000, followed by the Mediterranean (5 %), the eastern central Atlantic (4 %) and the north-west Atlantic (1 %).

— EEA aquaculture production increased from 1.1 million tonnes in 1990 to 1.8 million tonnes in 2000. The main producing countries are Norway (Atlantic salmon), Spain and France (molluscs).

— The size of the EEA fishing fleet has remained relatively stable during the last few years and amounted to a total gross tonnage of over 2.5 million tonnes in 2001.

Further reading:

Eurostat publications
— **Fisheries — Yearbook 2002**
— **European fisheries in figures**

Statistics in Focus — Theme 5
— **No 18 EEA fisheries in the north-west atlantic**
— **No 19 Fisheries production, 1999**
— **No 20 EEA fishing fleet in 2000**
— **No 21 Mediterranean fisheries**
— **No 22 European aquaculture, 1999**
— **No 24 Catches in the NE Atlantic**

Do you need more information?
— **Ask your Data Shop (see last page)**
— **http://www.europa.eu.int/comm/eurostat**
— **Eurostat's data serves the political discussion in Europe. Have a look at the website of the "Fisheries Directorate-General": http://europa.eu.int/comm/dgs/fisheries/index_en.htm**

4

Total aquaculture production. 1 000 t live weight

	1991	1992	1993	1994	1995	1996	1997	1998	1999	2000	2001	
EU-15	946	917	909	1 012	1 095	1 277	1 318	1 298	1 336	1 295	:	**EU-15**
B	1	1	1	1	1	1	1	1	2	2	:	**B**
DK	42	43	40	43	45	42	40	42	43	44	41	**DK**
D	68	90	63	42	58	75	59	67	74	60	:	**D**
EL	13	20	33	33	33	40	49	60	79	80	:	**EL**
E	225	169	126	178	224	232	239	317	324	316	:	**E**
F	245	250	277	281	281	286	287	268	265	268	252	**F**
IRL	28	27	30	29	27	35	37	42	44	51	:	**IRL**
I	175	170	166	176	215	232	238	209	210	217	:	**I**
L	:	:	:	:	:	:	:	:	:	:	:	**L**
NL	52	54	71	109	84	100	98	120	109	75	:	**NL**
A	3	3	3	3	3	3	3	3	3	3	:	**A**
P	6	6	6	7	5	5	7	8	7	8	:	**P**
FIN	19	18	18	17	17	18	16	16	15	15	16	**FIN**
S	8	7	6	7	8	8	7	6	6	5	:	**S**
UK	61	57	69	86	96	201	237	139	155	152	:	**UK**
IS	3	3	3	3	3	4	4	4	4	4	:	**IS**
NO	161	131	164	218	278	322	368	411	476	488	:	**NO**
EEA	1 110	1 050	1 076	1 234	1 377	1 602	1 690	1 712	1 816	1 786	:	**EEA**
CH	1	1	1	1	1	1	1	1	1	1	:	**CH**
CA	48	45	52	55	65	72	82	91	113	123	:	**CA**
JP	1 359	1 397	1 359	1 420	1 390	1 349	1 340	1 290	1 315	1 292	:	**JP**
US	364	414	417	391	413	393	438	445	479	428	:	**US**

4

Annual catches in all regions. 1 000 t live weight

	1991	1992	1993	1994	1995	1996	1997	1998	1999	2000	2001	
EU-15	6 386	6 713	6 420	6 824	7 233	6 672	6 827	6 711	6 292	6 062	:	EU-15
B	40	37	36	34	36	31	31	31	30	30	30	B
DK	1 751	1 954	1 492	1 844	1 999	1 681	1 827	1 557	1 405	1 534	1 510	DK
D	236	217	253	228	239	237	259	267	239	205	211	D
EL	139	153	159	181	152	149	157	109	119	99	:	EL
E	1 070	1 077	1 082	1 098	1 179	1 168	1 198	1 263	1 188	995	:	E
F	651	656	637	652	677	635	633	594	676	690	663	F
IRL	233	248	278	291	389	333	293	325	284	283	:	IRL
I	406	396	396	398	397	366	344	318	294	300	:	I
L	0	0	0	0	0	0	0	0	0	0	:	L
NL	405	432	462	420	438	411	452	537	515	496	:	NL
A	1	0	0	0	0	0	0	0	0	1	:	A
P	318	291	288	263	259	259	219	224	209	188	190	P
FIN	109	131	135	151	155	163	165	156	145	156	150	FIN
S	237	308	342	387	405	371	357	411	351	339	311	S
UK	791	813	860	878	910	868	892	920	838	746	:	UK
IS	1 057	1 583	1 727	1 571	1 624	2 074	2 225	1 700	1 754	1 982	1 981	IS
NO	2 012	2 431	2 415	2 366	2 524	2 650	2 863	2 861	2 628	2 702	:	NO
EEA	9 455	10 726	10 562	10 760	11 382	11 396	11 916	11 272	10 674	10 747	:	EEA
CH	4	3	2	1	2	2	2	2	2	2	:	CH
CA	1 471	1 317	1 154	1 046	872	923	998	1 037	1 059	983	:	CA
JP	8 651	7 936	7 420	6 752	6 116	6 086	6 075	5 378	5 321	5 108	:	JP
US	5 349	5 480	5 803	5 882	5 523	5 186	5 195	4 957	5 062	5 083	:	US

Fishing fleet. Total power. kW

	1991	1992	1993	1994	1995	1996	1997	1998	1999	2000	2001	
EU-15	:	:	:	:	8 140 679	7 921 283	7 942 347	7 797 787	7 734 172	7 547 034	7 434 614	EU-15
B	81 317	75 862	71 586	69 260	65 965	63 540	64 896	63 941	63 453	63 355	66 347	B
DK	495 757	459 330	409 666	418 196	404 981	392 392	376 409	370 419	368 256	371 866	364 087	DK
D	177 480	165 556	175 855	172 278	169 182	167 967	161 486	159 711	163 305	167 206	167 084	D
EL	705 674	694 409	668 056	666 459	655 290	654 607	653 065	649 201	622 802	626 881	628 142	EL
E	1 978 351	1 921 892	1 837 093	1 714 569	1 631 379	1 537 271	1 467 993	1 405 795	1 381 529	1 330 931	1 310 467	E
F	1 088 361	1 054 460	1 034 079	1 010 644	990 509	986 287	1 144 135	1 125 034	1 113 444	1 107 214	1 097 064	F
IRL	181 836	191 109	191 092	193 447	197 846	190 941	195 730	191 935	194 533	193 651	197 283	IRL
I	1 515 556	1 526 007	1 530 198	1 520 751	1 515 842	1 513 677	1 508 639	1 506 647	1 482 333	1 396 679	1 313 920	I
L	:	:	:	:	:	:	:	:	:	:	:	L
NL	540 059	533 336	537 935	512 398	506 990	497 555	480 101	470 384	487 877	507 759	504 963	NL
A	:	:	:	:	:	:	:	:	:	:	:	A
P	493 175	473 374	449 808	416 364	396 943	392 157	393 102	389 166	393 755	395 851	399 213	P
FIN	:	:	:	:	224 384	219 278	220 341	211 168	203 695	196 173	190 138	FIN
S	:	:	:	:	266 205	256 542	244 644	236 713	217 110	236 622	243 555	S
UK	1 191 878	1 200 025	1 202 421	1 163 059	1 115 163	1 049 069	1 031 806	1 017 673	1 042 080	952 846	952 351	UK
IS	:	:	:	:	:	:	:	502 563	513 774	528 711	554 559	IS
NO	:	:	:	:	:	:	2 225 643	2 290 027	2 379 360	2 443 145	2 522 728	NO
EEA	:	:	:	:	:	:	:	10 590 377	10 627 306	10 518 890	10 511 901	EEA

Agriculture and environment

Agriculture and the environment: a multifaceted relationship

The relationship between agriculture and the environment is twofold. On the one hand, agriculture contributes to the protection of biodiversity and to the preservation and enrichment of the landscape. On the other hand, it can affect the environment by intensive use of fertilisers or overuse of pesticides. Intensive animal husbandry produces emissions of methane and ammonia. Large-scale irrigation can lead to the lowering of groundwater and surface water levels with a negative impact on flora and fauna or the gradual salinisation of groundwater in coastal areas.

Organic farming

Organic farming is one example of sustainable farming. It has developed worldwide due to increased consumer awareness of, and demand for, organically grown products. The first EU regulation on organic farming (Regulation (EEC) No 2092/91) was drawn up in 1991. Since its implementation in 1992, many farms across the EU have converted to organic production methods. This regulation has established procedures for the Member States to report data on organic farming to the European Commission.

Intensive use of fertilisers

The intensive use of fertilisers impacts negatively on the environment. Maintaining a healthy balance between nutrients added to the soil and nutrients removed, for example, in crops is essential to ensure optimal use of resources and to limit pollution problems, particularly those associated with nitrogen (and phosphate) surpluses. A surplus of nutrient to immediate crop needs can be a source of potential environmental damage to surface- and groundwater, and to air quality. It may equally contribute to the global warming of the planet.

The Food and Agriculture Organisation (FAO) of the United Nations compiles information on commercial fertilisers. Country-level data are collected through: annual tailored questionnaires; electronic files and access to country web sites; national/international publications; country visits made by FAO statisticians; and reports of FAO representatives in member countries.

Overuse of pesticides

The overuse of pesticides, i.e. plant protection products, has a negative impact on biodiversity and increases the risk of them finding their way into drinking water and the food chain. Some agri-environmental measures in the common agricultural policy (Council Regulation (EEC) No 2078/92) have been designed to promote a reduction in the use of pesticides by farmers by compensating them for any loss of income attributable to lower levels of inputs, particularly of pesticides. The European Crop Protection Association produces data on plant protection products for Eurostat.

4

Consumption of commercial fertilisers. Phosphate. Tonnes of active ingredient

	1997	1998	1999	2000	
B/L	44 000	47 000	45 000	44 000	B/L
DK	50 000	47 000	41 000	37 000	DK
D	409 536	406 678	420 988	351 337	D
EL	132 000	120 000	119 000	113 000	EL
E	589 000	655 000	642 963	568 100	E
F	1 038 800	1 011 200	965 600	795 000	F
IRL	113 000	116 000	115 000	98 000	IRL
I	501 000	508 000	514 000	504 000	I
L	:	:	:	:	L
NL	60 000	62 000	58 993	55 000	NL
A	57 000	57 000	48 000	47 000	A
P	67 000	71 000	68 000	66 000	P
FIN	56 000	53 000	52 000	53 000	FIN
S	49 000	47 000	43 000	38 000	S
UK	408 000	345 000	317 000	284 000	UK

Volume of plant protection products sold. Total. Tonnes of active ingredient

	1991	1992	1993	1994	1995	1996	1997	1998	1999	2000	2001	
EU-15	:	:	295 289	291 183	285 623	284 310	305 188	313 676	321 386	326 870	:	EU-15
B	:	:	10 426	10 286	9 888	10 939	10 403	8 909	9 474	9 202	:	B
DK	:	:	4 566	4 103	3 919	4 809	3 669	3 675	3 619	2 874	:	DK
D	:	:	33 570	28 930	29 769	34 531	35 085	34 647	38 884	35 403	35 604	D
EL	:	:	8 390	9 283	9 973	8 525	9 870	9 034	11 479	10 153	11 131	EL
E	:	:	31 839	29 408	31 243	27 852	33 236	34 023	35 070	33 614	:	E
F	:	:	84 709	91 953	89 515	84 007	97 889	109 792	107 753	114 695	97 490	F
IRL	:	:	2 322	2 169	2 761	2 639	2 568	2 102	2 469	2 071	2 097	IRL
I	:	:	58 848	54 928	46 678	48 490	48 050	46 236	46 798	50 850	46 080	I
L	:	:	:	301	328	357	357	332	430	421	:	L
NL	:	:	15 921	11 761	11 169	10 923	9 918	10 397	10 722	10 232	:	NL
A	:	:	3 897	3 984	3 620	3 404	3 566	3 690	3 341	3 419	3 564	A
P	:	:	6 117	8 984	9 581	11 818	12 457	12 750	14 392	15 412	15 470	P
FIN	:	:	1 410	1 260	1 297	1 054	933	1 015	1 191	1 158	:	FIN
S	:	:	1 511	1 464	1 961	1 224	1 529	1 608	1 629	1 698	1 652	S
UK	:	:	31 738	32 346	33 903	33 723	35 540	35 466	35 355	35 668	:	UK

4

Please find the complete information of the Eurostat Yearbook on the annexed CD-ROM.

Business structures at a glance

- Turnover of mining and quarrying. Million EUR
- Turnover of manufacturing. Million EUR
- Turnover of electricity, gas and water supply. Million EUR
- Turnover of construction. Million EUR
- Turnover of wholesale and retail trade; repair of motor vehicles, motorcycles and personal and household goods. Million EUR
- Turnover of hotels and restaurants. Million EUR
- Turnover of transport, storage and communication. Million EUR
- Turnover of real estate, renting and business activities. Million EUR
- Value added at factor cost of electricity, gas and water supply. Million EUR
- Personnel costs of manufacturing. Million EUR
- Personnel costs of electricity, gas and water supply. Million EUR
- Personnel costs of construction. Million EUR
- Personnel costs of wholesale and retail trade; repair of motor vehicles, motorcycles and personal and household goods. Million EUR
- Personnel costs of hotels and restaurants. Million EUR
- Personnel costs of transport, storage and communication. Million EUR
- Personnel costs of real estate, renting and business activities. Million EUR.
- Number of persons employed in mining and quarrying
- Number of persons employed in manufacturing
- Number of persons employed in electricity, gas and water supply
- Number of persons employed in construction
- Number of persons employed in wholesale and retail trade; repair of motor vehicles, motorcycles and personal and household goods

- Number of persons employed in hotels and restaurants
- Number of persons employed in transport, storage and communication
- Number of persons employed in real estate, renting and business activities

Industry and construction

- EU-15 and euro-zone production indices, total industry (excluding construction)
- Industrial production index: main industrial groupings, trend series. 1995 = 100
- Share of value added in production. %. EU-15 estimates 1999
- Share of gross operating surplus in value added. %. EU-15 estimates 1999
- Employment index in EU-15, seasonally adjusted. 1995 = 100
- Hours worked index for total industry (excluding construction). Year on year growth rates. Gross
- Wages and salaries index for total industry (excluding construction). Year on year growth rates. Gross
- Producer prices, total industry (excluding construction). Year on year growth rates. Gross
- Employment index for construction. Growth rates. %. Gross
- Evolution of labour productivity. 1 000 ECU/EUR. EU-15 estimates 1992–2001

Distributive trades

- Retail trade, volume of sales in EU-15, seasonally adjusted. 1995 = 100
- Retail trade, volume of sales. Year on year growth rate, working days adjusted

Services, including financial services

- Credit institutions: Number of enterprises. Units
- Credit institutions: number of persons employed. Units
- Credit institutions: interest payable and similar charges. Million EUR
- Insurance: number of life insurance enterprises. Units

4

- Insurance: Number of non-life insurance enterprises. Units
- Insurance: number of composite insurance enterprises. Units
- Insurance: number of specialist reinsurance enterprises. Units
- Insurance: number of persons employed in life insurance enterprises. Units
- Insurance: number of persons employed in non-life insurance enterprises. Units
- Insurance: number of persons employed in composite insurance enterprises. Units
- Insurance: number of persons employed in specialist reinsurance enterprises. Units
- Insurance: gross premiums written by non-life insurance enterprises. Million EUR
- Insurance: gross premiums written by composite insurance enterprises. Million EUR
- Insurance: gross premiums written by specialist reinsurance enterprises. Million EUR
- Insurance: gross claims payments by life insurance enterprises. Million EUR
- Insurance: gross claims payments by non-life insurance enterprises. Million EUR
- Insurance: gross claims payments by composite insurance enterprises. Million EUR
- Insurance: gross claims payments by specialist reinsurance enterprises. Million EUR
- Pension funds: number of members. Units
- Pension funds: total pension contributions. Million EUR
- Pension funds: total expenditure on pensions. Million EUR

Transport

- Total length of railway lines in km
- Goods transport by road. Million tonne-km
- Goods transport by rail. Million tonne-km
- Goods transport by inland waterways. Million tonne-km
- Goods transport by oil pipelines. Million tonne-km
- Sea transport of goods. Million t
- Inland goods transport. 1 000 million tonne-km. EEA and Switzerland. 2000
- Worldwide commercial space launches
- Air transport of goods. 1 000 t
- Air transport of passengers. Millions

- Passenger transport. 1 000 million passenger-km. EEA and Switzerland. 2000
- Passenger car transport. Million passenger-km
- Bus transport of passengers. Million passenger-km
- Rail transport of passengers. Million passenger-km

Tourism

- Nights spent by residents in other collective accommodation establishments
- Nights spent by non-residents in other collective accommodation establishments
- Number of tourists
- Number of trips
- Arrivals of residents in hotels and similar establishments
- Arrivals of non-residents in hotels and similar establishments
- Arrivals of residents in other collective accommodation establishments
- Arrivals of non-residents in other collective accommodation establishments

Energy

- Production of coal and lignite. 1 000 toe
- Production of crude oil. 1 000 toe
- Production of natural gas. 1 000 toe
- Primary production of nuclear energy. 1 000 toe
- Production of renewable energy. 1 000 toe
- Net imports of crude oil and petroleum products. 1 000 toe
- Net imports of natural gas. 1 000 toe
- Gross inland consumption of primary energy. 1 000 toe
- Total gross electricity generation. GWh. EU-15. Euro zone
- Market share of the largest generator in the electricity market as % of total generation
- Electricity generation by origin: hard coal. GWh
- Electricity generation by origin: petroleum products. GWh
- Electricity generation by origin: natural gas. GWh
- Electricity generation by origin: nuclear. GWh

4

- Electricity generation by origin: hydroelectricity. GWh
- Electricity generation by origin: wind. GWh
- Consumption of electricity by industry, transport activities and households. GWh. EU-15
- Share of renewables. Contribution of electricity from renewables to total electricity consumption
- Final energy consumption of petroleum products. 1 000 toe
- Final energy consumption of electricity. 1 000 toe
- Final energy consumption of natural gas. 1 000 toe
- Final energy consumption by industry. 1 000 toe
- Final energy consumption by transport. 1 000 toe
- Natural gas prices for large industrial standard consumers (418 600 GJ per year). EUR per GJ. 1 January 2002
- Electricity prices for large industrial standard consumers (24 GWh per year). EUR per kWh. 1 January 2002
- Natural gas prices for industrial standard consumers: (41 860 GJ per year). EUR per GJ. 1 January 2002
- Electricity prices for industrial standard consumers: (2 GWh per year). EUR per KWh. 1 January 2002
- Natural gas prices for domestic standard consumers: (83.70 GJ per year). EUR per GJ. 1 January 2002
- Electricity prices for domestic standard consumers: (3 500 kWH per year). EUR per 100 kWh. 1 January 2002

Steel

- World production of pig iron. Million t. 1996 and 2001
- World production of crude steel. Million t. 1996 and 2001
- Imports of ECSC steel by country of origin as % of EU total imports
- Exports of ECSC steel by country of destination as % of EU total exports
- Exports of ECSC steel to third countries, of which plate and sheet and coils. Million t
- Imports of ECSC steel from third countries, of which plate and sheet and coils. Million t

Research and development

- Researchers in the business enterprise sector (head count)
- Researchers in the government sector (head count)
- Researchers in the higher education sector (head count)
- Total researchers in full-time equivalent
- Researchers in the business enterprise sector in full-time equivalent
- Researchers in the government sector in full-time equivalent
- Researchers in the higher education sector in full-time equivalent
- Women researchers in the business enterprise sector (head count) as % of total researchers
- Women researchers in the government sector (head count) as % of total researchers
- Women researchers in the higher education sector (head count) as % of total researchers
- Total women researchers in full-time equivalent as % of total researchers
- Women researchers in the business enterprise sector in full-time equivalent as % of total researchers
- Women researchers in the government sector in full-time equivalent as % of total researchers
- Women researchers in the higher education sector in full-time equivalent as % of total researchers
- Government research and development appropriations as % of GDP
- Civil research and development and defence as % of total government research and development appropriations. 2000
- Total European patent applications per country
- Patents (USPTO): number of US patents granted by the United States Patent and Trademark Office (USPTO) per million inhabitants
- Employment in high- and medium-high-technology manufacturing sectors as a share of total employment
- Employment in knowledge-intensive service sectors as a share of total employment

4

Information society

- Number of personal computers. 1 000s
- Personal computers per 100 inhabitants
- Personal computers per 100 inhabitants. 2001
- Number of Internet hosts. 1 000s
- Internet hosts per 100 inhabitants
- Internet users per 100 inhabitants
- Number of Internet users. 1 000s
- Internet users per 100 inhabitants
- Number of mobile phone subscribers. 1 000s
- Mobile phone subscribers per 100 inhabitants
- Price of telecommunications: national calls. Price level and evolution in the telecommunications market. EUR per 10 min call
- Price of telecommunications: calls to the United States. Price level and evolution in the telecommunications market. EUR per 10 min call
- Market share of the incumbent in fixed telecommunications — long-distance calls — as % of total market. 2000
- Market share of the incumbent in fixed telecommunications — international calls — as % of total market. 2000
- Market share of the incumbent in mobile telecommunications as % of total market. 2001

Agriculture

- Number of holdings, agricultural area < 5 ha. 1 000s
- Number of holdings, agricultural area 5-<20 ha. 1 000s
- Number of holdings, agricultural area 20-<50 ha. 1 000s
- Number of holdings, agricultural area >= 50 ha. 1 000s
- Area under cereals. 1 000 ha
- Holdings with cereals. 1 000s
- Area under sugar beet. 1 000 ha
- Area under sunflower. 1 000 ha
- Area under glass. 1 000 ha
- Fallow land. 1 000 ha
- Vineyards. 1 000 ha
- Grassland. 1 000 ha
- Number of cattle. 1 000s

- Number of sheep. 1 000s
- Total labour force. 1 000 AWU
- Family labour force. 1 000 persons
- Full-time regular labour force. 1 000 persons
- Part-time regular labour force. 1 000 persons
- Production of wheat. 1 000 t
- Production of wine. 1 000 hl
- Production of tomatoes. 1 000 t
- Production of apples. 1 000 t
- Production of butter. 1 000 t
- Production of milk powder. 1 000 t
- Production of cheese. 1 000 t
- Production of meat: poultry. 1 000 t
- Production of meat: sheep and goats. 1 000 t
- Producer price indices, nominal; total agricultural production. 1995 = 100
- Producer price indices, nominal; crop products. 1995 = 100
- Producer price indices, deflated; crop products. 1995 = 100
- Producer price indices, nominal; animals and animal products. 1995 = 100
- Producer price indices, deflated; animals and animal products. 1995 = 100
- Purchase price indices, nominal; total means of agricultural production. 1995 = 100
- Crop output. Million ECU/EUR
- Animal output. Million ECU/EUR
- Gross value added at basic prices of the agricultural industry. Million ECU/EUR
- Gross value added at basic prices of the forestry industry. Million ECU/EUR

Forestry

- Forest categories (TBFRA 2000)
- Total sawnwood production. 1 000 m³
- Total paper and paperboard production. 1 000 t

Fisheries

- Annual catches in all regions as % of total world catches
- Annual catches in the north-east Atlantic. 1 000 t live weight
- Annual catches in the north-west Atlantic. 1 000 t live weight

4

- Annual catches in the eastern central Atlantic. 1 000 t live weight
- Annual catches in the Mediterranean. 1 000 t live weight
- Fishing fleet. Total tonnage. GT

Agriculture and environment

- Organic land. ha
- Number of organic holdings
- Consumption of commercial fertilisers. Total. Tonnes of active ingredient

- Consumption of commercial fertilisers. Nitrogen. Tonnes of active ingredient
- Consumption of commercial fertilisers. Potash. Tonnes of active ingredient
- Volume of plant protection products sold. Fungicides. Tonnes of active ingredient
- Volume of plant protection products sold. Herbicides. Tonnes of active ingredient
- Volume of plant protection products sold. Insecticides. Tonnes of active ingredient
- Total sales of pesticides in EU-15. t of active ingredients

4

Annexes

Accident at work incidence rate

The incidence rate is defined as the number of accidents at work which occurred during the year per 100 000 persons in employment. The prevalence rate is the number of work-related health complaints suffered over the past 12 months per 100 000 persons in employment. The reference employment population in each country is based on the labour force survey of the corresponding year. Here, the incidence rate is measured in terms of full-time equivalent employment in order to allow for differences in hours worked both between men and women and between jobs in different sectors of activity.

Agricultural area (AA) or utilised agricultural area (UAA)

Agricultural area (AA) or utilised agricultural area (UAA) is the area utilised for farming, i.e. Categories : arable land, permanent pasture, permanent crops and kitchen gardens.

AIDS case definition

Different case definitions are used in different countries, depending on population factors (number of children or adults, relative occurrence of opportunistic infections) and on the laboratory infrastructure and training available, but the countries participating in the surveillance of AIDS in Europe use a uniform AIDS case definition definitively adopted in 1993. The European definition for AIDS differs from the definition used in the United States in that it does not include CD4+ T-lymphocyte count criteria. The WHO clinical case definition for AIDS is used in countries having limited diagnostic resources.

Annual work unit (AWU)

One annual work unit corresponds to the work performed by one person who is occupied on an agricultural holding on a full-time basis. 'Full-time' means the minimum hours required by the national provisions governing contracts of employment. If these do not indicate the number of hours, then 1 800 hours is taken to be the minimum (225 working days of eight hours each).

Aquaculture

The farming of aquatic organisms including fish, molluscs, crustaceans and aquatic plants. Farming implies some form of intervention in the rearing process to enhance production, such as regular stocking, feeding and protection from predators. Farming also implies individual or corporate ownership of, or rights resulting from contractual arrangements to, the stock being cultivated.

Asylum-seekers

People awaiting a decision on applications for refugee status.

Balance of payments

In the balance-of-payments framework, the balances of the miscellaneous accounts (goods balance, services balance, etc.) are calculated as the difference between exports (credits) and imports (debits). The balance is in surplus when exports are greater than imports, and the balance is in deficit when exports are less than imports.

— **Capital transfers**

In the balance-of-payments framework, capital transfers cover transfers of ownership of fixed assets, transfers of funds linked to, or conditional upon, acquisition or disposal of fixed assets or cancellation without any counterparts being received in return of liabilities by creditors.

— **Communications services**

In the balance-of-payments framework, this item covers two main categories of international communications between residents and non-residents: telecommunications services and postal and courier services.

— **Computer and information services**

In the balance-of-payments framework, this item covers computer data and news-related service transactions between residents and non-residents.

— **Construction services**

In the balance-of-payments framework, this item covers work performed on construction projects and installations by employees of an enterprise in locations outside the economic territory of the enterprise. The work is generally performed for a short time period. Goods imported by the enterprise for use in the projects are included in the value of these services rather than under goods.

— **Financial services**

In the balance-of-payments framework, this item covers financial intermediary and auxiliary services conducted between residents and non-residents.

— **Government services, not included elsewhere**

In the balance-of-payments framework, this item is a residual category covering all services associated with government sectors or international and regional organisations and not classified under other service sub-items (such as financial services, insurance services, communications services, etc.).

— **Income**

In the balance-of-payments framework, income contains two main items: compensation of employees that records wages, salaries and other benefits, in cash or in kind, earned by individuals for work performed for economic units whose place of residence is different from their own; investment income that covers income which a resident entity derives from the ownership of external financial assets and income non-residents derive from their financial assets invested in the compiling economy. This includes interest and dividends on direct, portfolio and other investments.

— **Insurance services**

In the balance-of-payments framework, this item covers the provision of various types of insurance to non-residents by resident insurance enterprises and vice versa.

— **Merchanting and other trade-related services**

In the balance-of-payments framework, this item covers commissions on goods and service transactions between: (i) resident merchants, commodity brokers, dealers and commissions' agents; and (ii) non-residents.

— **Miscellaneous business, professional and technical services**

In the balance-of-payments framework, this item covers a large variety of services such as legal, accounting, management, consulting and public relations services, advertising and market research services, research and development services, architectural, engineering and other technical services, agricultural, mining and on-site processing services, etc.

— **Operational leasing services**

In the balance-of-payments framework, this item covers resident/non-resident leasing and charters of ships, aircraft and transportation equipment without crew.

— **Other business services**

In the balance-of-payments framework, this item includes merchanting and other trade-related services, operational leasing services, and miscellaneous business, professional and technical services.

— **Personal, cultural and recreational services**

In the balance-of-payments framework, this item covers audiovisual and related services and other cultural services provided by residents to non-residents and vice versa.

— **Royalties and licence fees**

In the balance-of-payments framework, this item covers the exchange of payments and receipts between residents and non-residents for the authorised use of intangible, non-produced, non-financial assets and proprietary rights and for the use, through licensing agreements, of produced original prototypes.

Bonds

Securities issued by governments, companies, banks and other institutions. They are normally interest bearing and have a fixed redemption value on a given date.

Business services

These include technical services such as engineering, architecture and technical studies; computer services such as software design and database management; and other professional services such as legal, accounting, consultancy and management.

Catch

Catches of fishery products (fish, molluscs, crustaceans and other aquatic animals, residues and aquatic plants) taken for all purposes (commercial, industrial, recreational and subsistence) by all types and classes of fishing units (fishermen, vessels, gear, etc.) operating both in inland, fresh and brackish water areas, and in inshore, offshore and high-seas fishing areas. The production from aquaculture is excluded. Catch is normally expressed in live weight and derived by the application of conversion factors to the landed or product weight. As such, the catch statistics exclude quantities which are caught but which, for a variety of reasons, are not landed.

Causes of death

Here, these are based on the underlying cause of death, as indicated in Section B of the death certificate. Causes of death are defined on the basis of the World Health Organisation's international classification of diseases, adopted by most countries. Although definitions are harmonised, the statistics may not be fully comparable as classifications may vary when the cause of death is multiple or difficult to evaluate and because of different notification procedures.

Central government

All administrative departments of the State and other central agencies whose responsibilities extend over the whole economic territory, except for the administration of the social security funds.

Communicable diseases

Diseases that cause, or have the potential to cause, significant morbidity and/or mortality across the EU and where the exchange of information may provide early warning of threats to public health. They could also be rare and serious diseases, which would not be recognised at national level and where the pooling of data would allow hypothesis generation from a wider knowledge base and for which effective preventive measures are available with a protective health gain.

Compensation of employees

All payments in cash and kind by employers in remuneration for the work done by their employees during the relevant period. The payments cover gross wages and salaries, employers' actual social contributions and imputed social contributions (those directly supplied by the employers to their employees without involving a social security fund, an insurance enterprise or an autonomous pension fund).

Consumption of fixed capital

Value, at current replacement costs, of the reproducible fixed assets used up during an accounting period (usually one year) as a result of normal wear and tear, foreseeable obsolescence and a normal rate of accidental damage. Unforeseen obsolescence, major catastrophes and depletion of natural resources are not included.

Continuing vocational training (CVT)

Training measures or activities financed wholly or partly by enterprises for employees with employment contracts. For the purposes of the European Commission survey, 'employees' means the total number of persons employed, excluding apprentices and trainees.

Continuing vocational training courses

Events designed solely for the purpose of providing continuing vocational training that take place away from the place of work, for example in a classroom or training centre, at which a group of people receive instruction from teachers/tutors/lecturers for a period of time specified in advance by those organising the course.

Convergence criteria

Convergence criteria for European monetary union are as follows:
— price stability;
— government budgetary position;
— exchange rates;
— long-term interest rates.

— Price stability

Member States should have a price performance that is sustainable and an average rate of inflation, observed over the period of one year before the examination, that does not exceed by more than 1.5 percentage points that of, at most, the three best-performing Member States in terms of price stability.

— Government budgetary position

Member States are to avoid situations of 'excessive government deficits', that is to say that their ratio of planned or actual government deficit to GDP should be no more than 3 %, and that their ratio of (general) government debt to GDP should be no more than 60 %, unless the excess over the reference value is only exceptional or temporary or the ratios have declined substantially and continuously.

— Exchange rates

Member States should have respected the normal fluctuation margins of the exchange rate mechanism (ERM) without severe tensions for at least the two years before the examination. In particular, the Member State shall not have devalued its currency's bilateral central rate against any other Member State's currency on its own initiative over the same period.

— Long-term interest rates

Member States should have had an average nominal long-term interest rate over a period of one year before the examination that does not exceed by more than 2 percentage points that of, at most, the three best-performing Member States in terms of price stability.

Cover rate

The cover rate is calculated by 'exports/imports' in per cent. It gives an indication of the weight of exports compared to imports. When the cover rate is greater than 100 with a selected partner, this indicates that the EU is a net exporter (exports are greater than imports) towards this country. On the contrary, a cover rate less than 100 indicates that the EU is a net importer from the country.

Crude death rate (CDR)

The crude death rate (CDR) is a weighted average of the age-specific mortality rates. The weighting factor is the age distribution of the population whose mortality experience is being observed. Comparing the CDR from two or more populations is a comparison of a combination of different age-specific death rates and different population structures not reflecting the 'real' mortality differences but including also the effect of the population structure on the total number of deaths and on the crude death rates.

Current taxes on income, wealth, etc.

Current taxes on income and wealth cover all compulsory unrequited payments, in cash or in kind, levied periodically by general government and by the rest of the world on the income and wealth of institutional units, and some periodic taxes which are assessed neither on the income nor the wealth.

Day-to-day money rate

This usually denotes the rate at which banks lend and borrow among themselves overnight on the interbank market. This rate is a good indicator of the general level of short-term market interest rates. The day-to-day money rate is influenced, among other factors, by the level of central bank interest rates.

Death rate

Deaths per 100 000 inhabitants.

Deaths in road accidents

People killed outright or who died within 30 days as a result of the accident; this is calculated as a standard death rate (SDR).

Direct cost of CVT courses

Costs immediately associated with the provision of continuing vocational training courses: fees and payments to external training providers and training staff; travel and other sundry expenses and subsistence allowances; labour costs for internal training staff wholly or partly engaged in planning, organising and providing the courses; and costs of premises (including training centres) and equipment, together with the costs of materials.

Disease incidence

Incidence is a measure of the number of new cases arising in a population in a given period. Incidence might be expressed as the number of new cases of a disease (or disorder) per 1 000 or 100 000 population in a year. Incidence might refer either to the first onset of a disease (i.e. new cases) or to all episodes.

Disease prevalence

Prevalence is a measure of the number of cases of a given disease existing at a certain time. Prevalence might be expressed as the proportion of a population with a disease at any time in a year. For prevalence statistics from different studies to be comparable, the length of period under consideration must be the same.

Distributive trades

Wholesale businesses, sales agents, retail trade and repair of consumer goods and vehicles.

Dwelling

A room or a suite of rooms and its accessories, lobbies and corridors in a permanent building or structurally separated part thereof which, by the way it has been built, rebuilt or converted, is designed for habitation by one private household all the year. A dwelling is either a one-family dwelling in a house or an apartment in a block of flats. Dwellings include garages for residential use, even when apart from the habitation or belonging to different owners.

Earnings, gross

Remuneration (wages and salaries) in cash paid directly to the employee before any deductions for income tax and social security contributions paid by the employee.

Earnings, net

Gross earnings after the deduction of social security contributions and income taxes payable by employees and, where applicable, after the addition of family allowances.

ECHP (European Community household panel)

An input-harmonised, longitudinal panel survey using a common set of definitions and directed to a representative sample of private households in each EU Member State, designed to obtain information on income and related social issues by means of personal interviews, which was launched in 1994 and expired in 2001.

Economic territory

The economic territory of a country consists of the geographical territory administered by a government; within the territory, people, goods and capital circulate freely. It also includes the national air space, the territorial waters, the natural deposits in international waters if worked by resident units, the territorial enclaves abroad (own representations, own military bases, etc.) but excludes extraterritorial enclaves (representations of foreign countries or of the European Union's institutions, etc.).

Ecu

The former European currency unit may be considered as the cornerstone of the European Monetary System (EMS). It was composed of a basket of currencies (see below). In addition to its official use in the EMS, a private market for the ecu developed, allowing its use in monetary transactions and for denominating financial instruments including bonds. The ecu was replaced by the euro, the new European single currency, on 1 January 1999 at a ratio of 1:1.

Ecu basket

It was defined by specific amounts of 12 currencies of the Member States of the EU. At its inception on 13 March 1979, the ecu was made up of a basket of fixed amounts of the then nine currencies, which was identical at the outset to the European unit of account (EUA). The currency composition of the ecu basket was frozen from November 1993 until the euro was introduced in January 1999. The currencies of Austria, Finland and Sweden did not take part in the composition of the ecu basket because they were only members of the EU from January 1995.

EEA countries

At the beginning of 2001, the European Economic Area (EEA) consisted of the EU Member States as well as Iceland, Norway and Liechtenstein. In 1989, Jacques Delors, then President of the Commission, proposed a new form of partnership, which was to become the EEA Agreement. The EFTA States, at that time Austria, Finland, Iceland, Liechtenstein, Norway, Sweden and Switzerland, welcomed the ideas; formal negotiations began in June 1990 and the agreement was signed on 2 May 1992 in Oporto. The agreement entered into force on 1 January 1994 and covered the EU and all EFTA countries except for Liechtenstein and Switzerland. Since 1 January 1995, Austria, Finland and Sweden have participated in the EEA as EU Member States. Liechtenstein became a full participant in the EEA on 1 May 1995.

Emigrants

People leaving their country of usual residence and effectively taking up residence in another country. According to the 1997 United Nations recommendations on statistics of international migration (Revision 1), such a person is a long-term emigrant if they leave their country of previous usual residence for a period of 12 months or more. However, few countries are able to supply statistics based on these definitions. The statistics shown in this volume are generally based on national definitions that may differ greatly from the UN recommendations. Not all countries collect statistics on emigrants, and, in those that do, data sources and the scope of the collection vary.

Employees

Employees are defined as persons who work for a public or private employer and who receive compensation in the form of wages, salaries, fees, gratuities, payment by results or payment in kind; non-conscripted members of the armed forces are also included. An extensive concept of employment is used in international guidelines on labour statistics. Persons in employment as reported by the labour force survey are those who during the reference week did any work for pay or profit for at least one hour, or were not working but had jobs from which they were temporarily absent. Family workers are included.

Employment rate

Persons in employment as a percentage of the population of the same age.

EMS (European Monetary System)

Formally introduced on 13 March 1979, it was operational until 31 December 1998.

Its purpose was 'to create a zone of monetary stability in Europe through the implementation of certain exchange rate, credit and resource transfer policies'. The EMS had three components: the ecu, the exchange rate mechanism (ERM) and the credit mechanism. At the end of its existence, the currencies of all EU Member States except Sweden and the United Kingdom were members of the ERM.

EMU (economic and monetary union)

Union of 12 EU Member States which have adopted the single currency, the euro. These countries are officially considered to have fulfilled the convergence criteria. The third stage of EMU began on 1 January 1999, when 11 member currencies were permanently fixed to the euro, joined by the Greek drachma on 1 January 2001. The coins and notes were introduced on 1 January 2002 and national currencies progressively withdrawn.

ERM (exchange rate mechanism)

Part of the European Monetary System aimed at achieving greater exchange rate stability. It had two elements: a parity grid of bilateral central rates and fluctuation bands, and the divergence indicator, which measured the extent to which each currency was deviating from its ecu central rate. It ceased to exist at the start of the third stage of monetary union.

ERM 2

On 1 January 1999, the ERM was replaced by the new exchange rate mechanism, ERM 2. It is aimed at preparing 'pre-in' countries for participation in monetary union, while helping to ensure exchange rate discipline in the EU. The central currency in the system is the euro. At the end of 2000, the currencies of two countries were participating in ERM 2, with fluctuation margins of ± 2.25 % for Denmark and ± 15 % for Greece. Since Greece joined the euro zone on 1 January 2001, Denmark is currently the sole country in the system.

ESA

European system of (integrated economic) accounts, the methodology in national accounts. The new version, ESA 95 (the third one), has been gradually introduced since 1999 as an expanded and fuller version of the earlier ESA 79. In this way, national accounts data (including their main component, gross domestic product (GDP), which covers all goods and services produced by a country in a given period) are defined and will be measured with increasing accuracy and exhaustiveness. ESA 95 is compatible with SNA 93, the United Nations' system, like ESA 79 with SNA 68. The first version of ESA was ESA 70.

EU-SILC (EU statistics on income and living conditions)

An output-harmonised data collection tool which replaces the ECHP and which is designed to be the reference source of information on income and related social issues, containing both cross-sectional and longitudinal elements, and placing greater reliance on existing national sources in an attempt to improve timeliness and flexibility.

Euro

The third stage of European monetary union began on 1 January 1999 with the introduction of the euro, the European single currency. It replaced the ecu on a 1:1 basis. Since that date, the national currencies of 11 EU Member States (Belgium, Germany, Spain, France, Ireland, Italy, Luxembourg, the Netherlands, Austria, Portugal and Finland) were fixed to the euro at irrevocable conversion rates (see table below). They were joined by Greece on 1 January 2001. The euro existed until the end of 2001 as book money only (cheque, transfer, payment by card) and its use was voluntary (no compulsion — no prohibition). The coins and notes were introduced on 1 January 2002, when use of the euro became compulsory, and national currencies progressively withdrawn.

Fixed conversion rates (EUR 1 =)

13.7603	ATS
40.3399	BEF
1.95583	DEM
166.386	ESP
5.94573	FIM
6.55957	FRF
340.750	GRD
0.787564	IEP
1 936.27	ITL
40.3399	LUF
2.20371	NLG
200.482	PTE

The conversion rules of the national currencies to the euro and vice versa are very strict. The official conversion rate with six significant figures has to be used for each conversion without rounding or truncation. To convert into euro, the amount has to be divided by the conversion rate and for the opposite operation the amount has to be multiplied by the rate.

The conversion of a national currency of the euro zone to another currency of the euro zone has to be done via the euro using the conversion rates.

A conversion in another currency has to be done also via the euro but using the prevailing exchange rate of this currency to the euro.

Euro zone: EUR-12 (formerly EUR-11)

Countries initially participating in monetary union in January 1999: Belgium, Germany, Spain, France, Ireland, Italy, Luxembourg, the Netherlands, Austria, Portugal and Finland. On 1 January 2001, Greece joined the euro zone. Hence, the three concepts: EUR-11 (the initial 11 countries), EUR-12 (EUR-11 plus Greece) and the euro zone, the variable concept (EUR-11 until 31 December 2000, EUR-12 from 1 January 2001). Note that the letter 'R' after 'EU' is used to distinguish the euro zone from the European Union (for which the code is just EU).

Eurobarometer

Eurobarometer public opinion surveys have been conducted on behalf of the Directorate-General for Education and Culture of the European Commission each spring and autumn since autumn 1973. Besides general public opinion surveys, the Survey Research Unit of the Directorate-General for Education and Culture organises specific target groups, as well as qualitative (group discussion, in-depth interview) surveys in all Member States of the EU and, occasionally, in non-member countries.

European Patent Office (EPO)

The European Patent Office (EPO) is the executive arm of the European Patent Organisation, an intergovernmental body set up under the European Patent Convention (EPC), which was signed in Munich on 5 October 1973 and entered into force on 7 October 1977. Members of the European Patent Organisation are the EPC contracting States. The EPO grants European patents for the contracting States to the EPC. The activities of the EPO are supervised by the Organisation's Administrative Council, composed of delegates from the contracting States.
Source: EPO (http://www.european-patent-office.org).

European Union (EU)

Established on 1 November 1993 when the Maastricht Treaty entered into force. On 31 December 1994, the EU had 12 Member States: Belgium, Denmark, Germany, Greece, Spain, France, Ireland, Italy, Luxembourg, the Netherlands, Portugal and the United Kingdom. From January 1995, the EU had three new Member States: Austria, Finland and Sweden.

Exchange rate

The price at which one currency is exchanged for another.
See also 'Convergence criteria'.

External courses

Courses designed and managed by an organisation that is not part of the enterprise, even if they are held in the enterprise.

Extra-EU flows

All transactions between EU countries and countries outside the EU.

Final consumption expenditure

Final consumption expenditure consists of expenditure incurred by resident institutional units on goods or services that are used for the direct satisfaction of individual needs or wants or the collective needs of members of the community.

Foreign direct investment (FDI)

Foreign direct investment (FDI) is the category of international investment within the balance-of-payment accounts that reflects the objective of obtaining a lasting interest by a resident entity in one economy in an enterprise resident in another economy. The lasting interest implies the existence of a long-term relationship between the direct investor and the enterprise, and a significant degree of influence by the investor on the management of the enterprise. Formally defined, a direct investment enterprise is an unincorporated or incorporated enterprise in which a direct investor owns 10 % or more of the ordinary shares or voting power (for an incorporated enterprise) or the equivalent (for an unincorporated enterprise).

FDI flows and positions: through direct investment flows, an investor builds up a foreign direct investment position that features on the international investment position of the economy. This FDI position (or FDI stock) differs from the accumulated flows because of revaluation (changes in prices or exchange rates), and other adjustments like rescheduling or cancellation of loans, debt forgiveness or debt-equity swaps.

Forest

Forest is defined as land with tree crown cover (or equivalent stocking level) of more than 10 % and area of more than 0.5 ha. The trees should be able to reach a minimum height of 5 m at maturity.

General government

The general government sector includes all institutional units whose output is intended for individual and collective consumption, and mainly financed by compulsory payments made by units belonging to other sectors, and/or all institutional units principally engaged in the redistribution of national income and wealth. The general government sector is subdivided into four subsectors: central government, State government, local government, and social security funds.

General government debt

Total gross debt at nominal value outstanding at the end of the year and consolidated between and within the subsectors of general government.
See also 'Convergence criteria'.

Government bonds

Official debt instruments issued by governments in order to fund budget deficits and to cover debt which is being redeemed. Government bond yields usually refer to secondary market yields, i.e. derived from the market where securities which are already in circulation are traded.

Government budget appropriations or outlays for research and development

Government budget appropriations or outlays for research and development (GBAORD) are a way of measuring government support to R & D activities and include all appropriations allocated to R & D in central (or federal) government budgets. Provincial (or State) government is only included if the contribution is significant, whereas local government funds are excluded.

Gross domestic product at market prices (GDPmp)

Final result of the production activity of resident producer units. It corresponds to the economy's total output of goods and services, less intermediate consumption. Measured at market prices, it includes VAT on production and net taxes on imports. The new methodology ESA 95 somewhat extends the underlying concepts to increase its accuracy (moment of recording a transaction etc.) and exhaustiveness (new activities like leasing, stock options, etc.).

Gross domestic product in purchasing power standards

Gross domestic product converted into PPS (purchasing power standards) through a special exchange rate called PPP (purchasing power parity, based on relative prices ratios) and used to make reliable volume comparisons.

Gross fixed capital formation

Gross fixed capital formation (GFCF) consists of resident producers' acquisitions, less disposals, of fixed assets during a given period plus certain additions to the value of non-produced assets realised by the productive activity of producers or institutional units. Fixed assets are tangible or intangible assets produced as outputs from processes of production that are themselves used repeatedly, or continuously, in processes of production for more than one year.

Gross national income (GNI)

Gross domestic product plus net (= received from abroad minus paid abroad) entrepreneurial and property and labour income.
Gross national disposable income, compiled as GNI plus net current distributive transactions with the rest of the world and net operating subsidies from EU institutions, shows the income available for national use.
Net income from abroad covers, for example, property and entrepreneurial income from the rest of the world, accident insurance transactions and unrequited current transfers.
The concept of GNI (ESA 95) replaces the one of GNP (gross national product, ESA 79). Both are identical conceptually, but ESA 95 adds accuracy and exhaustiveness.

Gross national product (GNP)

See 'Gross national income'.

Gross value added at market prices

Final output minus intermediate consumption, plus subsidies minus taxes linked to production.
Gross value added usually makes up more than 90 % of GDP.

High-technology patents

High-technology patents are counted following the criteria established by the trilateral statistical report, where the subsequent

technical fields are defined as high technology: computer and automated business equipment; micro-organism and genetic engineering; aviation; communications technology; semiconductors; and lasers.

High-technology sectors

The classification of high- and medium-high-technology manufacturing sectors is based on the notion of R & D intensity (ratio of R & D expenditure to GDP). Following this criterion, high-tech manufacturing comprises manufacturing of office machinery and computers, manufacturing of radio, television and communication equipment and apparatus, and manufacturing of medical precision and optical instruments, watches and clocks. Medium-high-tech manufacturing includes the manufacture of chemicals and chemical products, manufacture of machinery and equipment n.e.c, manufacture of electrical machinery and apparatus n.e.c, manufacture of motor vehicles, trailers and semi-trailers, and manufacturing of other transport equipment.

Following a similar logic as for manufacturing, Eurostat defines the following sectors as knowledge-intensive services (KIS): water transport; air transport; post and telecommunications; financial intermediation; insurance and pension funding (except compulsory social security); activities auxiliary to financial intermediation; real estate activities; renting of machinery and equipment without operator and of personal and household goods; computer and related activities; research and development; other business activities; education; health and social work; and recreational, cultural and sporting activities.

Of these sectors, post and telecommunications, computer and related activities and research and development are considered high-tech services.

Hospital discharges

Discharge is the formal release of an inpatient by an inpatient or acute care institution. The discharge rates are expressed by the number per 100 000 population. Diagnostic chapters (using principal diagnosis) have been defined according to the international classification of diseases, ninth revision, clinical modification (ICD-9-CM).

Hours in CVT courses

The number of hours in CVT courses relates to the paid working time that a participant in total spent in CVT courses in 1999.

Household

According to the household budget surveys, household should be defined in terms of having a shared residence and common arrangements. A household comprises either one person living alone or a group of people, not necessarily related, living at the same address with common housekeeping, i.e. sharing at least one meal a day or sharing a living or sitting room.

Household consumption

The value of goods and services used for directly meeting household needs. It covers expenditure on purchases of goods and services, own consumption such as products from kitchen gardens, and the imputed rent of owner-occupied dwellings.

ICD diagnosis

Diagnoses and procedures associated with hospitalisations are classified in accordance with the ninth revision of the international classification of diseases (ICD-9). This classification is the result of close collaboration among many nations and non-governmental organisations, under the auspices of the World Health Organisation (WHO). Its original use was to classify causes of mortality. Later, it was extended to include diagnoses on morbidity. For example, the clinical modification of the ICD is used in categorising hospital diagnoses. In practice, the ICD has become the international standard diagnostic classification for all general epidemiological, as well as health management, purposes. Most Member States will adopt or are adopting the 10th ICD classification. The diagnostic categories used are based on the principal diagnosis, which is submitted as the first of several possible diagnoses coded on the discharge record. The principal diagnosis represents the 'condition established after study to be chiefly responsible for occasioning the admission of the patient to the hospital for care'.

Immigrants

Persons arriving or returning from abroad to take up residence in the country for a certain period, having previously been resident elsewhere. According to the 1997 United Nations recommendations on statistics of international migration (Revision 1), such a person is a long-term immigrant if he/she stays in his/her country of destination for a period of 12 months or more, having previously been resident elsewhere for 12 months or more. However, few countries are able to supply statistics based on these definitions. The statistics shown in this volume are generally based on national definitions that may differ greatly from the UN recommendations.

Not all countries collect immigration data, and, in those that do, data sources and the scope of the collection vary. A few countries (e.g. France) exclude national citizens from immigration statistics.

Implicit price index, GDP

Indicator of price evolution of all goods and services that make up the GDP. The word 'implicit' relates to the fact that the price index is a combination of the individual price evolution of its components.

Inpatient care beds

Beds accommodating patients who are formally admitted (or 'hospitalised') to an institution for treatment and/or care and who stay for a minimum of one night in the hospital or other institution providing inpatient care. Inpatient care is delivered in hospitals, other nursing and residential care facilities or in establishments which are classified according to their focus of care under the ambulatory care industry but perform inpatient care as a secondary activity.

Inactive

People not in the labour force. They are neither employed nor unemployed. Apart from retired and disabled people, they include young people still in education and people working without earning an income, whether they do housework or charity work.

Income from patents

Transactions involving trade in technical know-how and trade marks protected by licences and patents.

Intermediate consumption

Intermediate consumption consists of the value of the goods and services consumed as inputs by a process of production, excluding fixed assets whose consumption is recorded as consumption of fixed capital. The goods and services may be either transformed or used up by the production process.

Internal courses

Courses designed and managed by the enterprise itself, even if held at a location away from the enterprise.

Intra-EU flows

All transactions declared by EU countries with other EU Member States.

ISCED

International standard classification of education, set up by Unesco in 1976.

ISCED 97

The international standard classification of education (ISCED) is an instrument suitable for compiling statistics on education internationally. It covers two cross-classification variables: levels and fields of education with the complementary dimensions of general/vocational/pre-vocational orientation and educational/labour market destination. The current version, ISCED 97 (see http://unescostat.unesco.org/en/pub/pub0.htm), was implemented in EU countries, for the first time, for the collection of data from the school year 1997/98.

The change in the ISCED classification has affected the comparability of chronological series, especially for level 3 (upper secondary education) and for level 5 (tertiary education). ISCED 97 introduced a new level, i.e. level 4: post-secondary non-tertiary education (previously included in ISCED levels 3 and 5). ISCED 97 level 6 only relates to Ph.D. or doctoral studies. ISCED 97 distinguishes seven levels of education.

ISCED 97 fields

The classification comprises 25 fields of education (at two-digit level) which can be further refined into three-digit level. The following nine broad groups (at one-digit level) can be distinguished.

0 — General programmes

1 — Education

2 — Humanities and arts

3 — Social sciences, business and law

4 — Science, mathematics and computing

5 — Engineering, manufacturing and construction

6 — Agriculture and veterinary

7 — Health and welfare

8 — Services

ISCED 97 levels

Empirically, ISCED assumes that several criteria exist which can help allocate education programmes to levels of education. Depending on the level and type of education concerned, there is a need to establish a hierarchical ranking system between main and subsidiary criteria (typical entrance qualification, minimum entrance requirement, minimum age, staff qualification, etc.).

0: Pre-primary education

Pre-primary education is defined as the initial stage of organised instruction. It is school- or centre-based and is designed for children aged at least three years.

1: Primary education

This level begins between four and seven years of age, is compulsory in all countries and generally lasts from five to six years.

2: Lower secondary education

It continues the basic programmes of the primary level, although teaching is typically more subject-focused. Usually, the end of this level coincides with the end of compulsory education.

3: Upper secondary education

This level generally begins at the end of compulsory education. The entrance age is typically 15 or 16 years. Entrance qualifications (end of compulsory education) and other minimum entry requirements are usually needed. Instruction is often more subject-oriented than at ISCED level 2. The typical duration of ISCED level 3 varies from two to five years.

4: Post-secondary non-tertiary education

These programmes straddle the boundary between upper secondary and tertiary education. They serve to broaden the knowledge of ISCED level 3 graduates. Typical examples are programmes designed to prepare students for studies at level 5 or programmes designed to prepare students for direct labour market entry.

5: Tertiary education (first stage)

Entry to these programmes normally requires the successful completion of ISCED level 3 or 4. This level includes tertiary programmes with academic orientation (type A) which are largely theoretically based and tertiary programmes with occupation orientation (type B) which are typically shorter than type A programmes and geared for entry into the labour market.

6: Tertiary education (second stage)

This level is reserved for tertiary studies that lead to an advanced research qualification (Ph.D. or doctorate).

Labour costs, direct

See 'Total labour costs'.

Labour costs, indirect

See 'Total labour costs'.

Labour force

People in the labour market, i.e. employed and unemployed people.

Labour force survey (LFS)

A labour force survey is an inquiry directed to households designed to obtain information on the labour market and related issues by means of personal interviews. The EU LFS covers the entire population living in private households and excludes those in collective households such as boarding houses, halls of residence and hospitals. The definitions used are common to all EU countries and are based on international recommendations by the International Labour Office (ILO).

Life expectancy

Average number of years still to live for people of a given age under the prevailing conditions of mortality at successive ages of a given population.

Live weight of fishery products

Live weight of fishery products is derived from the landed or product weight by the application factors and is designed to represent the weight of the fishery product as it was taken from the water and before being subjected to any processing or other operation.

Local government

All types of public administration whose competence extends to only a local part of the economic territory apart from local agencies of social security funds.

Long-term interest rates

Here measured as the yield to redemption on 10-year government bonds.
See also 'Convergence criteria'.

Manufacturing industry

All activities included within Section D of NACE Rev. 1 (statistical classification of economic activities in the European Community). Both cottage industry (crafts) and large-scale activity are included. It should be noted that the use of heavy plant or machinery is not exclusive to Section D. It covers industries such as manufacture of non-metallic mineral products; chemicals; man-made fibres; manufacture of metal articles; food, drinks and tobacco; textiles; leather and leather goods; timber and wooden furniture; manufacture of paper and paper products, including printing and publishing; and processing of rubber and plastics. Not included are mining and extraction and building and civil engineering.

Market services

Recovery and repair, wholesale and retail trade, accommodation and catering, inland, maritime, air and auxiliary transport services, communications, and credit and insurance institutions and other market services. They are services produced for sale, normally with the aim of making a profit. In the nomenclature NACE Rev. 1, they include Sections G to P excluding Section L (public administration and defence; compulsory social security) which is non-market services. In ESA 79, recycling belonged to the services, while, in ESA 95, recycling belongs to manufacturing.

Migration, net (including corrections)

The difference between immigration to and emigration from the area. Since most countries either do not have accurate figures on immigration and emigration or have no figures at all, net migration is generally estimated on the basis of the difference between (total) population increase and natural increase between two dates. The statistics on net migration are therefore affected by all the statistical inaccuracies in the two components of this equation, especially population increase.

Mortality rate, crude

Deaths per 1 000 inhabitants.

Mortality, infant

Deaths per 1 000 live-born children aged less than one year.

NACE 70

General industrial classification of economic activities within the European Communities (with regard to data from 1970 to 1990).

NACE Rev. 1

NACE Rev. 1 is a revision of the general industrial classification of economic activities (with regard to data from 1991 onwards, see annex 'Classification of economic activities' below).

National citizens

Persons who are citizens of the country in which they are currently resident.

Net operating surplus

Gross domestic product at market prices minus compensation of employees paid by resident employers, taxes net of subsidies on production and imports levied by general government and by the rest of the world, including EU institutions, and consumption of fixed capital. Net operating surplus comprises total property and entrepreneurial income from production.

Non-market services

These are mainly general government services and are measured by their cost of production (as their 'market' value is not always representative). Other examples are private welfare institutions and outside domestic help. Non-market services do not include the production of goods and services by households using their unpaid labour for producing their own consumption. The value added generated by such activities is excluded from conventional macroeconomic aggregates because it does not enter the economic circuit. In the nomenclature NACE Rev. 1, non-market services are located in Section L (public administration and defence; compulsory social security).

Non-national citizens

Persons who are not citizens of the country in which they are currently resident.

NUTS

This nomenclature of territorial units for statistics was drawn up jointly by Eurostat and the other Commission departments in order to provide a single and coherent territorial breakdown for the compilation of EU regional statistics. The current NUTS nomenclature (version 2001) subdivides the territory of the European Union into 78 NUTS 1 regions, 211 NUTS 2 regions and 1 092 NUTS 3 regions.

Official external reserves

These reserves are held by countries' monetary authorities for the purpose of financing balance-of-payments deficits or for influencing their currency's external value. They are made up of monetary gold, foreign currencies, special drawing rights (SDRs) of the International Monetary Fund (IMF) and reserves held with the IMF.

Paper and paperboard

This is the sum of graphic papers; newsprint; sanitary and household papers; packaging materials and other paper and paperboard. It excludes manufactured paper products such as boxes, cartons, books and magazines, etc.

Participant in CVT course

This is a person who took part in one or more CVT courses at some time during 1999. Each person was counted once only, irrespective of the number of times he or she participated in a CVT course.

Population density

Number of inhabitants per square kilometre.

Population increase, natural

Births minus deaths.

Psychiatric care beds

Beds accommodating inpatients for mental health (including substance abuse therapy), but excluding beds for patients who are mentally handicapped if the principal clinical intent is not of a medical nature.

Purchasing power parities (PPPs)

Monetary exchange rates should not be used to compare the volumes of income or expenditure because they usually reflect more elements than just price differences (e.g. volumes of financial transactions between currencies, expectations in the foreign exchange markets). In contrast, purchasing power parities (PPPs) are exclusively determined by the differences between the price levels in different countries. Therefore, they truly reflect the differences in the purchasing power, for example, of households. Purchasing power parities are obtained by comparing the price levels for a basket of comparable goods and services that is selected to be representative for consumption patterns in the various countries. Purchasing power parities convert every national monetary unit into a common reference unit, the purchasing power standard (PPS), of which every unit can buy the same amount of goods and services across the countries (see 'Purchasing power standards').

Purchasing power standards (PPS)

Purchasing power standards help to compare incomes (or other disposable amounts of money) as well as expenditure in different countries. Purchasing power standards indicate, for the various countries, the national currency units needed to purchase the same basket of goods and services. If currency values (e.g. an amount of received income) are converted into purchasing power standards, the resulting values will be directly comparable in terms of the purchasing power of households.

Real values

Calculated by deflating an economic variable at current prices by the implicit price index of another variable, often the GDP (e.g. deflating the compensation of employees by the price index of household consumption). This is typically the case for financial flows. If a variable is deflated by its own price index, the result is said to be 'at constant prices'. 'Real' is sometimes used as a synonym of 'constant' (constant prices).

Refugee

Someone with a well-founded fear of being persecuted for reasons of race, religion, nationality, membership of a particular social group or political opinion (according to Article 1 of the 1951 United Nations Convention relating to the Status of Refugees).

It should be noted that many countries allow applicants for asylum to remain on a temporary or permanent basis even if they are not deemed to be refugees under the 1951 convention definition. For example, asylum applicants may receive a positive response to their application on humanitarian grounds. Such persons are not included in the refugee figures in this edition.

Research and development (R & D)

Research and development comprises creative work undertaken on a systematic basis in order to increase the stock of knowledge of man, culture and society, and the use of this stock of knowledge to devise new applications.

Resident producer units

Units engaged in production on the domestic territory of a country.

Roundwood production

Roundwood production comprises all quantities of wood removed from the forest and other wooded land, and trees outside the forest during a certain period of time.

Sawnwood

Sawnwood is wood that has been produced either by sawing lengthways or by a profile-chipping process and that, with a few exceptions, exceeds 5 mm in thickness.

Services

The terms 'service industry(ies)', 'service sector(s)' or simply 'service(s)' are generally used to refer to economic activities covered by Sections G to K and M to O of NACE Rev. 1 and the units that carry out those activities.

SMEs

Small and medium-sized enterprises employing less than 250 people. (According to the definition of the Directorate-General for Enterprise of the European Commission: very small enterprises: 1–9 employees; small enterprises: 10–40 employees; medium-sized enterprises: 50–249 employees; large enterprises: 250 or more employees.) SMEs form the backbone of the EU-15 enterprise culture where over 99 % of businesses employ fewer than 250 people.

Social benefits (other than social transfers in kind)

Social benefits (other than social transfers in kind) are those paid to households by social security funds, other government units, NPISHs (non-profit-making institutions serving households), insurance enterprises, employers administering unfunded social insurance schemes and other institutional units administering privately funded insurance schemes.

Social contributions

Social contributions are paid on a compulsory or voluntary basis by the employers, the employees and the self- and non-employed persons. They are of two types: actual and imputed.

Social security funds

Central, State and local institutional units whose principal activity is to provide social benefits, and which fulfil each of the two following criteria: (i) by law or regulation except regulations concerning government employees, certain groups of the population are obliged to participate in the scheme or to pay contributions; (ii) general government is responsible for the management of the institution in respect of settlement or approval of the contributions and benefits independently of its role as a supervisory body or employer.

Stability and Growth Pact

The Stability and Growth Pact has to be seen against the background of the third stage of economic and monetary union, which began on 1 January 1999. Its aim is to ensure that the Member States continue their budgetary discipline efforts once the single currency has been introduced.

In practical terms, the pact comprises a European Council resolution (adopted at Amsterdam on 17 June 1997) and two Council regulations of 7 July 1997 laying detailed technical arrangements (one on the surveillance of budgetary positions and coordination of economic policies and the other on implementing the excessive deficit procedure).

In the medium term, the Member States undertook to pursue the objective of a balanced or nearly balanced budget and to present the Council and the Commission with a stability programme by 1 March 1999 (the programme then being updated annually). Along the same lines, States not taking part in the third stage of EMU are required to submit a convergence programme.

The Stability and Growth Pact opens the way for the Council to penalise any participating Member State which fails to take appropriate measures to end an excessive deficit. Initially, the penalty would take the form of a non-interest-bearing deposit with the Community, but it could be converted into a fine if the excessive deficit is not corrected within two years.

Standard death rate (SDR)

Death rate of a population of a standard age distribution. As most causes of death vary significantly with people's age and sex, the use of standard death rates improves comparability over time and between countries, as they aim at measuring death rates independently of different age structures of populations. The standard death rates used here are calculated by the World Health Organisation on the basis of a standard European population.

Standard gross margin (SGM)

The gross margin of an agricultural enterprise means the monetary value of gross production from which corresponding specific costs are deducted.

The standard gross margin (SGM) is the value of the gross margin corresponding to the average situation in a given region for each agricultural characteristic.

SGMs are determined on the basis of three-yearly averages. In the 1997 structure survey, the '1994' standard gross margins were calculated from the arithmetic mean for the years 1993, 1994 and 1995.

Gross production is the sum of the values of the principal product(s) and of the secondary product(s). These values are calculated by multiplying production per unit (less any losses) by the farm-gate price, without VAT. Gross production also includes subsidies linked to products, to area and/or livestock.

State government

Separate institutional units exercising some of the functions of government at a level below that of central government and above that of the governmental institutional units existing at local level, except for the administration of social security funds.

Subsidies

Current unrequited payments which general government or the institutions of the European Union make to resident producers, with the objective of influencing their levels of production, their prices or the remuneration of the factors of production.

Tax rate on a married couple with two children

This tax rate has a similar basis to the tax rate on low-wage earners (structural indicator). The differences are as follows: (i) the tax rate applies to a married couple with two children (both between 5 and 12 years of age); (ii) there is only one working spouse; (iii) the total income of the family includes universal cash benefits (e.g. family allowances) as well as the employment income of the working spouse; (iv) the tax on earnings is equal to total income tax on gross wage earnings plus the employee's and employer's social security contributions less universal cash benefits; this tax on earnings is then expressed as a percentage of labour costs, precisely as defined for the tax rate on low-wage earners; (v) the working spouse is taken to be an adult full-time production worker in the manufacturing industry whose earnings are equal to 100 % of the average earnings of such workers in each country.

Tax rate on low-wage earners

For this structural indicator, the tax rate applies to a single earner without children; it is assumed that the taxpayer has no income source other than employment income. The total tax is calculated as the sum of income tax on gross annual earnings plus the employee's and employer's social security contributions. This income tax is then expressed as a percentage of labour costs, which are defined as gross wage earnings plus the employer's social security contributions and payroll taxes (if applicable). The calculated tax rate is therefore an average rate of tax. The wage earner is taken to be an adult full-time production worker in the manufacturing industry whose earnings are equal to 67 % of the average earnings of such workers in each country. Gross annual earnings include all cash payments during the reference year. Apart from overtime, shift premiums, vacation payments, bonuses and other regular pay, irregular bonuses and payments are also included (for example, 13th or 14th month payments, holiday bonuses, profit-sharing, allowances for leave not taken, etc.). The following are not included: payments in kind, severance payments and profit-sharing schemes which take the form of dividend distributions.

Taxes on production and imports

Compulsory unrequited payments, in cash or in kind, levied by general government, or by the institutions of the EU, in respect of the production and importation of goods and services, the employment of labour, and the ownership or use of land, buildings or other assets used in production.

Total cost of CVT courses

Total expenditure on continuing vocational training courses. This is the sum of direct costs, the labour costs of participants and the balance of contributions to national or regional training funds and receipts from national or other funding arrangements.

Total general government expenditure

According to Commission Regulation (EC) No 1500/2000 of 10 July 2000, total general government expenditure comprises the following ESA 95 categories: intermediate consumption; gross capital formation; compensation of employees; other taxes on production; subsidies payable; property income; current taxes on income, wealth, etc.;

social benefits other than social transfers in kind; social transfers in kind related to expenditure on products supplied to households via market producers; other current transfers; adjustment for the change in net equity of households in pension fund reserves; capital transfers payable; and acquisitions less disposals of non-financial non-produced assets.

Total general government revenue

According to Commission Regulation (EC) No 1500/2000 of 10 July 2000, total general government revenue comprises the following ESA 95 categories: market output; output for own final use; payments for the other non-market output; taxes on production and imports; other subsidies on production receivable; property income; current taxes on income, wealth, etc.; social contributions; other current transfers; and capital transfers.

Total health expenditure

Total health expenditure includes: the medical care households receive (ranging from hospitals and physicians to ambulance services and pharmaceutical products), and their health expenses, including cost sharing and the medicines they buy on their own initiative; government-supplied health services (e.g. schools, vaccination campaigns), investment in clinics, laboratories, etc.; administration costs; research and development; industrial medicine, outlays of voluntary organisations, charitable institutions and non-governmental health plans.

Total labour costs

Total expenditure borne by employers in order to employ workers. For presentational purposes, total labour costs can be subdivided into 'direct costs' and 'indirect costs'. Direct costs include gross wages and salaries in cash (direct remuneration and bonuses) and wages and salaries in kind (company products, housing, company cars, meal vouchers, crèches, etc.). Direct costs are dominated by wages and salaries in cash. Indirect costs cover employers' actual social contributions (i.e. statutory, collectively agreed, contractual and voluntary social security contributions); employers' imputed social contributions (mostly guaranteed remuneration in the event of sickness or short-time working, plus severance pay and compensation in lieu of notice); vocational training costs; recruitment costs and working clothes provided by the employer; taxes paid by the employer (based on the wages and salaries bill or on employment); minus subsidies received by the employer (intended to refund part or all of the cost of direct remuneration). Indirect costs are dominated by employers' actual social contributions, in particular by employers' statutory social security contributions.

Tourism and travel

On the debit side, there is expenditure by residents living abroad for less than a year for whatever reason: leisure, work, health or study. The credit side includes the same activities by foreign travellers on the national territory.

Tourist accommodation, demand for

This includes all types of accommodation: hotels and similar establishments, camping sites, holiday dwellings, youth hostels, etc.

Tourist accommodation, supply of

This refers to the number of bed places in an establishment where people can stay overnight in permanent beds, discounting any extra beds set up at the customers' request.

Transfers

Transfers cover international transactions in which goods, services, or financial items are transferred between the residents of one economy and the residents of foreign economies without something of economic value being received in return.

Turnover

Turnover comprises the totals invoiced by the observation unit during the reference period, and this corresponds to market sales of goods or services supplied to third parties. Turnover includes all duties and taxes on the goods or services invoiced by the unit with the exception of the VAT invoiced by the unit vis-à-vis its customer and other similar deductible taxes directly linked to turnover. It also includes all other charges (transport, packaging, etc.) passed on to the customer, even if these charges are listed separately on the invoice. Reduction in prices, rebates and discounts as well as the value of returned packing must be deducted. Income classified as other operating income, financial income and extraordinary income in company accounts is excluded from turnover. Operating subsidies received from public authorities or the institutions of the European Union are also excluded. For NACE

Rev. 1 classes 66.01 and 66.03, the corresponding title of this characteristic is 'Gross premiums written'.

Unemployed person

Persons are considered as unemployed if they fulfil three conditions: to be without employment during the reference week; to be available to start work within the next two weeks; and to have actively sought employment at some time during the previous four weeks. In addition, unemployed persons include those who had no employment and had already found a job to start later. The duration of unemployment is defined as the duration of search for a job or the length of the period since the last job was held (if this period is shorter than the duration of search for a job).

Unemployment rate

The unemployed as a percentage of people in the labour force.

United Nations (UN)

The United Nations (UN) was established on 24 October 1945 by 51 countries committed to preserving peace through international cooperation and collective security. Today, nearly every nation in the world belongs to the UN: membership totals 189 countries. When States become members of the United Nations, they agree to accept the obligations of the UN Charter, an international treaty that sets out basic principles of international relations. According to the Charter, the UN has four purposes: to maintain international peace and security; to develop friendly relations among nations; to cooperate in solving international problems and in promoting respect for human rights; and to be a centre for harmonising the actions of nations.

United States Patent and Trademark Office (USPTO)

The United States Patent and Trademark Office (USPTO) is a non-commercial federal entity and one of 14 bureaux in the Department of Commerce (DOC) of the United States. The mission of USPTO is to promote industrial and technological progress in the United States and strengthen the national economy by administering the laws relating to patents and trademarks, advising the Secretary of Commerce, the President of the United States, the administration on patent, trademark, and copyright protection and the administration on the trade-related aspects of intellectual property rights.

ACP: African, Caribbean and Pacific countries, signatories to the Partnership Agreement (Cotonou Agreement)

Angola, Antigua and Barbuda, Barbados, Belize, Benin, Botswana, Burkina Faso, Burundi, Cameroon, Cape Verde, Central African Republic, Chad, Comoros, Congo, Congo (Democratic Republic of), Cook Islands, Côte d'Ivoire, Djibouti, Dominica, Dominican Republic, Equatorial Guinea, Eritrea, Ethiopia, Fiji, Gabon, Ghana, Grenada, Guinea, Guinea-Bissau, Guyana, Haiti, Jamaica, Kenya, Kiribati, Lesotho, Liberia, Madagascar, Malawi, Mali, Marshall Islands, Mauritania, Mauritius, Micronesia (Federated States of), Mozambique, Namibia, Nauru, Niger, Nigeria, Niue, Palau, Papua New Guinea, Rwanda, Saint Kitts and Nevis, Saint Lucia, Saint Vincent and the Grenadines, Samoa, São Tomé and Príncipe, Senegal, Seychelles, Sierra Leone, Solomon Islands, Somalia, South Africa, Sudan, Suriname, Swaziland, Tanzania (United Republic of), The Bahamas, The Gambia, Togo, Tonga, Trinidad and Tobago, Tuvalu, Uganda, Vanuatu, Zambia, Zimbabwe.

APEC: Asia-Pacific Economic Cooperation

Australia, Brunei, Canada, Chile, China, Hong Kong, Indonesia, Japan, Korea (Republic of), Malaysia, Mexico, New Zealand, Papua New Guinea, Peru, Philippines, Russian Federation, Singapore, Taiwan, Thailand, United States, Vietnam.

ASEAN: Association of South-East Asian Nations

Brunei, Cambodia, Indonesia, Laos, Malaysia, Myanmar, Philippines, Singapore, Thailand, Vietnam.

Candidate countries

Bulgaria, Cyprus, Czech Republic, Estonia, Hungary, Latvia, Lithuania, Malta, Poland, Romania, Slovakia, Slovenia, Turkey.

CEECs: central and east European countries

Albania, Bosnia-Herzegovina, Bulgaria, Croatia, Czech Republic, Estonia, Former Yugoslav Republic of Macedonia, Hungary, Latvia, Lithuania, Poland, Romania, Slovakia, Slovenia, Yugoslavia.

CIS: Commonwealth of Independent States

Armenia, Azerbaijan, Belarus, Georgia, Kazakhstan, Kyrgyzstan, Moldova, Russian Federation, Tajikistan, Turkmenistan, Ukraine, Uzbekistan.

DAEs: dynamic Asian economies

Hong Kong, Korea (Republic of), Malaysia, Singapore, Taiwan, Thailand.

EEA: European Economic Area

EU, Iceland, Liechtenstein, Norway.

EFTA: European Free Trade Association

Iceland, Liechtenstein, Norway, Switzerland.

European Union (EU-15)

Belgium, Denmark, Germany, Greece, Spain, France, Ireland, Italy, Luxembourg, the Netherlands, Austria, Portugal, Finland, Sweden, United Kingdom.

Euro zone

Countries participating in economic and monetary union and having the euro as the single currency. In 2001, these were Belgium, Germany, Greece, Spain, France, Ireland, Italy, Luxembourg, the Netherlands, Austria, Portugal and Finland.

Extra-euro-zone (12)

Africa, America, Asia, Denmark, Oceania and polar regions, Sweden, United Kingdom, other European countries, miscellaneous (countries not specified) extra.

Extra-EU-15

Other European countries, Africa, America, Asia, Oceania and polar regions, miscellaneous (countries not specified) extra.

Latin American countries

Argentina, Bolivia, Brazil, Chile, Colombia, Costa Rica, Cuba, Dominican Republic, Ecuador, El Salvador, Guatemala, Haiti, Honduras, Mexico, Nicaragua, Panama, Paraguay, Peru, Uruguay, Venezuela.

MEDA: Mediterranean countries in the Euro-Mediterranean partnership

Algeria, Cyprus, Egypt, Israel, Jordan, Lebanon, Malta, Morocco, Palestinian Territories, Syria, Tunisia, Turkey.

Mediterranean basin countries

Albania, Algeria, Bosnia-Herzegovina, Ceuta, Croatia, Cyprus, Egypt, Former Yugoslav Republic of Macedonia, Gibraltar, Israel, Jordan, Lebanon, Libya, Malta, Melilla, Morocco, Palestinian Territories, Slovenia, Syria, Tunisia, Turkey, Yugoslavia.

Mercosur: Southern Cone Common Market

Argentina, Brazil, Paraguay, Uruguay.

NAFTA: North American Free Trade Agreement

Canada, Mexico, United States.

NICs: newly industrialised Asian countries

Hong Kong, Korea (Republic of), Singapore, Taiwan.

OECD, excluding the EU

Organisation for Economic Cooperation and Development, excluding the EU Australia, Canada, Christmas Island, Cocos Islands (or Keeling Islands), Czech Republic, Heard Island and McDonald Islands, Hungary, Iceland, Japan, Korea (Republic of), Mexico, New Zealand, Norfolk Island, Norway, Poland, Slovakia, Switzerland, Turkey, United States, Virgin Islands (US).

OPEC: Organisation of Petroleum Exporting Countries

Algeria, Indonesia, Iran, Iraq, Kuwait, Libya, Nigeria, Qatar, Saudi Arabia, United Arab Emirates, Venezuela.

SAARC: South Asian Association for Regional Cooperation

Bangladesh, Bhutan, India, Maldives, Nepal, Pakistan, Sri Lanka.

A.   **Agriculture, hunting and forestry**

B.   **Fishing**

C.   **Mining and quarrying**
CA.   Mining and quarrying of energy-producing materials
CB.   Mining and quarrying, except of energy-producing materials

D.   **Manufacturing**
DA.   Manufacture of food products, beverages and tobacco
DB.   Manufacture of textiles and textile products
DC.   Manufacture of leather and leather products
DD.   Manufacture of wood and wood products
DE.   Manufacture of pulp, paper and paper products; publishing and printing
DF.   Manufacture of coke, refined petroleum products and nuclear fuel
DG.   Manufacture of chemicals, chemical products and man-made fibres
DH.   Manufacture of rubber and plastic products
DI.   Manufacture of other non-metallic mineral products
DJ.   Manufacture of basic metals and fabricated metal products
DK.   Manufacture of machinery and equipment n.e.c.
DL.   Manufacture of electrical and optical equipment
DM.   Manufacture of transport equipment
DN.   Manufacturing n.e.c.

E.   **Electricity, gas and water supply**

F.   **Construction**

G.   **Wholesale and retail trade; repair of motor vehicles, motorcycles and personal and household goods**
50.   Sale, maintenance and repair of motor vehicles and motorcycles; retail sale of automotive fuel
51.   Wholesale trade and commission trade, except of motor vehicles and motorcycles
52.   Retail trade, except of motor vehicles and motor-cycles; repair of personal and household goods

H.   **Hotels and restaurants**

I.   **Transport, storage and communication**
60.   Land transport; transport via pipelines
61.   Water transport
62.   Air transport
63.   Supporting and auxiliary transport activities; activities of travel agencies
64.   Post and telecommunications

J.   **Financial intermediation**
65.   Financial intermediation, except insurance and pension funding
66.   Insurance and pension funding, except compulsory social security
67.   Activities auxiliary to financial intermediation

K.   **Real estate, renting and business activities**
70.   Real estate activities
71.   Renting of machinery and equipment without operator and of personal and household goods
72.   Computer and related activities
73.   Research and development
74.   Other business activities

L.   **Public administration and defence; compulsory social security**

M.   **Education**

N.   **Health and social work**

O.   **Other community, social and personal service activities**
90.   Sewage and refuse disposal, sanitation and similar activities
91.   Activities of membership organisations n.e.c.
92.   Recreational, cultural and sporting activities
93.   Other service activities

P.   **Activities of households**

Q.   **Extra-territorial organisations and bodies**

This nomenclature is accessible on the Eurostat web site:
http://europa.eu.int/comm/eurostat/ramon/ (option 'classifications').

0. **Food and live animals**
00. Live animals other than animals of Division 03
01. Meat and meat preparations
02. Dairy products and birds' eggs
03. Fish (not marine mammals), crustaceans, molluscs and aquatic invertebrates and preparations thereof
04. Cereals and cereal preparations
05. Vegetables and fruit
06. Sugars, sugar preparations and honey
07. Coffee, tea, cocoa, spices and manufactures thereof
08. Feedingstuffs for animals (not including unmilled cereals)
09. Miscellaneous edible products and preparations

1. **Beverages and tobacco**
11. Beverages
12. Tobacco and tobacco manufactures

2. **Crude materials, inedible, except fuels**
21. Hides, skins and fur skins, raw
22. Oilseeds and oleaginous fruits
23. Crude rubber (including synthetic and reclaimed)
24. Cork and wood
25. Pulp and waste paper
26. Textile fibres (other than wool tops and other combed wool), and their wastes (not manufactured into yarn or fabric)
27. Crude fertilisers, other than those of Division 56, and crude minerals (excluding coal, petroleum and precious stones)
28. Metalliferous ores and metal scrap
29. Crude animal and vegetable materials, n.e.s.

3. **Mineral fuels, lubricants and related materials**
32. Coal, coke and briquettes
33. Petroleum, petroleum products and related materials
34. Gas, natural and manufactured
35. Electric current

4. **Animal and vegetable oils, fats and waxes**
41. Animal oils and fats
42. Fixed vegetable fats and oils, crude, refined or fractionated
43. Animal or vegetable fats and oils, processed; waxes of animal or vegetable origin; inedible mixtures or preparations of animal or vegetable fats and oils, n.e.s.

5. **Chemicals and related products, n.e.s.**
51. Organic chemicals
52. Inorganic chemicals
53. Dyeing, tanning and colouring materials
54. Medical and pharmaceutical products
55. Essential oils and resinoids and perfume materials; toilet, polishing and cleaning preparations
56. Fertilisers (other than those of Division 27)
57. Plastics in primary forms
58. Plastics in non-primary forms
59. Chemical materials and products, n.e.s.

6. **Manufactured goods classified chiefly by material**
60. Complete industrial plant appropriate to Section 6
61. Leather, leather manufacture, n.e.s., and dressed fur skins
62. Rubber manufacture
63. Cork and wood manufacture (excluding furniture)
64. Paper, paperboard and articles of paper pulp, of paper or of paperboard
65. Textile yarn, fabrics, made-up articles, n.e.s., and related products
66. Non-metallic mineral manufactures, n.e.s.
67. Iron and steel
68. Non-ferrous metals
69. Manufacture of metals, n.e.s.

7. **Machinery and transport equipment**
70. Complete industrial plant appropriate to Section 7
71. Power-generating machinery and equipment
72. Machinery specialised for particular industries
73. Metalworking machinery
74. General industrial machinery and equipment, n.e.s., and machine parts, n.e.s.
75. Office machines and automatic data-processing machines
76. Telecommunications and sound-recording and reproducing apparatus and equipment
77. Electrical machinery, apparatus and appliances, n.e.s., and electrical parts thereof (including non-electrical counterparts, n.e.s., of electrical household-type equipment)
78. Road vehicles (including air-cushion vehicles)
79. Other transport equipment

8. **Miscellaneous manufactured articles**
80. Complete industrial plant appropriate to Section 8
81. Prefabricated buildings; sanitary plumbing, heating and lighting fixtures and fittings, n.e.s.
82. Furniture and parts thereof; bedding, mattresses, mattress supports, cushions and similar stuffed furnishings
83. Travel goods, handbags and similar containers
84. Articles of apparel and clothing accessories
85. Footwear
87. Professional, scientific and controlling instruments and apparatus, n.e.s.
88. Photographic apparatus, equipment and supplies and optical goods, n.e.s.; watches and clocks
89. Miscellaneous manufactured articles, n.e.s.

9. **Commodities and transactions not classified elsewhere in the SITC**
91. Postal packages not classified according to kind
93. Special transactions and commodities not classified according to kind
94. Complete industrial plant, n.e.s.
96. Coin (other than gold coin) not being legal tender
97. Gold, non-monetary (excluding gold, ores and concentrates)

Member States

EU-15	The 15 Member States of the European Union
EU-12	The euro zone with 12 countries participating (B, D, EL, E, F, IRL, I, L, NL, A, P, FIN)
€-zone / Eurozone	EUR-11 (B, D, E, F, IRL, I, L, NL, A, P, FIN) up to 31.12.2000 / EU-12 from 1.1.2001

B	Belgium
DK	Denmark
D	Germany
EL	Greece
E	Spain
F	France
IRL	Ireland
I	Italy
L	Luxembourg
NL	Netherlands
A	Austria
P	Portugal
FIN	Finland
S	Sweden
UK	United Kingdom

Candidate countries

BG	Bulgaria
CY	Cyprus
CZ	Czech Republic
EE	Estonia
HU	Hungary
LT	Lithuania
LV	Latvia
MT	Malta
PL	Poland
RO	Romania
SI	Slovenia
SK	Slovakia
TR	Turkey

Other countries

AF	Afghanistan
AM	Armenia
AR	Argentina
AZ	Azerbaijan
BA	Bosnia and Herzegovina
BR	Brazil
CA	Canada
CD	Democratic Republic of Congo
CH	Switzerland
CN	China
CO	Colombia
D-E	territory of the former East Germany
D-W	territory of the former West Germany

DZ	Algeria
FRY	Federal Republic of Yugoslavia
GB	Great Britain
HR	Croatia
IN	India
IQ	Iraq
IR	Iran
IS	Iceland
JP	Japan
KR	South Korea
LI	Liechtenstein
LK	Sri Lanka
LY	Libya
NG	Nigeria
NO	Norway
RU	Russian Federation
SA	Saudi Arabia
SG	Singapore
SL	Sierra Leone
SO	Somalia
TW	Taiwan
UA	Ukraine
US	United States of America
ZA	South Africa

Currencies

ECU	European currency unit, data up to 31.12.1998
EUR	euro, data from 1.1.1999 on
ATS	Austrian schilling
BEF	Belgian franc
DEM	German mark
DKK	Danish crown (krone)
ESP	Spanish peseta
FIM	Finnish markka
FRF	French franc
GBP	pound sterling
GRD	Greek drachma
IEP	Irish pound
ITL	Italian lira
LUF	Luxembourg franc
NLG	Dutch guilder
PTE	Portuguese escudo
SEK	Swedish crown (krona)
CAD	Canadian dollar
JPY	Japanese yen
USD	US dollar

Other abbreviations and acronyms

AA	agricultural area
ACP	African, Caribbean and Pacific States party to the Cotonou Agreement
AIDS	acquired immuno-deficiency syndrome
ASEAN	Association of South-East Asian Nations
AWU	annual work unit
BERD	business enterprise expenditure on R & D
BMI	body mass index
BSE	bovine spongiform encephalopathy
CAP	common agricultural policy
CCs	candidate countries
CDR	crude death rate
CEECs	central and east European countries
cif	cost, insurance and freight
CIS	Commonwealth of Independent States
CVTS2	continuing vocational training survey
DAEs	dynamic Asian economies
DG	Directorate-General
DG INFSO	Directorate General Information Society
DG PRESS	Directorate General Press and Communication
EAGGF	European agricultural guidance and guarantee fund
ECB	European Central Bank
ECHP	European Community household panel
ECHP-UDB	European Community household panel — user's database
ECMT	European Conference of Ministers of Transport
ECSC	European Coal and Steel Community
EEA	European Economic Area (EU + EFTA countries without Switzerland)
EEAICP	European Economic Area index of consumer prices
EFTA	European Free Trade Association (CH, IS, LI, NO)
EICP	European index of consumer prices
EITO	European Information Technology Observatory
EMS	European Monetary System
EPO	European Patents Office
ERDF	European Regional Development Fund
ESA	1. European system of national and regional accounts (ESA 95)
	2. European Space Agency
ESF	European Social Fund
Esspros	European system of integrated social protection statistics
EU	European Union
Eurostat	Statistical Office of the European Communities
Eurydice	information network on education in Europe (http://www.eurydice.org/)
fob	free on board
GBAORD	GBAORD government budget appropriation outlays for research and development
GCSE	GCSE general certificate of secondary education
GDP	GDP gross domestic product
GERD	GERD gross domestic expenditure on R & D
GJ	GJ gigajoule
GNI	GNI gross national income
GNP	GNP gross national product
GT	GT gross tonnage
GVA	GVA gross value added
GWH	GWh gigawatt hour (10^6 kWh)
ha	ha hectare

HICP	HICP harmonised index of consumer prices
hl	hl hectolitre
ICT	ICT Institute of Computer Technology
ILO	ILO International Labour Organisation
IMF	International Monetary Fund
IPI	industrial production index
ISCED	international standard classification of education
ISPO	Information Society Promotion Office
IT	information technology
kcal	kilocalorie
kg	kilogram
kgoe	kilogram of oil equivalent
kWh	kilowatt hour
LFS	labour force survey
LMP	labour market policy
m³	cubic metre
Mercosur	Southern Cone Common Market
MSTI/OECD	main science and technology indicators/Organisation for Economic Cooperation and Development
MUICP	monetary union index of consumer prices
n.e.c.	not elsewhere classified
n.e.s.	not elsewhere specified
NACE	general industrial classification of economic activities within the European Communities
NAFTA	North American Free Trade Agreement
NHS	national health service
NIS	new independent States (of the former Soviet Union)
NUTS	nomenclature of territorial units for statistics (Eurostat) (NUTS 1, 2, etc.)
ODs	overseas departments
OECD	Organisation for Economic Cooperation and Development
OECD-DAC	Organisation for Economic Cooperation and Development — Development Assistance Committee
OPEC	Organisation of Petroleum Exporting Countries
PPP	purchasing power parity
PPS	purchasing power standard
R & D	research and development
RON	research octane number
SDR	standard death rate
SI	structural indicator
SGM	standard gross margin
SIF	*Statistics in Focus*
SITC REV.3	standard international trade classification, third revision
sq. km/km²	square kilometre
TBFRA	temperate and boreal forest resources assessment
t	tonne (metric ton)
tkm	tonne-km
toe	tonne of oil equivalent
VAT	value added tax
WHO	World Health Organisation
UN	United Nations
Unesco	United Nations Educational, Scientific and Cultural Organisation
UNHCR	Office of the United Nations High Commissioner for Refugees
USPTO	United States Patent and Trademark Office

Installation

Insert the CD-ROM in the drive.

Click on the language of your choice to access information.

If you do not have Acrobat Reader, click on 'Acrobat Reader' to install it, following the instructions. N.B. Installation may require special rights, depending on your operating system. In this case contact your computer expert.

Contents of the CD-ROM

This CD-ROM contains the English, German and French versions of the Yearbook 2003 in PDF format. You can also find all the data files displayed in current office formats (tables, graphs, etc.).

The many functions of this product make it an efficient office tool : easy access to data, printing, text copying, searches, etc.

Use

Once the file is open, you can move swiftly around the document, using the bookmarks open on the left-hand side. If they are not present on the screen, click on 'Bookmarks'.

To copy to other software, print part of the document or search for key words, use the standard functions of Acrobat Reader (see relevant documentation).

On the CD-ROM, the references for further reading are linked electronically to the Internet presentation of the respective publication, or, if the publication can be downloaded free of charge, to the publication itself. The logo for the structural indicators is linked to the Internet pages presenting these indicators (see section 'Eurostat's structural indicators').

European Commission

Eurostat yearbook 2003

Eighth edition

Luxembourg: Office for Official Publications of the European Communities, 2003

2003 —317 pp. — 21 x 29.7 cm (printed version and CD-ROM), available as a combined product

Theme 1: General statistics
Collection: Panorama of the European Union
ISBN 92-894-4209-3 (printed version in English and CD-ROM: English, French and German)
ISBN 92-894-4210-7 (printed version in French and CD-ROM: English, French and German)
ISBN 92-894-4208-5 (printed version in German and CD-ROM: English, French and German)

The printed version and the CD-ROM are sold together as a combined product at a price (excluding VAT) in Luxembourg of EUR 50.

The book/CD-ROM has four chapters containing an introduction, tables, graphs and references for further reading. The chapters are followed by annexes including a glossary, the geographical nomenclature, the classifications of economic activities and of commodities, a list of abbreviations and acronyms and instructions for the installation of the CD-ROM.

The four chapters are:

1. 'Statisticians for Europe' which provides information on: Eurostat's service; The structural indicators ; The European Union in the global context; In the spotlight: the candidate countries.

2. 'People in Europe', with data on: A changing population: the EU population, families and births, and international migration; Life and its risks: life expectancy and mortality, and health and safety; Education and work: education, people in the labour market, continuing vocational training in enterprises, and labour market policy data; Households: household consumption expenditure, income and living conditions, and housing.

3. 'Economy and ecology', with data on: National accounts: economic output, consumption and spending, income of the input factors, government finances, and social protection; Prices, wages, and finance: consumer prices, wages and labour costs, and financial market indicators; International trade: balance of payments, trade in goods, trade in services, and trading partners; The environment: water, waste, environmental protection expenditure, air emissions and air quality, and transport.

4. 'Entrepreneurial activities', with data on: Business structures: business structures at a glance, industry and construction, distributive trades, and services, including financial services; Business sectors: transport, tourism, energy, and steel; Science and technology: research and development, and the information society; Agriculture, forestry and fisheries: agriculture, forestry, fisheries, and agriculture and the environment.

BELGIQUE/BELGIË

Jean De Lannoy
Avenue du Roi 202/Koningslaan 202
B-1190 Bruxelles/Brussel
Tél. (32-2) 538 43 08
Fax (32-2) 538 08 41
E-mail: jean.de.lannoy@infoboard.be
URL: http://www.jean-de-lannoy.be

**La librairie européenne/
De Europese Boekhandel**
Rue de la Loi 244/Wetstraat 244
B-1040 Bruxelles/Brussel
Tél. (32-2) 295 26 39
Fax (32-2) 735 08 60
E-mail: mail@libeurop.be
URL: http://www.libeurop.be

Moniteur belge/Belgisch Staatsblad
Rue de Louvain 40-42/Leuvenseweg 40-42
B-1000 Bruxelles/Brussel
Tél. (32-2) 552 22 11
Fax (32-2) 511 01 84
E-mail: eusales@just.fgov.be

DANMARK

J. H. Schultz Information A/S
Herstedvang 12
DK-2620 Albertslund
Tlf. (45) 43 63 23 00
Fax (45) 43 63 19 69
E-mail: schultz@schultz.dk
URL: http://www.schultz.dk

DEUTSCHLAND

Bundesanzeiger Verlag GmbH
Vertriebsabteilung
Amsterdamer Straße 192
D-50735 Köln
Tel. (49-221) 97 66 80
Fax (49-221) 97 66 82 78
E-Mail: vertrieb@bundesanzeiger.de
URL: http://www.bundesanzeiger.de

ΕΛΛΑΔΑ/GREECE

G. C. Eleftheroudakis SA
International Bookstore
Panepistimiou 17
GR-10564 Athina
Tel. (30-1) 331 41 80/1/2/3/4/5
Fax (30-1) 325 84 99
E-mail: elebooks@netor.gr
URL: elebooks@hellasnet.gr

ESPAÑA

Boletín Oficial del Estado
Trafalgar, 27
E-28071 Madrid
Tel. (34) 915 38 21 11 (libros)
        913 84 17 15 (suscripción)
Fax (34) 915 38 21 21 (libros),
        913 84 17 14 (suscripción)
E-mail: clientes@com.boe.es
URL: http://www.boe.es

Mundi Prensa Libros, SA
Castelló, 37
E-28001 Madrid
Tel. (34) 914 36 37 00
Fax (34) 915 75 39 98
E-mail: libreria@mundiprensa.es
URL: http://www.mundiprensa.com

FRANCE

Journal officiel
Service des publications des CE
26, rue Desaix
F-75727 Paris Cedex 15
Tél. (33) 140 58 77 31
Fax (33) 140 58 77 00
E-mail: europublications@journal-officiel.gouv.fr
URL: http://www.journal-officiel.gouv.fr

IRELAND

Alan Hanna's Bookshop
270 Lower Rathmines Road
Dublin 6
Tel. (353-1) 496 73 98
Fax (353-1) 496 02 28
E-mail: hannas@iol.ie

ITALIA

Licosa SpA
Via Duca di Calabria, 1/1
Casella postale 552
I-50125 Firenze
Tel. (39) 055 64 83 1
Fax (39) 055 64 12 57
E-mail: licosa@licosa.com
URL: http://www.licosa.com

LUXEMBOURG

Messageries du livre SARL
5, rue Raiffeisen
L-2411 Luxembourg
Tél. (352) 40 10 20
Fax (352) 49 06 61
E-mail: mail@mdl.lu
URL: http://www.mdl.lu

NEDERLAND

SDU Servicecentrum Uitgevers
Christoffel Plantijnstraat 2
Postbus 20014
2500 EA Den Haag
Tel. (31-70) 378 98 80
Fax (31-70) 378 97 83
E-mail: sdu@sdu.nl
URL: http://www.sdu.nl

PORTUGAL

Distribuidora de Livros Bertrand Ld.ª
Grupo Bertrand, SA
Rua das Terras dos Vales, 4-A
Apartado 60037
P-2700 Amadora
Tel. (351) 214 95 87 87
Fax (351) 214 96 02 55
E-mail: dlb@ip.pt

Imprensa Nacional-Casa da Moeda, SA
Sector de Publicações Oficiais
Rua da Escola Politécnica, 135
P-1250-100 Lisboa Codex
Tel. (351) 213 94 57 00
Fax (351) 213 94 57 50
E-mail: spoce@incm.pt
URL: http://www.incm.pt

SUOMI/FINLAND

**Akateeminen Kirjakauppa/
Akademiska Bokhandeln**
Keskuskatu 1/Centralgatan 1
PL/PB 128
FIN-00101 Helsinki/Helsingfors
P./tfn (358-9) 121 44 18
F./fax (358-9) 121 44 35
Sähköposti: sps@akateeminen.com
URL: http://www.akateeminen.com

SVERIGE

BTJ AB
Traktorvägen 11-13
S-221 82 Lund
Tlf. (46-46) 18 00 00
Fax (46-46) 30 79 47
E-post: btjeu-pub@btj.se
URL: http://www.btj.se

UNITED KINGDOM

The Stationery Office Ltd
Customer Services
PO Box 29
Norwich NR3 1GN
Tel. (44) 870 60 05-522
Fax (44) 870 60 05-533
E-mail: book.orders@theso.co.uk
URL: http://www.itsofficial.net

ÍSLAND

Bokabud Larusar Blöndal
Skólavördustig, 2
IS-101 Reykjavik
Tel. (354) 552 55 40
Fax (354) 552 55 60
E-mail: bokabud@simnet.is

SCHWEIZ/SUISSE/SVIZZERA

Euro Info Center Schweiz
c/o OSEC Business Network Switzerland
Stampfenbachstraße 85
PF 492
CH-8035 Zürich
Tel. (41-1) 365 53 15
Fax (41-1) 365 54 11
E-mail: eics@osec.ch
URL: http://www.osec.ch/eics

BĂLGARIJA

Europress Euromedia Ltd
59, blvd Vitosha
BG-1000 Sofia
Tel. (359-2) 980 37 66
Fax (359-2) 980 42 30
E-mail: Milena@mbox.cit.bg
URL: http://www.europress.bg

CYPRUS

Cyprus Chamber of Commerce and Industry
PO Box 21455
CY-1509 Nicosia
Tel. (357-2) 88 97 52
Fax (357-2) 66 10 44
E-mail: demetrap@ccci.org.cy

EESTI

Eesti Kaubandus-Tööstuskoda
(Estonian Chamber of Commerce and Industry)
Toom-Kooli 17
EE-10130 Tallinn
Tel. (372) 646 02 44
Fax (372) 646 02 45
E-mail: einfo@koda.ee
URL: http://www.koda.ee

HRVATSKA

Mediatrade Ltd
Pavla Hatza 1
HR-10000 Zagreb
Tel. (385-1) 481 94 11
Fax (385-1) 481 94 11

MAGYARORSZÁG

Euro Info Service
Szt. István krt.12
III emelet 1/A
PO Box 1039
H-1137 Budapest
Tel. (36-1) 329 21 70
Fax (36-1) 349 20 53
E-mail: euroinfo@euroinfo.hu
URL: http://www.euroinfo.hu

MALTA

Miller Distributors Ltd
Malta International Airport
PO Box 25
Luqa LQA 05
Tel. (356) 66 44 88
Fax (356) 67 67 99
E-mail: gwirth@usa.net

NORGE

Swets Blackwell AS
Hans Nielsen Hauges gt. 39
Boks 4901 Nydalen
N-0423 Oslo
Tel. (47) 23 40 00 00
Fax (47) 23 40 00 01
E-mail: info@no.swetsblackwell.com
URL: http://no.swetsblackwell.com.no

POLSKA

Ars Polona
Krakowskie Przedmiescie 7
Skr. pocztowa 1001
PL-00-950 Warszawa
Tel. (48-22) 826 12 01
Fax (48-22) 826 62 40
E-mail: books119@arspolona.com.pl

ROMÂNIA

Euromedia
Str.Dionisie Lupu nr. 65, sector 1
RO-70184 Bucuresti
Tel. (40-1) 315 44 03
Fax (40-1) 312 96 46
E-mail: euromedia@mailcity.com

SLOVAKIA

Centrum VTI SR
Nám. Slobody, 19
SK-81223 Bratislava
Tel. (421-7) 54 41 83 64
Fax (421-7) 54 41 83 64
E-mail: europ@tbb1.sltk.stuba.sk
URL: http://www.sltk.stuba.sk

SLOVENIJA

GV Zalozba
Dunajska cesta 5
SLO-1000 Ljubljana
Tel. (386) 613 09 1804
Fax (386) 613 09 1805
E-mail: europ@gvestnik.si
URL: http://www.gvzalozba.si

TÜRKIYE

Dünya Infotel AS
100, Yil Mahallessi 34440
TR-80050 Bagcilar-Istanbul
Tel. (90-212) 629 46 89
Fax (90-212) 629 46 27
E-mail: aktuel.info@dunya.com

ARGENTINA

World Publications SA
Av. Cordoba 1877
C1120 AAA Buenos Aires
Tel. (54-11) 48 15 81 56
Fax (54-11) 48 15 81 56
E-mail: wpbooks@infovia.com.ar
URL: http://www.wpbooks.com.ar

AUSTRALIA

Hunter Publications
PO Box 404
Abbotsford, Victoria 3067
Tel. (61-3) 94 17 53 61
Fax (61-3) 94 19 71 54
E-mail: jpdavies@ozemail.com.au

BRESIL

Livraria Camões
Rua Bittencourt da Silva, 12 C
CEP
20043-900 Rio de Janeiro
Tel. (55-21) 262 47 76
Fax (55-21) 262 47 76
E-mail: livraria.camoes@incm.com.br
URL: http://www.incm.com.br

CANADA

Les éditions La Liberté Inc.
3020, chemin Sainte-Foy
Sainte-Foy, Québec G1X 3V6
Tel. (1-418) 658 37 63
Fax (1-800) 567 54 49
E-mail: liberte@mediom.qc.ca

Renouf Publishing Co. Ltd
5369 Chemin Canotek Road, Unit 1
Ottawa, Ontario K1J 9J3
Tel. (1-613) 745 26 65
Fax (1-613) 745 76 60
E-mail: order.dept@renoufbooks.com
URL: http://www.renoufbooks.com

EGYPT

The Middle East Observer
41 Sherif Street
Cairo
Tel. (20-2) 392 69 19
Fax (20-2) 393 97 32
E-mail: inquiry@meobserver.com
URL: http://www.meobserver.com.eg

MALAYSIA

EBIC Malaysia
Suite 45.02, Level 45
Plaza MBf (Letter Box 45)
8 Jalan Yap Kwan Seng
50450 Kuala Lumpur
Tel. (60-3) 21 62 92 98
Fax (60-3) 21 62 61 98
E-mail: ebic@tm.net.my

MÉXICO

Mundi Prensa México, SA de CV
Río Pánuco, 141
Colonia Cuauhtémoc
MX-06500 México, DF
Tel. (52-5) 533 56 58
Fax (52-5) 514 67 99
E-mail: 101545.2361@compuserve.com

SOUTH AFRICA

Eurochamber of Commerce in South Africa
PO Box 781738
2146 Sandton
Tel. (27-11) 884 39 52
Fax (27-11) 883 55 73
E-mail: info@eurochamber.co.za

SOUTH KOREA

**The European Union Chamber of
Commerce in Korea**
5th Fl, The Shilla Hotel
202, Jangchung-dong 2 Ga, Chung-ku
Seoul 100-392
Tel. (82-2) 22 53-5631/4
Fax (82-2) 22 53-5635/6
E-mail: eucck@eucck.org
URL: http://www.eucck.org

SRI LANKA

EBIC Sri Lanka
Trans Asia Hotel
115 Sir Chittampalam
A. Gardiner Mawatha
Colombo 2
Tel. (94-1) 074 71 50 78
Fax (94-1) 44 87 79
E-mail: ebicsl@slnet.ik

T'AI-WAN

Tycoon Information Inc
PO Box 81-466
105 Taipei
Tel. (886-2) 87 12 88 86
Fax (886-2) 87 12 47 47
E-mail: euitupe@ms21.hinet.net

UNITED STATES OF AMERICA

Bernan Associates
4611-F Assembly Drive
Lanham MD 20706-4391
Tel. (1-800) 274 44 47 (toll free telephone)
Fax (1-800) 865 34 50 (toll free fax)
E-mail: query@bernan.com
URL: http://www.bernan.com

ANDERE LÄNDER
OTHER COUNTRIES
AUTRES PAYS

**Bitte wenden Sie sich an ein Büro Ihrer
Wahl/Please contact the sales office of
your choice/Veuillez vous adresser au
bureau de vente de votre choix**

Office for Official Publications of the European
Communities
2, rue Mercier
L-2985 Luxembourg
Tel. (352) 29 29-42455
Fax (352) 29 29-42758
E-mail: info-info-opoce@cec.eu.int
URL: publications.eu.int

.... Eurostat Data Shops

DANMARK

Danmarks Statistik
Bibliotek og Information
Eurostat Data Shop
Sejrøgade 11
DK-2100 København Ø
Tlf. (45) 39 17 30 30
Fax (45) 39 17 30 03
E-post: bib@dst.dk
URL: http://www.dst.dk/bibliotek

DEUTSCHLAND

Statistisches Bundesamt
Eurostat Data Shop Berlin
Otto-Braun-Straße 70-72
(Eingang: Karl-Marx-Allee)
D-10178 Berlin
Tel. (49) 1888-644 94 27/28
      (49) 611 75 94 27
Fax (49) 1888-644 94 30
E-Mail: datashop@destatis.de
URL: http://www.eu-datashop.de/

ESPAÑA

INE
Eurostat Data Shop
Paseo de la Castellana, 183
Despacho 011B
Entrada por Estébanez
Calderón
E-28046 Madrid
Tel. (34) 915 839 167 / 915 839
500
Fax (34) 915 830 357
E-mail:
datashop.eurostat@ine.es
URL: http://www.ine.es/prodyser/
datashop/index.html
Member of the MIDAS Net

FRANCE

INSEE Info service
Eurostat Data Shop
195, rue de Bercy
Tour Gamma A
F-75582 Paris Cedex 12
Tél. (33) 1 53 17 88 44
Fax (33) 1 53 17 88 22
E-mail: datashop@insee.fr
Member of the MIDAS Net

ITALIA - ROMA

ISTAT
Centro di informazione
statistica — Sede di Roma
Eurostat Data Shop
Via Cesare Balbo, 11a
I-00184 Roma
Tel. (39) 06 46 73 32 28
Fax (39) 06 46 73 31 01/07
E-mail: datashop@istat.it
URL:
http://www.istat.it/Prodotti-e/
Allegati/Eurostatdatashop.html
Member of the MIDAS Net

ITALIA - MILANO

ISTAT
Ufficio regionale per la
Lombardia
Eurostat Data Shop
Via Fieno, 3
I-20123 Milano
Tel. (39) 02 80 61 32 460
Fax (39) 02 80 61 32 304
E-mail: mileuro@tin.it
URL:
http://www.istat.it/Prodotti-e/
Allegati/Eurostatdatashop.html
Member of the MIDAS Net

NEDERLAND

Centraal Bureau voor de
Statistiek
Eurostat Data Shop —
Voorburg
Postbus 4000
2270 JM Voorburg
Nederland
Tel. (31-70) 337 49 00
Fax (31-70) 337 59 84
E-mail: datashop@cbs.nl
URL: www.cbs.nl/eurodatashop

PORTUGAL

Eurostat Data Shop Lisboa
INE/Serviço de Difusão
Av. António José de Almeida, 2
P-1000-043 Lisboa
Tel. (351) 21 842 61 00
Fax (351) 21 842 63 64
E-mail: data.shop@ine.pt

SUOMI/FINLAND

Statistics Finland
Eurostat Data Shop Helsinki
Tilastokirjasto
PL 2B
FIN-00022 Tilastokeskus
Työpajakatu 13 B, 2. kerros,
Helsinki
P. (358-9) 17 34 22 21
F. (358-9) 17 34 22 79
Sähköposti: datashop@stat.fi
URL:
http://tilastokeskus.fi/tk/kk/data
shop/

SVERIGE

Statistics Sweden
Information service
Eurostat Data Shop
Karlavägen 100
Box 24 300
S-104 51 Stockholm
Tfn (46-8) 50 69 48 01
Fax (46-8) 50 69 48 99
E-post: infoservice@scb.se
URL: http://www.scb.se/tjanster/
datashop/datashop.asp

UNITED KINGDOM

Eurostat Data Shop
Office for National Statistics
Room 1.015
Cardiff Road
Newport NP10 8XG
South Wales
United Kingdom
Tel. (44-1633) 81 33 69
Fax (44-1633) 81 33 33
E-mail:
eurostat.datashop@ons.gov.uk

NORGE

Statistics Norway
Library and Information Centre
Eurostat Data Shop
Kongens gate 6
Boks 8131 Dep.
N-0033 Oslo
Tel. (47) 21 09 46 42/43
Fax (47) 21 09 45 04
E-mail: Datashop@ssb.no
URL: http://www.ssb.no/
biblioteket/datashop/

SCHWEIZ/SUISSE/SVIZZERA

Statistisches Amt des Kantons
Zürich
Eurostat Data Shop
Bleicherweg 5
CH-8090 Zürich
Tel. (41) 1 225 12 12
Fax (41) 1 225 12 99
E-Mail: datashop@statistik.zh.ch
URL: http://www.statistik.zh.ch

USA

Haver Analytics
Eurostat Data Shop
60 East 42nd Street
Suite 3310
New York, NY 10165
Tel. (1-212) 986 93 00
Fax (1-212) 986 69 81
E-mail: eurodata@haver.com
URL: http://www.haver.com/

EUROSTAT HOME PAGE
www.europa.eu.int/comm/eurostat/

MEDIA SUPPORT
EUROSTAT
(only for professional journalists)
Postal address:
Jean Monnet building
L-2920 Luxembourg
Office: BECH A4/017 —
5, rue Alphonse Weicker
L-2721 Luxembourg
Tel. (352) 43 01-33408
Fax (352) 43 01-35349
E-mail:
eurostat-mediasupport@cec.eu.int